The History of Timur-Bec, Known by the Name of Tamerlain the Great, ... Being an Historical Journal. With Historical Notes and Maps. Now Faithfully Render'd Into English. In two Volumes. of 2

THE
HISTORY
OF
TIMUR-BEC,
Known by the Name of
Tamerlain the Great,
Emperor of the
MOGULS and TARTARS:
BEING

An hiſtorical JOURNAL of his Conqueſts in *Aſia* and *Europe*.

Written in *Perſian* by CHEREFEDDIN ALI, Native of *Yezd*, his Contemporary

Tranſlated into *French* by the late Monſieur *Petis de la Croix*, Arabick Profeſſor in the Royal College, and Secretary and Interpreter to the King in the Oriental Languages.

With hiſtorical Notes and Maps.

Now faithfully render'd into ENGLISH.

VOL. II.

LONDON Printed for J. DARBY in *Bartholomew-Cloſe*, E BELL in *Cornhill*, W TAYLOR in *Pater-noſter-row*, W and J INNYS at the Weſt End of St *Paul*'s Church-yard, J OSBORNE in *Lombard-ſtreet*, and T. PAYNE in *Stationers-Court*. MDCCXXIII.

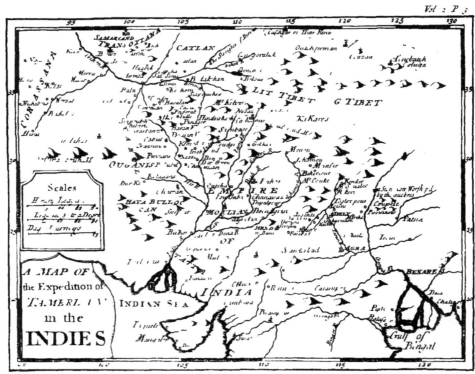

THE HISTORY OF TIMUR-BEC.

BOOK IV.

Timur enters India, and passes over the rivers Indus and Ganges. The taking of the citys of Moultan, Lahor, and Deli capital of that kingdom. A considerable battel between Timur and the Sultan Mahmoud, grandson of Firouz Chah emperor of India. The Tartars artifice in conquering the elephants in the wars with the Indians. The destruction of the temples of the Guebres. Several battels with these adorers of fire, and other idolaters of this great empire.

CHAP.

CHAP. I.

The cause of Timur's war in India.

TIMUR had given to his grandson prince Pir Mehemed, son of Gehanghir, the provinces of Condoz, Bacalan, Cabul, Gaznin, and Candahar, with their dependencys, as far as the frontiers of India, as we said before; and this Mirza being establish'd in these principalitys, endeavor'd to render 'em flourishing by his justice and goodness.

He receiv'd orders from court to assemble the troops of all the provinces, and to depart at their head for other conquests, and to make himself master of many towns and countrys in India. He accordingly set out with a great army commanded by good generals, the most valiant Emirs of his country.

They began with the plunder of the Ouganis, inhabitants of the mountain of Solyman Couh¹, which country they entirely ravag'd. They pass'd the Indus, invested Outchah², and also laid siege to Moultan³, which had then for its governor prince Sarenk, eldest brother of Mellou Can, who govern'd the empire of India for the young Sultan Mahmoud.

Timur resolv'd to make war in the empire of India, because since the death of Firouz Chah

---

¹ On the west of the Indus, between Cabul and Candahar.
² A town E. of the Indus, N of Moultan
³ A town of India on the Rave, long. 107½. lat. 29.

The history of Timur-Bec.

emperor of it, Mellou Can and Sarenk two brothers, who had been his generals, had usurp'd the sovereign power, and having plac'd on the throne Sultan Mahmoud, grandson of Firouz Chah, they reign'd over all India, Mellou Can residing at Deli [*], near Sultan Mahmoud, and his brother Sarenk at Moultan.

Moultan being besieg'd by our army, was briskly attack'd and batter'd without interruption: there were two assaults given every day, and the regiment of Timur Coja son of Acbouga, fought with more heat than all the others, because this Emir was not only an adviser, but the first actor in this enterprize.

Timur receiv'd the news with joy, and as he had already resolv'd to carry his arms to Catai or China, to root out the infidels, he got together all the troops of the empire. He had been before that inform'd, that the mahometan religion was then observ'd in many places of India, as at Deli and other citys, where the testimony of that faith was written upon their coins, nevertheless the greatest part of the provinces distant from this town were inhabited by idolaters. Timur, who design'd to partake of the merit and glory of the Gazie[*], and had rais'd this numerous army with intention to make war on the enemys of his religion, soon resolv'd on the conquest of India. He assembled his council, according to the custom Ma-

---

[*] Capital of India, long. 100. lat. 30. It consists of three Towns, Sari, Geharpena, and old Deli, all which make but one, as Paris consists of the city, university, and suburbs of St. Germain.

[*] Gaz e among the orientals signifys the wars the Mahometans undertake against those who profess a different religion. They imagine that whoever die in these wars, become martyrs, and of consequence inherit paradise.

homet had introduc'd, and propos'd his undertaking to the great Emirs of the state in these terms.

"Fortune, my dear friends, furnishes us with such happy conjunctures, that she seems to offer herself to us, and invite us to lay hold of the favorable opportunity's which present themselves, for as we have already seen the empires of Iran and Touran, and almost all Asia under our command, she shews us India, thro the disorders of the princes who govern it, opening its gates to receive us. My name has spread terror throughout the universe, and the least motion I make is capable of shaking the whole earth. It is therefore time to attack the kingdom of India, where having overcome what opposes our designs, we shall oblige this kingdom to acknowledg no other sovereign than me. What think ye, my dear friends, who are the companions of my victory's, of this great enterprize? Speak all in general, and every one in particular, your opinion of this proposal, which appears reasonable, since fortune has not yet withdrawn its protection from us."

Timur having thus made known his resolution to the captains and generals of his army, they fell upon the ground, and with sincere submission and perfect obedience, said, The order of the emperor was a law to all men, and more indispensibly so to them who were his slaves, that wherever he shou'd set his feet, there they shou'd be ready to lay their heads: that it was their glory punctually to obey his orders, even when he requir'd 'em to undertake the greatest difficulty's. Timur, pleas'd with this answer, heap'd favors on 'em, and thought of nothing

nothing more than the means of bringing this enterprize to perfection.

CHAP. II.

Timur brings his army into the field, to make war against the Guebres in India.

THE Alcoran says, the highest dignity man can attain to, is that of making war in person against the enemys of his religion. Mahomet adviseth the same thing, according to the tradition of the muslulman doctors · wherefore the great Timur always strove to exterminate the infidels, as much to acquire that glory, as to signalize himself by the greatness of his conquests.

For which reason in the year of the Leopard, that is, in the month of Regeb of the year 800 of the Hegira, having left Mirza Omar son of Mirza Miran Chah to govern the city of Samarcand, he took the road to India, having many kings of Asia for his attendence, who were come to his court as to an asylum, to render their services to this conqueror. *March 1398.*

He had in his army soldiers and even officers of all nations, but all the chiefs, and greatest part of the companys who were in posts of consequence, were Tartars : and he had also a great many lords of Kech.

Timur being arriv'd at Termed, there order'd to be made a bridge of boats over the Oxus, which he cross'd with his army · He rais'd many choice soldiers and of good appearance in the fine city of Culm, from whence he took the road to Aznic and Semencan ; and after having pass'd pass'd the mountains of Bacalan, he went to encamp at Enderabe.

CHAP. III.

Timur marches against the inhabitants of Ketuer. He defeats the Siapouches, who were cloth'd in black.

WHILST Timur was encamp'd at Enderabe, the inhabitants came to cast themselves at his feet, to complain of the insults and troubles they receiv'd from the idolaters of Ketuer[e], and from the Siapouches[f]: they represented to him that there were a great number of Mussulmans, from whom the infidels exacted every year excessive sums of money, under the name of tribute and Carage, which if they fail'd to pay punctually, they kill'd their men, and made their women and children slaves.

The emperor, touch'd with their complaints, and excited by zeal for the religion of which he was protector and defender, march'd immediately against these tyrants: he chose three soldiers out of every ten, and left the Mirza Cheroc to command the rest of the army and the baggage at Gounandictour[g], where they ordinarily pass'd the summer. Timur decamp'd twice a day, and march'd with so much diligence, that he made two days journy in one.

---

[e] A mountain of Bedakchan inhabited by idolaters, long. 115 lat. 35.

[f] An idolatrous nation cloth'd in black, inhabiting the mountains S. of the province of Becalchan.

[g] A cool place in the mountain near Enderabe.

He

He soon arriv'd at Perjan [9], whence he sent Mirza Rouftem, accompanied by Burhan A-glen, and other Emirs, with ten thousand men towards the left, to seek the Siapouches; and following his road, he arriv'd at Caouc [1], where he found a demolish'd citadel, which he caus'd to be rebuilt. Many Emirs and soldiers left some of their horses at Caouc, and ascended on foot the mountain of Ketuer, where tho the sun was in Gemini, the snow lay in so great abundance, that the feet of most part of the horses, which the lords wou'd have carry'd up, fail'd 'em, yet some of 'em were spur'd on so much during the night and the frost, that they were constrain'd to get up: but day being come, and the snow turn'd into ice, they kept these horses under tents till evening, when they continu'd to ascend the mountain, so that at length they arriv'd at the top, and then sent for the rest of the horses. And as the infidels dwelt in narrow passages and precipices, and there was no road to get to them, besides what was cover'd with snow; some of the Emirs and soldiers descended by cords, while others lying on the snow, slid down to the bottom. They made a sort of raft for Timur, to which they fasten'd rings, that they might tie cords to it of one hundred and fifty cubits in length: he sat upon it, while many persons let him down from the top to the bottom of the mountain, as far as the cords wou'd reach. Others dug with pickaxes in the snow a place where he might stand firm. They who were on the top

---

[9] A town in the province of Bedakchan, two days journy from Fnderabe near the Siapouches.

[1] A town at the foot of the mountain of Ketuer, long. 115 la. 36.

having

having gently descended, they let down Timur again in the machine. The place also was mark'd out where he shou'd stay next, and so on till the fifth time, when he arriv'd at the foot of the mountain. Then this monarch took a staff in his hand to rest on, and walk'd on foot a great way. These fatigues did not deter him, because of his confidence in the merit of the Gazie, which always increas'd his ardent zeal for the most difficult enterprizes. Those who work for God may rest assur'd of success. They also let down some of the emperor's horses, girding 'em about the belly and neck, with great precaution, but most of 'em thro the fault of the guides fell headlong down, so that there remain'd but two fit for service. Then Timur took horse, and all the army follow'd on foot.

The infidels of this country are strong men, and as large as the giants of the people of Aad[1]; they go all naked, their kings are nam'd Oda and Odachouh they have a particular language[2], which is neither Persian, nor Turkish, nor Indian, and know no other than this: and if it was not for the inhabitants of the neighbouring places, who are found there by chance, and having learnt their language, serve for interpreters, no one would be able to understand 'em.

These infidels were in a citadel, at the foot of whose walls passes a great river, and on the other side of this river there was a high mountain. As they had learnt the approach of Timur twenty four hours before his arrival, they abandon'd this post, cross'd the river, and car-

---

[1] Arabians in the time of Nimrod.
[2] The language of the people of Ketuer was heretofore unknown.

ry'd

ry'd their effects to the top of this mountain, imagining it inaccessible, especially with the intrenchments they had made there.

When the army after long fatigues arriv'd at the citadel, they found nothing there but some sheep the enemy had left, which they made themselves masters of: then having set fire to the houses, they immediately cross'd the river. The emperor order'd 'em to ascend the mountain by many narrow passages, which our soldiers did, and at the same time return'd thanks to God.

Cheik Arslan, at the head of the vanguard of of the left wing[1], attack'd the foremost of the enemys, and made himself master of a rising ground. They were also attack'd by Ali Sultan Ta'achi, who came down into the place where they were encamp'd. A colonel nam'd Chamelic signaliz'd himself by many great actions; and fourteen of our bravest soldiers fell from the top of the mountain to the bottom, and were kill'd. Mobacher also behav'd himself gallantly. Mengheli Coja advanc'd at the head of his company, and gain'd the top of the mountain. Sevindgic Behader did all that cou'd be expected from the greatest valor. Cheik Ali Salibert advanc'd as far as the ridge of the mountain with all his soldiers; he attack'd the enemy, and got possession of their post. Mouffa Reemal and the Emir Hussein Couitchi behav'd themselves with the utmost resolution, and at length all the Emirs of the Hezares and Couchons attack'd the infidels on all sides in the most dangerous places. The enemy defended themselves vigorously, notwithstanding the great slaughter of their men. The fight lasted three

---

[1] The Tartars have a vanguard to each wing, which they call Cambol.

nights

The history of Timur-Bec.

Obstinate fight of the men of Keruer.

nights with unheard-of obstinacy: but at length these unfortunate men finding themselves no longer able to make resistance, beg'd quarter with tears in their eyes. Timur sent to 'em Ac Sultan Kechi, with order to tell them that if they wou'd come to him with submission and obedience, abandon their errors, and take up a resolution to acknowledg but one God, and embrace the mahometan religion with sincerity, he wou'd not only give 'em their lives and effects, but also leave 'em to enjoy their principality as before. They had no sooner learnt this from an interpreter, than the fourth day they came to cast themselves at the feet of the emperor conducted by Ac Sultan Kechi: they abjur'd their idolatry, and embrac'd the mahometan religion, promising to submit entirely to the emperor, and obey all his commands. Timur, according to his wonted generosity, gave them clothes, and sent them away, after having encourag'd 'em by the most affectionate speeches.

Treason of the men of Keuer.

Night being come, these wretches, whose hearts were more black than their garments, fell upon the regiment of Chamelic, and put all the soldiers of it to the sword, except a few, who, tho wounded and lame, escap'd their hands.

Their punishment.

As soon as this treason was discover'd, our men few no more one hundred and fifty of 'em. All the army got up upon the mountain, and following the precept of Mahomet, who orders the women to be spar'd, they put to the sword all the old and young men of these infidels, and carry'd away their women and children. At length they built towers on the top of the mountain and the end of the bridge, with the heads of these traitors, who had never bow'd their head to adore the true God. Timur order'd to be engrav'd upon marble the history

of

of this action, which happen'd in the month of Ramadan in the year of the Hegira 800, and he added the particular Epocha which this people us'd, that their posterity might have some knowledg of the famous valor of the ever-victorious Timur. This pillar so inscrib'd gave the greater pleasure to Timur, in that these people had never been conquer'd by any prince in the world, not even by Alexander the great.

CHAP. IV.

Timur sends Mehemed Azad to gain intelligence of Mirza Rouftem and Burhan Aglen. His return to Ketuer.

AS there came no news of Mirza Rouftem and Burhan Aglen, who were gone against the Siapouches, the emperor order'd the inhabitants of Ketuer to furnish him with guides, and he sent Mehemed Azad and Doletchah, who had been rais'd to preferments in his court. Four or five Emirs accompany'd 'em, with four hundred Turks [4] and three hundred Tadgies [5], commanded by Mehemed Azad, who had orders to get information of Mirza Rouftem and Burhan Aglen. Mehemed after his departure, according to Timur's order, went up, by strait and difficult passages with extreme fatigue, high mountains cover'd with snow, which he afterwards slid down, having

---
[4] The Turks are those who descend from the Moguls and Tartars.
[5] The Tadgies are the inhabitants of the towns of Tranfoxiana, and all the country of Iran, who are neither Tartars, Moguls, nor Turks.

strongly

strongly fasten'd his buckler to his shoulders. He then march'd to the fortress of the Siapouches, where he cou'd not meet a single person, or hear one word, but he found the tracks of the feet of several men, who were gone to the other side of the mountain. These were the footsteps of the Siapouches, who having advice of the march of Mirza Rouftem and Burhan Aglen, were gone out of their fortresses, and retir'd to the mountains, where they lay in ambuscade in a very narrow passage. Some pass'd by 'em, and others without precaution got off their horses, which they let go loose · then the Siapouches, laying hold of the opportunity, came out of their ambuscade, and fell suddenly upon them. Burhan Aglen, thro his great cowardice, or rather by an unheard-of treason, flung off his coat of mail, and fled without fighting, which caus'd the defeat of his troops. When a general turns his back, we may say he is the murderer of his soldiers. The infidels seeing the Mussulmans fly, became more daring; and pursuing our men close, slew many of 'em with their axes and war-clubs, and among the rest Cheik Hussein Courtchi, Doletchah Gebagi, and Adna captain of the horse, who, after a vigorous defence, were destroy'd among the rest.

Affairs were in this miserable state, when Mehemed Azad observing the prints of the feet of the Siapouches, arriv'd in the passage where this tragedy happen'd he met 'em at their return, attack'd 'em with the greatest bravery, after a sharp fight utterly defeated 'em, and retook from 'em the bucklers, arms and horses of our Mussulmans He then went to rejoin Burhan Aglen with the horse which had fled, and every

every one knowing his own bucklers, arms and horses, they were restor'd.

Mehemed Azad then told Burhan Aglen that he must stay in that place all night, but this coward would not do it: he got up to the top of the mountain, whither he was follow'd by his troops, to the great regret of Mehemed Azad; for when a commander proves a traitor or a coward, his army never fails of being conquer'd. This action of Burhan was very infamous; and since the reign of Genghiz Can there has not been one prince of the race of Cayat [6], who has committed the like. Burhan had formerly done the same in the war of the Uzbecs, and receiv'd pardon by the singular goodness of Timur, who continu'd to honor him as before, and had even sent him on this expedition, in hopes he would repair his fault, and recover his credit, which in this last affair he entirely destroy'd.

After the conquest of Ketuer, and defeat of the idolaters, Timur sent Gelaleliffam and Ali Siftani with troops to seek an easy passage from the mountains, and to clear the ways: and he order'd them to ruin whatsoever they met belonging to the infidels.

These two Emirs having found a passage to their mines, open'd a way in the snow; and then Timur crofs'd the mountains, and went down to Caouc [7], where he left a strong garison. At this place he join'd the Emirs and soldiers, who for eighteen hours had constantly

---

[6] A Mogul hord, from whence Gerghiz Can sprung, which hord were the descendent of an antient Mogul prince nam'd Cayat, who was descended from Turc, son of Japhet, son of Noah.

[7] A town in Ketuer rebuilt by Timur.

fought

fought on foot, then they took horse, and accompany'd the emperor.

When Burhan Aglen and Mehemed Azad had join'd the imperial standard with their troops, Timur wou'd not admit the first into his presence, because without making any defence he had fled from the infidels he treated him with scorn as he met him by chance, and to shew his infamy, cited a passage of the Alcoran, which assures us, That twenty zealous Mussulmans are able to conquer two hundred infidels, provided they trust in God. and yet Burhan (said the emperor) at the head of ten thousand men fled from a handful of infidels, and put the Mussulmans in danger of being torn in pieces. Then Timur declar'd him criminal, and as a mark of disgrace banish'd him the court.

Mehemed Azad having fought on foot at the head of four hundred men only, and stood his ground against the same men, tho puff'd up with their victory, and having also put a great number of 'em to the sword, recovering from 'em all the horses they had got from us, Timur heap'd on him honors and riches, distinguishing him by great praises, and giving him the command of a regiment to reward his valor. The emperor distributed also largesses among those who had given marks of their courage in so dangerous an expedition.

CHAP.

CHAP. V.

Timur sends Mirza Charoc to Herat.

AT this place * Timur permitted his dear son Mirza Charoc, heir apparent to the crown, to return to Herat, capital of Coraſſana, of which he was governor. When he took leave of this prince, he gave him his advice, and us'd many expreſſions which shew'd a fatherly tenderneſs and affection, and after having embrac'd him, and recommended him to the divine protection, he diſmiſs'd him. Timur decamp'd at the same time, and march'd towards Cabul: he took the road to Tulle [8], aſcended the mountain of Hendou-Kech, paſs'd by Pendgehir [9], commonly call'd Pendgir, and went to encamp in a meadow of the country of Barin, about five leagues from Cabul. And as the design of this conqueror was chiefly to diſpenſe juſtice to the people, and to render the countrys and towns flouriſhing, he gave orders for a canal to be dug, which might join the river which paſſes thro thoſe quarters. He divided the land between the captains and ſoldiers, and in a ſhort time there was a great canal made five leagues long, which is yet call'd the canal of Mahighir · at length there were many large villages built upon it, and the valley, which before had not

* Caouc.

---

[8] A little town of Bedakchan.
[9] A town and mountain, where Abulfeda the geographer ſays there are two ſilver mines; and that the town is full of ditches dug to get out the oar. It is at the foot of the mountains of Cachmir to the weſt, between Caoul and Enderabe

been cultivated, became a fine and delightful garden

CHAP. VI.

The arrival of ambassadors from several places. Taizi Aglen returns from the country of the Calmacs, and Cheik Nouredin from that of Fars

TIMUR being encamp'd in the plain of Dourin [1], there arriv'd an ambassador from Timur Cotluc Aglen a prince of Capchac, and another from Emir Aidecou, a prince of Capclac, as also a third of Gete from Kefer Coja Aglen, who were presented before the throne by the Emirs and Nevians. After they had kiss'd the ground and perform'd other usual ceremonies, they began their harangue, wishing all prosperity to Timur, and highly extolling him then they declar'd the subject of their embassy, which was, to assure the emperor that their masters were faithful servants of his majesty, that tho for some time past there had been no good intelligence or agreement between 'em, which had made 'em depart from the obedience they ow'd him, and wander as vagabonds in the desarts, yet consideration and prudence having now brought 'em to see the deformity of their actions, they sincerely repented of 'em, and that if the emperor would be merciful and pardon their fault, they would for the future

---

[1] A village near Caran

be most obedient, and never disobey the orders of his officers.

Taizi Aglen, who for some difference which happen'd between him and the Can at Olug Yurt ¹, fled from the kingdom of Calmac ², came to this place to lay himself at the feet of the throne, and was receiv'd as handsomly as a prince of his rank cou'd expect. Timur embrac'd him, and presented him with a vest wove with gold, a belt set with precious stones, horses of great price, several mules and camels, tents and pavilions, and whatever cou'd be expected from a great emperor. At the same place also arriv'd Emir Cheik Noureddin, son of Sar Bouga, who had been left by Timur in Persia, after the five years campaign there, in order to receive the revenues of that kingdom and the neighboring countrys. He brought with him an immense treasure, with abundance of jewels of inestimable price, likewise animals proper for the chase, and birds of prey; leopards, gold mony, belts enrich'd with precious stones, vests wove with gold, stuffs of all colors, arms and all sorts of utensils for war, arabian horses with saddles of gold, great camels, several carriage and riding mules, fine stirrups, the straps embroider'd with gold and silver; umbrellas, canopys, pavilions, tents and curtains of scarlet and all colors; in short, there was so great a quantity of curious pieces of work, that the secretarys and comptrollers of the Divan employ'd three days and three nights

---

¹ That is, the great hord, seat of the kings of Calmac, or rather of the Mogul Cans or emperors, near Caracorom capital of Calmac.

² A kingdom, formerly call'd Caracatai, in Mogolistan, north of the kingdom of Courge or Leastung.

to register 'em, and write copys of 'em, which were presented to the lords of the court for their perusal.

The day for presenting petitions being appointed, the Emirs or generals, and the Nevians or foreign princes, presented Emir Cheik Noureddin before the imperial throne. This prince knelt down, and the whole day was spent in calling over before the emperor all his presents, than which none ever were seen so magnificent, not even in the reign of the great Feridon [a], or of Corzu Peruize [b].

Prince Taizi Aglen, the ambassadors of Capchac, and several princes of the race of Genghiz Can, who were present, were surpriz'd at it; not only at the sight of the riches, but but also considering that the power of Timur must be very great, since one of his subjects was rich enough to make so magnificent a present.

Timur distributed a great many of these raritys, and gave a very friendly reception to Emir Cheik Noureddin, who told the emperor that all these presents were too small for those who had resolv'd to sacrifice their lives to his service.

Timur being willing to treat the ambassadors of the Uzbecs [c] and Getes handsomly, gave 'em caps of gold, belts, vests and horses; he granted 'em whatsoever they ask'd, and loaded 'em with presents, as well for themselves as their masters, with letters in answer to those they had brought. At length Emir Cheik Noureddin knelt down, and ask'd pardon for Burhan Aglen, and the rest who accompany'd him at

---

[a] King of Persia of the first race.
[b] King of Persia of the third race.
[c] The princes of Capchac are here call'd Uzbecs.

The history of Timur-Bec.

the audience. Timur granted this with an excess of clemency and generosity.

He then sent to India Sultan Mahmoud Can [1], with the troops of the left wing, and all the princes and Emirs who had before receiv'd orders.

At this time Malek Mehemed, brother to Lechker Chah an Ougani, cast himself at the feet of the emperor, and in an humble manner told him, that Moufla, prince of the nation of the Kerkes, had kill'd his brother, who was an officer of his majesty, that he had ruin'd the town of Iijab [2], and pillag'd his Hezares; that he had made himself master of their effects by force, and that this villain constantly robb'd in the great roads, that no one cou'd pass those quarters: " For my part, says Malek, I, who " am a poor servant of your majesty, have fled " to save my life from the hands of this barba- " rous man, I have pass'd by Gazna, and staid " here on the good news I receiv'd of the " march of your imperial standard."

This advice rais'd Timur's passion, and he resolv'd to put a stop to these disorders, by some means or other. He order'd Malek to lie conceal'd, and to keep this advice secret, telling him he wou'd call Moussa to court, and if he came, he wou'd oblige him to do justice, and make entire satisfaction, but if he did not come, he wou'd give him an army, with which he might revenge himself on this murderer, for the death of his brother. Timur immediately sent

---

[1] True emperor of Zagatai, who serves under Timur as general of the army, and has only the name of Can, Timur being sovereign.
[2] Four days journy from Dourin, in the road to India.

a messenger to Mousla, to whom he gave orders to tell him as follows.

"The emperor having advice that you have demolish'd the city of Irjab, situate in the great road to India, does not think convenient that it shou'd remain in ruins, wherefore he wills and commands you to come forthwith to court, where he designs to invest you with the government of that country, not doubting but you will rebuild the place, and settle it in its former splendor."

The messenger having handsomly acquitted himself of this commission, Mousla came immediately with a resolution to cast himself at the feet of the throne, but Timur, who had resolv'd to put him to death, with all his accomplices, receiv'd him in a civil manner at first sight, and gave him a vest woven with gold, a belt, a sword with a gold handle, a horse well equip'd, with other curious things, and at last said to him, "We will assign you troops, with which it is expedient you shou'd go and rebuild that place: wherefore depart with thy domesticks and friends, and use all your efforts, that the place may be rebuilt before we arrive, and if there is need of any thing towards the perfecting of it, we will order it you, and then leaving you in the government of it, we will depart for India." Timur then sent him away, and order'd Mousla Recma', with three thousand brave men, to accompany him.

When Mousla was arriv'd at Irjab, he made dispatch in executing the orders he had receiv'd, and employ'd all his men and domesticks, about three hundred persons, in the rebuilding of this place.

CHAP

CHAP VII.

The repairing the fortress of Irjab, and the destroying of the Ouganis robbers.

TIMUR sent from the country of Dourin to Samarcand the august princess Serai Mulc Canum, and the Mirza Oluc Bei, who were at court, and then he decamp'd. In four days he arriv'd at the town of Irjab, which he found nearly repair'd there he fix'd his imperial tent, and the army encamp'd in order of battel, every one in his proper post. Timur order'd that the rebuilding of the town shou'd be continu'd, and the Emir Chahmelik and Gelalelillam had a commission for rebuilding of mosques and other public buildings, insomuch that all was finish'd in fourteen days. Timur had before commanded the Tavachis not to suffer any of the subjects of Moussa, employ'd in repairing the town, to re-enter it after once going out and this order was not given without cause, for on the seventeenth of Zilhadge Sept 16, in the morning, Timur having taken horse to 1398. view the place, with its ditches and wall, accompany'd with many princes and generals, who march'd on foot on each side him, he was perceiv'd by seven of Moussa's labourers, who were in an upper story of an house situate behind a gate of the town, and being within bow-shot of him, they let fly from a window with design to kill him. But they did not take good aim, and the rustling the arrow made only startled his horse. However Timur went into the town by another gate, and caus'd Moussa and his accomplices to be seiz'd the seven assassins who were in the house from whence the arrow was shot, took up their arms to defend themselves, and wounded some of our men, but at last Kelchi Sistan, broke open the house with some soldiers of his company, and put 'em to death.

At one a clock the same morning, Timur deliver'd to Malek Mehemed his enemy Moussa, with two hundred of his men, whom he had seiz'd. Malek, assisted by three of his servants, cut off all their heads, to revenge himself for the death of his brother whom they had slain, and made a tower of them. Then they pillag'd all his country and subjects, and put to death several leaders of those villains who were mix'd among our officers. The women and children, as also the goods and moveables of these tyrants, were given to the poor oppress'd people of Irjab, who, for being of Malek Mehemed's side, had suffer'd for several years great violence and injustice. And on this occasion we see that passage of the Alcoran fulfill'd, which threatens tyrants with confusion and ruin.

Timur gave the principality of Irjab to Malek Mehemed, and by this means deliver'd travellers from being infested by these insolent robbers. Thus as he render'd kingdoms flourishing by his goodness and equity, so he suppress'd disorders by his power and justice.

CHAP.

CHAP. VIII.

Timur marches to Chenouzan and Nagaz; and destroys the robbers of the nation of the Pervians.

TIMUR, after having settled the affairs of the country of Ijab, which requir'd as great authority as his to put it in order, the eighteenth of Zilhadge, in the year 800, march'd towards Chenouzan. After having past many forests and some mountains, he encamp'd near that place; where he staid the next day, and sent his son prince Calil Sultan to Banai [9], by the road of Captchagai [9], at the head of the baggage, accompany'd by several Emirs. Sept. 17. 1398.

Timur having march'd all night with great diligence, went with some thousands of horse towards the fortress of Nagaz, where he arriv'd early on the twenty-first of Zilhadge. Sept. 20.

It is to be remark'd, that the court having been before at Cabul, Emir Solyman Chah, and other commanders of the troops of Corassana, were come to Nagaz [1], according to Timur's order, to rebuild that place, and that they had work'd very hard there, so that it was compleatly fortify'd. Timur at his arrival there, was inform'd that the nation of the Pervians, a sort of Ouganis, to whom he had sent orders to appear before his throne with their troops, to serve in the army, had revolted, and refus'd

---

[9] Towns of Cabulestan near the Indus.
[1] A town of Cabulestan, between the Indus and the river of Cabul.

to send their men; for one day when Mirza Pir Mehemed, who had been to view some neighbouring places in India, was return'd with his troops and plunder, bringing with him to Cabul several captives, these inconsiderate men were so bold as to stop up their passage, to plunder 'em of part of the spoils, pass the river of Hir, and entrench themselves in the high mountains and forests, from whence they constantly went to rob on the high-ways. Timur had no sooner advice of this, than giving loose to his passion, he the same day march'd in search of these insolent people, whose end must of course be unfortunate. He came up to 'em in three days, and order'd all his soldiers to dismount, that they might march into the woods and mountains with more ease, and so seize and exterminate these rebels. They attack'd 'em with the greatest vigor, and after a weak defence cut 'em in pieces, made their children prisoners, and pillag'd their goods, having set fire to their habitations; and as there were some who fled, Timur would stay some time in this mountain, to deliver passengers from the fear of these robbers. At this place the deputys and Kelinters¹ of the nation of Oubel¹ came to cast themselves at his feet, to beg pardon, and implore his protection. This monarch, who sought nothing more than the welfare of his people, not only forgave their crimes, but receiv'd 'em into his protection, heap'd favors on 'em, and granted 'em many privileges, because of their descent.

---

¹ *………… O……*

The history of Timur-Bec.

Chap. 8

The Emir Solyman Chah having restor'd the town of Nagaz to its former splendor, learnt that the Kelatians [a], a strong and numerous people, had refus'd to obey the orders of the emperor, and to come to the camp with their troops. This news oblig'd him to fall on 'em, which he did with such bravery, that in two days and nights he defeated these giants, who before that time were esteem'd the most valiant men in the world. He pillag'd their country, cut to pieces a great number of 'em, put the rest in chains, made their children slaves, and burnt their houses. After this he left the country of the Kelatians, and return'd in triumph to the imperial throne, where he was receiv'd with all the respect his actions deserv'd.

The first of Muharrem in the year 801, Timur leaving the country of the Pervians, went down to view the neighbourhood of the town of Nagaz. He sent the Emir Solyman Chah to Moultan with good troops, to Mirza Pir Mehemed, and leaving Chah Ali Ferahi with five hundred foot in garison at Nagaz, he departed for Banou, in which he left Pir Ali Selduz, and the Emir Hussein Courtchi, with a sufficient garison.

Sept. 30, 1398.

Timur departed from Banou, and the eighth of Muharrem arriv'd at the river Indus, at the very place where Sultan Gelaleddin king of Carizme, when he fled from the wrath of Genghiz Can, swam cross the river. Genghiz Can encamp'd here, but did not pass the Indus.

Octob. 7.
See the history of Genghiz Can, Book IV. Ch. 5.

Timur had a bridge of boats and reeds made over this river, in which all the army were

---

[a] A nation among the Ouganis.

con-

Book IV constantly employ'd, and it was finish'd in two days.

At this place he dismiss'd the Ambassadors who came to pay their respects to him, among whom were the said Mehemed Medini, ambassador from Mecca and Medina [3], and from all the princes and Cherifs of Arabia, who pray'd this conqueror to honor 'em one day with a visit, and take 'em under his protection. Timur also dismiss'd the ambassador of Eskender Chah, prince of Cachmir [4], whom he had sent to beseech his majesty to receive him upon his obedience: he order'd him to tell his master that he receiv'd his offer with pleasure, and that he desir'd he wou'd not fail to come to him at the town of Dipalpour [5], and there join the imperial camp.

CHAP. IX.

Timur passes the river Indus.

Octob. 11. 1398.

THE twelfth of Muharrem in the year 801, which answers to that of the Leopard, Timur cross'd the Indus at the head of his army, and encamp'd at the entrance of the great desart of Gerou, which is call'd Tchol Gelali, because the Sultan Gelaleddin Carezem Chah, flying from the wrath of Genghiz Can, cross'd the Indus at this place, and enter'd this desart to avoid being put to death by the sword of

---

[3] The Cherifs of Mecca and Medina offer'd to declare Timur Calif, tho Bajazet was invested with that high dignity.
[4] A province, whose capital was Nagar.
[5] Town of India, S. of Lahor.

that

that conqueror. At Timur's arrival at this place, the Rayas, and the principal inhabitants of the mountain of Couhdgioud [6], came to make their submissions to him: they offer'd him presents, promis'd to remit to him considerable sums, and serve him on all occasions.

Some months before, Rouftem Tagi Bougai Berlas had been sent with an army towards Moultan, and having stopt some days at Couhdgioud, these same Rayas did him several important services, furnish'd him with provisions, and even mony to pay his soldiers. Timur was highly pleas'd with 'em upon these accounts, and resolv'd they shou'd enjoy the fruits of his clemency he prohibited every one from insulting 'em, and order'd they shou'd be treated with humanity and affection After which they return'd home joyful and contented, without either being molested or depriv'd of their usual place of residence These are the effects and fruits of civility The poet says, We ought always to be under the protection of our own actions.

CHAP. X.

Chehabeddin Mobarec Chah Temini commits hostilitys against the emperor after his submission.

CHEHABEDDIN Mobarec, who was prince of an isle of the river of Jamad [7], had a great number of officers under him, and was very

---
[6] A mountain S. E. of Cachmir.
[7] A river near the Indus. it is the continuation of the river Dendana, which comes from Cachmir.

rich

rich in men and moveables. When the Mirza Pir Mehemed Gehangir march'd to the frontiers of Moultan, Chehabeddin came to him to kiss his feet, and met with a handsom reception from him. He submitted to the emperor, and after he had staid some time to make his court to the Mirza, he took his leave, and return'd home, where he suffer'd himself to be overt'len with pride, and trusting in the strength of his isle, which he believ'd inaccessible, he fortify'd it with a good ditch and high walls. Timur at his arrival at the river of Jamad, had advice of his revolt, and the fourteenth of Muharrem order'd the Emir Cheik Noureddin to attack this isle at the head of his Toman, and as soon as he made himself master of it, to put to the sword every one he shou'd find therein. When the Emir came there, he and his soldiers cast themselves into the water to cross over. The besieg'd prepar'd to obstruct their passage; and there was as furious a battel fought as was ever heard of, which lasted till night. Chehabeddin at the head of ten thousand men came by the windings of the river to attack our army in the rear during night, and fought with great courage and bravery. The Emir Cheik Noureddin, a man of good conduct, receiv'd the enemy with the greatest intrepidity; and after several attacks entirely defeated 'em, constraining some to leap into the water, where they were drown'd, and killing the rest. Mansour and Dorege Temoura, officers of the emperor, perform'd many noble actions, and receiv'd several wounds.

Timur came with diligence to this place, and encamp'd near the isle. Chehabeddin, who till that time had never us'd precaution in an affair, was so imprudent as to get ready two hundred

dred flat-bottom'd boats, that he might escape Chap. 10.
if he shou'd be conquer'd. Whereupon at his
return from the night-attack, in which he was
vanquish'd, he fled with his domestics in these
boats. With a great deal of difficulty they
escap'd, rowing along the river Jamad, and at
length they came to Outcha [1], a town of India.

The Emir Cheik Noureddin had orders to
pursue him along the banks of the river; he slew
a great number of these Indians with arrows.
When he return'd, the emperor rewarded those
who had behav'd themselves gallantly on this
occasion, and were wounded, giving 'em vests,
and other things. Chehabeddin's boats arriving
near the frontiers of Moultan, the troops of
Mirza Pir Mehemed and Mirza Charoc, commanded by Solyman Chah, who had been sent
out as scouts, hinder'd their passage, and seizing the boats on the river, cut 'em to pieces.
Chehabeddin cast his wife and children into the
river, and half-dead gain'd the bank. As many
of this prince's subjects were retir'd into the
woods, Timur order'd Chamelik to enter 'em,
and if possible to exterminate all who were fled
there for refuge. Chamelik accordingly enter'd
the forests and bogs, and having slain a great
number of these miserable people, and pillag'd
their effects, return'd to the camp, laden with
booty, and a great number of captives.

After the success against Chehabeddin, the
army march'd five or six days on the banks of
the Jumad, and on the twenty-fourth of Mu- Octob. 23.
harrem it encamp'd on the borders of the Genave [2], at a fortress over-against which the Jamad and the Genave join in one stream, where

---

[1] On the Jamad above Moultan, long. 117. lat. 30.
[2] It falls into the Rave above Moultan.

the

the waves dashing against one another, make it appear like the troubled ocean. Timur order'd a bridge to be built over it, which was finish'd on the twenty-seventh of Muharrem, all the troops having been employ'd in it. We don't find in history that ever any one built a bridge over it before; and even Turmechirin Can [1], who formerly cross'd it, was oblig'd to swim over.

CHAP. XI.

Timur's arrival at Toulonba.

TIMUR pass'd this great river [2] with all his army, and encamp'd on the other side: the next day having entirely left the bridge to give free passage to the baggage and the rest of the army, he went to encamp over-against the town of Toulonba, on the bank of the river, thirty-five miles * from Moultan. The princes and Rayas, accompany'd by the Cheriffs and doctors, immediately came out of the place to cast themselves at Timur's feet, they kiss'd the ground on which he stood, and were handsomly treated by him.

*Gourouh

Octob. 28. The same day Timur pass'd the river of Toulonba, and the twenty-ninth of Muharrem staid on the other bank, till all the army was cross'd over. The first of Sefer he encamp'd in the neighboring plains of Toulonba.

Octob. 29.

---

[1] Descended from Genghiz Can; he conquer'd India, Anno Dom. 1240.
[2] Jamad and Genave join'd.

The ministers tax'd this town at two millions of crowns for the safety of their effects and lives. The Cheriffs, because of the nobleness of their race, and the doctors for their learning and virtue, were exempted from this tax. They had even presents made 'em of vests and other things, because Timur was naturally respectful to men of their character.

Some part of this tax was soon paid, but the inhabitants making a difficulty of paying the rest, the troops, who were in great want of provisions, had orders to carry away all the grain they cou'd find. During the night the soldiers, under pretence of making a search, march'd towards the town, which they sack'd and pillag'd, burning all the houses, and even making the inhabitants slaves, the Cheriffs and doctors being the only persons exempt from this misfortune.

Timur had advice that a number of Rayas and little princes in the neighbourhood of Toulonba, who had before submitted to the Mirza Pir Mehemed, had now revolted; whereupon he sent the Emir Chamelik, and the Cheik Mehemed Aicoutmur, with their regiments, to ravage the country of these Rayas, with orders to punish 'em severely, for an example to others. The Emirs immediately departed, and enter'd the forests whither the enemy was retir'd. They kill'd two thousand Indians, who became a prey to the wild beasts and birds, and carrying away their children prisoners, they return'd to the court, laden with the spoils of the rebels.

The eighth of Sefer, Timur departed from Nov. 5. Toulonba, and next day encamp'd on the borders of a deep lake, situate on the bank of the Biah *, within sight of the town of Chanavaz

---

* A river near Lahor, which falls into the Rave.

CHAP. XII.

Timur marches in search of Nusret Coukeri.

TIMUR, having advice that Nusret, brother of the Cheik Coukeri, had surrounded this deep and large lake with a wall, behind which he had retir'd with two thousand men, immediately took horse, and leaving the baggage, went to encamp with his army on the borders of this lake. He rang'd his soldiers in order of battel, and gave the command of the right wing to the Emirs Cheik Noureddin and Allahdad, the two greatest men of their time. The left wing was given to the Emirs Chamelik and Cheik Mehemed Aicoutmur. The main body was commanded by Ali Sultan Tavachi, with the infantry of Corassana. And being all in order, they prepar'd to give a vigorous assault. Nusret at the head of a thousand Indians posted himself on the borders of the lake in view of our men. Ali Sultan immediately attack'd him with his infantry, and tho the marshes and sloughs were very disadvantageous to our men, yet they gave marks of their invincible courage. Ali Sultan was wounded in the fight, as well as several others of our captains but the Emirs Cheik Noureddin and Allahdad, entering into the bogs, cut all the enemys to pieces, and fixing their heads on their lances, laid 'em at Timur's feet. It's uncertain what became of Nusret, whether he fled into the desart, or was slain. The soldiers set fire to the houses of these rebels, pillag'd their goods, and brought away a great number of cattel.

The

The tenth of Sefer the army pass'd this great lake, and the low-lands, which were full of bogs and marshes, notwithstanding the extreme difficulty of the ways; and went to encamp at Chanavaz, a great and populous town. Here they found several granarys full of corn, of which the soldiers took as much as they had occasion for.

Shortly after the Emirs had orders to depart. They cross'd the river of Biah, in pursuit of some soldiers of Nufret who had fled. They overtook 'em, and having cut 'em in pieces, brought away a great booty. Timur staid two days at Chanavaz, and set fire to the granarys which were left, in order to reduce the infidels to extremity, and on the 13th of Sefer he decamp'd, and went down to the banks of the river Biah over against the town of Dgendgian, to which place the baggage and main body of the army was come. Here he made all his troops pass the river. The same day Herimule, a faithful domestic of prince Charoc, came from Herat: he acquainted the emperor with this prince's good state of health, which very much pleas'd him, and excited him to read the Alcoran, and distribute alms in token of joy.

CHAP. XIII.

Arrival of prince Pir Mehemed Gehanghir from Moultan.

WE said in the chapter * which gives the reason of Timur's march into India, that the Mirza Pir Mehemed besieg'd the town of Moultan, where, after a siege of six months,

C 2   the

Book IV the inhabitants were in such great want of victuals, that they were constrain'd to eat uncleanly things, and even dead bodys: and Sarenk the governor being at length oblig'd to fly, the town was taken by our prince, who immediately sent advice of it to the emperor. In the mean while there happen'd an * inundation, which caus'd a mortality among our horses, and oblig'd us to carry the sick horses into the town, and there shut 'em up.

Upon this accident the Rayas of these countrys revolted, tho' they had before submitted. They declar'd war against us by acts of hostility, massacring the governors who had been set over 'em. And as our men had no horses, these insolent people advanc'd during night to the gates of the town, which extremely disturb'd our Mirza. but at length the enemy, on advice of Timur's approach, flung away their weapons, and fled.

No. 11. The Mirza being deliver'd from this trouble, came out of Moultan the fourteenth of Sefer, and march'd to the imperial camp, on the banks of the Biah; where he had the honor to kiss the emperor's feet, who tenderly embrac'd him, and gave him a handsom reception.

Juneid Bourouldai, his brother Bayazid, and Mehemed Dervich Taicani, who in the wars of Carezem had fled from the Emir Gehancha, and with great difficulty were got into India

---

* Pechehal is the name the Indians give to the great rains and inundations which happen in India at a certain time of the year; for then they say to travellers, Don't go now, it is the season of Pechehal. This inundation is caus'd by the great rains and snows, which falling off the mountains, cover the flat countrys, fill the rivers, and overflow like the Nile in Egypt; and this constantly happens in the months of July, August, September and October.

having

having heard that the Mirza Pir Mehemed had made himself master of Moultan, came from the very furthest parts of India to implore his protection. The Mirza carry'd 'em to the emperor, and procur'd 'em the honor to salute him, begging pardon for 'em. Timur granted their lives, but not their libertys, before they had been baftinado'd according to the laws of Genghiz Can. The fifteenth of Sefer, Timur crofs'd the Biah, and went to encamp at Dgendgian, forty miles diftant from Moultan In three days the foldiers pafs'd this river, fome in barks, and others by fwimming, notwithstanding its rapidity, without any damage

Timur ftaid four days at Dgendgian; and the eighteenth of Sefer, the prince Pir Mehemed made a fumptuous banquet, and offer'd his rich prefents, which confifted of crowns of gold, belts of gold, Arabian horfes with gold faddles, jewels of great price, ftuffs, curious veffels, bafons and pots of gold and filver; of which there was fo great a number, that the fecretarys and comptrollers of the Divan employ'd two days in regiftring 'em. Timur diftributed thefe prefents among the Emirs, Vifiers and officers of his court, according to their deferts: and as the Mirza's foldiers had loft their horfes in this campain, and fome were oblig'd to ride on oxen, and others to go on foot, he gave thirty thoufand horfes among 'em. Then Timur departed for Schoual [1]: on the twenty firft of Sefer he encamp'd at Afouan [2], where he ftaid one day, and at length went to Gehaoul [3].

---

[1] Towns S. of the river Biah.
[2] A town between Lahor and Dipalpour, S. of the Biah.

The inhabitants of Dipalpour [1] had formerly submitted to the Mirza Pir Mehemed, who plac'd over 'em a governor nam'd Meflafer Calat, with a thousand men: but there being a mortality among the horses of the Mirza, which consequently diminish'd his troops, these men join'd with the Goulam [2] guards of Sultan Firouz Chah, and slew Meflafer with the thousand men he commanded. On the report of Timur's approach, these rebels, thinking to escape the emperor's fury, retir'd with their effects into the fortress of Batn r. Timur, at his arrival at Gehenal, left the Lmir Chahmelik and Dolet Timur Tavachi, with the baggage and main-body of the army, which he order'd 'em to conduct by the way of Dipalpour, and to join him at Samane, a town near Deli. Then he departed with ten thousand horse, and got to Adjoudan on the twenty fourth of Sefer, the inhabitants of which town having been drawn from their obedience to the nephew of the Cheik Nouredin, by the Cheiks Munaver and Sad, had shamefully abandon'd their country: for these Cheiks after having seduc'd 'em, took 'em into their pay, and carry'd 'em to a town call'd Pati, except some few who fled to Deli with the Cheik Munaver.

The Cheiks and doctors, being inform'd of the respect Timur always shew'd to men of their character, were so far from being disturb'd at

---

[1] A town between Lahor and Deli.
[2] Goulams are the corps-de-garde of the Indian kings, who are commonly slaves turn'd Mahometans. They are educated by the kings orders in the noble exercise of arms and sciences. There are also such in Persia, who in their youth are call'd Goulams, and when grown up and incorporated among the guards, Cezelbashi.

these actions, that as soon as they had advice Chap. 14. of his arrival in their quarters, they came immediately to the foot of the throne, and met with a kind reception there. Timur gave the government of their town to Moulana Nasereddin Amor, and to Chahab Mehemed son of Coja Mahmoud, with orders to hinder the troops in their passage from molesting the inhabitants of that place. Thus Timur treated those civilly who rely'd on his protection, and extirpated those who refus'd to submit, pillaging their goods, and carrying away prisoners their women and children.

CHAP. XIV.

The taking the town of Bend, and the fortress of Batnir, the inhabitants of which places are put to the sword.

THE citadel of Batnir was the strongest and most noted place in India; situate in a desart, and out of the common road. The inhabitants have no water, except from a great lake near the gate of the town, which is never fill'd but in inundations; and as no foreign army ever came into these parts before, the inhabitants of Dipalpour, Adjoudan and other towns, fled for refuge into Batnir, to escape the fury of our soldiers. So many had retir'd hither, that the place not being large enough to contain all their cattel and effects, they had left without a great number of cattel, and several chariots fill'd with moveable goods.

Book IV
Nov. 22.

The twenty fifth of Sefer, in the morning, Timur enter'd Adjoudan; he visited the sepulchre of the Cheik Ferid Cheker Condge, whose protection he implor'd near God's throne. Then he departed for the conquest of Batnir, cross'd the river Dena, and encamp'd on the hill of Calescuteli, ten miles distant from Adjoudan, and fifty from Batnir, three miles, which they call Gourouh, making one Farsanga, or a Persian league. Timur read the noon-prayers at Calescuteli, and then he march'd all night by moonlight, and cross'd the great desart in one day.

Nov. 23.

The twenty sixth of Sefer, at ten in the morning, he came before Batnir, and immediately caus'd the drums to be beat, and the great cry Souroun to be made: and the soldiers pillag'd whatever they cou'd find without the place. Raoudouldgin the governor prepar'd to make resistance. He had a great many soldiers and domestics, and reign'd as a sovereign in that country. He forc'd the merchants and caravans to pay custom to him, no one being safe from his insults. The strength of the place, the many officers, and the abundance of effects he had, made him so insolent and proud, that he refus'd to obey Timur; for which reason the army march'd directly against the place. The right wing was commanded by the Emir Solyman Chah, the Cheik Noureddin, and Allahdad, and the left had for its leaders, the Mirza Calil Sultan, and the Cheik Mehemed Aicoutmur.

At the first attack our generals made themselves masters of the out-parts and suburbs, where they slew a great number of Indians, and got a vast quantity of booty; they also took the counterscarp: and at the same time the Emirs, colonels and captains invested the town,

and

The history of Timur-Bec.

and arming themselves with their bucklers, gave a second assault. Raoudouldgin posted himself at the gate of the town with the bravest of his Indians; but the Emirs Solyman Chah, Seid Coja and Gehan Mulc, who belong'd to prince Charoc's court, march'd to attack that gate. Seid Coja and Gehan Mulc fell briskly upon the enemy near the person of the Indian prince, and perform'd several heroic actions. Then all the soldiers began to advance at the sound of kettledrums, drums and trumpets, and the terrible Kerrenai. They gave many assaults, and as they were on the point of gaining the place, Raoudouldgin, despairing of being able to make any longer resistance, demanded quarter, and had recourse to the emperor's clemency. He sent a Cheriff to Timur, to desire a suspension of arms for one day, on condition that he came the next to cast himself at his feet. Timur granted his petition for the messenger's sake, who was of the race of Mahomet; he order'd his soldiers to retire from the gate of the town, and even from the suburbs, and to incamp in the open plain. Next day Raoudouldgin not keeping his word, orders were given that every Emir shou'd sap that part of the walls which was over-against his respective post, that they might the more easily take the town by assault. Every one obey'd, and all the fire, stones and arrows the besieg'd cast upon our men, cou'd not divert 'em. Raoudouldgin and all his court being astonish'd at their intrepidity, got upon the tops of their towers, and made signals that they implor'd the conqueror's clemency, acknowledg'd their fault, and wou'd for the future obey the emperor, only begging he wou'd save their lives. Timur, following the precepts of the Alcoran,

which

which tells us that pardon is the tithe of victory, hearken'd to their prayer: whereupon in the evening R...ouldgin sent his son Naib, with presents of animals and arabian horses, to the foot of the throne. Timur, after a handsom reception, gave him a vest of gold-brocade, a belt and sword; and then sent him back to his father. This prince took courage, and mov'd at Timur's civilitys, came out of the place the twenty-eighth of Sefer at nine in the morning, accompany'd by the Cheik Sadeddin Adjoudani, he kifs'd the threshold of the door, and at length approach'd the imperial carpet, he made several presents of animals and three sets of arabian horses, nine in a set, with saddles of gold to each. Timur recompens'd him with vests of gold, belts of gold, and a crown. And because the people who were in this place, were very numerous, especially those of Dipalpour and Adjoudan, the Emirs Solyman Chah and Allahdad had orders to guard the gate of the fortress. And on the twenty-ninth of Séfer, Timur order'd the people assembled there to come before him. They were put into the custody of some faithful persons, and near three hundred Arabian horses were taken from 'em, which Timur gave to the Emirs and bravest warriors of the army. Five hundred of the inhabitants of Dipalpour were put to the sword, and their wives and children made slaves, for having treacherously slain Messater Cabuli, and a thousand horsemen belonging to the Mirza Pir Mehemed. And as for the people of Adjoudan, who had abandon'd Timur, part of 'em were slain, and the rest made prisoners, after having their effects pillag'd.

Ke-

Kemaleddin, brother of Raoudouldgin, having Chap. 14.
seen the punishment of those who had deserv'd
it, was seiz'd with a panic fear, and next day,
tho Raoudouldgin was in the imperial camp,
he caus'd the gate of the town to be shut. This
so irritated Timur, that he caus'd Raoudgould-
gin to be put in chains, and order'd the siege
to begin again, and the place to be fill'd with
the blood of the inhabitants. The soldiers
having set themselves to sap the walls, the besieg'd soon found they shou'd not be able to defend themselves against so warlike a people, and
an ever-victorious prince, they were persuaded
that if the place shou'd be taken by assault,
they must not expect their lives, for repentance
wou'd then signify nothing. Whereupon they
resolv'd to beg pardon of the emperor. Accordingly Raoudouldgin's brother and son went
out, to beseech Timur to grant a general pardon, and deliver'd the keys of the town and
castle into the hands of our officers.

The first of Rabiulevel, the Emirs Cheik Nov. 28.
Noureddin and Allahdad enter'd the place to
receive the tribute for saving the people's lives,
but the Rayas and other chiefs wou'd not accept the tax: and as there were among the
rest Guebres and idolaters, disputes arose, which
cou'd not be terminated without commotions and
broils. Timur was incens'd at this proceeding;
and order'd that this rabble shou'd be put to
the sword, and the houses of the infidels raz'd
to the ground. The soldiers scal'd the walls,
and enter'd the place sword in hand. The
Guebres set fire to their own houses, casting
their wives, children and goods into the fires;
and those who call'd themselves Mussulmans cut
their wives and childrens throats. And thus
the men of these two sorts uniting together,
put

put themselves in a posture of defence, being resolv'd to die sword in hand. They fought in a cruel obstinate manner: and as these men were exceeding strong and courageous, tho ignorant, they may be compar'd to an army of satyrs, who fight only in despair.

Our men having enter'd the place, and cry'd out Allahou Ecber[1], fell upon these enrag'd people, who slew several Muslulmans, and wounded others. The Emir Cheik Noureddin, who to partake of the honor of this expedition, had resolv'd to dare the greatest dangers, advanc'd into the midst of the enemy, and struck with his sword one of the bravest of 'em, whom he disabled from fighting. But the Emir was immediately surrounded by a troop of Guebres, and was near being seiz'd by 'em, had not Ouzoun Mezid of Bagdad, and Firouz of Sistan made their way thro these infidels, and deliver'd him from danger. Victory at length declaring for our men, they slew ten thousand Indians, set fire to the houses which remain'd, and even ruin'd the walls of the town, so that it look'd like an uninhabitable place. The emperor distributed among the soldiers all the gold, silver, horses and habits that were in the place. He rewarded the wounded; and gave great gifts to Ouzoun Mezid and Firouz, who had acted with so much resolution in delivering the Emir Cheik Noureddin, and rais'd 'em to dignitys according to their merit.

---

[1] God is great. The Mahometants begin all their prayers with these words, which they often repeat, with their face towards the ground.

CHAP.

CHAP. XV.

Timur departs from Batnir, for Serefti, Fatabad and Ahrouni.

AFTER the ruin of Batnir, the multitude of dead carcasses which infected the air, oblig'd Timur to depart thence the third of Rabiulevel. When he had march'd about fourteen or fifteen miles, he came to Kenarei Haouz *, where he encamp'd. Next day he went to the castle of Firouze, and march'd as far as the town of Serefti, the inhabitants of which being infidels, eat swines-flesh. They fled on advice of Timur's arrival, who sent out a detachment of horse in pursuit of 'em. These cavalry overtook a great number, whom they put to the sword, and brought their horses and goods back to the camp; Adel Ferach being the only person on our side who was slain. Timur staid one day at Serefti, and the next march'd eighteen miles, as far as Fatabad, where he encamp'd. The inhabitants of this town were also fled. Some of our men pursu'd 'em, destroy'd several, and return'd loaden with booty, as silver, furniture and cattel.

The seventh of Rabiulevel, Timur pass'd by the town of Redgebuour, and went to encamp near that of Ahrouni, which was inhabited by a brutish people, unfit for making compliments to the emperor, or demanding his protection: wherefore part of 'em were destroy'd like beasts, and the rest made slaves by the soldiers, who carry'd away their corn, and set fire to their houses

Nov. 30.

* The bank of the bason.

Dec. 4.

Book IV
Dec. 5.

The eighth of Rabiulevel, the army departed from Ahrom, to encamp in the plains of the village of Touhene, a country inhabited by Getes, who had by force of arms made themselves masters of it a long time, and committed disorders there. They rob'd on the high-ways, insulted and pillag'd the caravans, and not having the least marks of religion, murder'd all who oppos'd their violence. On the report of the arrival of our troops, these wretches hid themselves in the midst of a wood, where almost all the trees were full of prickles.

The emperor sent against 'em a regiment commanded by Touhel Hindoui Carcara, and Moulana Naseieddin Amor. These two lords made so strict a search after these robbers, that they put to the sword near two thousand, render'd themselves masters of their cattel, and return'd to the imperial camp, dragging after 'em several of these wretches loaded with chains.

CHAP. XVI.

Timur marches against a nation of rebellious Getes

Dec. 6

TIMUR's intention in these wars being chiefly to exterminate robbers, tyrants and infidels, to put a stop to their disorders, and give peace and tranquillity to the people, he departed from Touhene the ninth of Rabiulevel, and having sent the baggage under the conduct of Solyman Chah towards Samane, he march'd beyond the castle of Mounec, where he encamp'd. Then he enter'd the deserts and woods, whither the Getes were retir'd

he

he exterminated two thousand of 'em, mak- Chap.16.
ing their wives and children slaves, and
pillaging their goods and cattel. Thus he deliver'd the country from the fear of their insults.

Several Cheriffs, who made their ordinary residence in a town in these quarters, came to cast
themselves at Timur's feet, and kiss'd his hands.
Timur receiv'd 'em with demonstrations of
esteem and affection, gave 'em vests and considerable presents, and fix'd a governor over
'em, to defend 'em from the insults of our soldiers.

The tenth of Rabiulevel, the Emir Solyman Dec. 7.
Chah departed with all the train of artillery
which was before Mounec, and march'd towards the town of Samane, where he staid one
night. The eleventh of Rabiulevel he arriv'd Dec. 8.
at the river of Kehker, at which place Timur
join'd him, after he had been against the Getes.
Here he staid four days, to wait the remainder
of the baggage. He departed hence the fif- Dec. 12.
teenth of Rabiulevel, and went to encamp near
the bridge of Foulcouble, where he was join'd
by the Emirs and soldiers of the left wing,
commanded by the Sultan Mahmoud Can, and
several others, whom Timur had sent from the
meadow of Cabul by a particular road into
India, where they had taken towns, ravag'd
the country, and brought into subjection several
people.

The sixteenth of Rabiulevel, the emperor, at Dec. 13.
the head of his army, cross'd the bridge of Foulcouble, and encamp'd on the other side. The
baggage and remainder of the army from Dipalpour, under the conduct of the great general
Chamelik, also arriv'd the same day at the imperial camp.

The

Dec. 17. The twentieth of Rabiulevel, the army departed from Foulcouble. They went but five miles that day, and encamp'd near the bridge Foulbeiran. The twenty first they arriv'd at the town of Kuteil, seventeen miles from Samane.

CHAP. XVII.

A review of the whole army marching in order of battel.

WHEN the several bodys of the army, which had taken different roads, had join'd the imperial camp, orders were given that every Emir shou'd repair to his respective post. The right wing was commanded by the Mirzas Pir Mehemed and Rouftem; the left by the great Sultan Mahoud, Can of Zagatai, with the princes of the blood, and several Emirs: and the main body was compos'd of divers Tomans and regiments, which march'd six leagues and two miles by the road of Deli.

Dec. 19. The twenty-second of Rabiulevel, they arriv'd at the town of Aflendi, seventeen miles from Kuteil. The inhabitants of Samane, Kuteil, and Aflendi, who were mostly idolaters, burnt their own houses, and fled to Deli; so that our men cou'd meet with no one in their country.

Dec. 20. The twenty-third, after a march of six miles, they encamp'd at Toglocpour, the inhabitants of which town were of a particular religion. They believ'd that the whole universe was govern'd by two beings, the first of which they call Yezdan, that is, God, and the other Ahrimen, that is, the devil. The former they

explain

The history of Timur-Bec.   49

explain by light, and the other by darkness, Chap. 17.
pretending that all good proceeds from God,
and all evil from the devil.

These idolaters, call'd Souloun, having all
fled, our soldiers set fire to the town. The
twenty-fourth of Rabiulevel the army arriv'd at Dec. 21.
Panipat, a town twelve miles from Toglocpour.
All the inhabitants had fled like the rest. There
was found in this place a granary of wheat, in
which were more than ten thousand Mans ' of
full weight, worth about a hundred and sixty
thousand Mans of common weight, which was
distributed among the soldiers. The twenty-   Dec. 22.
fifth they march'd about six miles, and encamp'd on the bank of the river of Panipat.
The twenty-sixth all the Emirs girded on their Dec. 23.
cuirasses, that they might be ready upon occasion, and then continu'd their march.

The twenty-seventh of Rabiulevel, the Emirs Dec. 24.
of the right wing had orders to march as far as
Gehannumai, a palace built by the Sultan Firouz
Chah on the top of a mountain, two leagues
from Deli, at the foot of which runs the great
river Jaoun. According to this order, they
march'd from Canighuzin as far as Gehannumai, putting to the sword all the officers they
met, and making slaves of the inhabitants of
that country, whom they pillag'd. On mon-
day the twenty-ninth, Timur departed from the Dec. 26.
town of Pelle, cross'd the Jaoun, and march'd
to the right of the town of Louni, where was
abundance of pasture: here he encamp'd the
same day. This place is situate between the
two rivers of Jaoun and Hilen. The latter is
a great branch which the Sultan Firouz Chah

' A Man is a pound, or thereabouts.

Vol II   D   had

had cut off from the river of Calini, which joins the Jaoun near the town of Firouzabad. The Emirs Gehan Chah, Chamelik, and Allahdad, were already come to the foot of this castle, the governors of which, nam'd Maimoun and Maichoum, far from coming to meet 'em with submission, resolv'd to defend themselves. At Timur's arrival there, an experienc'd old man came out to cast himself with respect at the emperor's feet, and demand his protection but the inhabitants, who were Guebres and the servants of Mellor, persisted in their rash resolution of resistance.

Then Timur order'd his men to besiege the town, and sap the walls. Accordingly they began to do it at noon, and by evening made themselves masters of the place, where the Guebres had burnt their houses, with their women and children. Timur repos'd himself this night

Dec. 27. without the place, and the thirtieth of Rabiulevel order'd that the inhabitants who were Mahometans, shou'd be separated from the Guebres and servants of Mellou Can, which being done, the latter were put to the sword. All the houses were pillag'd excepting those of the Cheriffs, for whom Timur always preserv'd a filial affection, because of their extraction: and then the rest of the town was set on fire.

Dec. 28. The first of Rabiulakher, Timur departed from the town of Louni, and went to the bank of the Raoun, before the palace of Gehannmai, so that observing himself the passages in these places, he might the better know how to give out his orders. He return'd to the camp in the evening, and assembled his imperial council, consisting of the princes his children, the great Emirs, and generals of his army. He propos'd to 'em the method of forming the siege of Deli,

capital

capital of India, which was not far off: and it was resolv'd, that a great quantity of corn and ammunition shou'd be got together forthwith, and kept in Gehanumai, and that this great city shou'd be block'd up.

Accordingly the Emirs Solyman Chah, Gehan Chah, and others, were order'd to pillage the granarys in the neighbourhood of Deli: whereupon they set out in the beginning of the month of Rabialakher. Next day Timur was for taking the diversion of walking in the palace of Gehannumai: he took horse with seven hundred cavaliers with their cuirasses on, pass'd the river Jaonn, and enter'd into this magnificent palace, to which the Sultan Firouz Chah had given the name of Gehannumai, that is, the mirror of the universe, because of its fine prospect, tho one wou'd think this name was rather given it, to prognosticate that it shou'd fall into the hands of the monarch of the universe.

After Timur had consider'd the beautys of this place, he took care to observe from this rising-ground the properest place for the field of battel, that he might draw the enemys thither in case they appear'd. In the mean time Ali Sultan Tavachi and Juneid Bourouldai, who had been sent out as scouts, return'd, Ali Sultan bringing with him Mehemed Selef whom he had seiz'd, and Juneid bringing another. Mehemed Selef was question'd concerning what had been transacted in the city, and then put to death. When Timur had pass'd the river, to observe the field of battel, four thousand horse, five thousand foot, and twenty-seven elephants, belonging to Mellou Can, were seen near Gehannumai. Our scouts, commanded by Seid Coia and Mobacher, to the number

D 2 of

of three hundred, attack'd their vanguard, and pretending to fly, led 'em as far as the bank of the river, where a furious battel ensu'd.

On notice of this, Timur sent Sevindgic Behader and Alahdad to succour Seid Coja; they cross'd the river with their regiments, and having join'd him, let fly a shower of arrows on the enemy, but as they were about to fall on 'em with their drawn swords, the Indians, unaccustom'd to such brave actions, gave ground at the first onset, and fled towards the city, which with difficulty they enter'd. Seid Coja pursu'd 'em, and flew a great number. In this fight an elephant fell and was wounded, which was a prognostic of our further victory.

CHAP. XVIII.

Timur marches to the east side of the town of Louni. Massacre of a hundred thousand Indian slaves who were in his camp.

THE third of Rabiulakher, Timur departed from Gehannumai, and went to encamp on the east side of Louni, where the emperor's sons *, the great Emirs, the colonels of the regiments, who were gone out to make inroads, came to the imperial camp. Being all assembled, Timur, who wou'd not give place to the greatest generals of the army, nor the most undaunted warriors, as well in policy and wisdom of government, as in war, believ'd it not improper to harangue the leaders, imitating in that the example of the antient emperors and the most illustrious conquerors. This he did with all the eloquence that cou'd be expected on the like occasion. He spoke to 'em of the manner of breaking thro ranks, of overturning squadrons, and how they shou'd repulse the enemy: he instructed 'em how to make retreats when overpower'd, and how rally the soldiers and return to the attack, how to sustain an obstinate fight, and how to free one's self from any eminent danger. In short, he explain'd to 'em, with so much energy and perspicuity, all the maxims of war, that his captains admir'd the extraordinary wisdom and experience which appear'd in his speech, saying that the discourses of great princes are the most beautiful, insomuch that being excited by the livly reasons and learned maxims which he had inculcated, they were fill'd with zeal and ardor, and prepar'd to confront the greatest dangers in his service. They answer'd every thing he propos'd by generous vows for his prosperity, and the continuation of his victorys, they kiss'd the ground on which he stood, to testify their respect and joy at being the officers of so great a conqueror.

Timur harangues the army.

The same day the Emir Gehan Chah and the other generals remonstrated to Timur, that since his crossing the Indus, they had made above a hundred thousand Indians slaves, who were mostly Guebres and idolaters; that they were now in the camp, and wou'd probably in any obstinate battel, take part with the men of Deli, and falling upon our soldiers, make us lose the battel. This remonstrance was back'd by those who had observ'd, that when the officers of Mellou Can came out of Deli with their elephants to attack us, the slaves seem'd highly pleas'd. Timur having made a serious reflection on all the circumstances of this affair,

pass'd

Book IV. pass'd an order, that those who had any Indian slaves shou'd put 'em to death, and he who defer'd or refus'd doing so, shou'd be put to death himself, and his wives, children and effects be given to him who shou'd inform against him.

As soon as this order was made public, they began to put it in execution, and in less than an hour were put to death a hundred thousand Indians, according to the smallest computation. Among others, Moulana Nasereddin Amor, one of the most venerable doctors of the court, who could never consent so much as to kill a single sheep, was constrain'd to order fifteen slaves whom he had in his house to be slain. Timur afterwards order'd that one soldier out of every ten, shou'd keep watch over the Indian women and children, as also over the camels they had taken in the pillage.

After these precautions, Timur resolv'd to march to the siege of Dehli: he set out on the third of Rabiulakher at noon, to encamp on the bank of the Jaoun. The astrologers and sooth-sayers secretly disputed concerning the disposition of the heavens, and of the fortunate or unfortunate aspects of the planets at his departure; but Timur told 'em that neither joy nor affliction, adversity nor prosperity, depended on the stars, but on the will of the Creator of them, of men, and of the universe. "I confide, " says the emperor, "in the assistance of the Al- "mighty, who has never abandon'd me. " What avail the triplicities or conjunctions of "the planets? I'll never delay one moment the "execution of my projects, when I have taken "sufficient measures and precautions to bring "'em to perfection." Next morning our hero made the public prayer, and order'd an Ac-

The history of Timur-Bec.

coran to be brought him, from whence he might Chap 19.
judg of the event of his expedition. Here
he found a very favorable answer, which point-
ed out the destruction of a people by a wonder-
ful effect of the almighty providence. He explain'd the passage in his own favor, and having
shewn it to all the army, became assur'd of the
victory. Our warriors being thus animated by
the Alcoran, which promis'd 'em the divine
protection, Timur despis'd the stars, and on
the fifth of Rabiulakher 801, cross'd the river Jan 1.
of Jaoun, and encamp'd on its banks on the
other side. The soldiers thro precaution made
a ditch to surround 'em, near a hill nam'd Pouch-
tei Behali, here they fix'd palisados of branches
of trees, and for a rampart bound several great
buffalos neck and heels, behind which they
prepar'd their bucklers and ensigns.

CHAP. XIX.

*Timur gives battel to Sultan Mahmoud, em-
peror of India.*

TUESDAY-morning the seventh of Ra- Jan. 3.
biulakher, Timur drew up his army in
order of battel. He gave the command of the
right wing to prince Pir Mehemed Gehanghir,
accompany'd by several Emirs. The left wing
was led by the Mirzas, Sultan Hussein, and Calil Sultan, also assisted by many great generals.
The rear was given to the Mirza Roustem,
in conjunction with several illustrious Emirs
and the main body was commanded by Timur
himself, it being fit that this prince, who was
D 4   the

Book IV. the very life of the soldiers, shou'd be fix'd in the heart of the army. Every thing being thus settled, they march'd in good order.

The enemy also advanced in order of battel. Their right wing was brought up by Tagi Can, Mir Ali Coja, and other Indian princes. The left had for its leaders Malek Moineddin, and others; and the main body was commanded by the Sultan Mahmoud Can, grandson of Firoz Chah, emperor of India, he having for his lieutenant-general Melou Can. This army consisted of ——thousand horse well equipp'd, and ——thousand foot arm'd to advantage; besides several elephants of war, arm'd with cuirasses, having between their long teeth great poison'd daggers, and on their backs wooden towers in form of bastions, on which were mounted a great many cross-bow-men and archers who cou'd fight under covert as in fortresses; and on the side of the elephants march'd those who were arm'd with pots of fire and melted pitch, as also rockets arm'd at the ends with iron, which give several blows one after another wherever they fall.

Our soldiers were not much disturb'd about this Indian army; but as they had never seen any elephants before, they ignorantly imagin'd that the arrow and sabre had no effect on the bodies of these animals, that they were so very strong that they overthrew trees only by shaking the earth as they pass'd along, that they cou'd throw down the strongest buildings, and that in battel they cou'd toss both horse and horsemen to a vast height in the air. This dispirited several of our side; so that when the posts were fix'd for the officers and lords of the court, Timur, who always shew'd respect to men of learning, civilly demanded of 'em what posts they

they wou'd chuse. Several of these doctors, who were always near Timur's person, being frighten'd at what they had read and heard of the elephants, answer'd immediately, "If it please your majesty, we chuse to be near the ladys."

Timur being sensible of his soldiers fear, took all necessary precautions to arm 'em with courage. He order'd that a rampart of bucklers shou'd be made before the ranks, and a ditch dug before the rampart. then he caus'd buffalos to be tied by the neck and feet with long pieces of leather, close to each other, after which on each side of 'em and on their heads were fix'd brambles. Besides this were made iron-hooks, three-fork'd, and fix'd to stakes, so that when the elephants shou'd come to the attack, these hooks shou'd be planted in their way, and the brambles on the buffalos set on fire to put the elephants into disorder. But victory declar'd for us before we had occasion to make use of these machines.

Timur's artifice to overcome the Indian elephants.

As soon as the two armys were in view, Timur got upon an eminence in the middle of the field of battel, near the foot of the hill of Ponchtei Behan, whence he observ'd the motion of both armys. When they were on the point of coming to blows, he fell on the earth, and after several times bowing, besought God to give him the victory, which he must expect from the divine goodness, and not from his own valor, and the number of his soldiers.

While Timur was at prayers, a strange accident happen'd, which was, that the Emirs of the rear, Cheik Noureddin, Chamelik and Alahdad, imagin'd that if the emperor shou'd send recruits from the main body to the right wing, and even to the rear, this wou'd be a certain token

Book IV. token of victory. Accordingly after prayer Timur order'd Ali Sultan Tavachi, and Tagi Bouga, who commanded the regiment of Sanfiz of the Toman of Rouftem, which belong'd to the main-body; as also Altou Bacchi Peferi, and Moufla Recmal, to go with their regiments to fuccour the right wing, and at the same time he sent another squadron of Emirs to re-inforce the rear. This so excited the courage of our warriors, that they rush'd impetuously upon the enemy, whom they attack'd with so much vigor, that the Indians were constrain'd to give ground, and the great and strong elephants suffer'd themselves to be drove like oxen.

This advantage augmented the valor of the other battalions, who also fell upon the enemy, praising God. So hot a battel was ne'er seen before. The fury of foldiers was ne'er carry'd to so great excess, and so frightful a noise was never heard: for the cymbals, the common kettledrums, the drums and trumpets, with the great brass kettledrums which were beat on the elephants backs, the bells which the Indians founded, and the cries of the foldiers, were enough to make even the earth to shake; and there was not a man, how dauntless foever, who was not somewhat dismay'd at the beginning of the fight. But our vanguard, compos'd of the regiments of many illustrious Emirs, perceiving the enemy's vanguard advancing, retir'd behind the right wing to lie in ambuscade, till they had pass'd by 'em, then they came out of their ambuscade, and fell on the enemy sword in hand like roaring lions, and in a moment flew between five and six hundred men. The prince Pir Mehemed, who was at the head of the vanguard of the right wing, assisted by the Emir Soliman Chah, attack'd the left of the enemy, which

which confided in the valor of Tagi Can this Chap.19 he did with so much conduct, that he drove 'em beyond the bason of Havizcas. Then Pir Mehemed fell upon the elephants, and these furious animals, finding themselves closely press'd, enter'd among the ranks of the enemy's left wing, and caus'd a further disorder. Our left wing, conducted by the Mirza Sultan Hussein, perform'd several great actions, thro the valor of that prince, of Gehan Chah Behader, Cayafeddin Tercan, and others, for they made the enemy's right wing, commanded by Moineddin and Malek Hani, give ground, and those who escap'd the edge of the sword, were repuls'd as far as the gate of the city. While the enemy's wings were thus gaul'd, their main body, sustain'd by the elephants in good order, came to the attack: they had a warm reception from the Mirza Roustem who commanded the rear, and was posted over against 'em. A bloody battel ensu'd, in which the Emir Cheik Noureddin gave marks of extraordinary valor. The Emir Chamelik also perform'd the most heroic actions, rushing furiously into the midst of the elephants, with Dolet Timur Tavachi, and Mengheli Coja. With their lances they overthrew those who were mounted on the elephants, and with their sabres and arrows cut off the trunks of these terrible animals, whom they wounded in all parts of their bodys; so that in a short time the field of battel was cover'd with the elephants trunks, and the heads and bodys of the slain.

The most valiant Indians always endeavor'd to defend themselves, but this defence seem'd rather like the struggling of sheep going to the slaughter, than a vigorous resistance. Thus these poor Indians were constrain'd to turn their

their backs with their elephants; to which this passage of the Alcoran may be well apply'd. " Do you not see how the Lord thy God has " dealt with the men of the elephant? "

The Sultan Mahmoud, and his head-general Meilk Can, fled into the city, the gate of which they shut.

The Mirza Caul Sultan, who commanded our left wing, brought to Timur one of the elephants bound with cords, after having very much mauld it with the sword, he overthrew its guards, and made it walk before him, as the husbandman does the ox in the plow. Timur and all the court were surpriz'd that a child, of but fifteen years old, shou'd dare to attack, and be able to conquer and bind a war-elephant, which had struck terror into the whole army.

When the flight of the enemy had assur'd us of [...], Timur spur'd his horse towards the gate of Deli, and carefully examin'd the walls and fortifications; and as it was the time of noon-prayer, he went down to the bank of the Havzee, which is a round bason, above an arrow's shot in diameter, built by the Sultan Firouz Chah, and as in any inundations it is fill'd with rain-water, it furnishes the inhabitants of Deli with water for an intire year. On its bank is the tomb of Sultan Firouz Chah.

Timur being encamp'd here, the princes and generals came before him to kiss the earth, they congratulated him on his victory, and gave thanks to the princes of the blood, the Emirs, and other brave men, who had signaliz'd themselves in the battel.

[...] an epocha call'd the

Timur

The history of Timur-Bec.

Timur upon hearing these strange adventures, Chap 20. burst out into tears of joy; he bless'd God for having given him such brave children, and such faithful and valiant subjects. Was it not surprizing, that this great prince, who on some occasions cou'd exercise extraordinary severitys, had at this time so tender a heart, that he cou'd not refrain his tears, while he return'd thanks to God for his favors? Timur had in the person of Calil Sultan a son worthy of himself, who in magnificence, valor and generosity, surpass'd Menoutcher¹, Feridon and Kei Cosru*; he was as virtuous as Alexander, and as rich as Darius. He was at first nam'd the friend of God, Calil Allah, and the glory he afterwards acquir'd, was the reason of his being call'd Sultan.

* Cosroes.

CHAP. XX.

Flight of Sultan Mahmoud, and his general Mellou Can, prince of Moultan. Reduction of Deli capital of India.

THE Sultan Mahmoud and Mellou Can, being vanquish'd, re-enter'd the city, repenting they had ever undertaken to go out but repentance now being useless, they cou'd have recourse only to flight. They departed at midnight while it was very dark the Sultan went out by the gate of Havaderam, and Mellou by that of Barake, both which are si-

¹ Son of Feridon, king of Persia.

tuated

tracted south of Gehanpenah, and they retir'd into the deserts.

Timur being inform'd of this flight, sent several Emirs in pursuit of 'em; they seiz'd on some of their officers who fled with 'em, and return'd with a great quantity of booty, taking prisoners the prince Seif Can, sirnam'd Malek Cherefeddin, and the prince Cedadad, son of Mellou Can.

The same night the Emir Allahdad, and other colonels of our regiments, had orders to make themselves masters of the gates by which the princes went out, as also to guard the other gates of the city, that no one might escape.

The eighth of Rabiulakher, Timur erected his standard on the walls of Deli, and went in person to the gate of the capital, where he sat on the Aidgiah, or throne whereon the Indian emperors sit in their royal robes on the great festi-days. This gate is in the quarter of Gehanpenah, over against the bason of Havizeas. In this place a tent and tribunal were prepar'd for him, where he gave audience. Then the Cheifs, Cadis, and principal persons of the city of Deli, came to cast themselves at the foot of the throne, and had the honor to kiss the imperial carpet. Fadlallah Bacchi, lieutenant of Mellou Can, at the head of the whole Divan of Deli, was the first who came to make his submission, and the Cherifs, the men of learning, and the old men, address'd themselves to the princes the emperor's sons, and to the great Emirs, to obtain quarter for the Mirza Pir Mehemed, and the Emirs Solyman Chah and Gehan Chah, at a proper time presented their petition.

According to custom they carry'd the horse's tails and kettledrums, which were fix'd upon

the

the gate, and the conforts of mufic were per- Chap. 20.
form'd on this occafion on the tune Rihavi, us'd
only on victorys And to preferve the memory
of fo confiderable a conqueft, an ingenious poet
made thefe verfes, the letters of which form
the epocha of this memorable day [*].

> *On wednefday the eighth of the month of Rabiulak-* Jan 4
> *her, the ever-victorious emperor Timur made* 1399.
> *himfelf mafter of Deli, the fun being in Ca-*
> *pricorn*

All the elephants and rhinoceros's were
brought to Timur. Thefe animals, being before inftructed, fell down before the emperor
in an humble pofture, and at the fame time
made a great cry as if they demanded quarter.
There were an hundred and twenty of thefe
elephants of war, which at the return from
India were fent to Samarcand, and to the provinces of the empire, where Timur's fons refided Two were carry'd chain'd to Tauris,
one to Chiraz, five to Herat, one to Chirvan
to the Cheik Ibrahim, and one to Arzendgian
to the lord Taharten The tenth of Rabiulak- Jan. 6.
her, the doctor Nafereddin Amor was order'd
to enter the city, with the other lords and Cheriffs of the court, to preach in the grand mofque,
and make the public prayers and Coutbe in the
auguft name and titles of the invincible empe-

---

[*] The Orientals have an alphabet, the leters of which they
make ufe of inftead of cyphers, and by which they compofe
a verfe to the praife of any one who has perform'd fome remarkable action, and the letters of this verfe us'd for cyphers,
denote the day, month and year wherein this action was perform'd.

or Timur, and not in the name of Firou Chah, as was done before.

The Debirs, Menehis and other secretarys sent a relation of this expedition, in their letters of conquest, into all the parts of the empire, and even to the princes in alliance with Timur, tho it were a year's journey to go round to em all, so that public rejoicings might be made for these great advantages with which God distinguish'd the reign of Timur.

The Bitictechis, or controllers of the Divan also enter'd the city, where having taken an estimate of the mony due for saving the peoples lives, the receivers-general took care to receive it

In the mean while the principal lords of the court, and the emperor's favorites remonstrated to his majesty, that after having suffer'd the fatigues and difficultys of this war, victory inspir'd 'em with thoughts of renewing their diversions and pleasures, that Feridon and the Keis had always done the same, and that it was in justice due to 'em after they had thus fatigu'd themselves The emperor willingly consented, and gave orders for a feast, which was to continue for several days. Timur began the rejoicings by presents to the princes of the blood, the Emirs and generals of the army, in consideration of their services and great actions: and afterwards the musicians perform'd consorts of music in amerous and drinking tunes, which so charm'd the hearts of all, that they forgot the rigors of war, and the fatigues of a campain

Jan. 12. The sixteenth of Rabiulakher, a great number of our soldiers being assembled at the gate of Deli, insulted the inhabitants of the suburbs The great Emirs were order'd to put a stop to these disorders, but God, who had predestin'd the

the ruin of this place for the chastisement of the inhabitants, permitted its destruction by second causes. Our soldiers coming into the place was one cause, and the despair of the Guebres, who remain'd in great numbers in the towns of Seiri, Gehanpenah and old Deli, was another. The curiosity of the Sultanesses to see the rarities of Deli, and particularly of the famous palace, adorn'd with a thousand columns, and built by the antient king of India, Melik Jouna, induc'd 'em to go into the city with all the court, which was very numerous, and the gate was left open to every one, so that above fifteen thousand of our soldiers got in unperceiv'd. Besides the Emirs and comptrollers of the Divan, who were set at the gate to receive the tribute for saving the inhabitants lives, other officers in commission had the same liberty to enter the city: but there remain'd a far greater number of troops in a large place between Deli, Seiri, and Gehanpenah. The disorders our men committed in the two last places caus'd a great bustle among the Guebres, who in despair fell upon our men, and several of 'em set fire to their houses, wherein their wives and children were burnt. Our men perceiving this desolation among the Guebres, pillag'd 'em, because of their evil designs. As other troops were let into the city to seize on the inhabitants of the neighbouring towns and villages who had fled for refuge thither, the confusion very much increas'd, and the troops within the place employ'd themselves intirely in plundering and burning the houses of the Guebres. The Emirs, to quell this disorder, caus'd the gates to be shut, that the troops without might not enter: but the soldiers within open'd the gates to their comrades, by

morning all the army enter'd, and the soldiers
ruſh'd in upon the Guebres or Idolaters, who oppos'd
their entrance. So on the seventeenth of Ra-
biul'eſſel, this great and proud city was
deſtroy'd.

The next day paſs'd in the ſame manner,
and there were ſome ſoldiers who took a hundred and fifty ſlaves, men, women and children, whom they carry'd out of the city, and
ſome ſoldiers brought twenty ſlaves to their
own ſhare. The other ſpoils of precious ſtones,
pearls, rubies, diamonds, ſtuffs, ſilks, gold and
ſilver veſſels, money, plate, and other curioſitys,
were innumerable, for the Indian women and
girls were adorn'd with precious ſtones, and
had chains on their feet and hands, and even on their
toes, bracelets and rings, of which our men
had ſuch great numbers, that they refus'd to
carry away a vaſt quantity of precious oint-
ments of inestimable value.

The nineteenth of Rabiulakher they did the
ſame in old Dehli, whither the reſt of the Guebres were retir'd. Theſe Indians aſſembled together in the great moſque, and prepar'd to defend themſelves, but the Emir Chamelik and
Ali Sultan Tavatchi came thither with five hundred men, and having forcibly enter'd the
moſque, ſent to the pits of hell the ſouls of
theſe infidels, of whoſe heads they erected
towers, and gave their bodys for food to the
birds and beaſts of prey. Never was ſuch a
number of fugitives and deſtruction heard of. As
old Dehli was pillag'd the ſame day, they made
ſlaves of theſe inhabitants lives, whom they loaded with chains, tho' they had promis'd 'em
their lives. Several men were employ'd in
making 'em quit the city, and as they went
out, every Emir of a Tuman or regiment
took

took a number of 'em for his service; and as there were several thousands of tradesmen and artizans, some were distributed among the princes and Emirs who serv'd under Timur, and others were sent to the officers of the emperor's sons, and to the other Emirs in their respective governments. The emperor likewise order'd that all the masons shou'd be kept for his particular service, as he design'd to build a spacious mosque in Samarcand of stone.

But it may not be amiss to give a description of the three towns which compose the city of Deli.* That of Seiri is surrounded with a wall in form of a circle, old Deli is the same, but much larger; and from the walls of Seiri on the north-east, to the walls of old Deli, which is on the south-west, there are two other walls, one on each side, and the ground which lies betwixt 'em is call'd Gehanpenah, and is larger than old Deli. Three gates of Seiri look towards Gehanpenah, and the four others have the prospect outwards. Gehanpenah has thirteen gates, six to the north-west, and seven to the south-east, so that when one speaks of Deli, we comprehend the three towns together, which have in all thirty gates.

---

* Description of Deli, as it was in the author's time, for at present what they call Deli is a new city, situate in a different place, built by Gelaleddin Ecber, and call'd Ecber Aba, from the name of that king, the father of Humaioun Chah.

CHAP XXI.

Timur departs from Deli, and pursues his conquests in the remoter parts of India, near the Ganges.

TIMUR continu'd fifteen days at Deli, the destruction of which place was caus'd by the ill conduct of the inhabitants: then having resolv'd to exterminate the idolaters of India, as well as the robbers and rebels, he march'd towards the other most famous places of this empire. At his departure he order'd the Cherifs, Cadis, doctors and Cheiks of the city, to assemble in the great mosque of Gehanpenah, and to chuse a governor over 'em, to protect 'em from the insults of the soldiers, who were by this render'd insolent.

The twenty-second of Rabiulakher, at ten in the morning, the army decamp'd from Gehinpenah, and march'd down to Firouz Abad, three miles from Deli. Here Timur staid an hour to view this delightful place; and after having made two Rekaats in the mosque belonging to it, which is built of stone on the banks of the Jaoun, to return thanks to God for his conquests, he departed out of this town.

About this time the lord Chandedoim, one of the Cherifs, who was sent with Aladin Nabi Letenin and the Cadi Codbeddin, who had been sent embassadors to the town of Coutele, return'd from their embassy: they brought advice that Bender Nagor, prince of these quarters, had willingly submitted to the emperor.

and hop'd next friday to have the honor to Chap. 22.
kiss the ground before his majesty, and offer
him his services. Timur being encamp'd on
the other side of Gehanama near Vezir Abad,
the embassadors presented him two white parrots, from Behader Nehar. These birds had
liv'd ever since the time of Toglac Chah, and
had been kept many years in the antichambers
of the emperors of India. Timur took this
curious present for a good augury, and continu'd his road six miles farther to a place call'd
Moudai, having before cross'd the Jaoun.

The twenty-fourth of Rabiulakher, he march'd Jan. 20.
six miles and encamp'd at Kece, where Behader Nehar with his son Coultach had the honor to kiss the imperial carpet, to offer a great
many rich presents, and assure the emperor of
their obedience. The twenty-fifth the army Jan. 21.
march'd to Baghbout, which for its beauty is
compar'd to the delicious garden of Durbehar,
and to the magnificent temple of the idols of
Fercar, which places are distant from each o-
ther six miles. The twenty-sixth they march'd Jan. 22.
also six miles, and encamp'd at Asar, situate
between two rivers, where Timur staid to repose himself.

CHAP. XXII.

Conquest of Myrthe. The Guebres are flea'd alive.

THE town of Myrthe being one of the most noted places of the empire of India, Timur resolv'd to make himself master of
it:

it; whereupon the twenty-fixth of Rabvulakher he fent thither from Afar the lord's Rouftem, Yagi Bouga, Chimenk, and Allahdad. The twenty-eighth thefe lords fent advice to the emperor, that Elias Ougani, and the fon of Moulana Ahmed Tohaneferi, with a Guebre nam'd Sefi, had fortify'd the town, and were back'd by a company of Guebres, that they had refus'd to fubmit, and had not only declar'd that they refolv'd to defend themfelves, but even dar'd to ufe fome infolent expreffions, faying that the emperor Tarmechirin Can once came to befiege the place, but was oblig'd to raife the fiege, and that they hop'd the fame would be our fate. This news difquieted Timur, and their fpeaking contemptuoufly of Turmechirin Can, whom they tax'd with cowardice, highly incens'd him. On Tuefday at the hour of morning-prayer he took horfe at the head of ten thoufand men, and in two days and one night, march'd twenty miles.

The twenty-ninth of Rabvulakher at noon he arriv'd at the town of Myrane, where he order'd the captains of the companys to undermine the walls. At night they vifited the works, not afore they had already advanc'd ten or fifteen cubits breadth to each baftion and courtine. All this fo furpriz'd the Guebres, that they ceas'd from defending themfelves.

Next day the Emir Allahdad, with his regiment, and more the fifth, confifting of the antient peers of the Cotchins, attack'd the gate of the town. A young lad, one of his domefticks, nam'd Serai, fon of Calender, boldly caft a net upon the battlement and mounted the walls. He was follow'd by Rouftem Penas, and a great many brave men, who rufh'd into the town, where in great [numbers they found?] Elias Ougani, and

and the son of Ichaneseri, governors of the place, whom they carry'd to the foot of the imperial throne. The Guebre Sefi, one of the princes of this place, was kill'd in the assault, and his body cast into the fire which he ador'd.

The first of Jumaziulevel they flea'd alive all the Guebres of this place, and made slaves of their wives and children; they set fire to every thing and raz'd the walls, so that this town was soon reduc'd to ashes, tho' Turmechirin Can, great emperor in Asia, cou'd not make himself master of it.

It is remarkable, that before the army's marching to this place, Timur had resolv'd to write a letter to the inhabitants, to reduce 'em by good-nature and promises; but the secretary being about to write these words, " Why " do you compare us with Turmechirin Can?" Timur reprimanded those who had order'd the secretary to write in such a manner, saying, " What am I to Turmechirin Can? He was a " greater lord than me, of stricter virtue, and " better conduct; but my design is to revenge " the affront these villains have put upon so " powerful and august a monarch." So without suffering the letter to be concluded, he march'd to exterminate 'em. This was Timur's modesty, which ought to serve as an example to others.

CHAP.

CHAP. XXIII.

Several battels upon the great river Ganges, *against the militia of the* Guebres.

THE same day that Myrthe was taken, Timur order'd the Emir Gehan Chah to depart with the left wing by a different road, to ravage the country of the Guebres, for which purpose he embark'd with his troops on the Jun. The emperor gave the command of the baggage to the Emir Cheik Noureddin, with orders to conduct it along the river of Ca fou, and then departed in person towards the great river of Ganges, fourteen miles from Myrthe. The Emir Solyman Chah join'd him on the road, and having march'd six miles, they encamp'd at Mensoura, where Timur stay'd one night. The second of Jumaziulevel, he set out at three in the morning, and at sunrising arriv'd at Piroeznour on the Ganges, where they march'd three miles to find an easy passage. Some time after they came to the ordinary passage, which was very difficult and dangerous; several horsemen swam over there on horseback, but not without great risque. Timur going to do the same, the Emirs on their knees besought him to the contrary, telling him that the Mirza Pir Mehemed and the Emir Solyman Chan, having cross'd the river near Piroeznour, were on the point of perishing. In the mean while several brave men swam over, as the Tomans of the Mirza Charoc, Said Coja son of Cheik Ali Behader, and Gehan Malek son of Melket. Then Timur march'd two miles further along the Ganges, and encamp'd. The third of Jumaziulevel, he went towards Tocloepour, a town on the bank of the Ganges, twenty miles from the place whence they set out. When they had march'd fifteen, advice was brought the emperor, that a great number of Guebres were got together on the bank of that river. Timur immediately sent thither the Emir Mobacher, Ali Sultan Tavacin, and other Emirs of Tomans, and captains, to the number of fifty thousand horse, and continu'd his road towards Tocloepour. At this time the emperor was seiz'd with a very troublesom swelling in his arm, which much impair'd his health, but this distemper did not continue long, thro the care and assiduity of his officers.

In the mean while advice was brought that a vast number of Guebres in forty-eight boats, advanc'd against us upon the Ganges. This news stir'd up the emperor's fury, and the pleasure of having an opportunity of acquiring glory and merit in this war against the infidels, made him forget his distemper. He took horse with a thousand of his particular officers, and march'd along the banks of the river. He had no sooner perceiv'd the enemy, than several of our brave men spur'd their horses into the water sword in hand, with their quivers fasten'd to their sides. The unskilful enemys only let fly their arrows upon 'em, with their bucklers laid over their heads, while our men continually advanc'd, and laying hold on their flat-bottom'd vessels, enter'd 'em, notwithstanding the resistance of the enemy, whom they cut in pieces, and cast their bodys into the Ganges, making their women and children slaves. When they were become masters of these great boats, they

they went in search of ten others mann'd with Guebres, who prepar'd themselves for fighting, and fasten'd their boats to one another, that they might the better defend themselves, and make a kind of naval fight. Our soldiers, after having discharg'd a vast number of arrows, boarded their vessels, giving praise to God, and with their swords flew the remainder of these unfortunate Indians.

C H A P. XXIV.

Timur's three Gazies, or expeditions against the Guebres.

AFTER the taking of the flat boats on the Ganges, Timur decamp'd for Toclocpour; and when he was arriv'd there, on the fourth of Jumaziulevel, a little after midnight, two men came from the Emirs Allahdad, Bajazet Coutchin, and Altoun Bacchi, the leaders of our scouts, who brought advice that having found an easy passage where they cross'd the Ganges, they had met on the banks of that river a great number of infidels well-arm'd, who had for their leader a king nam'd Mobarek Can, who was resolv'd to defend himself.

Timur on advice of these motions, took horse before morning at the sound of drums and kettiedrums, being lighted by a vast number of flambeaux and torches: he cross'd the Ganges, and read the morning-prayer after having march'd a mile on the other side that river. Then our soldiers, with their cuirasses on, advanc'd against Mobarek Can, who had rang'd ten thousand horse, and some infantry, in order of battel, and expected us with his ensigns displa'yd, tho' he risk'd his crown on this occasion.

Timur hereupon imagin'd that these Indians being far more numerous than we, and our two wings at a great distance, we cou'd use no precautions, but must entirely resign our selves to the will of God. And as he was thus disquieted about the success of the battel, five hundred horse of the Tomans of Mirza Charoc arriv'd, which had cross'd the water with Seid Coja and Gehan Mulc, to make inroads in several places, and they join'd us at so proper a time, that one wou'd have thought they had been appointed to meet us here, or that heaven had sent 'em express to succour Timur when he had such need of 'em. Whereupon he return'd God thanks for his kindness to him, and order'd the Emirs Chamelik and Allahdad to attack the enemy with a thousand horse, and not to regard their number, or resistance.

Our brave men, in obedience to this order, and in resignation to the will of God, rush'd with fury upon the enemy, who thinking that our men were not alone, but only the vanguard of a great army, suddenly grew afraid, and fled like hinds before a roaring lion, and like Chacals * hid themselves in the woods. Our warriors pursu'd 'em, and put a great number to the sword, carrying away captive their women and children, with a considerable booty of oxen and other animals. Timur encamp'd in

---

* Chacal is an animal which partly resembles a dog, and partly a fox. It digs up dead bodys to devour 'em, and hath a languishing voice.

this

this place, and at the same time receiv'd advice that a great number of Guebres were rendezvous'd in the defile of Coupele, east of the Ganges. Whereupon he departed with five hundred horse for that place, leaving the rest to guard the spoils. The emperor at his arrival at these mountains, met a great number of Guebres. The Emirs Chamelik and Ali Sultan Tavachi, notwithstanding the enemy were superior to 'em in number, fell upon 'em sword in hand, giving praises to God. These infidels at first defended themselves but our men put 'em to the rout, notwithstanding their great number, while the soldiers were employ'd in collecting the booty. Timur being left with only a hundred horsemen of his guards, a Guebre, nam'd Malek Cheika, fell briskly upon him with a hundred men, partly horse and partly foot. Timur oppos'd these rash fellows, but while the two partys were about to let fly a shower of arrows, one of our soldiers, thro mistake, told Timur that this man was the Cheik Coukeri, one of his faithful servants. This false alarm caus'd the emperor to return to the bottom of the mountain, which the Guebre perceiving, he attack'd some of our men. Timur then return'd against this infidel, shot him in the belly with an arrow, and unhors'd him with a cut of his sabre on his head: he was then bound with cords, and drag'd after our men. Timur being willing to question him concerning the condition of the enemy, but he presently gave up the ghost. Some time after advice was brought that in the defile of Coupele, two miles from this place, a great many Guebres were assembled, that in the passages of these mountains were only thick woods, and trees twined one within another, with reeds

and

and canes so large and strong that a man cou'd scarcely grasp 'em.

Timur, who had already taken horse twice this day to fight, and was in great want of sleep, had no sooner heard this news, than preferring the treasures of eternal rewards to his quiet here, he march'd towards this defile at the head of some officers and Emirs of the vanguard. As he was oblig'd to go thro woods almost unpassable, and the Indians were far more numerous, Timur said to his men, " If " my son Pir Mehemed and Solyman Chah " shou'd arrive here presently, they wou'd be " of great service to us: but that cannot be; " seeing it is but three days since I sent 'em " to make inroads beyond the Ganges, which " they have cross'd at Pirouznour." While Timur was thus speaking, on a sudden they perceiv'd these brave men, who were over-joy'd to meet the emperor in this place. The pleasure, as one may easily imagine, was not less on Timur's side. They march'd together against the Guebres, on whom they discharg'd showers of arrows, and then rushing on 'em sword in hand, they made a cruel slaughter: they took a vast quantity of booty from these infidels, as well camels, oxen, and other cattel, as gold and silver belts, which the enemys wore.

Thus Timur was in three battels the same day, which never happen'd to any prince before him, that we find mention'd in history. The field of battel being so strait, and full of woods and thorns, that it was impossible to encamp here, in the evening they were oblig'd to return to the place where the second Gazie was fought.

CHAP.

CHAP. XXV.

Timur exterminates the Guebres assembled in the famous defile of Coupele. Description of a marble statue of a cow ador'd by the Indians.

THE defile of Coupele is situate at the foot of a mountain near the Ganges, and fifteen miles higher than this defile is a stone carv'd in form of a cow, from whence springs this great river. For this reason the Indians adore this stone, and in all the neighbouring countrys, within a year's journy, when they are at prayers they turn towards it. One of their customs is to burn themselves alive, and to have their ashes flung into the Ganges, believing they shall merit salvation by it. They also cast into this river their gold and silver, and a chief part of their devotion is to wash themselves in it, and there shave their beard and head, upon which they pour water, which they esteem as useful as the Mahometans imagine the Abdeste [a] necessary, when they go in pilgrimage to Mecca.

Abounair Otbi, in his book call'd Yemini [b], gives a relation of the superstitions of these Indian idolaters, and of the ridiculous notions they entertain concerning this river. We are told in this book, that Nasareddin Subuctekin,

---

[a] The ablution which the Mahometans are oblig'd to make before prayer.
[b] A famous history of the Sultan Mahmoud Subuctekin of India.

The history of Timur-Bec.

and his son the Sultan Mahmoud, for several years made war on these idolaters of India, and by degrees conquer'd the towns and castles of this kingdom, that God bless'd their undertakings, and permitted the Sultan Mahmoud at the end of these wars, to march into the kingdom of Cannoudge* with the mahometan army. The interpreter of the Yemini remarks, that this war in the country of Cannoudge is the most celebrated of any that Yemin Eddole Mahmoud was ever engag'd in

But to return to our subject: we must know that when Timur took up a resolution to carry his arms into India, he sent several Emirs with considerable troops by one road, and with the rest of his army march'd himself another, that these two armys took all the cities, castles, fortresses, towns and villages, in their way; that they exterminated the idolaters; and met together before Deli, as we have already mention'd, and that after the reduction of Deli, they cross'd the Ganges Thus Timur accomplish'd his undertaking in India, for the extirpation of idolatry in that country. But as there yet remain'd a prodigious multitude of Guebres in the mountains of Coupele, who possess'd a

---

* A town and kingdom on this side the Ganges. The geographer Abulfela says that the Ganges runs towards the east of the kingdom of Cannoudge, at forty leagues distance; and that the capital of Cannoudge is in long 104 lat 26 Naferedam Toadh says it is in long 115 5° lat. 26 35 which is consistent with the former, because the one counts the longitude from Hercules's pillars, and the other from the fortunate isles Elmeglebi remarks that Cannoudge is 232 leagues east of Moultan Adem is a town of the kingdom of Cannoudge, seven days journy from the city of the same name. Bengid tells us that Cannoudge is between two arms of the Ganges.

great

great quantity of riches, cattel, and movable goods, he resolv'd to attack 'em. Whereupon the fifth of Jumaziulevel the army began its march towards this defile, where the infidels, who were destin'd to perish, dar'd to wait their arrival, and rashly prepar'd to sustain the attacks of our warriors, and make a vigorous defence. At sun-rising the mahometan army was rang'd in order of battel, and arriv'd at the defile in very good order. The right wing was commanded by the Mirza Pir Mehemed, and the Emir Solyman Chah, and the left by other Emirs of great reputation. The Emir Chamelik and other captains famous for their valor, led the vanguard of the main body.

When the noise of the drums, the great and little kettledrums, and trumpets, accompany'd with the usual great cry, had echo'd in these mountains and narrow passages, the infidels were confounded, and lost all courage. fear got possession of their hearts, and wou'd not suffer 'em to wait the attack of our warriors, but oblig'd 'em to conceal themselves in the mountains, whither they were pursu'd by our men, and great part of 'em slain, some sav'd themselves, yet their effects, which consisted of furniture and other riches, fell to the conquerors.

This kingdom being thus deliver'd from these idolaters, the army return'd the same day, and cross'd the Ganges, on the banks of which Timur read the noon-prayer, returning thanks to God for the advantages and victorys he had gain'd thro his goodness. Then he took horse, and after five miles march encamp'd towards the lower part of the river, pleas'd with the conduct of all the captains and soldiers of his army, to whom he gave rewards for their brave actions in this war.

CHAP

CHAP. XXVI.

Timur's resolution to return to the seat of his empire.

TIMUR being satisfy'd with having march'd as far as the eastern frontiers of the empire of India in one campain, and having acquir'd the merit of the Gazie, departed from the bank of the Ganges the sixth of Jumaziulevel, to join the baggage. Every one march'd in his respective post, and the quartermasters and harbingers had orders to meet the baggage, and conduct it to the army. The seventh, they march'd six miles, and encamp'd four miles distance from the baggage

Jan. 31

Feb. 1.

In the mean while advice was brought that in the mountain of Soualec, one of the most considerable mountains of India, which stretches over two thirds of this vast empire, there were assembled a great number of Indians, with design to insult us. Timur order'd the troops which accompany'd the baggage to decamp, and march towards Soualec, while himself went in person to a place but five miles from thence, where the Mirza Calil Sultan and the Emir Cheik Noureddin join'd him with the baggage The Emir Solyman Chah and the other generals on their knees besought the emperor to stay in the camp, and not continually expose his sacred person, while they wou'd go and exterminate the Indians. Timur told 'em, the Gazie produc'd two considerable advantages; one was, that it procur'd for the warrior eternal

nal merit; the other, that he acquir'd by it worldly spoils and goods that as they had these two advantages in view, they shou'd be willing that he might partake of 'em also, since his intention in all his fatigues and labors, was only to render himself well-pleasing to God, and so treasure up good works for his eternal happiness, and riches to bestow upon his soldiers, and do good to the poor.

Then he sent orders to the Emir Gehan Chah, who had been gone out a week to make inroads on the Jaoun, to come to the camp, that he might partake of the merit of this expedition as well as the other Emirs. This Emir accordingly obey'd the order, and return'd to join his majesty.

CHAP. XXVII.

Timur's irruption on the mountain Soualec.

Feb. 4

ON saturday the tenth of Jumaziulevel, Timur departed for the mountain of Soualec, where a Raya nam'd Behrouz had assembled a number of Guebres in a narrow passage, and confiding in the strength of the mountain, and a strong place he had in possession, which he imagin'd inaccessible, had resolv'd to give us battel. Our army advancing in good order, Timur went down to the entrance of this defile, where he stopt. Our soldiers fell suddenly upon the infidels, who made but a weak defence, so that with their swords and half-pikes they slew a great number of 'em. Having reduc'd 'em thus low, they became masters of their cattel and effects, and took those prisoners who escap'd the sword: but as

the

the booty was unequally divided, the rich and powerful having got four or five hundred oxen, Timur order'd the spoils shou'd be equally distributed, that the poor and weak might have their share. The following night Timur lay in the tent of the Mirza Pir Mehemed; and next day he went to Behre, near Bekeri, commonly call'd Meliapour

The twelfth of Jumaziulevel he march'd four Feb. 6. miles, and encamp'd at Chaefarfava. The soldiers were so laden with booty, that they cou'd scarce march four miles a day Next day they went four miles, and encamp'd at Kender.

CHAP. XXVIII.

Several combats in the woods near Soualec.

THE fourteenth of Jumaziulevel Timur Feb. 8. cross'd the Jaoun, and encamp'd in another part of the mountain of Soualec, where advice was brought that a Raya nam'd Ratan had caus'd the trumpets to be sounded to assemble the people, and fall upon our army, that by this means an infinite number of Indians were got together under his command, and had retreated into thick and inaccessible woods.

Timur wou'd not stay till night was over before he began his march against 'em; but caus'd torches and flambeaus to be lighted, and order'd the captains to keep a constant march in order of battel The soldiers employ'd all their strength in cutting down the trees to make roads, and the same night they advanc'd twelve miles

F 2 The

Book IV
Feb. 9

The fifteenth before morning they arriv'd between the two mountains of Soualec and Couke, where the Raya was prepar'd to give battel, having form'd two wings and a main body: but he had no more courage than the rest, for as soon as the noise of the drums, trumpets and kettledrums, with the soldiers cries, were heard in this mountain, they fled, and the Raya himself turn'd his back, and retir'd to the bottom of a wood. Our soldiers pursu'd the enemy, and cut in pieces a great number, enriching themselves with the spoils, and carrying away an innumerable company of captives.

The same day our right wing went into another defile of these mountains, where, after having exterminated the Guebres, they gain'd a considerable booty: the left wing also made inroads in another place, and massacred several Indians, but got no spoils. The following night the two wings return'd to Timur. The

Feb. 10.

sixteenth, Timur quitted this narrow passage, and re-enter'd the mountain of Soualec, where he encamp'd in a place fifteen leagues from Bekircout, all which country is full of forests and craggy mountains. Then he resolv'd to go in person into the most dangerous places; and sent back the left wing, compos'd of the troops of Corassana, to make inroads, because they were return'd without any booty.

In the mean while Sainte Maure, at the head of the scouts, arriv'd at nine in the morning; bringing advice that there were so many Guebres in these quarters, that it was impossible to number 'em. This news oblig'd Timur to stay in this place, while the left wing shou'd go out to make inroads.

Then

Then advice was brought from the body of troops commanded by the Emirs Cheik Noureddin and Ali Sultan Tavachi, that several Guebres, with abundance of cattel, were got together in a defile on the left side. Timur immediately march'd towards this place, ordering the Emirs Cheik Noureddin and Ali Sultan to fall upon the Guebres. They soon became conquerors, putting the enemys to the sword, in the emperor's presence, who had set up his imperial standard on the very brink of the mountain, to encourage his men. Some of the wounded sav'd themselves by flight; but all their effects and cattel fell into the hands of the victors. Timur staid upon the mountain till evening, and caus'd part of the booty to be distributed among those who cou'd get none, so that every one had as much as he cou'd well take care of. At night they encamp'd in this defile, where there were abundance of monkys, who came to steal away the soldiers goods.

Thus we may truly say, there were twenty battels fought in thirty days, during which time our men conquer'd seven of the most important fortresses of India, which wou'd not give place to Caiber [s]. These seven fortresses were at one or two leagues distance from each other, and the inhabitants were at continual variance among themselves. They had formerly paid tribute to the emperors of India; but were some time since brought to subjection to the Mussulmans, from whom they revolted, refusing to pay tribute to 'em, and thus they merited the punishment they receiv'd. One of these places, which

---

[s] A strong place in Syria, inhabited by Jews, formerly conquer'd by the prophet Mahomet.

belong'd to Cheikou, a relation of the Cheu Couker*, had willingly submitted to Timur, thro the interposition of the Muſſulmans who liv'd with 'em but this was mere ſhew, for they ſoon gave us marks of their treaſon and malice, and when the cuſtomary tax for the ſaving of their lives was impos'd on 'em, they made uſe of tricks and equivocations. In the mean while one of Timur's officers invented a ſtratagem to oblige 'em to pay the mony with leſs reluctance, which was, that we ſhou'd buy up all their old bows, which they accordingly ſold our men upon their offering a good price, ſo that they had ſcarcely any more arms left. Then it was order'd that forty Guebres ſhou'd be liſted in the ſervice of Hendou Chah Cazen, one of the emperor's officers: which they wou'd not conſent to, but ſlew ſeveral Muſſulmans.

This oblig'd us to treat 'em as enemys, and beſiege their place in form, which having taken, we put two thouſand Guebres to the ſword, as a puniſhment for their paſt crimes.

The place belonging to Malek Djuradge, and five others, were taken with the ſame eaſe in a very ſhort time, ſo that this country was clear'd of this generation of idolaters, their temples were ruin'd, and the mahometan religion afterwards flouriſh'd there.

* Prince of Lahor.

CHAP

CHAP. XXIX.

Timur's Gazies and expeditions in the province of Tchamou.

THE Gazies on the mountains of Soualec being finish'd to Timur's satisfaction, he departed from Mansar the sixteenth of Jumaziu- lahher, and after a march of six miles, encamp'd at Baila, a town of the province of Tchamou, where he was join'd by the Emirs Cheik Mahemed Aicoutmur, Mobacher, and Ismael Berlas, of the Toman of Mirza Calil Sultan. March 12. 1399

The inhabitants of this town were valiant men, and their forests very difficult of access: they had fix'd their bucklers round their woods, where they prepar'd for a vigorous resistance. Our soldiers were eager to fall upon 'em, but there came an order from the emperor to defer the attack till next day, because he design'd to be there in person.

The seventeenth Timur took horse, and having rang'd his army in order of battel, caus'd the great cry to be made, and the instruments of war to be sounded; but the enemy abandon'd the town, and fled into the woods, to hide themselves. Part of our soldiers were posted on the side of the wood, while the others enter'd the town without opposition, and made themselves masters of a great quantity of mony and ammunitions; so that the army was furnish'd with all necessarys March 13.

The same day the army departed thence, to encamp four miles further. Olaia Timur, Toncator, and Coulad, as also the Mirza Roustem, and

Book IV. the faithful Zeineddin, who had been sent ambassadors from Deli into Cachmir, arriv'd at the camp with letters from prince Chah Eskender, from whom there likewise came ambassadors, who assur'd Timur that their prince, full of respect to him, had resolv'd to demand his protection, with all the submission that cou'd be expected from a subject, who was entirely resign'd to his orders; and that as a mark of his sincerity, he was upon his way to meet the emperor, being already arriv'd at a place nam'd Gebhan, where he was rejoin'd by the doctor Noradin, one of his ambassadors, who told him that the Emirs of Timur's Divan had tax'd him at thirty thousand horses, and a hundred thousand Derefts of gold, each Dereft weighing two Medicales and a half. Chah Eskender immediately return'd to collect the mony he was tax'd at, that he might the sooner have the honor to kifs the imperial carpet. Timur, on advice of this, disapprov'd of this order, because they had impos'd a tax upon Eskender, which he was not able to pay, since it was more than his little kingdom was worth and as the ambassadors at the same time represented to the emperor how willingly Chah Eskender had submitted to him, Timur order'd that he shou'd be treated with civility, and sent to tell him that the payment of this tax shou'd not detain him from coming before him.

March 1. The eighteenth of Jumaziulakher, the ambassadors of Chah Eskender and of Motamedzeineddin were sent back to Cachmir, with orders for Chah Eskender to come to the bank of the Indus in ten days. Then the army on their road pillag'd three towns: but Aratmour, officer of Timur's houshold, was wounded with an arrow

March 15. The nineteenth of Jumaziulakher, they encamp'd over-against the capital of Tchamou, after

after having march'd four miles. In their road Chap. 29. they found four leagues of cultivated land, ready for harvest; which serv'd for forage, and our horses were let loose among the grass in this pasture-ground.

The twentieth of Jumaziulakher, Timur enter'd the defile from whence the river of Tchamou springs, which the army had cross'd several times. It is situate at the foot of a mountain, on the left side of the city of Tchamou, having on its right the town of Menou. It was inhabited by strong and tall Indians, who were resolv'd to defend their lives, and having sent their wives and children into the mountains, had intrench'd themselves in almost inaccessible woods, upon a cragged mountain, having their king at the head, and like dogs barking at the rising moon, they houl'd, if one may so say, when they discharg'd their arrows

Timur imagin'd it better to surprize 'em by artifice, than to attack 'em openly in so dangerous a place: whereupon he order'd our soldiers to leave 'em, and to go to pillage the town of Menou, which was accordingly executed The troops also enter'd the town of Tchamou, whence they brought away ammunition and spoils enough for their pay and sustenance. Then Timur posted some regiments of active and resolute men in the woods where the enemy had fortify'd themselves, and in the mean while he departed with the cavalry.

The twenty first he cross'd the river of Tchamou, march'd four miles, and encamp'd on the bank of the Genave, in a plain of four leagues in length, full of pasturage.

As soon as the imperial army had quitted the defile of Tchamou and Menou, the Indians, like foxes coming out of their holes, when they imagin'd the

forests

forests void of lions, came out of their mountain to re-enter their houses: but they were soon attack'd by our regiments who lay in ambuscade, and who falling upon 'em, cut 'em in pieces, not giving quarter to any one.

Dolet Timur Tavachi, an officer of the Toman of Cheik Noureddin, assisted by Hussein Melik Coutchin, took the king of Tchamou prisoner, with fifty officers of consideration, whom he brought to Timur. The emperor return'd thanks to God, and thus address'd these Emirs "Blessed be the almighty King of heaven and "earth, who hath humbled these proud Guebres, "the enemys of his name, who but yesterday "insolently brav'd the faithful from their craggy "mountains, having no regard to any one but "to day God has deliver'd 'em up to us, bound "like malefactors. To him be blessing and glo-"ry for ever." Then he order'd that the captives shou'd be loaded with chains, and left groveling upon the earth, except the king of Tchamou, who had been wounded in the fight, he was heal'd of his wound, and treated with civility, as well because of his character, as for that they imagin'd they might the more easily get the mony due to the mahometan army for the town of Tchamou, and the saving the lives of the king and his men. In the mean while they treated this prince with so much kindness and respect, instructing him in the beautys of the musulman religion, that he resolv'd to make profession of mahometanism, and quit his errors and idolatry. So he declar'd his belief of the unity of God, and eat the flesh of oxen with the Mussulmans, which is prohibited these miserable Indians.

This change of religion caus'd him to be honor'd and caress'd by Timur, who consented to
make

King of Tchamou taken prisoner.

make a treaty with him, by which he was re- Chap. 39.
ceiv'd under the protection of our monarch.

The twenty third of Jumaziulakher the ar- March 19.
my ſtaid on the banks of the Genave, to wait
for the troops which were gone to Lahor.

CHAP. XXX.

*Relation of what paſs'd at Lahor, with regard
to Chicai Couker, prince of that city.*

IN the mean while advice was brought that
the princes and Emirs, who had been ſent
towards Lahor, had made themſelves maſters of
that city, and actually receiv'd the tax for re-
deeming the inhabitants lives, having made Chicai Couker priſoner of war.

Deceit, ſays the poet, may at firſt have a good
appearance, but in the end it makes the perſon
bluſh who practiſes it · wherefore Timur, who
was an enemy to tricking, made uſe of the following words for the motto of his ſeal, *Safety
conſiſts in fair-dealing.*

But that every one may be ſufficiently appriz'd
of the affair of Chicai Couker, they muſt know
that this prince of Lahor, at the beginning of
this war, accompany'd Timur every where, from
whom he obtain'd ſo much favor and reſpect,
that if any of the Indians made uſe of his name,
they were neither pillag'd nor made priſoners.
When the army was between the two rivers of
Ganges and Jaoun, he beg'd leave to go into his
own country, which was granted him · and he
even agreed about the preſents he ſhou'd make to
the emperor upon his meeting him again at the
bank of the Biah, which is alſo call'd the river

BookIV. of Lahor. Thus Chicai Coaker return'd into his own country, where he pass'd some time in plays and diversions, forgetting what he had promis'd before the august tribunal of Timur and he not only neglected the performance of his promise, but even gave marks of his disregard to us; for several of our officers having past thro his city coming from Transoxiana, as the doctor Abdallah Sedre, Hendouchah Cazen, and others, thro whose protection he might have advanc'd himself in honor and power, he did not give 'em a handsom reception, nor shew the least marks of civility, pretending ignorance of their being in the city. This procedure drew on him Timur's indignation, who order'd that his country shou'd be pillag'd, and his person seiz'd. Thus our monarch punish'd ingratitude.

March 20. The twenty fourth of Jumaziulakher, Timur cross'd the river of Genave, and encamp'd after having march'd five miles. The same day officers arriv'd from Tauris from the Mirza Miran Chah, bringing news of the good health of that prince, his children, and principal Emirs. They also brought an account of the affairs of Bagdad, Egypt, Syria, Anatolia and Capchac, as likewise the condition of the fortress of Alengic.

The twenty fifth, several sick soldiers were drown'd in the river, which oblig'd Timur, who was the most merciful prince in the universe, to give those who were in want of 'em, proper horses and mules out of his own stable, upon which they cross'd the river. The same day the emperor sent Hendouchah Cazen to Samarcand, with advice that he was about to return home, to comfort the people who impatiently expected him. That day there likewise came an officer from Persia from the Mirza Pir Mehemed,

med, son of Omar Cheik, who brought news of this prince's health, and the state of his kingdom he likewise presented Egyptian swords, damask'd blades, and other curiositys.

The twenty sixth of Jumaziulakher the army decamp'd from the bank of the Genave, and after six miles march encamp'd in the desart; and the same day the emperor sent again to Samarcand one of the ambassadors who came from Tauris, to order the princes his sons to come and meet him. Then Timur designing to cross the river Dindana before the rest of the army, set out before 'em.

The twenty seventh he march'd six miles, and encamp'd at the entrance of a wood: they saw a lion in a meadow, which every one attack'd, and the Emir Cheik Noureddin kill'd.

Then the Mirzas Pir Mehemed and Roustem, with the Emirs Solyman Chah and Gehan Chah, arriv'd at the camp from Lahor, after having slain several Indians, and taken a considerable booty. They kiss'd the imperial carpet, and made their presents to Timur, which consisted of nine pieces of each sort Timur gave great largesses to these brave men; and particularly distinguish'd Mehemed Azad, to whom he presented a vest, a quiver, and a gold-belt. The greatest lords only sought to be favorably regarded by our monarch.

The same day Timur order'd that all the Emirs of both wings, the colonels of regiments, and the captains of companys, shou'd return home by the different roads mark'd out for 'em. Then he made presents to every one according to their rank and mettle, beginning with the princes of the blood, the Emirs, dukes, foreign princes call'd Nevians; and then the Emirs of Tomans, the colonels of Hezares, and the centurions.

The

The Mirza Pir Mehemed, son of Gehanghir had a present made him of a belt and crown set with precious stones

He also honor'd with his liberalitys the lords of India, the Emirs and Cherifs, who had the good fortune to accompany him, and giving 'em letters-patent for their principalitys, he permitted 'em to return into their respective countrys

Timur assign'd the government of the city and province of Moultan to Keder Can, who having been arrested by order of Sarenk brother of Mellou Can, and laid in irons in a citadel, had escap'd thence, and fled to Biana, a place dependent on Deli, to the king Ahoudan a Mussulman, and who having heard of Timur's arrival in that country, had with an humble confidence fled for refuge to the foot of the throne, and had the honor to accompany his majesty from that time.

As in this country there was a plain, which for its vastness, and the great quantity of game in it, seem'd to invite passengers to the chace, (for there were lions, leopards, rhinoceros's, unicorns, blue stags, wild peacocks, parrots, and other uncommon animals) Timur spent some time in that diversion He sent several thousands of soldiers to form the great circle, and having first pursu'd the idolaters, he chas'd the wild beasts, and afterwards went a fowling. The falcons and hawks destroy'd all the peacocks, pheasants, parrots and ducks in this country. The soldiers took a great deal of game, and slew several rhinoceros's with their sabres and lances, tho this animal is so strong, that it will beat down a horse and horseman with a single blow of its horn; and has so thick a skin, that it cannot be peirc'd but by an extraordinary force.

The

The twenty eighth of Jumaziulakher the army march'd eight miles, and encamp'd at Gebhan, a delightful residence on the frontiers of Cachmir. *March 24.*

CHAP. XXXI.

Description of the little kingdom of Cachmir, or Kichmir.

AS Cachmir is one of the most noted countrys in the world, has so particular a situation, and so few people ever see it, because it is not the ordinary passage into any other countrys, we will give a short description of it, which we have receiv'd from the natives, and the truth of which we are fully satisfy'd of

Cachmir is a principality near Hac, in the middle of the fourth climate, which according to Ptolomy, begins at 34 deg. 37 min. of lat. its middle is at 36 deg. 22 min. and its end at 38. 54 The latitude of Cachmir is 35 degrees; and its longitude from the fortunate isles 105.

The country is of an oval form, surrounded with high mountains on all sides: it looks southwards upon Deli and the country of India, northwards on Bedakchan and Coraflana, westwards upon the hords of the Ouganis, and eastwards upon Tobbot or Thebet.

In the extent of its province are ten thousand flourishing villages, full of fountains and green plains: but the common opinion is that the whole principality of Cachmir consists of a hundred thousand villages, as well in the plains as mountains. The air and water are very wholesom, and the beauty of the Cachmirian

rian women hath pass'd into a proverb among the Persian poets and orators. They have vast quantitys of good fruit; but the winter is hurtful, because of the great abundance of snows which fall there. The summer-fruits, as dates, oranges and citrons, never come to maturity, but are brought thither from the warm neighboring countrys. The flat country in the middle is twenty leagues in breadth from one mountain to the other

The prince and court reside at the city of Nagaz, thro the middle of which, as at Bagdad, runs a river as large as the Tigris: and what is very surprizing, this river is exceeding rapid, tho it is form'd from a single fountain in the same country, call'd the fountain of Vir. The inhabitants have built upon this river more than thirty bridges of boats, with chains cross the chief passages seven of these bridges are in the city of Nagaz, which is the center and capital of the country. When this river hath pass'd the limits of Cachmir, it takes different names, from the several countrys it washes, as Dindana and Jamad. above Moultan it joins the Genave, and both together having pass'd by Moultan, fall into the Rave, which runs by the other Moultan. at length the river Biah joins 'em, and near the town of Outcha, they all fall into the Indus or Absend, which disembogues into the sea of Omman *, at the end of the country of Tatta.

* The Arabian sea.

The mountains which surround this country serve as fortifications against the insults of an enemy; the inhabitants being under no apprehensions of their being ruin'd, either by times rains or storms.

There are three roads into this country: that of Corassana is so very difficult, that the inhabitants, who are accustom'd to that sort of labor, are

The history of Timur-Bec.

are oblig'd to carry bales of merchandize and other burdens upon their backs, which the beasts of carriage are not able to do. The road of India is equally difficult. That of Tobbot or Thebet is easiest; but for several days journy passengers meet with venomous herbs, which poison their horses

Thus God has given this country natural defences, so that the inhabitants have no occasion for arms or armys

The twenty-ninth of Jumaziulakher, Timur departed from Gebban, march'd four miles, and encamp'd on the bank of the river Dindana, which he cross'd on a bridg built by his order; and which was an ease to the fatigu'd soldiers, as well Turks as Tadgics'. The Emirs Chamelik and Gelalelislam had orders for conducting the army over this bridg.

March 25.

CHAP. XXXII.

Timur returns to the seat of his empire.

ON the thirtieth of Jumaziulakher in the morning, Timur departed for Samarcand before the army, that he might get there in good time: he march'd twenty miles on the Dindana, and encamp'd at Sanbaste, a town in the mountain of Joudis. The first of Regeb he encamp'd at the castle of Beroudge: he took horse after noon-prayer, and enter'd the desart of Gelali *, from whence he came out in the even-

March 27.

* Gerou.

' The Turks are native Tartars. the Tadgics are inhabitants of conquer'd citys and countrys.

ing,

ing, and encamp'd in a cavern, where there yet remain'd some water of the Pechecals, or great rains of the last winter. This cavern is but three miles from Peroudge.

The 2d of Regeb at ten in the morning, he came to the Indus, over which the Emirs Pir Ali Selduz, and others, who had the care of the frontiers of Nagaz and Banou, and of the roads of those quarters, had caus'd a bridg of boats to be built.

Timur having crofs'd the Indus, staid till noon on its banks, and then leaving the Emir Allahdad at the foot of the bridg, that he might cause the baggage, and part of the army which was behind, to pass over, he departed in the afternoon, and march'd ten miles before he encamp'd.

March 29. The third of Regeb he stop'd at Banou, where the Emirs Pir Alitaz, Hussein Coutchin, and others, who had been left there to keep the Ouganis in obedience, had the honor to pay their respects to him: having not seen him for a month, they presented him with nine horses and a thousand oxen. Timur gave 'em back their horses, and order'd that the oxen shou'd be restor'd to the right owners, and then he commanded Pir Alitaz to stay in that place, till all the army had pass'd it.

April 2. The 7th of Regeb, which is the first of Ferverdin of the Gelalian epocha, as also the first day of the spring, he took the road to Nagaz, where he arriv'd next day.

The same day the officer of Mirza Miran Chah was sent back into Azerbijana, with advice of the emperor's conquests, and the good condition of his troops. Mahmoud, son of Berat Coja, and Hendoucha, were likewise sent to Cabul, to bring troops from thence, to destroy

The history of Timur-Bec. 99

the Ourganis, against whom the Emir Soliman Chap 32. Chah had caus'd the castle of Nagaz to be built before the emperor's departure for India, to oppose their insults; which establish'd quiet and security among the Mussulmans of that country.

On one side of the castle without the walls was a delicious fountain, which Timur was desirous shou'd be within the enclosure of the castle: for which reason, notwithstanding his great desire to see the princes his dear children, he prefer'd the good of the public before his private satisfaction, and staid in that place till the walls of the castle and the building over the fountain were finish'd. This lasted no longer than from tuesday till monday evening, because every one assisted in it, and the Emirs themselves, to set an example to others, carry'd the tiles to the masons. Then the emperor gave the government of this castle of Nagaz to Nusret Comari, an officer of the Mirza Pir Mehemed, with three hundred men of the regiment of Sama Aglen, whose captain was Yarek Aghil, to whom he join'd four hundred deserters of the Uzbecs. He gave the government of Irjab and Schenouzan to the Cheik Hassan, nephew of the Cheik Nouredin. Timur at length departed to encamp at the dome of the Cheik Mobareschah.

The ninth of Regeb he went to Kermadge, April 4. where the Cheik Ahmed Ougani, prince of that place, had the honor to kiss his hand, being introduc'd by the great Emirs. but Timur was not pleas'd with the entertainment he gave him; for these mountaineers are neither acquainted with civility, good-breeding, or even the laws of hospitality.

In the evening they went to encamp at Acsica, where the Cheik Abdal gave the emperor

G 2 as

Book IV. as handsom an entertainment as he was able,
with which he was very much pleas'd.

April 5.   The 10th of Regeb, Timur encamp'd in the defile of Rame, and the same day sent the doctor Nimet to prince Charoc to acquaint him with his arrival. The 11th they stopt at a town, from whence they departed the same day at nine in the morning for Cabul, where Timur left the empress Tchelpan Mulc Aga, with some troops, whose horses and mules were exceedingly fatigu'd: he also left Mobacher there, to conduct 'em leisurely. At night Timur arriv'd at the mouth of Joui Neu, a canal very full of fish, which he had caus'd to be dug. The 12th he went to encamp at Garban; where he built a great hospital of brick, because several roads meet at this place, which was soon finish'd.

April 8.   The 13th the court pass'd the mountain and defile of Cheberto, and went to encamp in a plain at two leagues distance. The same day the emperor being struck by some evil eye [a], or malign influence, fell sick, and had on his feet and hands painful ulcers, which hinder'd his taking any repose, and retarded 'em a whole day's march, and because of this accident this place was call'd the dry and unfortunate camp. The night following an officer arriv'd from Huat from prince Charoc, with very agreeable news.

Timur departed from this place on the third day in a commodious litter carry'd by mules, he not being able to ride on hoseback. and as his sickness yet encreas'd, the officers

---

[a] The Turks, as well as the Italians, are so superstitious as to believe that certain persons bring misfortunes to every thing they look upon; and that their eyes are so venomous as to kill children. The Italians call this, *il cattivo occhio*, the evil eye.

The history of Timur-Bec.

of his chamber fasten'd leathern straps to the poles fix'd to the litter, and so carry'd him by the bottom of the river in a very narrow passage of the mountain Siapoutch, which they were oblig'd to pass From the beginning of this defile to the mountain they cross'd the river twenty-six times; and twenty-two times from the mountain to the end of the defile.

The 15th of Regeb, the domestics of the empresses Serai Mulc Canum and Touman Aga, and of the other ladys and children of the emperor, arriv'd at Samarcand, where they made presents to his majesty, assuring him of the empresses and princes health. Timur sent Corluc Timur, an officer of Touman Aga, to the baggage, to bring from thence the elephants. In the mean while his majesty's indisposition disquieted the whole court, till the 17th of Regeb, when they cross'd the river of the defile, at which time it pleas'd God to restore him his health.

The 18th he went in a litter from Surab towards Bacalan, and encamp'd at the town of Aker, where he staid a little to refresh himself, and afterwards encamp'd at Cara Boulac. The ladys of the Mirza Pir Mehemet, and of the Emir Gehan Chah, with the Emirs and chiefs of Bacalan, came to meet the emperor, and make their presents.

The 19th at ten in the morning he arriv'd at Semencan, whence he departed the same day, to encamp at Gaznic. The 20th he march'd to Culm; and setting out from thence at noon, he arriv'd at the Gihon before Termed at midnight.

Chap. 32.

April 10.

April 12.

G 3 CHAP.

CHAP. XXXIII.

Timur crosses the Oxus, and is met by the princes and princesses of the blood.

April 15   THE 20th of Regeb, at nine in the morning, Timur having cross'd the Oxus in a boat, met on the other side the Mirza Ouloucbek, the Mirza Ibrahim Sultan, the princess Beghisi Sultan his daughter, with the empresses Serai Mulc Canum, Tekil Canum, and Touman Aga, accompany'd by all the princes, Mirzas, Emirs, lords and Cherifs of Samarcand, with others who came to meet his majesty, who gave 'em a handsom reception. This charming company, and especially the ladys, congratulated him on his conquests, and sprinkled over him so great a quantity of gold and precious stones, that it seem'd as if the sand had been transform'd into 'em.

The court staid at Termed two days, where they were entertain'd with a sumptuous banquet by the great Cherif Alael Mulc, who made several handsom presents.

April 18   The 23d of Regeb the court went to the Kichlac of Gehan Mulc, and the 24th to the bath of Turki: the 25th they pass'd the iron-gate of Coluga, and encamp'd at the river of Baric. The 26th they encamp'd at Tchekedalic; the 27th at Couzimondac, and the 28th they arriv'd at Dourbildgin, where the Mirza Charec, who was come from Herat, had the honor to kiss the emperor's hands: he congratulated him upon his victorys, made him presents, and sprinkled upon him, according to custom

The history of Timur-Bec.

custom, gold and precious stones. The great conqueror most affectionately embrac'd his dear son, whom he tenderly lov'd, and loaded him with favors and honors.

At this place likewise the Mirza Omar, son of Miran Chah, whom Timur at his departure for the Indian war had left at Samarcand, had the honor to kiss his majesty's feet, who gave him a very kind reception, because of the love and care he had always shewn to his people, and the justice he had so exactly render'd

On monday the 29th of Regeb, Timur went to encamp on the bank of a little river *, and the 30th, in the delicious fields of Kech. He immediately went to pay his devotions at the tombs of the great Santons, Chamfeddin Kelar, and others, and at length at that of his illustrious father, the Emir Tragai, of blessed memory: and then he visited those of his noble children Here he staid fifteen days, giving alms to the poor of that country

He departed from this place the 14th of Schaban, to encamp on the bank of the river of Roudec. The 15th he encamp'd at Tchenar Rebat, or the town of plane-trees the 16th he pass'd the mountain, and encamp'd at Cotlocyur The 17th he went to Tact Caratchah, which himself had built and the 18th he encamp'd at the Kiochk ' of Gehannuma. The 19th he arriv'd at the pleasure-house of Dolet-Abad: and monday the 20th, at nine in the morning, he came to the Kiochk of the garden of Dilcu Chah, the palace of which had been lately finish'd and to consecrate that palace to joy and pleasures, a royal banquet was prepar'd, at

Chap 33.

April 24.
* Toum.

May 9.

' Kiochk is a building in form of a cupola.

which the empresses, the emperor's children, the princes of the blood, the Emirs or dukes, and the Nevians and foreign princes, assisted. They cast so much gold and precious stones upon his majesty, to congratulate him on his victorys and happy arrival, that the earth seem'd sown with 'em, and all the officers were loaded with riches.

The 21st of Schaban, Timur made his entry into his capital city of Samarcand, where, after he had been at the baths, to make his ablutions, he went to visit the tomb of the venerable Santon Farcadcatam, son of Abbas; and there he gave presents to the officers belonging to this mausoleum: then he went to the hospital founded by the empress Touman Aga. After noon-prayer he honor'd with his presence the garden of planes, and the palace of Nakchidgehan, where he was diverted with feasts and plays. From thence he went to the delicious garden of Baghi Behicht, which is indeed a true paradise, as its name imports. Then he came to the palace of Baghi Bolend, at which place the elephants and baggage arriv'd. The inhabitants of Transoxiana, who had never before seen any elephants, were surpriz'd at these huge animals of such an extraordinary figure, and gave praise to the Almighty, whose works are incomprehensible.

The emperor distributed the curiositys and riches he had brought from India, among the princes of the blood, the Cherifs, and chief persons of the kingdom, according to their different rank and quality: among which were precious stones, gold, beautiful male and female Negroes.

Timur sent Sarenk, eldest brother of Mellon Can prince of Moultan, with two chains of elephants, and other curiositys, to the Mirza Mehemed Sultan. He made other presents to the
Emirs

Emirs who had been left in Transoxiana, that every one might partake of the benefits of his conquests. Then he permitted his son prince Charoc, to return to the seat of his kingdom of Corassana, after having loaded him with favors

CHAP. XXXIV.

Building of the great mosque of Samarcand.

THE Alcoran expresly assures us, that the greatest proof of a prince's faith is his erecting temples to the honor of God: whereupon our conqueror, being persuaded that this work of piety wou'd be the crown of the merits he had acquir'd in his wars and Gazies against the infidels, where he had destroy'd the temples of the false gods, and exterminated the idolaters, resolv'd to build a great mosque in Samarcand, large enough to contain all the faithful of that capital city, when they shou'd assemble at friday-prayers, and to this effect he issu'd out his orders for the foundations to be laid.

The architects chose a happy moment to begin it, viz on the 4th of Ramadan 801, which answers to the year of the Hare, the moon being then in Leo, going out of the sextile aspect of the sun, and entring the sextile aspect of Venus. The masons, brought from foreign countrys, as mention'd before, gave the greatest proofs of their art and skill, as well in the solidity and beauty of the angles, as in the strength of the foundations of this noble edifice. In the inside of the mosque were employ'd two hundred masons froms Azerbijana, Persia and India: five hun-

May 28.
1399.

hundred men likewise work'd in the mountains in cutting and hewing of stones, which were sent into the city. Several other artisans, of different trades, perform'd their parts with the utmost application. Ninety-five chains of elephants were made use of in drawing large stones with wheels and machines, according to the laws of mechanics. The princes of the blood and Emirs were appointed to oversee the workmen, that not one moment might be lost in finishing this stupendous building.

In the mean while the Mirza Mehemet Sultan, who ordinarily resided at Andecan, on the frontier of Gete, arriv'd with a great attendance of officers. He had the honor to pay his respects to the emperor in the hospital of Touman Aga, where he made his presents, and sprinkled gold and precious stones upon his majesty, according to the custom of the Tartars, Moguls, and indeed of almost all the nations of the Turks. Timur embrac'd this young prince with all the tenderness that cou'd be expected from so good a father. He then went to visit the works, to animate the workmen by his presence; and he did not stir either from the college of Canum, which is near this mosque, or from the hospital of Touman Aga; at which places he distributed justice, sat in council, and decided the affairs of religion and of the state.

At length, under his conduct, this great edifice was finish'd. It contain'd four hundred eighty pillars of hewn stone, each seven cubits high. The arch'd roof was cover'd with marble, neatly carv'd and polish'd: and from the architrave of the entablature to the top of the roof were nine cubits. At each of the four corners of the mosque without was a Minaret *. The doors were of brass: and the walls, as well with-

* A kind of steeple.

without as within, as also the arches of the roof, were adorn'd with writing in relievo, among which is the chapter of the cavern, and other parts of the Alcoran. The pulpit, and reading-desk, where the prayers for the emperor were read, were of the utmost magnificence: and the nich of the altar, cover'd with plates of iron gilt, was likewise of perfect beauty.

Chap. 34.

After the month of Ramadan was past, and the feast of Bairam come, Timur went to the palace of Dilcu Chah, where he order'd preparations to be made for the most sumptuous banquets, and all sorts of plays and diversions. The empress Rokia Canica on this occasion gave a noble entertainment, accompany'd with consorts of music and fine dancing.

The end of the fourth book.

BOOK

BOOK V.

Two wars of Timur in Georgia. The conquest of Syria and Mesopotamia. The famous war with Bajazet the Ottoman emperor, who after the loss of a battel is taken prisoner, and dies in the Tartars camp.

CHAP. I.

The causes which oblig'd Timur to make war in the country of Iran, that is, in the western parts of Asia, from the river Gihon to the Mediterranean sea.

An. Dom. 1399.

IN the autumn of the year of the Hegira 801, which answers to that of the Mouse, the Mirza Miran Chah¹, conducted by his evil destiny, went to take the diversion of hunting in the neighborhood of Tauris, where the tomb of Pir Omar Naq Chirban is to be seen

---

¹ Son of Timur, and viceroy of Media, which is call'd by the Persians Azerbijana. The great Moguls of India are descended from him.

He

He met a roe-buck, which he was desirous to take with his hands: but as he was stooping down to that purpose, he fell off his horse, tho he was one of the best horsemen of Asia, and the violence of his fall cast him into a swoon, in which he lay a long time. All the lords of his court were extremely concern'd at it, and got round him to comfort him. He continu'd in fits for three days and nights: and his physician, being an ignorant fellow, or rather a knave, which has since been most suspected, fail'd in the application of remedys; by which means this prince was seiz'd with a giddiness in his brain, which impair'd his senses. Thus this great man, who till that time had possess'd the throne of Hulacou, and of the kingdom of Azerbijana, with so much applause and glory, by the administration of justice and by his liberality, was depriv'd of his understanding. Upon a bare suspicion he slew a man, and prodigally squander'd away the treasures of the state, destroy'd the most noted buildings, and did many things contrary to the good sense and dignity of a prince.

One of his actions, which plainly discover'd the alteration of his judgment, was, that at the beginning of summer, he departed at the head of all his troops to besiege the city of Bagdad: he march'd day and night, going two days journy in twenty-four hours, imagining that the bare rumor of his approach wou'd strike a terror into the heart of the Sultan, and make him abandon the city. But affairs took a quite different turn, for when Miran Chah was at the dome of Ibrahim Lic, he receiv'd advice from Tauris, that a great number of the principal men of the kingdom were confederated against him, which nevertheless did not hinder his progress to Bagdad. But the Sultan Ahmed, knowing it was not

not a proper season to besiege the place, because of the great dryness and heat of the weather, resolv'd to defend himself. In the mean while couriers came incessantly from Tauris with reiterated advice of the conspiracy, and even of the revolt of the principal inhabitants; so that the Mirza, two days after the arrival of the great standard before Bagdad, was constrain'd to return to Tauris with expedition: he was no sooner enter'd into that capital of Media, than he put all those to the sword who were accus'd of being in the conspiracy, of which number was the Cadi* During this autumn he suspected that the Cherif Ali, prince of Cheki, of the tribe of Erlat, wou'd revolt from his obedience: for which cause, without examining into the truth of it, he march'd into the field at the head of his army, and went to pillage his country

* The judg.

When the Georgians, who by their acts of hostility had already drawn on themselves Timur's anger, were inform'd of the Mirza Miran Chah's small application to public affairs, they became so insolent, that during Timur's expedition in India they revolted At the same time the Sultan Taher, son of the Sultan of Bagdad, was with his troops in the fortress of Alengic, which had been besieg'd a long time, according to Timur's orders, by the Sultan Sendger, son of Hadgi Seifeddin ². The besiegers, the better to carry on the siege, had built a great wall round the place, so that no one cou'd get in or out This conjuncture caus'd the Georgians to get together a great number of troops and even the Cherif Ali, tho a good Mussulman,

---

² An old general of Timur's army, and his favorite, who had attended him ever since the beginning of his rise.

join'd

join'd these infidels, to revenge himself for the Mirza Miran Chah's having pillag'd his country. The Georgians came before Alengic with a great army, being resolv'd to deliver the Sultan Taher, who had been so press'd, that his heart, as one may say, was in his mouth, and entring Azerbijana, they sack'd the country, pillag'd the Mussulmans effects, and committed all imaginable disorders.

Sultan Sendger, on advice of this, rais'd the siege, and march'd to Tauris to give an account of this strange accident to Miran Chah, who immediately order'd his son the Mirza Aboubecre to march with four or five Emirs before Alengic, to repulse the Georgians, and put a stop to their disorders, which they cou'd not do with so much expedition, but that the Georgians got first to the place, from whence having made the Sultan Taher go out, they plac'd Alengic in the hands of Hadgi Saleh, and three famous Oznaours [1] of Georgia, and then return'd home, their design being only to deliver the Sultan Taher. Yet by chance they met the army of Tauris, which being far less numerous, endeavor'd to avoid 'em, but that being impossible, the Oznaours resolutely advanc'd as if assur'd of the victory: at the first onset they broke thro the wings of the army of Tauris; and the Cherif Ali, perceiving Aboubecre, rush'd upon him out of the main body sword in hand, to revenge the ruin his father had brought upon his country: but this young prince, who was but eighteen years old, kept his ground, and let fly an arrow of walnut-wood against the

---

[1] The Oznaours are the principal lords of Georgia, as the Emirs and Mirzas are with the Persians and Tartars.

Cherif,

Cherif, with so much skill, that he struck him near the collar of his helmet of gold, which he pierc'd, and the arrow stuck in his neck; so that the rash Cherif fell down dead on a sudden. This vigorous action of the young prince did not hinder the Georgians gaining the victory, for they totally defeated the army of Tauris, and then return'd into their own country, while the Mirza Aboubecre sav'd himself by flight.

These melancholy events were the consequences of the Mirza Miran Chah's being lunatic, which yet appear'd in a more shameful manner in his excesses and debauches, for he employ'd almost all his time in drinking and gaming. And as one vice is always attended by another, he fell into greater extravagances. As he was one day in conversation with his wife the princess Canzade, he reproach'd her with a fact which wounded her honor, with which this chaste princess was so sensibly touch'd, that she us'd all her endeavors to discover the source of this calumny, in which search the lives of several men and women were sacrific'd; and even the Mirza's Visier, Dolet Coja Einac, was oblig'd to fly with his wife to Beyan Coutchin at Rei, leaving all he had got during the time of his ministry to be plunder'd. The aversion of the Mirza and Canzade so far increas'd, that the princess, being highly incens'd, was oblig'd to go to Samarcand, where she arriv'd just as Timur return'd from the Indian war, and had begun to take some recreation after the fatigues of that expedition, and inform himself of the present affairs of the empire. This was a favorable time for the princess to be reveng'd; for Timur had been already inform'd of the many disorders committed in the kingdom of Iran, and especially in Azerbijana, thro the ill conduct of the
Mirza.

Mirza Canzade at her arrival had the honor to kiss the imperial carpet in the castle of plane-trees, where she acquainted his majesty with her husband's distemper, assuring him that if he did not march towards that kindom, the Mirza wou'd not fail of revolting, since he now made flight of the imperial mandates and prohibitions, and had squander'd away the treasures of Azerbijana in debauches and prodigality.

These reasons oblig'd Timur, before he had repos'd himself after the fatigues of the last campain, from which he had not return'd above four months, to take up a resolution to carry his arms into the countrys of Iran, to put a stop to the disorders which had crept in there, to succour the weak, curb the insolent, and deliver those who were fallen under the weight of injustice and tyranny.

CHAP. II.

Timur's departure for a campain of seven years.

TIMUR, to whom the universal empire of Asia was destin'd, was no sooner on his return from India, where he had suffer'd the fatigues of a tiresom war with the infidels for a whole year, than he resolv'd to march towards the western parts of Asia, for the reasons given in the preceding chapter. The exempts immediately sent messengers into all the provinces, with orders for the officers of the army to assemble their troops, as well cavalry as infantry, for a campain of seven years, and repair immediately to court to receive his maje-

majesty's orders Timur sent to Herat three Emirs of the court of the Mirza Charoc, to signify to that prince that he must march into Azerbijana at the head of the troops of Corassana, and that the Emir Solyman Chah * shou'd go before at the head of the vanguard to Tauris.

* Charoc's Visier.

The Mirza Charoc having learnt the emperor's will from the Emirs, employ'd himself in getting ready the army of Corassana; and the Emir Solyman Chah departed at the same time with the Seid Coja, whom Timur had sent. As soon as the troops were assembled, the Mirza at their head took the road to Bestam and Damgan. When he was arriv'd at Jadgeron, he met Toukel Carcara, who was come from the imperial camp, which had already cross'd the Gihon, and who brought orders for the army of Corassan to take the road to Chasuman, Esterabad, and Sari, because the imperial army must pass by Bestam and Damgan. Whereupon the Mirza turn'd towards Chasuman, but many of his horses perish'd in their march, as well by reason of the difficulty of the ways, as for that the roads were full of poisonous herbs: and after a tedious journy he arriv'd at Firouzcouh. Timur before his departure gave the government of all the country of Touran to the Mirza Mehemed Sultan, whom he left at Samarcand, the seat of this great empire He fix'd several Emirs in employments near the Mirza's person, whose business was to defend the frontiers, and he gave the government of Andecan to the Mirza Eskender, to whom he entrusted the care of the limits of Turkestan. At length, recommending himself to God, he order'd the great imperial standard to be brought into the field, and at the beginning of autumn, the eighth of Muharrem 802, which answers to the year of the Hare,

Oct. 11.
1399.

his great conqueror departed for a campain of Chap. 2. seven years, the date of which day is found in the letters of Fateh Carib, which signifys, easy conquest. Timur went directly to encamp at Caratoupa, which mountain he afterwards pass'd, and went down to Kech, where he visited the tombs of the prince his father, and of the Cheik Chamseddin Kelar: here he distributed alms, and then went to Termed, where he did the same in the tombs of the Cherifs, as well as in that of Coji Mehemed Ali, the great philosopher of Termed, and in that of the illustrious Aboubecre Verrac, and other famous Santons, imploring their intercession with God for the good success of his arms.

He cross'd the Gihon, and went down to Balc, where he encamp'd in a meadow situate at the foot of the fortress of Hendouan he likewise visited at Balc the tombs of these holy men, Coji Olia Chah, Coja Rommane, Sultan Ahmed Kezrouye, Fdailayaz, Sefian Thaouri, and others, whose assistance he besought: and he did the Emir Yadghiar Berlas, governor of Balc, the honor to lodge in his house This Emir was not wanting in performing his devoirs, as well in sprinkling gold and precious stones at the emperor's feet, as in preparing for him a magnificent banquet and presents, and giving him all the marks of a profound respect and perfect obedience Timur departed from Balc, and after several days march, came to Sarek Camich Dgicm, where he was join'd by the Mirza Charoc's houshold, and by the princesses Melket Aga *, and Ghioher Chad Aga *, with their children, who came from Herat.

* Charoc's wives.

The emperor took pleasure in seeing 'em, and receiv'd their presents, and the precious stones they sprinkled on him, with so much the more satisfaction,

Book V

June 1399.

satisfaction, in that they presented to him the young Mirza Siorgatmich, who was born of Melket Aga but four months before, under the ascendent of Virgo, the eighth of Ramadan 801. The emperor was tenderly affected at the sight of the Mirza his grandson, whom he loaded with blessings.

The Emir Acbouga came to the same place to pay his respects to his majesty, making presents, and sprinkling precious stones at his feet. The emperor gave him a handsom reception, with a vest, and permitted him to return to Herat. Then he went to visit the tomb of the celebrated Mufti Ahmed Dgiam, where he distributed alms as usual, to implore the protection of this famous Santon: and from thence he sent the Mirza Rouftem to his eldest brother the Mirza Pir Mehemed at Chiraz, with orders that these two brothers shou'd march together towards Bagdad, and he commanded the Emir Sevindgic to accompany him with a thousand horse. Timur then took the diversion of the chace in the plains of Khergherd and Feragherd, where in two days they slew an excessive number of beasts, and afterwards he continu'd his road by Nichabour and Beftam, and distributed victuals and ammunition among the troops he pass'd by the province of Rei and Khouvar, and being encamp'd at the town of Aivanic, he was join'd by the Mirza Charoc, who according to his instructions had march'd by the road of Mazendran.

CHAP.

CHAP. III.

The transactions of the Emir Solyman Chah.

THE Emir Solyman Chah, who had taken the road to Tauris with the vanguard, being arriv'd at Rei, heard from Beyan Coutchin, governor of that town, of the Mirza Miran Chah's being lunatic: whereupon, not thinking himself secure if he shou'd go to wait upon this prince, he resolv'd to march to Hamadan. But the Mirza Aboubecre having held a council with his father's Emirs, they consented to write a letter to Solyman Chah, in which they invited him to come to Tauris, assuring him that he shou'd receive all manner of satisfaction. On this promise the Emir went there, and with so much conduct wrought upon Miran Chah, that he persuaded him to set out two days after to meet the emperor, with a numerous retinue, while the Mirza Aboubecre gave this brave Emir a magnificent entertainment in the meadow of Comtoupa, without the city of Tauris, honoring him with a vest, and making him a present of several fine horses, to gain his good-will, as he did also Seid Coja, who accompany'd the Emir Solyman Chah. And then they went together to Chehriar. When Timur had pass'd by Chehriar, the Mirza Miran Chah arriv'd at the imperial camp, but he cou'd not obtain audience till the next day. The same day a messenger, nam'd Aman, arriv'd from Chiraz, and offer'd presents to Timur from the Mirza Omar Cheik: he had a handsom reception, and the honor to kiss the imperial carpet. Next

H 3   day

day the Mirza Miran Chah had also the honor to kifs the emperor's feet he offer'd his presents on his knees; but he was not receiv'd by the emperor with any tokens of kindness, because of the faults he had committed. Then Timur fent to Tauris before the reft, Timur Coja fon of Acbouga, and Gelaleliflam, to carry information of the deportment of Miran Chah. These two commiflarys, at their arrival there, caus'd the principal officers and lieutenants of this Mirza to be feiz'd and bound, and the regifters of the Divan to be brought to 'em. And whereas the Mirza had fquander'd away two parts of the revenues for four years belonging to the Divan, these commiflarys wou'd not pafs his accounts for the fame. But as information was given the court, that the principal caufe of the diforder of the province came from the Mirza's excefles, and he was buoy'd up in this evil paffion by the inftigation of certain profligate muficians, and others, who made it their bufinefs to excite him to pleafures and drunkennefs, that these parafites never ftir'd from the prince's perfon, but took care to furnifh him with new fubjects for debauches, the emperor iflu'd out an order that they fhou'd be all hang'd, not excepting one man, to ferve for an example to others. Thus all the Mirza's favorites were feiz'd, and even the moft ingenious men, who were of that number, were not fpar'd, but ferv'd as a warning to others, as the incomparable Moulana Mehemed Couheftani, fo famous for all fciences, and fo celebrated a poet, whose converfation and agreeable wit had render'd him the wonder of his age.

Timur, at his arrival at Sultania, gave audience to Muzaffer of Neteuze *, who came

* A town near Cachan.

from

from Ispahan; and presenting to Timur jewels and precious vessels, he kiss'd the imperial carpet. Timur continu'd his march towards Carabagh, by the way of Caraderra and Ardebil: he hunted in the plains of Moucam¹ and Actam¹, and encamp'd on the banks of the Arana⁴, which he cross'd the next day upon a bridge of boats, and went to Carabagh Arran. He distributed the winter-quarters among his troops, which were to be in the neighbourhood of Coutourknt, where the hord and lordship of Omartaban lay. At Carabagh the Mirza Aboubecre, and the Emir Solyman Chah, had the honor to pay their respects to the emperor, and all the Emirs and chief lords of Miran Chah's court, and the generals of his army, made their presents to his majesty, according to their ability.

We have already related how the Cherif Ali king of Cheki, of the hord of Erlat, had join'd the Georgian army, that he came with 'em to the gates of Alengic, and lost his life by the hands of the young Mirza Aboubecre, son of the Mirza Miran Chah. Since that time, his son, the Cherif Sidi Ahmed, who had taken upon him the reins of government, fell into an extreme inquietude, fearing lest his father's fault shou'd justly draw upon him Timur's vengeance; this reflection oblig'd him to seek the protection of the Emir Cheik Ibrahim, king of Chirvan, and to fly to him for refuge, because this Emir was honor'd with Timur's particular favor, who lov'd him because of his sincerity, and distinguish'd him among his greatest officers. Wherefore this king of Chirvan, relying entire-

---

¹ Towns of Azerbijana.
⁴ A river frontier of Azerbijana and Arran.

ly on the emperor's goodness, carry'd the Cherif to the foot of the throne, designing to beg pardon for him, and procure him the honor to kiss the imperial carpet. In effect, Sidi Ahmed kiss'd the ground with a profound submission, and the Cheik Ibrahim ask'd pardon for his faults. The emperor full of clemency was willing to give him that mark of his affection; and not only pardon'd the Cherif on his account, but even gave him a handsom reception, and moreover confirm'd him in the principality of Cheki, which the Cherif Ali his father formerly possess'd The Cheik Ibrahim, in quality of king of Chirvan, paid also his particular devoirs; and to testify his joy at the emperor's coming into his country, he prepar'd great banquets, and caus'd so great a number of horses and sheep to be slain, that all the cooks in the court were not sufficient to dress 'em. Besides this banquet, he entertain'd the court with all other pleasures, which usually accompany any famous feasts, and afterwards he offer'd his presents, which consisted of curious animals, beautiful boys and girls, divers stuffs, belts of gold set with precious stones, several sorts of cuirasses and other arms; and lastly, six thousand horses of great price and beauty.

CHAP. IV.

The arrival of good news from several parts.

DURING these transactions, advices were brought from all parts, which were very advantageous to us: among the rest we were inform'd of the death of Timur Cotluc Aglen, who

The history of Timur-Bec. 121

who having fled for refuge to Timur, after the defeat and ruin of Tocatmich Can, had thro the protection of Timur been establish'd on the throne of the Cans of Capchac, and the empire of Touchi, and yet forgetful of all the favors he had receiv'd from Timur, thro an unparallel'd ingratitude, had revolted, and declar'd war against him: they had advice, I say, of the death of this ungrateful prince, as also of the miserable state of the kingdom of Capchac from seditious and intestine wars.

Chap. 4.
Death of the grand Can of Capchac.

At the same time we also heard that Malek Laher Barcoc, king of Egypt and Syria, had pass'd from this world into the other, that discord having crept among the Emirs and Mamalues, the affair had ended in a civil war, in which several of the principal Emirs had been massacred that Farrudge, son of Barcoc, who was declar'd heir and successor to the kingdom, had neither credit nor authority· and, that the kingdoms of Egypt and Syria were entirely fallen into disorder

Death of the Sultan of Egypt.

There came also advice, that Tangouz Can, emperor of China, where he had reign'd a long time, professing idolatry, was dead. and that the Chinese who had revolted, had caus'd great contentions in that empire

Death of the emperor of China.

They also learnt that Kezre Coja Aglen, king of Gete, had paid the tribute to the angel Israel, and that after his death dissensions arose among his four sons, Chamadgehan, Mehemed Aglen, Chirali, and Chadgehan, thro the motions of some seditious people

Death of the king of Gete.

The same day they also heard that the Mirza Iskender, son of Omar Cheik, was departed from Andecan at the head of his Emirs and army, and had enter'd Mogolistan, where, thro Timur's good fortune, he had gain'd the advantage

tage over the Moguls, whom he utterly defeated.

These advices, which were of so great importance to the designs of our conqueror, arriving the same day, fill'd the hearts of all the emperor's faithful servants with joy.

As the affair of the Mirza Eskender is of such great consequence, we have thought proper to give the reader a detail of it. Dissension having crept in among the people of Gete[7] after the death of Kezre Coja Aglen, the Mirza Eskender laid hold on this favorable opportunity, and got together the troops of Andecan, and tho' he was but fifteen years old, he put himself at their head, accompany'd by the Emirs of his court, and by those who in compliance with Timur's orders, guarded the frontiers of Gete, and boldly enter'd into the lands of the Mogols.

When he was come near to Cachgar[8], and the Emirs had join'd him, they advanc'd all together to pillage and ravage the town of Yarkent[9], then they march'd on farther, and did the same to Sarek Camich, Kelapine, Aligheul, Yar Courgan, Tchartac, and Keiouc Bagh[1]; they at length arriv'd at the province of Aoudge in Mogoustan, and almost all the people, whose hords were in those quarters, came to meet 'em with submission and obedience. They took those prisoners who refus'd to obey, and carry'd 'em with 'em towards the citadel of Acsou, which they besieg'd, and with great difficulty made themselves masters of it. This citadel consists of

---

[7] The author seems to make no difference between the Getes and the Mogols, either because the action is the same, or that the Mogols at that time inhabited the country of Gete.
[8] Capital of Turkestan.
[9] Town of Gete.
[1] All towns of Mogolistan.

The history of Timur-Bec.

...ree caftles, which have a communication with
...ne another, and is efteem'd fo ftrong, that the
...nhabitants of all the neighboring provinces
...onfider it as a fure afylum in time of war. The
Mirza foon encamp'd with his Emirs without the
place, and being prepar'd to attack it vigo-
roufly with inftruments for fapping the walls,
fcaling-ladders, battering-rams, and other machines, he caus'd feveral affaults to be given
immediately after one another, for near forty
days, when the befieg'd were oblig'd to furren-
der to which purpofe they fent prefents to the
Mirza, and made feveral very rich Chinefe merchants go out of the place, who had been fhut
up there with their effects. Then the Mirza
fent men to make inroads at Bai and Coufan,
the former of which is a cool place fit for the
fummer, and the latter a warm place proper for
winter. The fcouts pillag'd thefe two towns,
and brought away captive the princefs Hadgi
Melik Aga, wife of the Emir Kezre Chah, and
her daughter Ifan Melik, with other ladys. At
length they went to pillage the town of Tarem,
whence they brought the inhabitants away prifoners.

After thefe conquefts the Mirza Eskender departed from Acfou for Cotan ^a, one hundred and
fifty feven days journy from Cambalec *, capital of the northern China, call'd Catai, which
is a flourifhing and populous country, with abundance of water: for we count from Cotan to
Cara Coja thirty-five days journy, from thence
to l'etcaoul, frontier of China, thirty-one days
journy, where there is a wall fituate between two
mountains, in which wall is a great gate, and

Chap. 4.

* Pequin.

The Chi-
nefe wall.

feveral

^a Capital of a kingdom of the fame name.

several Yam Canes, or inns to lodge passengers, and several soldiers are always at this place to guard the frontiers and entrance of the wall. From hence to Ghendgian Fou, a city of China, is fifty-one days journy; and forty from that place to Cambalec. It is also forty from Ghendgian Fou to Nemnai. We are assur'd there is another road, by which to go from Cotan to the frontiers of China in forty days: but there is not one dwelling-place in it, the sands make it very tiresom, and tho the water, which is drawn out of the wells in its desarts, is easily come at, yet in several places it is venomous, and kills the animals which drink of it; and what is very surprizing, out of two wells at a small distance from each other, the water of one is poisonous, and the other perfectly good. From Cotan to Cachgar is fifteen days journy, and from Cachgar to Samarcand twenty-five. In Cotan are two rivers, Oraccach, and Caracach, the stones of which being jasper, are carry'd to other countrys. These two rivers have their source in the mountain of Carangoutac.

To return to our subject: at the Mirza Eskender's arrival at Cotan, the inhabitants came out to salute him, and bring him presents, and he behav'd himself with so much prudence, that all the places and castles of this frontier-province were reduc'd to the emperor's obedience. He at length departed from Cotan, and came to Carangoutac, a very steep and rugged mountain, into which the inhabitants of Cotan and the neighboring places fly for refuge in time of war. When the Mirza was fully inform'd of the strength and inaccessibleness of Carangoutac, he did not judge it convenient to hazard his troops there, but chose rather to return, and spend the winter at Cachgar. He chose two com-

companys of Mogul young women, the most beautiful of Cotan, nine in each company, whom he sent as a present to the emperor by the Cheik Yesaoul he likewise sent by the same person nine young women and nine horses to the Mirza Mehemet Sultan, who being extremely incens'd against him, refus'd his presents.

The reason of this discord was as follows: the Mirza Mehemed Sultan was come into Turkestan with an army to join the Mirza Eskender, and go with him to the war against the Getes, but Eskender, instead of waiting for him as he ought, went before, and march'd directly into Mogolistan, that he might not serve under Mehemed Sultan This excited Mehemed's hatred, so that he wou'd not accept of his presents, and he return'd to Samarcand with his army, without putting any designs in execution.

When spring was come, the Mirza Eskender return'd to Andecan, from whence he took the road to Samarcand, to visit Mehemed Sultan; but he learnt at the mountain Ackioteb, that the Mirza being highly incens'd against him, had a design to seize him. This advice made Eskender jealous, so he return'd to Andecan, and enter'd the castle but the Emirs, Pir Mehemed, son of Tagi Bouga, and Pir Hadgi son of Melik, tax'd him with a design to revolt They assembled the militia of Andecan, and besieg'd the castle, upon which the Mirza Eskender came out, and went to lodge in a garden built by the Mirza Omar Cheik, after having confer'd with 'em with a deal of good-nature. Then the Emirs seiz'd his domestics, and bound 'em; of which they sent advice to the Mirza Mehemed Sultan at Samarcand, as also of Eskender's entring the castle, and design to revolt. Mehemed Sultan dispatch'd an express to bring Eskender to Samar-

Samarcand, with the officers of his houſhold They deliver'd this prince to him at the bank of the river of Couhec, and having bound him, they put to death his Atabec [1], Beyan Timur, ſon of Bikidgeh, with twenty-ſix of his domeſtics.

CHAP. V.

Timur marches into Georgia, and to the defile of Comcha.

TIMUR deſigning to carry his arms into Georgia, in obedience to the precept of the Alcoran, which teaches us to wage war upon all who disbelieve the muſſulman religion, he began to make preparations from the winter of 802, being then encamp'd at Carabagh Arran.

An. Dom. 1399.

He gave a veſt to the Cheik Ibrahim of Chirvan, and another to Sidi Ahmed of Cheki, and after having loaded 'em with his favors, he permitted 'em to return home. He choſe three men out of every ten to ſerve as ſcouts, whom he order'd to take victuals for ten days: and he commanded the baggage and reſt of the army to ſtay in this place. He went to join theſe ſcouts with the Mirzas his ſons; and being arriv'd at the river of Cyrus *, he croſs'd it with his troops on a bridge of boats. Soon after he was join'd by the Cheik Ibrahim of Chirvan, and Sidi Ahmed, prince of Cheki, who came to follow the court

* Abcor.

---

[1] Atabec is a prince's governor.

The imperial army pass'd by Cheki [4], and took the road to the defile of Comcha [5], where the infidels dwelt: and as this defile was full of thick woods, the trees of which were very closely interwoven with one another, the soldiers had orders to cut 'em down to facilitate their passage. Accordingly they made a road with their axes and saws ten days journy in length, and broad enough for five or six companys to march in front. At that time it snow'd exceedingly for twenty days together, but that cou'd not hinder Timur from arriving with his army in Georgia. Our men made the great cry, *Allah Ec-l-*, and fell upon the enemy with so much fury, that the surface of the mountain which the snows had before render'd white, with the blood of these infidels became as red as fields sown with tulips, and no quarter was given to any they met. Comcha the chief of these infidels, who disbelieve any future judgment, was oblig'd to abandon his effects and family, and fly. Our soldiers pursu'd him as far as the defile of Acsou, and return'd with a great many oxen, sheep, and other cattel. After Comcha's flight, and retreating into the woods, they set fire to his houses, and pillag'd and ruin'd all his villages. And as wine was absolutely necessary for this people; their men, women, and little children being so accustom'd to it, that when they were on their death-bed, they entreated that some might be buried in their sepulchres with 'em, and order'd by their wills that after their deaths their bodys shou'd be wash'd with wine, and their coffins made with vine-tree for this consideration,

---

[4] A town on the south frontiers of Georgia near the Caspian.
[5] A defile in Georgia, belonging to prince Comcha.

that

that they might do 'em the more damage, and entirely ruin 'em, the vine-trees were diftributed among the troops, who rooted up all of 'em, which they had with fo great difficulty cultivated; they alfo cut down the other trees, and peel'd feveral. They afterwards raz'd the great edifices of this country, and efpecially the temples, where they paid their adorations, which were fo difagreeable to God. And what is remarkable is, that in the winter of the preceding year, which was that of the Leopard, Timur deftroy'd the Guebres of India, and ruin'd their temples at Deli, and upon the Ganges, and that this winter, which was the year of the Hare, he was carrying on the fame war of religion in Georgia, and razing the temples of the Georgians. The poet fays, that he had one foot on the eaftern frontiers of India, and the other upon the weftern limits of the country of Arran.

CHAP. VI

Timur's return from the defile of Comcha.

TIMUR ftaid near a month in this defile, and his foldiers had made themfelves mafters of all the mountains, after having flain an infinite number of brave Oznaours, whofe prince Comcha was retir'd to fo great a diftance, that no advice cou'd be got of the place he was in; and the enemy's country was entirely ruin'd befides all this, the cold was very violent, and the ways were clog'd up with fnow, fo that the horfes had nothing to eat but the barks of trees, and even feveral of 'em died with hunger.
Where-

Whereupon Timur resolv'd to return: he repass'd the river of Cyrus, and came back with glory to Curabigh, where he enter'd his imperial tent with the acclamations of all the lords and princes of his court. The joy at his presence was augmented by the birth of a son to the Mirza Calil Sultan; this young prince was nam'd Berlas, and several days were spent in sprinkling gold and precious stones upon him: they had banquets and plays, accompany'd with music, to celebrate this happy birth. Soon after a severe order was issu'd out, for prosecuting those in a council of war, who had not behav'd themselves as they ought in the battel fought by the Mirza Miran Chah against the Georgians, in the neighborhood of Alengic. The Mirza Charoc was commission'd to see to the putting this order in execution, who having examin'd all the facts, in council with the Emirs of the Divan, he presented a memorial to the emperor, with the several interrogatorys, informations and proofs; upon which Timur order'd the punishment due by the laws of Genghiz Can to be executed. The bastinado was given to Hadgi Abdalla Abbas, and Mehemed Casgan: Yumne Harizai Aperdi, who had fled first, was order'd to be put to death, but the Chah Zades, or emperor's children, obtain'd the favor of his being repriev'd after the bastinado before and behind, and each of these three lords was fin'd thirty horses. They also fin'd the principal officers of the Mirza Miran Chah, some at fifty, some at two hundred, and some at three hundred horses, which horses were distributed among the foot-soldiers.

Timur bestow'd many favors and honors on the Mirza Aboubecre, because of the valor he had shewn in the fight, when he unhors'd Sidi Ali

Ali king of Cheki. At the same time the prince Burhan Aglen was likewise put to death, for having committed some considerable faults, very unworthy of his birth, in several skirmishes. His son was treated in the same manner; and his regiment, officers, and domestics were given to Roustem Foulad.

CHAP. VII.

Continuation of the history of the Mirza Roustem, who was gone from Dgiam to Chiraz. A great crime committed by his eldest brother, the Mirza Pir Mehemed.

WE have said before that the emperor had sent the Mirza Roustem from Dgiam [a] to Chiraz, and that he was accompany'd in his journy by the Emir Sevindgic at the head of two thousand horse. They happily arriv'd at Chiraz by the road of Yezd and Abrecouh. The Mirza Pir Mehemed gave him a handsom reception, and a sumptuous banquet, in the garden of Carabagh [b], and presented him with a vest and a hundred thousand Dinars Copeghis. Some time after the Mirza Roustem, accompany'd by the Emirs Sevindgic, his nephew Hassan Jandar, and Hassan Jagadaoul, who were at Chiraz, took the road to Bagdad, according to the emperor's order, and pass'd by Behbehan and Tostar, leav-

---

[a] In Corassana towards Bactriana: the same with Sark Carnich Dgiam.
[b] A royal garden at Chiraz, different from Carabagh near Tauris.

ing at Chiraz, to govern that city, the Emirs Said Berlas, and Alibek Aifa, a relation of the Emir Abbas, as Timur had commanded him. But the Mirza Mehemed, who had the same orders to depart at the head of this army, delay'd his departure, till a long time after; then pretending sickness, he return'd to Chiraz by Nobendgian in Chouleftan.

This did not deter the Mirza Rouftem with his Emirs from ravaging Lorafterec, in the country of Ramhermez [8], from whence he brought a great quantity of booty he made the same hafte in paffing by the village of the bridge, call'd Dezfoul. he pillag'd in the plain of Dombar all the fubjects of the princes Saki and Febli. From thence he went to plunder Bad [9] and Bacfa [9], whence he brought away several flaves; and in the month of Jumaziulevel 802, he arriv'd at Mendeli [1]. The Emir Ali Calander, the governor of it for the Sultan of Bagdad, put himself in a pofture of defence; but he being repuls'd at the first onfet, they feiz'd on eleven of his men, whose heads they cut off, and then permitted the foldiers to pillage the place.

In the mean while the Mirza Pir Mehemed, who under pretence of sickness had turn'd back, arriv'd at Chiraz, where by the inftigation of certain Tadgics, who had lifted themselves in his fervice, he fell into some extravagances; undertaking to compofe poifons and fafcinations, the defigns of which he was utterly ignorant of. The Emir Said Berlas, governor of Chiraz, being inform'd of it by some of this young prince's fervants, immediately made a ftrict fearch into

Chap. 7.

March 1400.

[8] A town of Lorestan. long. 86. lat. 31.
[9] Towns of Chaldea.
[1] A town of Arabia, dependent on Bagdad.

the matter, and learnt from his very officer the whole of it, even before the Mirza's face Upon these inconteſtable proofs the Emir Said impriſon'd Pir Mehemed in the inner fortreſs, and lodg'd himſelf in the caſtle to guard him, leaving Alibec Aiſa in the city to govern it in his ſtead, and he ſent advice to court of what had paſs'd at Chiraz. The meſſenger of the Emir Said gave an accouut of this to Timur in the winter-quarters at Carabagh, who immediately ſent the Emir Allahdad to Chiraz, to proſecute thoſe wicked Tadgics, who had taught the Mirza to make the poiſons, that they might be put to death he was likewiſe order'd to ſettle the Mirza Rouſtem upon the throne of Perſia, in the room of his eldeſt brother, whom he was to bring bound to court. Accordingly the Emir Allahdad, at his arrival at Chiraz, put to death Moulana Mehemed Calife, Seid Dgerrah, and Rouſtem Coraſani, who were convicted of having taught the Mirza how to compoſe the poiſons, he caus'd Maſtaoui Couchtchi's legs and arms to be cut off; and put in irons Mobarec Coja, Muhib Cherberdar, and Cheik Zadei Ferid, who were accus'd of having been concern'd in the ſame crime Allahdad then ſent the emperor's letters-patent to the Mirza Rouſtem, in Irac-Arabi, by which he was inſtall'd in the government of the kingdom of Perſia. This prince receiv'd 'em at Mendeli, after he had gain'd the victory over Mir Ali Calander. As ſoon as he had read the emperor's orders, he departed for Chiraz the Emirs Haſſan Jandar and Haſſan Jagadaoul, who accompany'd him, return'd back, and the Emir Sevindgie took the road to Crepchemal, for Carabagh Arran, where the army lay then encamp'd

Mir

Mir Ali Calander, who had fled from Mendeli, being arriv'd at Bagdad, gave an account to the Sultan Ahmed of what pass'd: this prince fell into a great inquietude, and order'd the gates to be shut, and the bridge of the city to be destroy'd.

About this time there happen'd a very remarkable affair, of great service to Timur. This monarch having given the government of Coureltan to one nam'd Cherouan, this governor immediately gave himself up to the getting of many at any rate: he exacted great sums from Chamseddin Dehdar, and other principal men of the country, he even put to death the governors of Haviza [1], and what was worse than all this, he revolted, and with a thousand horse well-equip'd went to Bagdad, where he offer'd his services to Sultan Ahmed, who gave him a handsom reception, loading him with honors and caresses. Cherman did not rest there, but endeavor'd to win over to him the Sultan's principal officers, and to that purpose secretly gave 'em considerable sums, from ten thousand to three hundred thousand Dinars of Bagdad. But it happen'd very unluckily to this traitor, that the memorandum of the sums paid to each of these lords was lost thro the negligence of his secretary, and fell into the hands of Cayre Behader, one of the Sultan's officers, who presented the note to his master, at a time when the affrighted Sultan had caus'd the gates of the town to be shut. This affair greatly increas'd his jealousy, and particularly a sum of ten thousand Dinars, set down to the name of Rafe, whom the Sultan immediately caus'd to be arrested, and cut off

---
[1] A town in the province of Coureftan, call'd also Ahouaz.

Book V. his head with his own hand. In the mean while, as he had already sent Cherouan, with Coutoub Haideri, Mansour, and other Emirs, to ravage Ourat; he immediately difpatch'd Yadghiar Ectatchi, with orders to the Emirs to flay Cherouan, which was accordingly executed, and his head brought to Bagdad, where the Sultan in less than eight days put to death near two thousand of his officers. He sent to Vafet the lady Vefa Catoun, who had nurs'd and educated Cherouan from his infancy, where she was smother'd by a pillow laid over her face. He slew with his own hand most part of the other ladys and officers of his houshold, whom he order'd to be cast into the Tigris: and afterwards he shut himself up in the Seraglio, not suffering any one to come to him; and even when the Bavertchis, or stewards, brought him his dinner, they knock'd at the door, deliver'd in the dishes, and then return'd without entring. He spent several days after this manner, and then order'd six of his most faithful servants to convey secretly six horses out of his stable to the other side the Tigris, which river he cross'd one night in a boat, and with those six persons rode into the country subject to Cara Yousef prince of the Turcomans. In the mean while the stewards, as usual, carry'd the king's dinner to the gate of the Seraglio, and deliver'd it to an officer who was in the secret, the people having no knowledg of the Sultan's absence. This prince join'd Cara Yousef, and persuaded him to come with his troops to pillage the town of Bagdad. When they were come there, he affign'd quarters on the other side of the water for the troops of Cara Yousef. the Sultan cross'd the river in a boat, and came to his palace, and he gave so much ready mony, stuffs, arms, Arabian horses, gold

gold belts, and other riches, to Cara Youfef and his men, that those Turcomans were content with what they had got. The Sultan wou'd by no means permit 'em to insult the city; but as he very much fear'd being attack'd by the army of Zagatai, he sent out spys on all sides, who gave him a true information of the condition of Timur's affairs.

In the month of Zilhadge 802, Timur being on his march to Sebafte, the Sultan of Bagdad imagin'd that if the formidable armys of this conqueror shou'd again enter Natolia and Syria, all the passages wou'd be block'd up, whilst he must be oblig'd to save himself by flight. He therefore resolv'd to leave Farrudge governor of the city of Bagdad, whence he design'd to go out with Cara Youfef, his wives and children, and his jewels, with whatever he cou'd carry away worth taking. So they cross'd the Euphrates, for Natolia; and being arriv'd at Aleppo, Temourtach, who commanded there, came out with his Emirs to oppose his passage. A battel ensu'd: but those of Aleppo being defeated, the Sultan and the rest pursu'd their road, and came to Natolia. As they were on their march towards the city of Sebafte, capital of Roum, they were met by a party of Timur's army: but what pass'd between 'em we'll relate hereafter.

CHAP. VIII.

A diet in relation to the affair of Georgia.

AFTER winter was over, that is, in the beginning of the year of the Crocodile, Timur left his winter-quarters at Carabagh. He assembled a diet, whereto the princes his sons, the Emirs, the lords and general officers did not fail of coming: he held a council with 'em, in which it was unanimously resolv'd that the war with the infidels of Georgia was preferable to all others, as well for the good of religion, which ought to be the principal object of war, as for the increase of the power of monarchy, and the conjuncture of the present affairs. The usual feast was made after the diet, and the banquet, which was very sumptuous, was accompany'd with all sorts of plays and pleasures. Timur, excited by a desire of liberality, distributed the treasures among the Chah-Zades, his sons, the Emirs and all the soldiers of the army, and gave horses to those who were on foot. He afterwards inform'd himself of the roads and quarters of Georgia, where they shou'd encamp, and had 'em very exactly set down in writing and then imploring the divine assistance, he departed from Carabagh, taking the road to Georgia, the country of Malek Ghourghin. In ten days he arriv'd at the plain of Berdaa, where he encamp'd, and gave audience to Taharten, prince of Arzendgian upon the Euphrates, who had already gain'd his majesty's favor by his good services. This prince kiss'd the earth before Timur; made a discourse in his praise, full

full of vows for his prosperity; and offer'd his presents. Timur being willing to distinguish him by very particular favors, not only gave him a vest, a cap and a belt, but he further honor'd him with a horse-tail, a standard, and two kettle drums, which are the signs of sovereignty: and then he permitted him to return to Arzendgian, after having given him instructions concerning the application and care he ought to use in the government of the city in the present conjuncture, and expresly recommended to him to use circumspection to preserve his frontiers from the insults of the Ottomans; to which purpose he ought to be watchful, cautious, and liberal to his soldiers, and neglect nothing to protect himself from his enemys artifices, who are very politic and dangerous.

Timur departed from Berdaa, and after several days journy, arriv'd at the frontiers of Georgia. He immediately dispatch'd an express to Malek Ghourghin, to send to the camp the prince Taher, son of Sultan Ahmed Gelair. The messenger acquitted himself of his commission; but the king of Georgia, Ghourghin, return'd him a very uncivil answer. The express came back without obtaining any thing, and gave an account to Timur of all that had pass'd in the audience. The rashness of this refusal kindled his wrath against these infidels; wherefore leaving the baggage, he went before, and order'd his troops to enter the lands of these Georgians, and to put every thing to fire and sword. The soldiers slew every one they met, ruin'd the houses of the Georgians, and even rooted up the trees; they destroy'd the vines, spoil'd the fruits, and brought a terrible desolation upon this country. The affrighted Georgians fled for refuge into their high mountains, where

Book V. where no one had ever yet conquer'd 'em, for here were fortify'd caverns, and houses upon craggy rocks, which it wou'd in vain to think any one cou'd enter by force of arms. They had entrench'd themselves in those places, and carry'd with 'em whatever they cou'd find worth taking. Timur's soldiers, without examining the dangers to which they were expos'd, and full of confidence in their prince's good fortune, ascended these mountains, and then laid themselves in boxes, to which strong cords were fasten'd, and so were let down by their comrades from the tops of the mountains to the caverns of the Georgians, where discharging their arrows, they approach'd the enemys, and slew the most advanc'd. then taking lances in one hand, and swords in the other, they enter'd the caverns, notwithstanding the vigorous resistance of the enemys, of whom they made a horrible slaughter. Among these craggy places there were some so well defended, that our men were oblig'd to cast a great quantity of combustible matter, as well to dissipate the enemys, as to burn their wooden houses, and the entrenchments they had made. Thus by the assistance of heaven, tho these infidels fought with all imaginable resolution, the mussulman soldiers had the advantage over 'em, according to the promise of the Alcoran, taking fifteen noted places, on which they very much rely'd. Those who wou'd turn Mussulmans obtain'd quarter: but those who, thro the temptation of the devil, stubbornly continu'd in the disbelief of the Alcoran, were beheaded.

Timur left several of the best troops of Corassana in the garison of the city of Teflis, capital of Georgia, and then went to encamp in the plain of Mocran. The king Ghourghin

being

being terrify'd at the success of the Mahometans, fled into the desarts, and as a vagabond wander'd about the uninhabited mountains: but the greatest part of the Oznaours of Georgia, seeing themselves reduc'd to the utmost extremity, submitted; they came in a humble manner to the gate of the imperial pavilion, where they begg'd quarter and pardon of the victorious Timur, making divers excuses to avert his vengeance When our troops had reduc'd this country, they raz'd the temples and monasterys, where the Georgians had for a long time exercis'd their religion; and erected chappels and mosques, in which they proclaim'd the Ezan [1], and read the prayers of the mussulman religion with the usual ceremony, to the glory of Timur

CHAP. IX.

Timur marches against prince Jani Bec, a Georgian.

AFTER the conquest and destruction of the country of Malek Ghourghin, Timur resolv'd to attack the other provinces of Georgia. He departed with expedition from the plain of Mocran, and leaving the baggage, march'd towards the defile of Jani Bec. When they were arriv'd there, the troops surrounded all the country, pillag'd it, and brought away a considerable booty. Jani Bec soon abandon'd

---

[1] Ezan is the cry the Mahometans make from the top of the Minarets (or steeples) of their mosques, to call the people to prayer.

his mountain and fortress, and with an entire submission came before the emperor. In the mean while our soldiers ravag'd the villages, burnt the houses, and slew every one they met; they carry'd away the Georgians effects, and while they enrich'd themselves in this world, they were laying up treasures of merit in the other. Afterwards they return'd to join the baggage, and Timur sent, by the way of Semave, the Seid Coja, son of the Cheik Ali Behader, to make inroads in other parts of Georgia, he order'd the Emir Gehan Chah to pass the defile with the troops of the left-wing, and the main body, commanded by Timur, pass'd by Semave, where it was join'd by all the troops which were gone out to make inroads in the provinces, from whence they return'd loaden with spoils, bringing away a great number of horses and sheep; and, to mortify the Georgians the more, our soldiers destroy'd all the standing corn, and ruin'd their temples and other edifices. At the mouth of the defile was a fortress nam'd Bil, which was very high and difficult of access; nevertheless our army was no sooner arriv'd there than they had orders to besiege it, and the siege and conquest of the place were almost perform'd at the same time. Having taken it, they raz'd it, lest it shou'd be of use to the enemy on another occasion. From thence the army went to encamp in the true antient Georgia; and Timur sent the Emirs into all parts in search of king Ghourghin, who, like wolves and chacals, wander'd as a vagabond in uninhabited woods and mountains but not being able to find him, they return'd to join the imperial camp with a great quantity of spoils, and some of Ghourghin's officers whom they had taken. Timur at length decamp'd, cross'd the river of Cyrus, and happily encamp'd camp'd on the other bank, loaded with good fortune, and pleas'd with his victorys.

CHAP. X.

The taking of the fort of Zerit, and the town of Suanit.

DURING thefe tranfactions, the fpys brought advice that a great number of Oznaours were retir'd into the caftle of Zerit, fituate on the ridg of a narrow mountain, which had never been taken by any conqueror. On this, Timur, to whom nothing appear'd impoffible, march'd with expedition towards this place, and order'd it to be befieg'd. The machines and battering rams were got ready, and after feveral attacks neceffary at a fiege, a general affault was given feven days after Timur's arrival. The fort was taken fword in hand, and raz'd the fame day, after putting all the Georgians to the fword. Then they went out to make inroads, and brought away a great number of prifoners bound, whom the emperor order'd to be put to death, becaufe they wou'd not turn Mahometans. They afterwards receiv'd advice that king Gourghin was in the town of Suanit. Timur order'd the roads to this town to be taken down in writing; and that the troops which were gone out to make inroads, fhou'd return to the camp. He left one half of the army with the baggage; and with enfigns difplay'd march'd with the reft. But Gourghin, who had his fpys about him, had advice of Timur's approach; he went out of Suanit,

Suanit, and fled towards Abkhaze [*]. The troops, at their arrival at Suanit, carry'd it upon the first assault, and then went in pursuit of Ghourghin, several of whose officers they slew, but this prince, reduc'd to the greatest misery, cross'd the rivers of Aigar and Corlan [5], and had the good fortune to save himself from the dangers wherewith he was surrounded. Then seeing himself, in a manner, ready for the slaughter, he found it was not for so weak a prince as himself to protect the son of the Sultan of Bagdad, against the powerful emperor Timur: whereupon he oblig'd Taher to seek an asylum in the country of the Ottomans, whither he had heard the Sultan Ahmed his father was likewise fled. At length Gourghin sent to the court of Timur an ambassador nam'd Ismael, who made known to him the great misery and extremity to which his master was reduc'd, deplor'd the ruin of his state, and destruction of his country, and with his face turn'd towards the ground, he spake thus to the emperor with all the submission that cou'd be expected from a miserable and vanquish'd prince: " I have seen
" the evil success of the methods I have so un-
" fortunately taken; I have tasted the fruits of
" my imprudence, and the bitterness of the pu-
" nishment I have merited: but if the great
" emperor, whose generosity after victory, I
" may venture to say, surpasses the fury of his
" arms in battel, will take pity upon me, who
" am his servant, and confess my fault, and is
" willing to pardon me for what is past, and
" grant me my life, I will not only be intirely
" obedient to him, but my life shall always be

---

[*] A town of Georgia on the frontiers of Circassia.
[5] Rivers of Capchac.

" employ'd in his service. I will take great care
" not to hurt the Mussulmans in any manner:
" and moreover I consent to pay the annual tri-
" bute to the imperial treasury; likewise pro-
" mising to send what number of troops his ma-
" jesty shall order into his service, at the time
" appointed."

CHAP. XI.

Timur marches against the Georgian prince Atvani.

TIMUR, upon hearing this discourse of Ghourghin's ambassador, was touch'd with the condition of this prince, and did not doubt the truth of what he said, considering the great misery and necessity to which he was reduc'd, his sincere confession of his fault, and his repentance for having dar'd to give protection to the Sultan Taher These considerations, join'd with the promises he had made, and confirm'd with an oath, to be always ready in the emperor's service, and punctually to pay the annual tribute, caus'd Timur to grant him the pardon he demanded; who then went out of his country, and march'd towards the lands subject to prince Aivani, one of the most powerful sovereigns of Georgia. The soldiers having enter'd his country, ravag'd and pillag'd all they met, and as there was no army to oppose 'em, they dispers'd themselves up and down, ruining the towns and castles, and destroying every thing with fire and sword. After they had entirely laid this country waste, they pass'd into that of Cara Calcanlic *, the inhabitants of which,

* A tribe of Georgians.

which, arm'd with black bucklers, were skilful mountaineers, and good horsemen. They were not treated with more mildness than the others, for their country was ravag'd, and the places raz'd whither they were retir'd, their houses burnt, and themselves put to the sword, after our soldiers had got what spoils they cou'd from 'em, which were very considerable.

CHAP. XII.

Timur returns from Georgia.

TIMUR being satisfy'd with the conquests he had gain'd, and having reveng'd himself on the Georgians, gave orders for his return. After several days march he encamp'd at Yeilac Mencoul, but having advice that the enemy were again assembled in a place nam'd Farasgherd in Georgia, he sent the Emir Cheik Noureddin thither with his troops, and being willing to be in person at the execution of all important affairs, he decamp'd some days after, and leaving the baggage, march'd to Farasgherd. In five days he made himself master of seven fortresses of the Georgians, which he caus'd to be raz'd, after having slain an infinite number of these infidels, and from thence he return'd with all his army to Mencouh, where he staid several days.

About this time there came ambassadors from an European prince, who brought with 'em the son of the Emir Amurat, the Ottoman emperor, whom they had taken prisoner: and by the intercession of the principal Emirs of the court, they were admitted into Timur's audience; to whom they made known the high esteem their
master

The history of Timur-Bec.

master had conceiv'd of his actions, and his desire to enter into an alliance with him, which he shou'd account a great honor. Timur receiv'd the ambassadors with all manner of civility, granted 'em what they desir'd, and after having given 'em rich vests, dismiss'd 'em, and they return'd home by the way of Trebizond [c], pleas'd with the honors they had reciv'd at court. The army lay encamp'd two months in the meadow of Mencoul, that the horses might have some rest after their fatigue, and to wait the arrival of the Emirs and troops which were dispers'd up and down the country.

CHAP. XIII.

Reasons which oblig'd Timur to march against the city of Sebaste, capital of Anatolia.

PHILOSOPHERS tell us that the relation between a king and his kingdom is the same as between the soul and body, for when the soul and body harmonize in the rules of moderation, the body is in perfect health; but if the contrary happens, it is attack'd with distempers, and at length falls into corruption: and so when a king neglects to do justice, his kingdom falls into decay. This moral may with justice be apply'd to the case of the Ottoman emperor, and the Sultan of Egypt; for these two princes priding in their power, committed several violent actions, which drew upon 'em

---

[c] Capital of the kingdom of the same name, in Anatolia, on the shore of the black sea; long. 70. 30. lat. 42.

Book V Timur's anger, and caus'd the destruction of their country and the desolation of their subjects. Timur being irritated at their proceedings, tho but newly return'd from a toilsom campain, and notwithstanding the great distance of these Sultans dominions, did not fail of undertaking the conquest of their empires, which by the grace of God he brought into subjection, so that all the citys, towns and villages of these great countrys were pillag'd by his soldiers: which calamity was brought upon the poor innocent people thro the bad conduct of their princes.

But to come to a particular detail of this history, we must know that Ildurum [7] Bajazet, sirnam'd the Thunder, who was then emperor of the Ottomans, surpass'd most of his predecessors in power, and the vastness of his dominions· he had brought into subjection a great part of the country of Roum *, to wit, the provinces of Aidine, Mentecha, Kermian, and Caramania, which his ancestors had never been able to do: and he had likewise extended his dominions the space of four months journy in Europe. After he had taken prisoner Cara Ofman, son of the Cadi Burhaneddin, prince of Sebaste, and had put to death the Cadi, he brought an army into the field, and having made himself master of Sebaste, he push'd his conquests towards Malatia [8], a town on the Euphrates, and bordering upon the province of Aleppo He even besieg'd and took the city of Malatia, which had been a long time dependent on Syria. He made the

* Anatolia.

---
[7] Ildurum signifys lightning or thunder.
[8] Long. 71. lat. 37.

Emir

Emir Muſtafa governor of Sebaſte, to whoſe ſon he gave the government of Malatia. At length, as if he cou'd find no one to diſpute his conqueſts, he return'd victorious and loaded with ſpoils to the ſeat of his empire. He had a great number of troops and officers belonging to his houſhold, and among the reſt, near twelve thouſand dog-keepers. His magnificence, riches, and power, render'd him ſo proud, that he forgot the ſentence which teaches us, that God, the creator of the univerſe, hath made thoſe who are ſuperior to them who pride themſelves in their ſtrength. He had the boldneſs to ſend an ambaſſador to Taharten, to ſummon him to his court, and ſend the tributes of Arzendgian, Erzerom, and their dependences, to his treaſury; which order was in ſuch haughty terms, that it did not become him to uſe. Taharten ſent advice of this to court; and Timur was very much ſurpriz'd at the deſigns of the Ottoman, who was not ignorant that Taharten was under his protection whereupon he reſolv'd to write a letter to him, to endeavor to bring him to a ſenſe of his fault by ſweetneſs and friendſhip.

CHAP. XIV.

Timur's letter to the Caiſer Roum, that is, the Ottoman emperor.

TIMUR commanded a ſecretary to be call'd to him, whom he order'd to write a letter to Ildurum Bajazet, mix'd with counſel and reproaches, hoping by that means to make him reflect upon what he had done. The ſecretary began the letter in an eloquent manner,

with

Book V. with praises to God, and blessings on Mahomet he made use of this passage of the Alcoran for the subject of his letter, *God blesses those princes who know what use they shou'd make of their power, and go not beyond the bounds prescrib'd 'em* and he continu'd it with expressions which were as daggers to the heart of Bajazet, and ought to have shewn him his duty. The letter was as follows

To the emperor of Roum, Bajazet the Thunder.

" After the usual compliments, we let you
" know, that by the infinite grace of God,
" the greatest part of Asia is in subjection to
" our officers, which we conquer'd by our
" strength, and the terror of our arms. Know
" likewise that the most powerful Sultans of the
" earth are obedient to our commands, that
" we govern our dominions by our self, and
" have even constrain'd fortune to take care of
" our empire, that our armys are extended
" from one sea to the other, and our guard con-
" sists of sovereign kings, who form a hedge be
" fore our gate. Where is the monarch who
" dares resist us? Where is the potentate who
" does not glory in being of the number of our
" courtiers? But for thee, whose true origin ter-
" minates in a Turcoman sailor, as every one
" knows, it wou'd be well, since the ship* of thy
" unfathomable ambition has suffer'd shipwreck
" in the abyss of self-love, if thou wou'dst lower
" the sails of thy rashness, and cast the anchor of
" repentance in the port of sincerity, which is

---

* This metaphorical way of expression is very common among the Orientals: but it sounds more proper in this place, because of the race of Bajazet being related to a sailor.

" the

"the port of safety, left by the tempest of our
" vengeance you shou'd perish in the sea of the
" punishment which you merit. But as we have
" learnt, that in obedience to the precept of
" the Alcoran, which orders us to wage war
" with the enemys of the Mussulman laws, you
" have undertaken a vigorous war with the Eu-
" ropeans; this consideration hath hinder'd us
" from making any insults in the lands which
" are subject to you: and the reflection that
" your country is the bulwark of the Mussul-
" mans, hath oblig'd us to leave it in a flou-
" rishing condition, for fear the passage of our
" armys into it shou'd raise a division among
" the inhabitants, and cause the Mussulmans
" to be disquieted, and the infidels to rejoice.
" Then take care of your self, and endeavor by
" your good conduct to preserve the dominions
" of your ancestors, not suffering for the future
" your ambitious foot to wander out of the li-
" mits of your power, which is but small.
" Cease your proud extravagances, lest the cold
" wind of hatred shou'd extinguish the flam-
" beau of peace. You may remember the pre-
" cept of Mahomet, to let the Turks remain in
" peace, while they are quiet: don't seek to
" wage war with us, which no one ever dar'd
" to do, and prosper'd. The devil certainly
" inspires you to ruin your self. Tho you
" have been in some considerable battels in the
" woods of Natolia, and have gain'd advanta-
" ges upon the Europeans; it was only thro
" the prayers of the prophet, and the blessings
" of the Mahometan religion of which you
" make profession: don't be proud at these
" advantages, nor attribute 'em to your own
" valor. Believe me, you are but a pismire:
" don't seek to fight against the elephants; for

K 3 " they'll

"they'll crush you under their feet The dove
"which rises up against the eagle destroys
"self. Shall a petty prince, such as you are
"contend with us? But your rodomontade
"are not extraordinary, for a Turcoman
"never spake with judgment. If you don't
"follow our counsels, you will repent it. These
"are the advices we have to give you; do
"you behave your self as you think fit."

This letter was seal'd with the imperial signet, and deliver'd to Bajazet by envoys who knew how to carry on the intrigues of princes. When they were come to Bajazet, they presented him the letter, acquainting him with the reasons of their coming, and their master's pretensions: but pride had taken too deep root in the breast of the Ottoman, for a letter, or the words of an ambassador, to have any effect upon him: he gave 'em therefore a very haughty answer. "It is a long time, said he,
"since we have been desirous of carrying on
"a war with you God be thank'd, our desire has had its effect, and we have taken
"up a resolution to march against you at the
"head of a formidable army. If you don't
"advance against us, we will come to seek
"you, and pursue you as far as Tauris and
"Sultania. We shall then see in whose favor
"heaven will declare, who of us will be rais'd
"by victory, and who abas'd by a shameful defeat."

CHAP.

CHAP. XV.

Timur marches to Sebaste, and takes that city.

THE envoys at their return from Natolia, gave an account to the emperor's officers of Bajazet's haughty answer. Whereupon Timur, being incens'd against this Turcoman, caus'd his ensigns to be display'd, in order to make war on him, and he immediately march'd towards Natolia. Being arriv'd at Avenic, he met the Emir Allahdad, who had been sent to Chiraz to bring from thence the Mirza Pir Mehemed bound like a criminal, which he accordingly did. Timur order'd that the Mirza shou'd be interrogated by the council of war, and that after his prosecution, he shou'd be punish'd according to his deserts. Accordingly, after judgment was given, he receiv'd the blows of the bastinado, order'd by the laws call'd Yasa; after which his chains were taken off, and himself set at liberty. In pursuance of the same laws, the Cheik Zade Ferid, and Mobarec Coja, who were then in irons, were put to death, for having corrupted the Mirza, and taught him magic.

Then the emperor sent to Sultania the empress Serai Mulc Canum, Canzade, and the wives of the princes his sons, with the Mirza Oloucbek, and the other young princes of the imperial houshold, under the care of the Mirza Omar, and some Emirs. After that he caus'd the great imperial standard to be display'd, and march'd at the head of his army. At his arrival at Erzeron, he was saluted by Taharten prince of Arzendgian. Two days after he decamp'd, and

march'd

march'd beyond Arzendgian, to enter the frontiers of the country of Roum, or Natolia, which was then subject to the Ottomans.

Sept. 1. 1400.

The first of Muharrem 803, Timur enter'd the country of the Ottomans, and march'd against Sebaste. When he was come before the city, he encamp'd upon an eminence, to view its condition and situation, and the troops encamp'd round about it. He saw the place full of men lifting up their heads to heaven, and singing and rejoicing with musical instruments in their hands: the walls, whose marble foundations were at the bottom of a ditch full of water, lifted up their battlements to the very clouds; and the soldiers in garison, arm'd with cuirasses, rais'd a great cry towards heaven. Then advice was brought that the vanguard of Bajazet's army, commanded by his son Kerichtchi, and Temourtach, one of the greatest Emirs of the Ottoman empire, who had been sent to Sebaste, having learnt the march of Timur's army towards that city, were fled, and return'd into the very heart of Natolia. The Emirs Solyman Chah, Gehan Chah, and others, were order'd to pursue 'em with expedition, which they did, and came up with 'em beyond Cæsarea in Cappadocia, where they briskly attack'd 'em, and cut 'em in pieces; after which, they made inroads, pillaging all the places near Cappadocia. They then return'd to the imperial camp before Sebaste, laden with the spoils of the Ottomans.

The city of Sebaste had walls of an extraordinary strength, being built of free-stone from the battlements to the very foundations, and each stone was three cubits long, and one thick. The wall was twenty cubits in height; ten in depth at the foot, and six at the top. There were seven gates, and those which open'd were of iron. It was built by Aladin Keicobade[1], and surrounded on the east, north and south sides, with a great ditch full of water, so that it was impossible to sap the walls on those sides, for they had no sooner sapp'd a cubit than the water enter'd: but it was not difficult to sap on the west side. The place was commanded by Mustafa[2] with four thousand horse, who prepar'd to make a vigorous defence, being furnish'd with all sorts of arms and machines for war. The besiegers rais'd a plat form higher than the town, over-against the gate of Irac, upon which they planted their machines to shoot stones. There were Arades[3], Mangenies[4], and Basolics[5], as they likewise prepar'd battering-rams to beat down the walls. On the west-side the sappers kept continually at work, while arrows were discharg'd from both sides, which did a great deal of damage.

After the siege had continu'd eighteen days, the violence of the battering-rams, and the great stones which were shot, began to shake the walls, and make breaches. On the other hand, the sappers had work'd with so much diligence, that the towers were propt only by stakes, which Timur order'd shou'd be set on fire, and so the towers fell. This struck terror into the hearts of the besieg'd, who perceiving that the troops wou'd soon enter the city, and take it by assault, chas'd Mustafa the governor out of it;

---

[1] A Seljukide king.
[2] The Arabian *history of M. Vatier says, that Solyman, son of the emperor of Bagdad, was governor of Sebaste, which is a mistake.   *Arab-chah.
[3] Machines to cast fire.
[4] Machines to hurl stones.
[5] A kind of battering rams.

and the Cherifs, Cadis, and doctors, full of hopes, came to cast themselves at the emperor's feet, begging quarter and pardon for them and the garison. Their prayers, mingled with the cries of the women and children, soften'd Timur's heart: he granted quarter to all the Musfulmans of the city, on paying the right of amnesty; but order'd that all the Armenians, and other Christians, shou'd be made slaves. And as the major part of the cavalry, which had so stubbornly defended the place for Bajazet, were Armenians, he gave orders that four thousand horse shou'd be divided among the Tomans of the army, and flung into pits, and then cover'd with earth, to serve as an example to those who shou'd follow their steps He afterwards caus'd the walls of Sebaste to be raz'd.

During the siege, advice was brought that Sultan Ahmed Gelair had fled from Bagdad, with Cara Yousef prince of the Turcomans, into Natolia. This oblig'd Timur to order some squadrons of horse to go in pursuit of 'em, which they accordingly did, and overtook their baggage, which they pillag'd, and brought away captive the Sultaness Dilchade, eldest sister of Cara Yousef, with his wifes and daughter. But he sav'd himself from our hands; and being come safe before Bajazet, our troops return'd to the imperial camp

CHAP.

CHAP. XVI.

Timur marches to Abuleſtan.

WHILE Timur was employ'd in the ſiege of Sebaſte, ſome robbers of Abuleſtan, which is the country of Zulcaderia, were ſo daring as to come and ſteal away the horſes of our ſoldiers, who were then buſy'd in the ſiege. For which reaſon, after the taking of the city, Timur march'd to Abuleſtan, to revenge himſelf on theſe robbers. He then ſent the lord Taharten to Arzendgian to guard his frontiers; and the Mirza Charoc ſet out in quality of chief of the ſcouts, accompany'd by the Emir Solyman Chah, and a ſelect troop, which compos'd the vanguard. The name of the ſoldiers were regiſter'd; and they had orders not to abandon the Mirza one moment. They ſoon arriv'd at Abuleſtan, from whence, on advice of their march, a great number of Turcomans fled into the mountains and deſarts. The Mirza purſu'd 'em ſo briskly, that he overtook 'em: theſe miſerable people ſeeing themſelves cloſely preſs'd, endeavor'd to ſave their lives by fighting; but after a weak defence, they were all routed and ſlain, as a puniſhment for their raſh enterprizes. The Emirs return'd to the imperial camp laden with ſpoils, and a great many horſes, mules, oxen and ſheep. Afterwards Timur ſent a courier to Malatia, to ſummon the inhabitants to ſubmit to him. Muſtafa's ſon, who was governor of it, blinded with ignorance, which is an inſeparable quality of the Turcomans, and eſpecially of thoſe of Natolia, impriſon'd the meſſenger,

Book V. senger. Timur on this was incens'd against the governor, and march'd towards that place. On the first advice these cowards had of the march of the imperial standard, Mustafa's son fled out of the place with all his party. Timur at his arrival at Malatia, carry'd it the same day. The Georgians and Armenians were made slaves, but quarter was given to the Mussulmans, after they had paid the tribute for an amnesty, which mony was distributed among the soldiers. Timur order'd the Emir Gehan Chah to go, with other Emirs, to make inroads in the country of Malatia: he harangu'd 'em, and with the most charming eloquence set before 'em the excellence of good warriors above other men, he told 'em that they ought utterly to exterminate the enemy, to take from 'em all means of renewing the war; and he spoke with a great deal of force of the punishment they ought to execute upon those who after pardon us'd hostilitys After this discourse, he chose out of each Toman some good soldiers, whom he gave to the Emirs to strengthen their body of the army, and then he dismiss'd 'em. According to these orders they departed, and ravag'd the country on all sides, not stopping in one place· they gave no quarter to any one, and left not one habitation unpillag'd, so that from Malatia to the castle of Kakhta [1], they made themselves masters of a great many places, some by fair means, and others by force, and after having constrain'd the natural princes of the country to submit to Timur, they return'd with a great quantity of riches, and join'd the imperial camp at Malatia, the government of which Timur gave to Cara

---

[1] A castle in the country of Roum, frontier of Syria.

Osman

Osmin a Turcoman Thus the frontiers of the two kingdoms of Natolia and Syria were in a short time brought in subjection to Timur, whose fame spread it self thro all parts of the world; so that there was not one prince who was not struck with terror at the rumor of his conquests.

CHAP. XVII.

The reasons of Timur's carrying his arms into Syria and Mesopotamia.

MAHOMET has told us, that when God resolves to destroy any one, he deprives him of common sense; conceals from him the methods he shou'd pursue, to protect himself from his destiny; and permits him to commit imprudent actions, which become the causes of his destruction, that the will of God may not fail of an accomplishment. The truth of these words was apparent in the fate of the countrys of Syria, for the governors of the citys of this kingdom, being blinded with excessive pride, turn'd from the ways of peace and justice, and committed actions as infamous as extraordinary, violating the rights of nations, and trampling upon the laws. Thus in the year 795, Timur, having made himself master of Bagdad, and conquer'd all Irac Arabi, sent to the Sultan Barcoc in Egypt an ambassador, a doctor of Savé, whose learning, birth and genius distinguish'd him from the chief persons of the empire, as as we have said before *. This Cheik being arriv'd at Rahhaba,

An. Dom. 1393.

*Book III. Chap. 32.

haba [1], he was seiz'd according to custom, that advice might be given the Sultan of Cairo of the arrival of an ambassador on his frontiers Barcoc, being excited by the evil counsels of the Sultan Ahmed Gelair king of Bagdad, order'd this ambassador to be put to death, not reflecting on the consequences of so enormous a crime, nor the infamy of the action, since to insult an ambassador is to violate the right of nations. What is most surprizing is, that such a king as the Sultan of Egypt shou'd be ignorant how Sultan Mehemed, king of Carezem, in the same manner put to death the ambassador and merchants of the great emperor Genghiz Can; and what was the tragical end of so black and barbarous an action [*], which wou'd be too long to recite here. However the destiny, which caus'd the ruin of Syria, blinded the mind of Barcoc, and procur'd the causes of his destruction.

[* See history of Genghiz Can, Book II. Ch. 5.]

Moreover, after the conquest of Azerbijana, and Irac Arabi, Timur being gone to make war in Capchac, and in Russia, Muscovy, Circassia, and the northern countrys, there was a battel between Atilmich Coutchin, governor of Avenic for Timur, and Cara Yousef, prince of the Turcomans, in which Atilmich was made prisoner. Cara Yousef loaded him with chains, and sent him to Sultan Barcoc at Cairo, who without any reflection upon the matter, continu'd his hostilitys against Timur, and confin'd Atilmich in a very close prison.

Timur being on the frontiers of Malatia, sent an ambassador with the following letter to Farrudge son of Barcoc, who succeeded his father in the throne of Egypt and Syria.

---

[1] A town upon the Euphrates, otherwise call'd Rahabat Malec Ben Taouc, frontier of Syria, long. 75. lat. 34.

" The

"The Sultan your father hath committed se-
"veral criminal and odious actions against us;
"and among the rest, the murder of our ambaſ-
"ſadors without the least ſhadow of a cauſe,
"and the impriſonment of Atilmich, one of
"our officers, whom he hath ſeiz'd inſtead of
"ſending him back to us. As your father hath
"ſurrender'd up his life to God, which he had
"only upon truſt, the puniſhment of his crimes
"muſt be brought before the tribunal of the ge-
"neral judgment. but as for your part, it is
'neceſſary you ſhou'd have regard to the pre-
'ſervation of your ſelf and your ſubjects; and
"to that effect you ought forthwith to ſend back
"Atilmich, leſt, the effects of your wrath and
"vengeance, falling upon the people of Syria,
"and even of Egypt, our furious ſoldiers make
"a cruel ſlaughter of their perſons, and burn
"and pillage their effects. If you are ſo ſtub-
"born as to reject our counſel, you'll be the
"cauſe of the effuſion of the muſſulman blood,
"and the total loſs of your kingdom."

The ambaſſadors, at their arrival at Aleppo, were ſeiz'd according to cuſtom, that advice might be given the Sultan of their arrival. Farrudge, to imitate his father's example, ſent meſſengers to bind the ambaſſadors, and put 'em in priſon.

It is not to be wonder'd at, that a plebeian ſhou'd commit actions of cowardice: what then may we expect from a Circaſſian ſlave? Barcoc had been ſold ſeveral times; and when his power encreas'd thro the kindneſs of his gover-nor, who was alſo a Mameluc ſlave, he trai-terouſly ſlew his benefactor, and uſurp'd the kingdom: and as there had never been any king of his race, ſo he had not in him the leaſt appearance of royalty. Thus was Barcoc; and
his

Book V. his son Farrudge was the crooked branch of an evil stock. He mounted his father's throne, tho but a child, no one having taught him how he ought to live: he had neither suffer'd heat nor cold, and was ignorant of policy and the art of war. In short, the father was of an ill character, and the son without merit.

Timur being inform'd of Farrudge's rashness, was transported with anger; and the fire of vengeance, which had lain lurking in his heart since the crimes committed by Barcoc, did so far exasperate him, that he immediately resolv'd to enter the Sultan's kingdom, and destroy every thing with fire and sword: which resolution he the more easily took up, in that Bajazet, with all his pride and menaces, had not dar'd to appear in the field of battel, and this proud Ottoman quietly saw our army besiege, take, ruin and pillage Sobaste and Malatia, and all the citys and towns of his kingdoms, as far as Kakhta, without making the least defence. But these are all the hidden decrees of providence.

CHAP. XVIII.

Timur marches into the kingdoms of Syria and Egypt.

THE heroes who are destin'd to execute great affairs, are also endu'd with a discerning spirit, which makes those enterprizes appear easy to 'em; and with resolution to carry 'em on with all the strength and power they are possess'd of: so that they easily compass those designs, which every one else accounts impossible. In effect, the Sultan of Egypt and Syria

The history of Timur-Bec.

Son having added to his father's crimes, by the arresting and imprisoning of Timur's ambassadors, on advice of it, the wrath of our emperor was kindled, so that he resolv'd forthwith to chastise him for his fault, and tho the execution of this project appear'd impossible to the eyes of the politicians, or at least exceeding dangerous and difficult, yet the boundless zeal of Timur, made this great and perillous enterprize appear easy to him. The Emirs and principal lords of the state on their knees remonstrated to him, that being but a short time since the troops return'd from the long campain in India, they had not repos'd themselves, before they march'd to the Georgian war, where they had been extremely fatigu'd, after re-iterated inroads in the mountains and rocks, and the conquest of the towns of that country, that after this they had march'd to Natolia, and conquer'd Sebaste, and all the citys and towns between that and Aleppo, where they had perform'd actions of the greatest valor, that therefore at present the expedition into Syria and Egypt appear'd very toilsom and difficult, as well in that the country was full of towns and fortresses, with lofty walls and impregnable castles, as in that the army of the Syrians was very numerous, good warriors, and provided with arms and every thing necessary to a vigorous resistance. for which reasons they besought his majesty to have the goodness to disband the troops, and send back the soldiers into their own countrys, to repose themselves for some time; and that afterwards fresh preparations might be made suitable to the greatness of this undertaking. Timur answer'd them, that victory was a gift which God liberally bestows on the princes whom he loves, that the great number of soldiers and arms had nothing to do with victory, which he

Vol II.   L   had

had often prov'd he put 'em in mind of the conquests he had gain'd with 'em, and the difficult enterprizes they had gone thro, tho they had believ'd 'em impossible, that it was requisite they shou'd have the greatest ambition, and then he wou'd answer for the success, provided they trusted in God. The Emirs perceiving the emperor firm in his resolution, loaded him with praises and applause, resolving to follow him, and thinking only of the expedition into Syria, and the means of making themselves masters of that kingdom.

Then Timur put his army in order; and causing the brass-drum to be beat, which is a sign of his departure, all the soldiers began their march, every one in his proper post, and they took their road towards Syria.

CHAP. XIX.

The taking of the castles of Behesna and Antapl.

TIMUR order'd the Mirza Charoc to depart with several great Emirs, as chief of the scouts. Being arriv'd at Behesna [*], they encamp'd there, where they were soon join'd by Timur with the whole army, who encamp'd on an eminence near the castle, to view the situation of the place, which is in a defile where several torrents flow its walls were high and strong, being built on the ridge of a steep mountain. The troops soon made themselves masters of the lower town, which they entirely ravag'd. The

---

[*] A fortress of Syria, between Aleppo and Malatia.

governo

governor of the castle for the Syrians was nam'd Mocbel, who relying upon the strength of the castle, put himself in a posture of defence. While Timur was examining the condition of the place, the besieg'd discharg'd a great stone from their machines against the emperor's person, which fell upon the ground near his tent, and roll'd into the very tent. This stir'd up Timur's wrath, who immediately order'd the siege to be form'd, and shar'd the walls among the Tomans of the army, round which they erected twenty machines, and one of 'em upon the very spot where the stone fell. The first stone cast from this machine struck that of the besieg'd, and broke it to pieces, which was reckon'd as a good omen. Then the Mirza Rouftem arriv'd from Chiraz with the Persian army, and join'd the imperial camp. The siege was continu'd, and the sappers follow'd their work close, while the Emirs and other brave men attack'd the place on all sides, and soon made breaches in several parts of the walls, propping the foundations with stakes. Mocbel seeing himself reduc'd thus low, was seiz'd with fear, and resolv'd to surrender: he sent messengers several times to the emperor, to acquaint him with his weakness and want of power, and alledg'd as an excuse for not coming before him, the dread he had of his imperial majesty; beseeching Timur to grant him quarter, which cou'd not in the least prejudice him or his officers. Timur made answer, that he wou'd grant him his liberty, but not till after the taking of the place, because as this castle was esteem'd impregnable, if the army shou'd raise the siege, those who had but little insight into things, would imagine that our soldiers were not able to take it by force; and that a conqueror should not be thought to have spar'd his enemy.

The 7th of Selel 803, they were order'd to set fire to the breaches, and so the towers began to fall; which when the besieg'd seeing, they were struck with fear, and Moebel lost all hopes. He sent the Cadi, the Imams and the Cheiks, with all the pearls and curiositys he had, as a present to Timur. They address'd themselves to the Mirza Charoc, whom they besought to be their advocate and protector. These doctors let the emperor know that Moebel was the meanest of his majesty's servants, that he sincerely repented of his fault, humbly demanded pardon for it, and hop'd that the emperor wou'd not refuse him the favor of sparing his life. Timur, at Charoc's intercession, pardon'd not only Moebel, but even all the garison, and the envoys contentedly return'd back, praising the emperor, and making vows for the prince Charoc. As soon as this good news was brought to the city, new gold and silver mony was coin'd, and friday prayers read in the name of the invincible Timur.

After this, the army decamp'd and march'd towards Antapa [1]. The walls of this city were exceeding strong, being built of hewn stone, and surrounded with a ditch thirty cubits deep, and near seventy broad, with a draw-bridge: the counterscarp, which is of stone, has also a cover'd way, broad enough for a man to pass on horseback, which post was assign'd the archers. The Tartar army on their arrival at this place,

---

[1] A town of Syria near Aleppo.

A Note taken from Arab Chah.
Timur left Calar-Erroum without attacking it; which he dar'd not do, because this place was very strong, and Naseri Mehemmed, son of Moussa, son of Sakari, made some advantageous sallys upon Timur's army, and very much molested him.

The history of Timur-Bec.

...d the principal persons gone out [1], and only ... of citizens left, who had shut the gates ... but the city was full of goods, and ...tion. When Timur came before the ..., the gates were open'd, and the keys ... out to him he fix'd a governor over it, ...d it to his dominions

CHAP. XX.

The siege and taking of the city of Aleppo.

MAHOMET tells us, that the sole terror of his name made his conquests extend a ...'s journy and we may with reason say, that ... had the honor to resemble him in that, ...the terror of his name was so great, that upon ... of the approach of his troops [2], kings and ... were so terrify'd, that they abandon'd ... dominions, fear blinded their eyes, and ...'en'd their understanding, so that all their ... tended to their destruction.

...hile the army was in the quarters of Behes-... and Antapa, Temourtach, [3] governor of A-...po for the Sultan of Egypt, dispatch'd a cou-

---

[1] The Arabian of M. Vatier says, that the governor of Antapa, ...'d Aquemar, sally'd out to defend himself; and being a-...on and wounded, he fled to Aleppo, but was not pursu'd

[*] A city of Syria in the province of Cannaserin, it is the ...ent Berœa, long. 72. 25. lat. 35. 35.

[2] The Arabian says, that according to the computation of ...m, Timur's comptroller, his army consisted of eight ...ed thousand men.

[3] ...ab Chah says, that Temourtach had agreed with Timur ...y the Sultan of Egypt.

rier to Grand-Cairo to give advice of it to his master. Whereupon the Sultan sent orders to the troops of all the towns and countrys of Syria, to march towards Aleppo, with all the arms and ammunition necessary for a vigorous defence. According to these orders, Chadoun [6], chief of the Emirs of Damascus, march'd to Aleppo at the head of a great army. The governors and generals of Hemse [7], Hama, Antioch, Tripoli, Napolos-Samaria, Balbec, Canaan, Gaza, Ramla or Rama, Jerusalem, Kerek, Calat-Erroum and all the other countrys and lordships of the kingdoms of Syria, came to the same place, well equip'd and arm'd cap-a-pie; and in a short time there were got together a very numerous army. [8] Temourtach, governor of Aleppo, who was esteem'd one of the most considerable lords, assembled the chiefs of all those troops, and made the following speech to 'em, in order to know their opinions of the matter. "We ought not,
" sirs, said he, to regard this affair which is
" coming upon us as a slight thing, and it is
" requisite we shou'd reflect seriously upon it before
" it happens. The prince who is this day
" come against us, is exceeding powerful, he
" and his officers have perform'd such extraor-
" dinary actions, as are no where recorded in
" antiquity. Wheresoever he hath march'd, he
" hath always conquer'd the towns and fortres-
" ses; and who ever attempted to resist him
" always repented in the end, and suffer'd the

---

[6] M. Vatier calls him my lord Sudon.
[7] Principal city of Syria.
[8] The Arabian tells us, that Timur sent an ambassador or herald to Aleppo, to summon the inhabitants to surrender; and that his herald was immediately put to death by Chacoun's order.

'most rigorous chastisement. Consider, sirs,
' now in a very short time he has reduc'd many
' vast and flourishing empires, as those of Ca-
' razem, Turkestan, Corassana, Zabulestan, and
' India, as far as the great river of Ganges, the
' kingdoms of Tabarestan, the two Iracs, Per-
" sia, Couhestan, Georgia, Azerbijana, and
" Dierbekir, with all their dependences, which
' he has wrested out of the hands of the most
' powerful Sultans, and the most illustrious em-
" perors of the universe. He has establish'd
' himself in those places with such an absolute
' authority, that one of his lieutenants, with a
' few officers, maintains a whole city under
" his obedience, so that in the vast extent of
" the countries of Iran and Touran, there is not
" a soul who dares act the least thing against his
" orders. It seems as if the great rise of this
" prince was owing to the peculiar protection
' of Heaven; if so, we ought not to tempt God.
' My advice therefore, in this conjuncture, is to
' treat with him by the ways of submission and
' obedience, to coin our mony, and to say the
' public prayers in his name, and to make use
" of the Cherifs, Imams, and doctors, as our
' mediators with him, seeing there are none but
" men vers'd in the law, and pious persons, who
" have any access to him, or whom he in the
' least regards. At the same time we'll send
' him presents and jewels, the most suita-
" ble to his grandure, that we may endeavour
' to keep him from coming near us, and by that
" means preserve the repose of the city, and per-
' haps of the whole kingdom. He is a prince
' favor'd by fortune, powerful, active, glorious
" and ambitious, his wrath burns and consumes
' a thousand times fiercer than fire; and if
" it is kindled, the sea it self won't be able to

" quench

"quench it. Therefore now conclude to ——
"something, chuse either peace or war, q——
"or misery."

Temourtach having finish'd his speech, those
who had most experience applauded his sentiments, and agreed that it was the best method
they cou'd take; but the majority, and especially Chadoun governor of Damascus, were of
a contrary opinion. Pride and presumption
were rooted in their hearts, and ignorance had
so stupifi'd 'em, that they gave no heed to
what Temourtach had said, and were so far
from applauding him, that they made use of some
haughty expressions, and tax'd him with cowardice, saying, that he who is afraid, is already
frustrated of his desires. "What comparison,
" say they, is there between this kingdom and all
" those you have mention'd? Their towns were
" built only of mud and brick, but ours are
" all of solid stone, cut out of the almost im-
" penetrable rock, they are fill'd with good
" garisons, and furnish'd with plenty of ammu-
" nitions of war and victuals, so that it wou'd
" require a whole year's siege to force a single one.
" Why therefore has fear got possession of your
" hearts? Is it the great number of their cavalry
" and infantry, or of their arms and equipages,
" which terrifys you? Only view ours, and
" you'll see the difference: our bows are of Da-
" mascus, our swords of Egypt, our lances of
" Arabia, and our bucklers of Aleppo. In the
" reigisters of this kingdom are sixty thousand
" villages, out of each of which taking but a
" few brave men, we shall complete an army,
" which our vast plains won't be able to hold.
" The houses and walls of these Tartars are on-
" ly of cords and canvas, while we live in good
" fortresses, which are of hewn stone from the bat-
" tlements

...ments to the very foundations." Thus fate, having resolv'd upon the destruction of these unhappy Syrians, inspir'd sentiments of pride in 'em, and these obstinate people persisted in their error, notwithstanding what Temourtach, and other men of sense, cou'd say to divert 'em from the evil steps they had resolv'd to take, who represented to 'em that the way of peace was always the most secure, considering the inconstancy of fortune, and the small hopes they cou'd reasonably expect of gaining the advantage over that powerful enemy. The others on the contrary said, they need only have courage and resolution, which if they had not, all sorts of disorders and losses wou'd happen among 'em. After a great struggle on both sides, the latter carry'd it by a plurality of voices; and it was resolv'd and concluded, that no one shou'd go out of the city, but that they shou'd fortify it with entrenchments, and with arrows and stones hinder the enemy from approaching the walls.

Timur departed from Antapa with joy, and made two days journy of six or seven leagues each; he afterwards gave orders that they shou'd march but half a league a day, and at each encampment dig a trench round the army, and make a kind of rampart with their bucklers, so that in a whole week they march'd but one day's journy, and that with extraordinary precautions. The Syrians, ignorant of the art of war, attributed the slowness of their march to fear, believing the Tartars mistrusted their own strength: at which they became haughty and insolent, for abandoning their first resolution of not going out of the city, and which indeed was the least dangerous, they rang'd themselves in order of battle, and pitch'd their tents in the open plains

The

Book V
Nov. 8.
1400.

The 9th of Rabiulevel 803, which answers to the year of the Serpent, the army of Timur arriv'd in the neighborhood of Aleppo, and the Mirza Sultan Huffein, with fome great officers, met the enemy's fcouts. he fell upon 'em, tho fuperior to him in number, and at the firft onfet unhors'd a cavalier, whom he collar'd, and carry'd prifoner out of the field of battel. His officers alfo perform'd fome glorious actions, and took two prifoners. the reft of the Syrian army fled into the city.

The fame day the Mirza Aboubecre advanc'd with fixty men, and a great number of the enemy made a fally to repulfe him, After a fharp skirmifh, the two partys return'd to their feveral camps. The next day fome brave Tartars advanc'd to skirmifh, and having fhewn themfelves to the enemy, not one dar'd to attack 'em. The third day at fun-rifing, Timur order'd the whole army to take horfe, and with enfigns difplay'd, and at the found of drums and kettledrums, to march towards the enemy's camp. Every one having on a coat of mail, a cuirafs, and a helmet, they advanc'd in order of battel. The right wing was commanded by the Mirzas Miran Chah and Charoc, accompany'd by feveral great Emirs, as Solyman Chah and others; and the vanguard of this wing was led by the Mirza Aboubecre. The Sultan Mahmoud, whofe lieutenant was the Emir Gehan Chah, had the command of the left wing, and his vanguard was brought up by the Sultan Huffein. The main body was commanded by Timur himfelf, who had before him a rank of bulky elephants, which had been taken in India, equip'd and caparifon'd in the moft magnificent manner. They ferv'd as a rampart to this body of the army, for the towers on their backs were fill'd with archers and

and flingers of wild-fire and these animals had drawn in their snouts like serpents. When the army was rang'd in order of battel, a Toman of the best horse of the army was order'd to post themselves on an eminence on the right side of the field of battel, and to keep their ground there, when the Syrians shou'd be put to the rout, and fly.

The Syrian army was likewise rang'd in order; it was compos'd of a right and left wing, and a main-body, and advanc'd with its ensigns display'd. The kettle-drums and trumpets were the signal to begin, and both partys made the great cry of Allah Ecber *. The battel began by the skirmishers, who rush'd furiously out of their squadrons into the midst of the enemys, and who after some brave action, as either the slaughter of some noted person, or the taking a prisoner from the midst of the opposite batallion, return'd glorious to their post. Our right wing immediately fell upon the enemy's left with so much vigor, that it was routed, thro the valor of the Mirza Aboubecre, who enter'd the field of battel like a lion, and forc'd many of the enemy to fling away their arms, and abandon their ensigns, while others were slain, and the ground soon cover'd with helmets, head-pieces, and sabres, mix'd promiscuously among the dead carcasses. Our left wing likewise defeated the Syrians right, and entirely dispers'd 'em, some crying out for quarter, and others saving themselves by flight. Our main-body did not in the least yield to the other; and the elephants enter'd into the midst, and with their trunks toss'd some up into the air, and trampled others under their feet, no one being able to stop them.

Chadoun and Temourtach having seen the strange manner of our soldiers fighting, quitted their

Chap. 20.

* God is the greatest.

their former fierceness, they trembled at the sight of the dreadful slaughter which was made in so short a time, and seeing no other remedy, they fled, and enter'd the city by the gate of Mancoula. The soldiers, perceiving their generals measures, likewise fled and dispers'd themselves; the major part took the road of Damascus, and were pursu'd by our men, who slew a great number, taking their arms and horses from 'em, so that out of this prodigious number of Syrians there escap'd but one horseman, who fled to Damascus to carry the news of the defeat.

After the rout of this army, part of 'em enter'd the city. The disorder was so great in the chief street of Aleppo, and the gates so crouded, that one cou'd hardly pass. Here was the greatest slaughter ever mention'd; for to avoid the fury of the sword, they flung themselves upon one another into the ditches, which were soon fill'd with men and horses. On the other hand, our men with a single pike often run three or four of the enemy thro at a time, in the throng at the gate, so that the dead bodys were pil'd upon one another to the very plinth of the walls, and at length a passage was made over the ditch upon those bodys, level with the draw-bridge. There one might see the horses and their riders mix'd promiscuously together, and cover'd with blood and dirt, some pierc'd with arrows, and others with their brains dash'd out, one with a coat of mail, his head bending beneath the blow of a war-club, another falling without his head, with his sword fast clasp'd in hand.

During this horrible slaughter, a body of the army was sent to pillage the Syrians camp, wherein they found the governor's pavilion, with his tents, furniture, arms, and several beautiful horses such ly harnefs'd. Each of the foldiers took one of the fpoils, of which there were an abundance. At length all the army pufh'd with fo much vigor to the general affault, that they enter'd the city the fame day, which was the 11th of Rabiulevel 803. Timur permitted 'em to pillage the city of Aleppo, and they fpar'd neither the markets nor any of the houfes: they carry'd away the women and children, the horfes, mules, and all the cattel, befides a prodigious quantity of gold and filver, arms, curious furniture, precious ftones, pearls, veffels of gold, the women's rich habits and ornaments. All thefe were taken by the foldiers, who render'd no account of 'em to any one.

Nov. 11. 1400.

C H A P. XXI.

The caftle of Aleppo attack'd and taken.

CHADOUN and Temourtach, not imagining themfelves fecure in the city, enter'd the caftle, which was a fortrefs upon the ridge of a high fteep rock [1], furrounded with a ditch thirty cubits wide, and fo deep that there is a fufficient quantity of water to carry a boat [2]. From the furface of the water to the bottom of the walls of the caftle, which is the fhelving of the mountain, is about

---

[1] The caftle of Aleppo is not built on a rock, but on a mountain of earth cover'd with free-ftone.
[2] The author feems not to have feen the ditch any more than the caftle; for if the ditch was full of water, a veffel might fail in it.

Book V. a hundred cubits, and it is so smooth and steep, that 'tis impossible to ascend it on foot, because this shelving is cover'd with free-stone and flat polish'd bricks. The strength of this place render'd these two governors insolent, they undertook to make a vigorous defence, resolving to die rather than surrender: they made great crys in token of their resolution; and ran upon the walls and towers, to give orders to the garison. They caus'd the great and little kettle-drums to be beat, and in good earnest began to insult the besiegers · they cast a great quantity of wild-fire, and pots fill'd with sulphur, which in their effects resembled a thunderbolt, as likewise stones and arrows. by which they let us know that they were in a condition to defend themselves.

Timur having enter'd the city as a conqueror, encamp'd over-against the castle, ordering his troops to range themselves round about the ditch, for the out-parts consisted only of a single key unguarded: then there were nothing to be seen but showers of arrows, which the besiegers incessantly discharg'd with so much vigor, that none of the besieg'd dar'd to get upon the walls. In the mean while the sappers went down into the ditch, and favor'd by the archers, cross'd the water upon floats; and being come to the other side, they began to work upon the bottom of the mountain, and to shake the stones of the walls. but the besieg'd having perceiv'd their design, five of their bravest men went out by the great gate, and being resolv'd either to lose their lives or succeed in the design, they ty'd a cord to their waste, the end of which others held from the top of the walls, that they might descend and get up again, notwithstanding the steepness of the shelving, without fear

of

of talking These five men accordingly went down, and ran sword in hand upon the sappers; but the Tartars, who had orders to back the sappers, sally'd out of their tents, and slew 'em with their arrows. The besieg'd on this were afraid, and drew up again the five dead bodys with the cords. From that time no one dar'd so much as look thro the loop-holes of the walls, so far were they from making sallys. Then Timur, whose advantages were consider'd rather as the scourge of God, than as an effect of human power, sent by an ambassador the following letter to the besieg'd, who now began to conclude that obstinately resisting him wou'd in the end produce repentance. " The Almigh-
" ty having reduc'd under my command the
' greatest part of the kingdoms of Asia, my
" armys can't be stop'd either by walls or for-
" tresses the great number of soldiers or arms
" are not able to oppose the just effects of my
" wrath, nor ward off the deadly blows of my
" vengeance. I believe the best way you can
" now take, is to have pity on your own lives;
" otherwise you'll be the murderers of your
" selves, your wives and children, and must
" answer for the crime of having shed their
" blood."

The besieg'd seeing no other refuge, were constrain'd to give way to force. Chadoun and Temourtach took the keys of the castle, treasurys, and magazines; and being accompany'd by the Cherifs, Cadis, Imams and nobles of the country, open'd the gate, and in an humble manner came to cast themselves at Timur's feet Chadoun, Temourtach, and other chiefs, with a thousand soldiers, were shar'd among the Tomans, and put in irons. Soldiers were sent to the castle, who brake down the battlements of the wall. Timur sent in embaſſ. to Grand Cairo, to the ſon of Barcoc, Eſſen Bougai Davatdar, whom they had ſeiz'd in the caſtle, with advice that he had laid Chadoun and Temourtach in irons, by way of repriſal for Atilmich, and that he wou'd not ſet 'em at liberty till he ſhou'd come back to him, that he muſt ſend Atilmich immediately, if he was willing to preſerve the lives and libertys of theſe two governors, and of all the other ſlaves he had detain'd. Timur fix'd the place where Eſſen Bougai was to meet him at his return: then he went to the caſtle of Aleppo, to take the diverſion of a very beautiful proſpect, and alſo to view the ſituation of the city and country, and he ſtaid there two days. He order'd the Emir Gehan Chah to guard the gate of the caſtle, and the riches within it, which conſiſted of the treaſures which ſeveral kings had amaſs'd there, and an infinite number of jewels and furniture which the citizens had carry'd into it to preſerve 'em from pillage. The whole amounted to immenſe ſums, part of which he diſtributed among the Emirs and ſoldiers. He afterwards left the baggage and cumberſom things belonging to the army, with his treaſure, in the caſtle of Aleppo: and he nam'd eight conſiderable Emirs for governors of this ſtrong place, and as guardians of the treaſures he left there. Then, after fifteen ³ days reſidence at Aleppo, he began his march, to continue his conqueſts in the reſt of Syria.

CHAP.

---

³ *A note taken out of the hiſtory of Tamerlan by Arab Chah his enemy.*

During the fifteen days that Timur ſtaid at Aleppo, he order'd the doctors to come before him, to perplex 'em with hard queſtions, and from thence get an opportunity to put 'em to death. He ſaid to Ahmed Ben Arab Chah (author of the Arab is

CHAP. XXII.

The taking of the towns and castles of Emessa and Hama.

WHEN Timur lay encamp'd without the city of Aleppo, he sent the Mirzas Pir Mehemed and Aboubecre, with the Emirs Solyman Chah, Sevindgic and others, as scouts, towards Hama*. These lords soon made themselves masters of the lower town, but they cou'd not take the castle, because it was exceeding

---

Arabian history of M. Vatier) There have lately been slain some of our men, and some of yours; which of the two are martyrs? This question, said Arab Chah, was formerly propos'd to Mahomet by an Arabian peasant, and I'll return the same answer as he did. Timur demanded what answer he gave. The peasant, answer'd Arab Chah, said to Mahomet, Lord, apostle of God, some fight thro shame, others thro valor, others thro a zeal for religion: who is the martyr? He who fights for religion, answer'd Mahomet, and for the honor and advantage of the word of God. Very well, says Timur, you cou'd not have given a better answer: and then he related to 'em all his victorys. I have one foot, says he, in the grave, but yet I have employ'd my life to a good purpose; for I have conquer'd, &c. Arab Chah then said, In gratitude for the favors you have receiv'd from heaven, pardon these men of learning. I never put any one to death, answer'd Timur, purposely, you are the cause of your own deaths: but thro God I grant you quarter. Then every one had liberty of speaking, and endeavor'd to answer first, as in the college.

When Timur, says the Arabian, design'd harm to any one, he did it without delay; but when good, he remitted the execution of it to another.

Timur cut off several heads to erect a trophys.

* A town of Syria, of which the geographer Abulfoda was prince, long. 70. 40. lat. 35.

Vol II M strong

Book V. strong. After the affair of Aleppo was finish'd to Timur's satisfaction, he went to Hama, and in his way took three or four castles. At the arrival of the great imperial standard before Hama, those who were in the castle, seeing this innumerable multitude of troops from the top of their walls, imagin'd it would be best for 'em to go out immediately with what presents they had, to offer the keys of the place, and submit to Timur. They accordingly did so, and addressing themselves to the Mirzas who were come before as scouts, they besought 'em to intercede and obtain quarter for 'em. The Mirzas promis'd 'em this favor, and quarter was granted 'em, but their spoils were given to these scouts. Timur staid twenty days at Hama, for the refreshment of his troops and horses, during which time he had apartments built for himself, the Mirzas, and principal Emirs of his court, and a magnificent Divan-Cané, where the councils of the state were held; so that this place in less than two or three weeks, became a second city.

In the mean while the Emirs made another attempt, to persuade the emperor to stay at this place, representing, that for two years past the troops had been either on the march, or employ'd in a battel, that the enemy had a great number of cavalry, whose horses were fresh and not fatigu'd, and being in their own country, had vast advantages over us, and that if his majesty approv'd of it, they would go and repose themselves on the sea-shore at Tripoli in Syria, where they would take up their winter-quarters, so that the horses might have some rest after their fatigues, and at the beginning of the spring they might march with vigor to exterminate the enemy. Timur would not hearken to

their

...en reasons, tho they were plausible, but an-
...wer'd, that they ought to make dispatch, that
...e enemy might have no time to recover them-
...elves. Whereupon he order'd 'em to take horse,
...nd march towards Emessa ⁵ One of our
...reat Emirs went thither first as a scout; and
...ad the good nature to advise the inhabitants,
...elling 'em that their resistence wou'd serve
...nly to ruin 'em, and it wou'd be pity so many
...ou'd be destroy'd, that if they wou'd go meet
...he emperor, and submit to him, he wou'd an-
...wer for the success, and their lives and even
...heir effects shou'd be spar'd. These words,
...hich on one hand caus'd fear, and on the o-
...her hope, in the people of Emessa, made an
...mpression upon 'em; so that the principal men
...f the city took up a resolution to obey Timur:
...hey came out loaded with presents, and ran to
...eet him; they cast themselves at his feet,
...issing the earth, which they cover'd with gold
...nd precious stones. they presented him with the
...eys of the town; upon which Timur had the
...oodness to prohibit any one's insulting 'em
...ither in their persons or goods. He gave 'em
...r their governor Ali Ecber, whom he order'd
...o have a singular regard to 'em, and to be
...heir protector on all occasions.

⁵ Emessa or Hims, a town of Syria near Hama.

CHAP. XXIII.

Conquest of the town of Balbec.

TIMUR decamp'd from Emessa, and continuing his road towards Balbec, he march'd a day's journy, and encamp'd near a salt-pit, from whence he sent out a body of the army to make inroads towards Seid and Barut, and to pillage the country along the shore of the Mediterranean. When the imperial standard was arriv'd at Balbec, all the army admir'd the beauty of the walls of this town: the stones are of a prodigious size, and there is one at the corner of the castle, which looks towards the gardens, twenty-eight cubits long, sixteen broad, and seven high. This town is very famous, as well for the beauty of the walls, as for the height of its buildings; and it's believ'd to have been built by Solomon's order, by dæmons and genii, over whom he had an absolute command. Notwithstanding these advantages, it was reduc'd by our troops as soon as ever they appear'd before it. There were in it so great a quantity of fruits, pulse, and goods, that our soldiers were furnish'd with all manner of necessarys for a long time. Then Timur order'd the Emirs Cheik Noureddin, Chamelik, Sevindgic, and others, to advance towards Damascus at the head of thirty thousand horse.

CHAP.

CHAP. XXIV.

Timur marches to Damascus, capital of Syria.

THEY staid not long at Balbec, because it was situated near a mountain, which render'd the air exceeding cold, and it being the beginning of winter, there fell abundance of snow and rain.

The 3d of Jumaziulevel, the sun being in the Jan. 3. 1400. sixth degree of Capricorn, Timur departed from Balbec, and after having march'd a day's journy, he halted to visit the tomb of the prophet Noah, whose blessings having besought, he set out for the conquest of Damascus. The body of the army, which had been sent out to make inroads towards Seid and Barut, return'd, after having ravag'd all the maritim country of Syria; and join'd the imperial camp, loaded with the spoils of that country. As Syria was at that time under the dominion of the Sultans of Egypt, the Syrians were continually sending couriers, to carry the news of our army's march, to Farudge son of Barcoc, their king, whom they continu'd to press so assiduously to come to oppose Timur, that at their persuasion he rais'd an army, which he equip'd with great expence and magnificence, and above all, the cavalry, which was the best in the world. In this condition he took the road to Damascus, which he was no sooner enter'd, than he us'd all his precautions to examine the fortifications, to post guards and centinels every where, to put the walls in good order, and to augment the entrenchments as well of the city as of the castle.

M 3

Book III In fine, he took all needful precautions and using policy with strength, he sent to Timur, in quality of ambassador, an eloquent and perfect villain, who the better to cover his intention took the habit of a poor religious. He order'd him for his companions two young assassins, to each of whom he gave a poison'd dagger, with orders to use their endeavours to murder Timur during the audience of the ambassador. At Timur's arrival near Damascus, these villains join'd the court, and came to the foot of the imperial throne to pay their compliments: they had several times the honor to approach his majesty, and very favorable opportunitys to execute their designs; but the Almighty, who was always Timur's guardian and protector, wou'd not suffer 'em ever to come to perfection. Coja Mafaoud Semnani, one of the great secretarys of the council, imagin'd by the proceedings of these rash fellows that they had some evil intention; wherefore he communicated his thoughts to some, who related 'em to the emperor, who order'd 'em to be search'd; and they found in their boots poison'd daggers. The chief of the villains perceiving himself and his companions discover'd, declar'd the truth, and the resolution they had taken to assassinate Timur. The emperor return'd thanks to his sovereign protector, and said, "It is not the "maxim of kings to murder ambassadors, yet it "wou'd be a crime to suffer this rascal, or his "comrades, to live, who tho cloth'd in the ha- "bit of a religious, is a monster of corruption and "perfidy." Then he order'd, that according to the passage which tells us that treason falls upon the head of the traitor, he shou'd be slain with the same dagger with which he wou'd have com-

mitted

mitted this abominable action, and his infamous carcase to be burnt for an example to others. His two assassins had their nose and ears cut off, but were not put to death, because Timur wou'd send 'em back with a letter to the Sultan of Egypt.

Timur took horse; and having fix'd his troops in good order, march'd towards Damascus, near which he encamp'd at the foot of a hill near Cobbei Seiar: a trench was dug for precaution round the army, and fortify'd with bucklers and pallisados. Then Timur ascended the hill to examine the situation of Damascus and its outparts. He sent scouts to skirmish with the enemy, and to keep 'em in play: the Emirs Sevindgic, Sainte Maure, and others, advanc'd, and were back'd by the Seid Coja of the right wing, and the Mirza Rouftem of the left, at the noise of kettle-drums, hautboys and flutes, mix'd with the soldiers crys. By next morning they attack'd the enemy's scouts, whom they put to flight, after having slain several, and taken others prisoners. Then Timur, to revenge himself for the scandalous action of the Sultan of Egypt, order'd Chadoun and the other prisoners brought from Aleppo, to be put to death.

The same night there happen'd an affair as ridiculous as extraordinary. The Mirza Sultan Hussein, after a debauch, was excited by some seditious Persians to revolt against the emperor his grandfather, and he accordingly went to the city of Damascus, and lifted himself into the Syrian service: which adventure gave the Syrians a great deal of satisfaction, imagining it wou'd produce to 'em considerable advantages. They conducted the prince into the city with a great

M 4 deal

Book V. deal of pomp and ceremony[c]. Farrudge, imagining the union with this prince wou'd deliver him from all troubles, and cause a calm after the storm was over, treated him with all possible respect. The officers of this Mirza, Adouc, and Hussein son of Barat Coja, gave advice of what had pass'd to the Emir Chamelik, who inform'd the emperor thereof. At break of day they decamp'd, and after a league's march towards the south-side of Damascus, which looks upon the country of Canaan, Egypt, and the desart of Arabia, they encamp'd again, and built a wall about the height of a man round the camp, and dug a trench round the wall. The scouts went out to ravage the country in the neigborhood of Damascus and Timur plac'd both infantry and cavalry round the walls of the camp to guard them in the night.

Two days after Timur sent Padi Chah Baouram ambassador to the Sultan of Egypt, with the following letter. "You are not ignorant
" of the effects which circumspection and ex-
" actness produce, and know that emulation and
" jealousy, mix'd with ambition, are the mo-
" tives which oblige conquerors to raise armies,
" undertake the most dangerous wars, and
" make themselves masters of countrys and king-
" doms, and that by this means they preserve
" the honor of their crown, and acquire eternal
" fame. All this great noise of the world is not
" so much to heap up riches, as to acquire ho-
" nor, for half a loaf every day is sufficient for

---

[c] The Arabian remarks, that the Mirza Sultan Hussein had a handsom head of hair, which they shav'd off; and having honor'd him with a robe, dress'd him after the fashion of the country, and that he had quitted Timur, being asham'd to see him with his army in so miserable a condition.

" the

"the nourishment of a man. We have several
' times demanded Atilmich of you, and you
" have not once offer'd to send him to us;
" but have always started some difficultys,
" and delay'd an affair of such consequence.
" This hath oblig'd us to make war in your
" country, which will bring ruin and desolation
" upon your subjects. If rocks cou'd speak,
" they wou'd tell you that this action of yours
" portends no good to you. Yet, notwithstand-
" ing your unreasonable proceedings, if you'll
" cause the mony to be coin'd, and the public
" prayers to be read in our name, that shall stop
" our fury. This you ought to do, if you have
" any compassion for your self or subjects.
" Our soldiers are like roaring lions, which
" want their prey, they seek to kill their ene-
" my, pillage his effects, take his towns, and
" overturn his edifices to the very foundations
" There are but two ways to chuse: either
" peace, the consequences of which are quie-
" and joy; or war, which produces disorde-
" and desolation. I have set both before you: it
" is your part to follow one or other. Consult
" your prudence, and make your choice Fare-
' well "

The ambassador having carry'd this letter,
he, receiv'd him with very particular honors,
contrary to their usual custom· at which reception they practis'd all the ceremonys us'd
towards the most illustrious men. And as fire-
works are very often made in this country, they
assembled a great many persons of this trade,
who pass'd in review before the ambassador, to
shew their strength and power: but they were
not ignorant that these were no more than atoms
in comparison of the court of Timur After
they had endeavor'd to please the ambassador by

abun-

abundance of civil treatment, and several honors bestow'd on him, they sent him back, and he was follow'd by several lords of the court of the Sultan of Egypt, who came to cast themselves at the foot of the imperial throne, and spoke to Timur in these words. " Most excellent and formidable emperor, we " know that we appear before your majesty as " your meanest servants; yet we are full of " respect and submission. We have resolv'd to " send Atilmich to your august court within " five days: and if after that you deign to " pardon our faults, we'll omit no occasion of " giving you marks of a perfect obedience; " and as far as depends on the power of the " Sultan, and the capacity of his subjects, they " shall endeavor to merit by their services the " good-will of your majesty, and the friend- " ship of the illustrious lords and officers of " your imperial court." The emperor, being touch'd with their discourse, which was color'd over with an appearance of sincerity, gave 'em a kind reception, worthy of his clemency he made 'em presents of vests, and with very obliging expressions assur'd 'em of the sincerity of his heart, he afterwards sent 'em back very well contented and pleas'd with having succeeded so well in their embassy. And this appearance of an acommodation occasion'd joy to the inhabitants of Damascus

CHAP.

CHAP. XXV.

Timur gives battel to the Sultan of Egypt, and gains the victory.

AFTER ten days encampment, an account was taken of the state of the army: upon which Timur order'd they shou'd depart from thence directly to encamp at Gouta, that the horses might feed in that delicious place. The army had no sooner began this motion, than thro their ill-fortune, the inhabitants of this country imagin'd that this march proceeded from weakness, and that our troops were fled towards the Levant. They likewise thought that so numerous an army cou'd not decamp without falling into some disorder, and that if they laid hold on this opportunity to attack the rear of the Tartar army, they cou'd not fail of defeating 'em, that the surprize wou'd so embarass the soldiers, that they must be constrain'd to disperse and fly, and that this action wou'd be a great honor to 'em in all future ages. In this hope the whole army of Syria took horse, and made a sally out of Damascus: the populace join'd with the soldiers, some having swords, and others sticks and stones in their hands, and as there were prodigious numbers of 'em, they had the rashness to fall on our rear. There came so great a multitude out of the city, that the whole plain was cover'd with horse and foot. The cavalry were arm'd with cuirasses, and were perfectly well equip'd, the infantry were arm'd with bows and arrows, swords, bucklers and ..., presuming in victory, and there were never

Book V. ver seen before so great a multitude assembled together.

Timur being inform'd of this ridiculous rash action, knew that fate had resolv'd on the Syrians destruction: he implor'd the assistance of God, and reflected seriously upon the conduct he ought to use in this conjuncture. He gave orders that the whole army shou'd face upon the enemy, and that all the cavalry shou'd dismount to encamp: he caus'd a kind of wall to be made with the bales of the baggage, prop'd up with great stones, and being thus entrench'd, they erected their tents and standards. Then Timur got upon an eminence with fifty of his favorites, and according to custom, on his knees address'd himself to God in prayer: he order'd his cuirass and other arms to be brought him, and then he took horse full of confidence, commanding the drums to be beat, and the great cry made. In the mean while the troops of our left wing arriv'd all in good order: and as the Syrians were already very near us, Timur sent instructions to the Mirzas Miran Chah, Charoc, and Aboubecre, who commanded the right wing, to attack the enemy on one side, while the Emirs of the left wing shou'd fall upon 'em on the other In this order they advanc'd against the enemy, and gave 'em battel. The Emirs Sevindgi Chamelik, Seid Coja, Sainte Maure, and others as well of the vanguard as of the rear, began the fight, being back'd by the main-body. And as the two wings fell furiously upon the unfortunate Syrians, there was so great a slaughter, that the whole plain was cover'd with blood. After an obstinate battel, victory inclin'd to Timur · the Syrians were defeated, and repuls'd as far as to the gates of Damascus, having above half their soldiers slain, and a great part dispers'd,

The history of Timur-Bec. 189

dispers'd; but this part was afterwards over- Chap.26.
taken by the Tartars, who slew vast numbers of
'em There were nothing to be seen but heaps
of dead bodys, and rivulets of blood, armor,
and standards, mix'd together. Scarce any escap'd
the fury of our soldiers, except those who enter'd the city This signal victory was gain'd
the 19th of Jumaziulevel 803, which answers to Jan. 19.
the year of the Crocodile. During the heat of 1400.
the battel, the Mirza Sultan Hussein, who commanded the Syrians left wing, was sent against
the Mirzas Miran Chah and Charoc; but Topalic
Coutchin, an officer of the Mirza Charoc, fell
upon him, and having seiz'd his horse's bridle,
brought him to his master, who gave advice of
it to Timur. His majesty being incens'd, gave
orders that Hussein shou'd be put in prison, and
loaded with chains, as a punishment for his action:
but he was shortly after set at liberty, thro the
intercession of the Mirza Charoc, yet not till
they had given him the bastinado, as order'd by
the law of Yasac. This was not so much a punishment to him, as the shame and continual reproaches he receiv'd from the whole court: and
he was never permitted to enter the emperor's
hall

CHAP. XXVI.

Taking of the city of Damascus.

THE next day our army decamp'd, and
went to erect the standard near the city at
the foot of a hill, while the news of the late
victory spread it self every where. At length
they departed at the noise of drums and trumpets;
and

and Timur order'd that the army shou'd march in order of battel, and place before 'em a great rank of elephants, as well to augment the magnificence of the army, as to strike terror into those who had never seen such things. It is remarkable, that from one end of the right wing to the extremity of the left, the Tartar army took up between three and four leagues of ground Then having their elephants at their head, the army got upon a rising-ground, from whence there was a prospect of the city, that the enemy might see their power, and be dishearten'd. By this means all the inhabitants of the country, as well soldiers as others, were satisfy'd of the multitude of this army, of which before they had had but an imperfect knowledge All the cavalry being upon this hill, the drum was beat, and the whole army made the usual great cry: and then they advanc'd nearer the city, to encamp on the bank of a deep rivulet, which serv'd instead of a trench; and with their great and little bucklers they made a sort of rampart round the camp. After these precautions, both the cavalry and infantry cross'd the rivulet; and the army, according to custom, rang'd themselves in order of battel in sight of the enemy. There was a vast number of Syrians, but the disadvantages they had had the preceding day had so discourag'd 'em, that they dar'd not advance. The Sultan of Egypt held a council with his great Emirs, as Norouz Hafezi, Yach Bec, Chadountaz, Cheiki Hajeki, and others, upon what they shou'd do in this conjuncture. Some, who were attach'd to the inhabitants interest more than to the Sultan's, said, that tho' they had receiv'd a great shock, the city and walls were entire, that there yet remain'd a vast number of soldiers, who were dispos'd to fight; that the

...best way wou'd be to make a second sally, Chap. 26.
...afterwards to defend the city and fortress.
...others who had greater experience, and
...more attach'd to the Sultan's interest, were
...another mind: they thought that men of sense
...wou'd not be prepossess'd with chimeras; that
...when the Tartars were disorder'd by a decamp-
...ment, without precaution, or being upon their
...guard, and not in the least expecting a battel,
...the Syrians with their great numbers, and in
...good order, went to surprize 'em, and attack
...their rear, with all possible diligence and arti-
...fice, yet every one knows what the success was:
...from whence they concluded, that the best reme-
...dy wou'd be for them to take the road of Egypt
...in the night, under favor of the darkness, accor-
...ding to the proverb, which tells us, That he who
...gains his life, gains all; that in the town and
...castle there were a great number of soldiers, as
...well as inhabitants, who were capable of defend-
...ing themselves, and wou'd use all their efforts to
...preserve their lives, their wives and familys, that
...if fortune favor'd 'em, and they sav'd the city,
...the king wou'd always continue master of it, but
...on the contrary, if the Tartars took it, and burnt
...and destroy'd every thing, the king and court at
...least wou'd be secur'd from the public desola-
...tion.

The whole Egyptian council was of this opinion, upon which Farrudge sent an ambassador
with presents to Timur, and a letter in these
terms "The affair which happen'd yesterday
" was a popular sedition, in which we had no
" hand: a number of ignorant young fellows of
" the common sort, had the rashness to sally out
" of the city, and receiv'd the punishment they
" merited. For our part, we have no other de-
" sign than to keep our words, as we promis'd be-
" fore.

Book V "fore. and if your highness is willing to grant
"a cessation of arms for this day only, to mor-
"row we will execute whatever you shall or-
"der, and endeavor to repair the fault com-
"mitted against our will, and obtain pardon
"for it."

The ambassador acquitted himself of his instructions: and after he had made known to the
emperor the subject of his coming, he order'd
the army to return, and encamp a second time

When night was come, the Sultan of Egypt
took horse, accompany'd by the principal lords
of his court; and having dispos'd every thing
in a proper order for his departure, he went out
of Damascus at midnight, and took the road to
Grand-Cairo. A Tartar deserter nam'd Thacmac, came with expedition to find the Mirza
Charoc, to whom he gave an account of all that
had pass'd. This Mirza ran to inform Timur of
it, carrying Thacmac with him. He order'd
that the troops of the right wing, under the
command of the Mirza Aboubecre, shou'd invest the city on one side, and those of the left
wing, commanded by the Emir Gehan Chah, on
the other, that no one might get out. At the
same time Timur sent some of the most famous
Emirs of his army, with a great body of cavalry,
in pursuit of the Sultan. These brave men
march'd with so much diligence, that they overtook him: they flew several of his men, and
oblig'd the others to abandon their horses, mules,
camels, and all their equipage, to save their lives,
so that the ways were cover'd with goods which
they had cast away to fly the better On break
of day, Timur took horse, and order'd the
Jan. 23. suburbs of Damascus to be pillag'd Next day,
the 23d of Jumaziulevel, after sun-rising, the
whole army were commanded to march in order

The History of Timur-Bec.

of battel; and after having pass'd the gardens and suburbs, to invest the city. This order was exactly executed; and Timur went to lodge in the palace of Casrablac, situate over-against the fortress, and built by Malek Ezzaher, formerly Sultan of Egypt. The Mirzas, Emirs, and soldiers took up their quarters in the suburbs; where they found a great quantity of furniture, arms, stuffs, and all sorts of merchandize.

Timur, who never omitted any opportunity of paying his devotion, visited the tombs of Oumme Selma and Oumme Habiba, two of the wives of Mahomet; and afterwards that of Belalhabachi, whose intercession he implor'd: and then he return'd to his camp. As soon as the inhabitants of Damascus saw themselves besieg'd in form, they were so seiz'd with fear, that all the Cherifs, the Cadis¹, Imams, doctors, and other lawyers of the city, open'd the gates themselves, and with an entire submission went out, and carrying with 'em presents, cast themselves at the foot of the imperial throne. They represented their misery, and the great displeasure they had at what was pass'd: and they besought the emperor to have pity on the Mussul-

---

¹ *An extract out of Arab Chah.*
The chief of this deputation was the Cadi Veliddin, son of Cheldoun, who very much pleas'd Timur in his discourses with him. this prince made him, and the others who were with him, dine at his own table. And as Veliddin had travel'd into Africa, Timur was desirous of hearing him discourse concerning the kings of that country: for Timur was well vers'd in the historys of princes and states, and was not ignorant of what pass'd either in the east or west.

Timur gave robes of honor to these lawyers, and sent 'em away contented.

He esteems him who comes to see him, according to the value of his presents, and presently after gives him up as a prey to death.

mans, and only grant 'em quarter for themselves, and for their familys. They made several presents to the officers; and after having submitted to pay the tribute for ransoming their lives, they return'd home. Timur gave a commission to the Emirs for receiving the tax, and sent 'em into the city. These Emirs were Cheik Noureddin, Chamelik, and Allahdad, accompany'd by the comptrollers Coja Massoud Sermnani, and Gelaleliflam, who enter'd into Damascus, and according to custom wall'd up seven gates of the city, leaving open only the gate of Elferadis, without which they kept their office. The receivers having drawn from the city the sums agreed upon, brought 'em to the Emirs. The friday following the Coutbe, or prayer for the king, was read in the famous mosque of the Ommades Califs, in the name and titles of the august emperor Timur.

CHAP. XXVII.

Taking of the castle of Damascus.

THO the condition of the city was as bad as we have represented, yet Yezdar Coutual, governor of the castle, confiding in the strength of this place, which was one of the most noted fortresses in the world, resolv'd to defend himself. Its walls were of great pieces of rock, very high and regularly built. It had round it a ditch of about twenty cubits; and

---

* Timur caus'd some of his soldiers to be crucify'd, for having us'd violence after the publication of quarter.

the

the place was supply'd with all sorts of ammunition. The garison began first to cast stones out of their machines, as also arrows, and pots full of naphtha and wild-fire, to hinder our approach. Nevertheless orders were given to all the generals of l'omans and Hezares to advance towards the castle, and besiege it in form. The necessary preparations were made, and the battering-rams and machines to cast stones were got ready; and the soldiers rais'd three platforms of such a height, that they commanded the castle. They afterwards entirely drain'd the ditch: then the sappers advanc'd to the foot of the wall, and began to work with all imaginable diligence, notwithstanding the great stones the besieg'd continually shower'd on 'em; which were answer'd by those from the machines erected on the platforms, and which hinder'd the besieg'd appearing so often in view. From our machines were likewise cast pots fill'd with wild-fire like theirs, besides the arrows which constantly fell upon the place like hail. The siege being divided among the Emirs, every one shook the walls on his side with battering-rams and other machines.

During these transactions, Timur order'd the Mirzas Miran Chah and Charoc, and the Emirs Sol'sman Chah, Gehan Chah and others, to go and take up their winter-quarters near Canzan, that their soldiers might refresh themselves, and their horses might get some pasture. The rest of the army advanc'd in the siege with a great deal of vigor: they heated great pieces of the rock by putting fire underneath, and casting vinegar there; and then with their hammers they broke 'em, and took 'em out of the walls: and when the wall and bastions were ready to fall, they prop'd 'em up with great stakes left they shou'd fall on a sudden. In this manner they soon finish'd finish'd sapping the bastion of Tarma, which was the largest of any: and the place which Altoum Bacchi inspected was soonest finish'd. This being done, orders were given to set fire to 'em, and at the same time this high and famous tower fell, and made a vast breach by its fall. The soldiers ran with their bucklers on their heads to enter by this breach: but on a sudden another part of the wall fell, which rais'd a prodigious dust, and crush'd to death eighty men of the troops of Corassana and Sistan. This misfortune stop'd the ardor of our men, who wou'd advance no farther and the besieg'd laying hold on the occasion, clos'd up the breach, and fortify'd themselves behind. These breaches struck terror into 'em, and they had willingly surrender'd, if they had not despair'd of pardon. The other props were then order'd to be set on fire, and great part of the castle soon fell. This accident entirely taking away all hopes from the besieg'd, Yezdar governor of the place caus'd the gate to be open'd, and being constrain'd to go out, he came full of grief to deliver up the keys of his castle, and of the treasury and magazines within it. The other sides of the walls, which had been prop'd up with stakes, were not set on fire.

Timur gave orders that the governor Yezdar shou'd be put to death, because he had waited too long before he surrender'd. They found in the castle great quantitys of riches, jewels, curious stuffs, and raritys which had been kept there for many ages. There was a famous granary full of corn, being the revenues of the two renown'd citys of Mecca and Medina. Timur, who was sincere in his religion, prohibited any one from touching 'em: and Herimulc, one of the Tavatchis, having taken a hundred Batmans

of

barly, he was baſtinado'd both before and behind, and the mony he had receiv'd for em taken from him. Timur order'd the intendant of this magazine to fell him some corn at the price of three Dinars Copeghis for each Batman or pound, becauſe the war had render'd proviſions extremely dear. This intendant got a great ſum of mony for the corn, and the whole ſum was diſtributed among the officers of the above citys, who were ſent back to Jeruſalem, after having receiv'd a great deal of civil treatment from Timur.

The gariſon were made ſlaves, and diſtributed among the Mirzas and Emirs, it was moſtly compos'd of Circaſſians, Mamalucs, Ethiopian ſlaves, and Zanghebars: all the women, children and old men had the ſame fate. The tradeſmen were ſeparated from the reſt, and ſhar'd among the Emirs, with thoſe who had been taken out of the city, to be conducted to Samarcand. Moulana Jumaleddin, and Moulana Sulleman, two celebrated phyſicians, were alſo carry'd with 'em. Then Timur went from the palace of Caſrablac to lodge in the houſe of Boutecach, one of the great Emirs of Syria, which houſe was the moſt charming and noble of any in that country. At the ſight of all this magnificence, Timur cry'd out, " Is it not
" a ſhame that in a kingdom of ſo large an ex-
" tent, where men give themſelves up only to
" pleaſures, they ſhou'd build all theſe fine edi-
" fices to pleaſe their ſenſes, and not have the
" charity to erect a ſingle mauſoleum of four
" walls for the holy wives of Mahomet, who
' lie underneath theſe tombs?" Whereupon he immediately order'd that two magnificent domes ſhou'd be built over the ſepulchres of theſe holy ladys. The commiſſion was given to the

Mirzas

Book V. Mirzas Aboubecre and Calil Sultan, and to the Emirs Cheik Noireddin, Ali Sultan, and Mengheli Coja, who made the workmen proceed with so much diligence, that the whole was finish'd in twenty five days. These two domes were of white marble, full of sculptures and chisel-work.

As the Syrian money was of a base alloy, Timur caus'd new money to be coin'd both of gold and silver, which was refin'd by the coppel: there were pieces of a hundred, of fifty, and of ten Medicales, which were all honor'd with the name and titles of the august emperor Timur. The money was so common among the soldiers, that the Divan got about six hundred thousand Dinars Copegni out of the single revenue for money.

Timur commanded the principal secretarys of state to prepare letters of conquest, to send to Samarcand, and all the capital citys of the kingdoms of Iran and Touran, which were subject to his empire, with advice of the reduction of Syria, and to command the governors to make public rejoicings for his victorys. These letters were dispatch'd by couriers, who likewise carry'd with 'em several of these new-coin'd pieces of gold and silver, to be distributed among the curoucties, the princes of the blood, and chief lords of the kingdoms of Iran and Touran.

Timur sent Coja Haflan to the Mirzas Mirancha and Charoc, that they might order the Emirs Soliman Chah and Gehan Chah to make inroads along the coast of the Mediterranean, as far as the town of Akka. These Emirs having departed according to order, made havock in all this country, from whence they brought away a great quantity of booty, and return'd to Canaan.

During

During these transactions, Timur was attack'd with a distemper, which proceeded from a flux of humors which fell upon his back, and turn'd into an imposthume. He was very bad with it: and one of the Emirs who attended his person, nam'd Aratmur, was sent into Canaan, to order the princes of the blood and the Emirs to return with expedition, but at their arrival the distemper went off, and the emperor recover'd Then Timur reflecting upon the history of Syria, assembled his privy-council to communicate his sentiments to 'em. " I have heard, says he, " that in the wars which the Merouanian Om- " miades Califs wag'd against the children of " Mahomet, and particularly with Ali, his son- " in-law, nephew, and lawful heir, where they " exercis'd all the massacres and cruelty's they " cou'd invent, the Syrians kept an intelligence " with 'em, encouraging 'em in all these abomi- " nable actions Nothing shou'd be more won- ' der'd at than this · for how can a nation be ' thought to be of the sect of a prophet, and " be drawn from the abyss of error and infi- " delity by the light he has afforded 'em, when " it becomes so far the enemy of his family as " to unite with its most cruel adversarys, and suffer all sorts of cruelty and injustice to be ' us'd towards 'em? This is what I can't com- " prehend We ought not to disbelieve this " tradition for if it were false, so rigorous a ' sentence wou'd not have come from the tribu- ' nal of God's justice, in consequence of which " they have suffer'd so cruel a punishment at this " time, notwithstanding all their strength and " power "

Timur having related this piece of history, with which he was perfectly acquainted, they explain'd his highness's thoughts among one another;

Book V

March 28.

ther, and the officers of his houshold were constantly reasoning on it. It was so insinuated into the minds of the warriors, that on the first of the moon of Schaban the troops forcibly enter'd the city without orders, and made a terrible slaughter, committing all manner of violences they made both men and women slaves, took from 'em their jewels, and pillag'd their goods, which consisted of an infinite quantity of gold, precious stones, curious merchandizes, rich stuffs, and all sorts of raritys. They got so much riches, that all the horses, mules, and camels, which they had taken from Sebaste as far as Damascus, were not able to carry 'em away: so the soldiers were oblig'd to fling away a great part, and especially several pieces of gold and silver stuffs, and curious belts of Egypt, Cyprus and Russia, which they had pillag'd at the beginning of the campain. This circumstance I have heard from several credible persons who were eye-witnesses of it.

The first floor of the houses of Damascus are built of stone, and the two upper ones of wood, and most of the cielings and even of the walls of 'em are varnish'd, which renders 'em very inflammable so that when any place has took fire, the judges and governors, notwithstanding all their precautions, are not able to stop it, and it commonly burns a great way This often happens in time of peace

March 29.

The 12th of Schaban, the city took fire by an accident, and every one strove in vain to quench it · it increas'd so much, that no place was free from the scent occasion'd by the ebony and sandarac, of which the varnish was compos'd, and the houses became exceeding black.

Timur, whose regard for religion was unparallel'd, sent the Emir Chamelik to preserve

the

the famous mosque of Ommiades from the fire: but tho the roof was made of wood cover'd with lead, instead of being varnish'd, God made his wrath appear against these people; for notwithstanding the soldiers endeavors to quench it, they cou'd not hinder the eastern Minaret of this mosque's being reduc'd to ashes, tho it was built of stone: whereas the Minaret of Arous, otherwise nam'd Mounar Beiza, remain'd safe, on which the Mussulmans believe, that the lord Messiah Jesus, on whom, as on our prophet, may blessings and salvation be shower'd, will descend from heaven, when he shall come to judg both the living and the dead. And what was most miraculous is, that this latter Minaret, tho built of wood, and plaster'd over with lime on the out-side, remain'd intire, while all Damascus was burnt down, and the immense riches within it pillag'd and sack'd, as well as the rest of Syria.

Then Timur took up a resolution to return back, and to give the inhabitants of Syria some marks of his clemency, after having made 'em feel the effects of his wrath, he order'd that all the slaves of Damascus and the rest of Syria, men, women and children, shou'd be set at liberty. Gelalelislam had the commission for executing this order, and conducting all the slaves to the city of Damascus; which was exactly observ'd.

†

CHAP.

CHAP. XXVIII.

Timur returns out of Syria.

March 31. 1401.

THE fourth of Schaban 803, which answers to the beginning of the year of the Serpent, the sun entring Aries, Timur decamp'd from Coubaibat, and march'd to Gouta, where he encamp'd. He there caus'd two orders to be drawn up; the one to the Mirza Mehemet Sultan, to leave the government of the frontiers of Mogolistan, to the Emirs Codadad Hussein, Birdi Bei, Sarbouga, and others, and to come forthwith to the foot of the throne, to receive the crown and investiture of the empire of Hulacou Can, which was granted him in consideration of his merits and services. The second order was, that the august empress Touman Agā and the young princes his children, shou'd come to meet the emperor. These two orders were seal'd, and sent by Dané Coja.

Timur being departed from Gouta, pass'd by Caraoun Bec, and in three days he arriv'd at Emessa, the inhabitants of which had continu'd firm in their obedience, for which reason the troops did not molest 'em in their passage. Then a council was held, and Timur order'd the Mirzas Roustem and Aboubecre, with the Emirs Soliman Chah and Cheik Noureddin of the right wing, to march with ten thousand horse to the town of Tedmir, built by the prophet Solomon, the houses of which were of free-stone, and to pillage the subjects of Zulcader, who were in the territories of this town. He commanded the Mirza Sultan Hussein and the Emir Berem

...e of the left wing, to march to Antioch at the ...ad of five thousand horse; and he sent the ...irza Calil Sultan, the Emir Rouſtem Tagi ...ouga Berlas, Temour Coja, Acbouga, and o-...ers, with fifteen thousand horse of the main ...dy, against the Turcomans of Coubec, who ...e encamp'd on the banks of the Euphrates.

Thoſe of the right wing soon arriv'd at Ted-...r, from whence they brought away about two ...ndred thousand sheep belonging to the Zulca-...enians, who were conſtrain'd to fly into the ...ſarts of Arabia with their horses and camels. ...fter this the troops return'd, pass'd the desart, ...nd came to the banks of the Euphrates, along ...hich they advanc'd

Those of the left wing being arriv'd near An-...ioch, cou'd scarcely enter it, because of the ...eat waters, sloughs and marshes; they pillag'd ...he city and country, and then turn'd towards ...leppo, where they join'd the troops selected out ...f the main-body, and commanded by the Mir-...a Calil Sultan; with these they march'd into ...e neighborhood of Calat-Erroum, towards the ...phrates. Here they met the Turcomans, who ...ad the boldness to wait their coming, and pre-...re for battel; they were briskly attack'd, and ...ourageously defended themselves; but the ...d Huſſein, son of Coubec, their leader, ...ing ſlain, his brothers and the reſt of the chiefs ...ere conſtrain'd to fly to the desart. Several ...f 'em were kill'd, and abundance of horses, ...amels, sheep and other spoils taken, which be-...ing join'd to the other booty of our soldiers, ...hey counted above eight hundred thousand ... and the soldiers were so fatigu'd, that ...hey cou'd not carry away the reſt of the cat-...

When

Book V. When Timur was arriv'd in the neighborhood of Hama, the evil deftiny of the inhabitants excited 'em to commit acts of hoftility againft our men. they deftroy'd the edifices our foldiers had built when they were there the firft time This action inflam'd Timur's wrath, who permitted 'em to be pillag'd: the inhabitants were made flaves, and their houfes fet on fire, after they had taken from 'em their beft effects.

The army march'd from Hama to Aleppo, from whence to Damafcus are feventy leagues. After fome days journy they came near Aleppo, and the Emirs Seid Azeddin, Hezaregher, Chah Chahan, and Mouffa Tui Bouga, who were in the caftle belonging to that city, raz'd the walls, burnt the houfes, as well of the caftle as of the town, and join'd the imperial camp. After four days journy the army arriv'd at the banks of the Euphrates, and the Mirzas Rouftem and Aboubecre, with the Emirs of the right wing, arriv'd there at the fame time, coming from the lower part of the river. The Mirzas Calil Sultan and Huffein Sultan, with the Emirs of the main-body, came there alfo by water: and they had all the honor to kifs the imperial carpet, and offer prefents of the booty they had taken in their inroads. There was fo great a number of cattel in the camp, that a fheep was fold for a Dinar. As the Mirza Sultan Huffein had perform'd feveral brave actions, and done the duty of a good fubject in the laft inroads, he obtain'd a pardon for his former fault, and kifs'd the emperor's feet, who promis'd to reftore him his beft favors, and take care of his advancement.

CHAP.

CHAP. XXIX.

Timur crosses the Euphrates, and hunts in Mesopotamia.

AFTER all the Mirzas and Emirs had join'd the imperial camp, orders were given to repass the Euphrates: and accordingly two boats were brought from the town of Bire, on the east side of this river, to transport the emperor's baggage. The Mirzas, Emirs and soldiers swam over, and encamp'd near Bire, the governor of which came out to salute the emperor, bringing him presents: and in acknowledgment of his services, his highness confirm'd him in his government, and the inhabitants receiv'd no damage from our troops. Cara Osman arm'd at this place, and kissing the imperial carpet, made his presents; and he had a handsom reception.

The army being departed thence, Timur had a desire to hunt in Mesopotamia: the soldiers of the right and left wing form'd the great circle of five days journy in circumference: and the circle growing less and less, they found so much game of all sorts near the fine fountain of Raselain, that they took the beasts with their hands. After the chace, tables were erected for a general banquet, to eat the game which had been taken, wherein the most delicious wines were serv'd up: and as an incentive to drinking, they eat roe-bucks and antilopes, whose flesh is very tender, and the best-tasted of any creatures of the desart.

Then

Book V Then they decamp'd from Bire; and when they were come to the town of Edessa [1], the principal persons came out with presents to salute Timur, who treated 'em handsomly, assur'd 'em of their lives, and sent 'em back contented. Passing farther, they found a castle inhabited by Armenian robbers. Timur gave orders for their being exterminated, and they were accordingly put to death, their goods seiz'd on, and the place raz'd. During these transactions Hendou Chah Cazandgi arriv'd from Samarcand; he had an audience of the emperor, to whom he gave an account of the good state of affairs in Transoxiana. There also came an officer from the empresses Toukel Canum and Touman Aga; and another from Sultania, from the empress Serai Mulc Canum, with presents of stuffs and jewels: and all these messengers inform'd the emperor of the good health of the princes his sons.

CHAP. XXX.

Timur marches to the town of Merdin.

THEN the army march'd towards Merdin. Timur sent back Hendou Chah Cazandgi, and the officers of the empresses, giving 'em presents, and letters full of affection for the princes his children. To the same place came the Sultan of Husni Keifa [2], and the Sul-

---

[1] The same as Ruhha and Orpha.
[2] Corruptly call'd Hasan Keif, a town on the bank of the Tigris between Amed and Moussel.

The history of Timur-Bec.

...n of Arzine, with the other princes and
...ds of those quarters. They brought presents
...d precious stones to lay before the emperor,
...d they had the honor to kiss the imperial
...rpet.

As to the Sultan of Merdin, we have already
...ark'd, that he being reduc'd to obedience,
...d been imprison'd by the emperor's order
... the castle of Sultania; that Timur in com-
...ion to him had pardon'd him, and given
...m a vest, with much civil treatment; and
...at he had promis'd to become a faithful servant
...long as he liv'd, and let flip no opportunity
...giving marks of it, that so he might render
...mself agreeable to the emperor, and merit
...s favors. After this it became him to follow
...e army into Syria with his troops; or if thro'
...e nearness of the enemys, there was any dif-
...ulty in that, he ought at least to have sent
...e of his sons or brothers. But as he had fail'd
...this particular, he was conscious of his fault;
...d dar'd not come to meet his highness. Ne-
...rtheless Timur, being arriv'd near his fron-
...ers, had the goodness to ask after him, or-
...ering him to come before him in very oblig-
...g terms: but this unhappy prince, giving
...ay to his evil destiny, had the insolence to
...fuse to come, and dreamt of defending his
...own, being persuaded, that it cou'd not be
...ken by force. In effect, as a long siege
...as necessary to the carrying it, tho in the
...ighborhood were abundance of fertile plains
... of pasturage, and proper to encamp
... Timur * was contented with ruining and
burning

---

* Timur cou'd not take the castle of Merdin, which was
upon an inaccessible rock, large enough to contain
much

burning all the houses of the lower town, as well as the markets: and he order'd Cara Ofman, governor of Malatia, after having honor'd him with a vest, to form the blockade of Merdin, and shut the inhabitants up so close, that no one might be able to escape.

Timur us'd abundance of civility to the Sultans of Husni Keifa, Arzine, and the other neighboring places, who were come to pay their devoirs to him at his arrival. He gave to each a robe wove with gold, a belt set with precious stones, and a sabre with a gold handle; and he permitted 'em to return to their own countrys. Then Timur sent the Emir Allahdad to Samarcand, with orders to march afterwards to Achpere, to take care of the frontiers of Gete.

CHAP. XXXI.

Timur sends troops into Georgia, and to Bagdad.

THE army being departed from Merdin, Timur order'd the Mirzas Sultan Huffein, Pir Mehemed, Omar Cheik, and Aboubecre, as also the Emirs Gehan Chah, Temour Coja, Sei Coja, and others, to march with a great body of the army to Alengic by the way of Amed

much plough'd lands. Here are great springs of water; the garison stand in no need of the out-parts to maintain 'em.

The Arabian says, that to be desirous of taking Merdin is to seek the friendship of an envious man, or to make sign to the blind.

The history of Timur-Bec.

to make themselves masters of Alengic, and Chap. 31. from thence to pass into Georgia. The Mirzas and Emirs departed according to order: but as Alengic had been besieg'd already two years by others of our troops, (for when the army march'd towards Sebaste, the Cheik Mehemed Deroga, with the troops of the Mirza Miran Chah, Firouz Chah, and the Mirza Charoc, went to besiege it, and press'd it so closely, that most of the inhabitants died of hunger; they being in so great want of victuals, as to be oblig'd to eat old leather, skins and such like things, to appease their hunger; and even these things failing 'em at last, constrain'd 'em to go out and deliver up the place) Alengic, I say, having been besieg'd two years, when the Mirzas and Emirs came near Avenic, and heard of the reduction of Alengic, instead of marching to it, they turn'd towards the right for Georgia. They made great haste to surprize the Georgians, whose country they ravag'd. This exceedingly disturb'd Malek Gourghin, who sent an ambassador to the Mirzas, to acquaint 'em with the great surprize he was in at their coming into his country, seeing he was one of the emperor's most faithful servants, and to assure 'em that as soon as his highness shou'd come into those quarters, he wou'd not fail of paying his obedience to him. The Mirzas sent an express to court with advice of Ghourghin's submission; they ceas'd ravaging his countrys, and staid at Mencoul, which is a place proper to pass the summer in, to wait the answer of the court, and know whether the emperor wou'd grant quarter to Ghourghin. The same day an order was issu'd out for the Sultan Mahmoud Can, the Mirza Rouftem, the Emir Solyman Chah, and other Emirs, to march at the head of their

Vol. II.   O   Tomans

Book V.

Tomans and companys towards the city of Bagdad. These lords set out immediately, and after several days march arriv'd at Bagdad, and encamp'd on the south-side. Farrudge, of the Mogul hord of Gelair, was governor for the Sultan Ahmed. The vast multitudes of Turks and Arabians, who were assembled in this city, render'd Farrudge insolent, and confiding in the strength of his walls, and the number of his soldiers, he even dar'd to sally out to oppose the Tartar army, and rang'd his men in order of battel in the view of ours.

As soon as the rumor of the arrival of our army was spread, the Emirs Ali Calander of Mendeli*, and Dgian Ahmed of Bacou*, began their march against us, and pass'd the Tigris at Medaine. On the other hand, Farruk Chah of Hille, and Micail of Sib, also departed with the same design, and join'd together at Serser, and with three thousand men well arm'd advanc'd to fight. The Mirza Roustem, the Emir Soliman Chah, and others, immediately took horse with their troops, and surrounded the enemy. They repuls'd 'em as far as the Tigris, and a bloody battel ensu'd near the castle of the Emir Ahmed. Dgian Ahmed was there slain, with a great number of his bravest soldiers: many cast themselves into the river and were drown'd, while the rest escap'd with a great deal of difficulty. After the defeat, one wou'd have thought Farrudge shou'd not have held out any longer, but this peasant, who had never before been master of a government, and had attain'd this only by cowardly intrigues, cou'd not resolve to quit his new dignity of governor, but found a pretence to excuse himself. " The Sul" tan Ahmed my master, says he, made me " swear, that if Timur shou'd come in person,
" I

* In Coureftan.

" I wou'd surrender the city, for fear of bring-
" ing the people into misery. but if that em-
" peror shou'd not come in person, whatever
" number of troops approach'd, I wou'd make a
" stout defence, and not deliver up the place:
" and I must obey my master's orders."

Under this sly pretence, he gain'd over the inhabitants and militia, whom he posted upon the walls to defend the city. There he us'd all his efforts, for he excited the soldiers upon the walls, and advanc'd upon the water in a boat, discharging a shower of arrows on our men in the rear

In the mean while Timur advanc'd towards Tauris. he pass'd by Nasibene [1], a strong place, which he gave orders to besiege and raze, but the inhabitants coming out with presents, and bringing the keys of the fortress, Timur gave 'em quarter, and they receiv'd no damage from the passage of our troops. The army being arriv'd at Moussel [6], they built a bridge over the Tigris, which all the troops cross'd in a week.

CHAP. XXXII.

Timur besieges and takes Bagdad.

THE Emirs who were before Bagdad, sent an express to the emperor, to acquaint him with Farrudge's sentiment, and the pretence with which he color'd over his obstinacy in defending the city. On this advice Timur

---

[1] A town of Courdistan, long. 76. 30. lat. 37.
[6] A town of Mesopotamia, long. 77. lat. 36. 30.

Book V chose the bravest men of his army; and leaving the empress Tchelpan Mulc Aga, with the rest of the troops and baggage, under the care of the Mirza Charoc, accompany'd by the Emir Chamelik, whom he order'd to march to Tauris by Tchinaran and Calaghi, he departed in person for Bagdad, by the way of Altoun Cuprue * where being arriv'd, he encamp'd at the lower part of the river, over-against the gate of Cariet Ulacab, and all the troops encamp'd round the city. He immediately order'd the sappers to begin to work. The Mirzas and great Emirs of the Tomans, Hezares and Couchons, fix'd their sappers each before his post, and some bodys of the troops to sustain 'em. Farrudge being desirous to know whether Timur was there in person, sent one to him whom he had confidence in, in quality of ambassador, because this person knew him, having had the honor to see him before. The ambassador met with a handsom reception, and after his audience was honor'd with a vest, and at length dismiss'd. At his return he gave Farrudge an exact account of what had pass'd; but this governor, tho he well knew he spoke the truth, accus'd him of dissembling, and put him in prison, lest others shou'd likewise know the truth from him, and then giving out that Timur was not there in person, he continu'd to defend himself, and committed hostilitys, not considering what the consequence wou'd be. Then the Cojas Masaoud Semnani, and Mengheli, who were employ'd in building a platform, which might have a prospect upon the city of Bagdad, were wounded with arrows, and soon after expir'd.

---

* A bridge on the river of Altoun Sou, near Mouffel.

Tim

Timur sent Locman Tavachi to the Mirza Charoc, to order him to return to Bagdad with the baggage and the rest of the army. Locman join'd the Mirza at Calaghi, and accompany'd him in his way to Bagdad. When this great army was assembled together, Timur review'd it, and the astonish'd inhabitants no longer look'd upon their city as the house of peace *, but as the palace of hell and discord. The troops encamp'd on both sides the river, and surrounded the city, tho it was more than two leagues in circumference. A bridge of boats was built over the Tigris below Cariet Ulacab; and several skilful archers were laid in ambuscade down the river, to hinder any from flying. The care of the upper part of the river, was given to the Mirzas Miran Chah and Charoc, who encamp'd over-against Souqs Essultan. On the other side of the Tigris were Mehemed Azad, and Tangri Birmich Coja, to guard the fore-part of the city, that no one might get out that way. In fine, it was so block'd up and environ'd on all sides, that tho the Tigris pass'd thro the middle of it, and there was a great number of boats, yet it was impossible to get out. During these transactions, Ahmed Ogoulkhai, governor of the castle of Alengic, who was seiz'd after the taking of the place, was brought to Timur, who order'd that he shou'd be put to death, and the castle committed to the care of Malek Mehemed Aoubehi. The execution of this order was given to him who had brought Sidi Ahmed to court.

At the same time the Emir Moussa arriv'd from the Mirza Mehemed Sultan at Transoxi-

---

* Bagdad is sirnam'd Daresselam, that is to say, the house of peace.

an], and gave the emperor an account of the good state of affairs in that kingdom He presented him with a piece of a balass ruby, weighing one hundred and twenty Medicales, dug out of the mine of Bedakchan.

In the mean while Farrudge and the inhabitants of Bagdad were struck with fear; so that they fought not so much out of bravery as from despair they perform'd actions of the greatest rashness, which almost exceeded human power for as soon as the Tartars having made a breach had set fire to it, and a side of the wall was about to fall, the besieg'd immediately repair'd the breach with mortar and brick, and entrench'd themselves behind. It was then summer, the sun being in Cancer: and as Bagdad was situate in a country near the tropic, the violence of the heat was so great, that the birds fell down dead, and as the soldiers had on their cuirasses, one may say they even melted like wax nevertheless they rais'd a high platform, which commanded the city, from whence they incessantly cast great stones out of their machines The Mirzas and Emirs fell several times to their knees before the emperor, begging leave to make a general assault, that they might take the city sword in hand: but Timur wou'd not consent to it, saying, perhaps the besieg'd may come to a sense of their fault, beg pardon, and deliver up the place, that they may save themselves from being slain or made slaves, and that the kingdom may not be entirely ruin'd. But fate had fix'd it otherwise, for these unfortunate people continu'd in their stubbornness notwithstanding the dearness and scarcity of provisions, the siege having already lasted forty days

The

The 27th of Zilcade 803, at noon, when the inhabitants by reason of the heat of the sun, not being able to stay upon the walls, had retir'd into their houses, and fix'd their helmets upon sticks which they had erected in their places, our army undertook to give a general assault. The Mirzas and Emirs furiously advanc'd, and having fix'd their scaling-ladders against the walls, the Emir Cheik Noureddin mounted first, and erected his horse-tail upon the wall, crown'd with a half-moon. He caus'd the trumpet to be sounded, and the drums and kettle-drums beat. immediately all the captains in their respective posts mounted the walls, and then cast them down into the ditch: the troops enter'd the city sword in hand, and Timur advanc'd to the foot of the bridge which had been built below Bagdad. The soldiers being in the place, the inhabitants endeavor'd to get out by all the ways they cou'd, but in vain: so they were constrain'd to cast themselves into the Tigris, where escaping the swords of the Tartars, they became the prey of the fishes. Several got into boats, and others swam, to gain the lower part of the river, but they were no sooner come to the bridge than they were shot by the soldiers arrows, who lay in ambuscade. Farrudge embark'd with his daughter, and found means, notwithstanding all Timur's precautions, to escape by water. He was pursu'd along the banks of the Tigris by our soldiers, who discharg'd upon him a vast number of arrows, whom not being able to resist, he was constrain'd to cast himself and daughter into the water, where they were both drown'd, and the boat sunk to the bottom. The boatmen had orders to fish up Farrudge, and having drawn 'im up out of the water, they cast his unfortunate

Chap 32
July 23. 1401.

nate carcase upon the bank. As there had been several Tartar soldiers slain in the general assault, each soldier was order'd to bring one head [*] of the men of Bagdad; which they accordingly did, and spar'd neither old men of fourscore, nor children of eight years of age. No quarter was given either to rich or poor, and the number of the dead was so great, that no one cou'd count 'em up, tho the Tavachis had orders to register it. Towers were made of these heads, to serve as an example to posterity. Some learned men found means to cast themselves at the feet of the emperor, who granted 'em pardon and quarter, and even gave 'em vests and horses, with a convoy to conduct 'em to what place of security they desir'd: all the rest of the inhabitants were exterminated. Afterwards Timur gave orders that there shou'd not remain one single house in the city unraz'd, but that the mosques, colleges and hospitals shou'd be spar'd. Accordingly they ruin'd the markets, caravanseras, hermitages, cells, monasterys, palaces, and other edifices. Thus, says the Alcoran, *The houses of the impious are overthrown by the order of God.*

---

[*] Arabschah says two, and that there were ninety thousand inhabitants of Bagdad slain in cold blood. They flung away the bodys, and made trophys of the heads pil'd together. There were one hundred and twenty towers made of the heads for trophys.

CHAP

CHAP. XXXIII.

Timur's return from Bagdad, and march towards Tauris.

AFTER the Tigris was grown red with the blood of the inhabitants of Bagdad, and the air began to be infected by the dead bodys, Timur decamp'd from that city the beginning of Zilhadge, and march'd a league towards the upper part of the river. He encamp'd near he tomb of the great Imam Abou Hanifa, chief of one of the four orthodox sects among the Mahometans, to implore the intercession of this saint. Then he sent a messenger with letters and orders to Mousike, who was come from Transoxiana; which messenger he order'd to be accompany'd by Nemedee, Deroga [1] of Khivak [2], that this Nemedee might have the care of the government of Carezem in the absence of Mousike, and till his return to the Mirza Mehemed Sultan.

Timur order'd the Sultan Mahmoud Can, and the Mirza Caleb Sultan, accompany'd by several great Emirs and a good number of troops, to make inroads in the neighbouring places. They hasten'd to obey this order, pass'd by Hille, and went as far as Mechad Nedgef [3];

---

[1] Deroga is the particular governor of a town.
[2] A town south of the Gihon, in the kingdom of Carezem.
[3] A place in Irac Arabi near the Euphrates, where Hussein, grandson of the false prophet Mahomet, was slain by the soldiers of Yezide, son of Muavias. To this place they go in pilgrimage from all parts of Asia.

but

but instead of attacking that holy place, they paid their devotions there: then they ravag'd Hille and Vaset, and return'd to court laden with booty.

Timur took the road to Chehrezour and Calghi, and leaving the care of the baggage and main of the army to the great Emirs, he order'd 'em to march slowly behind, while no one shou'd separate from his Toman or company. The emperor made haste, accompany'd by the Mirzas Miran Chah, Charoc, and Calil Sultan: but while they were on their march, the Courdes were so rash as to attack those who were separated, tho at ever so small a distance from the army, and rob 'em. Timur being inform'd of their boldness, plac'd soldiers in ambuscade round the roads; and as soon as these villains appear'd, our men sallying out of their ambuscades, seiz'd 'em, and hang'd 'em upon the spot on the chesnut trees which grew in the roads. As to these chesnut-trees, I have heard it reported by very credible persons, that one year they produce chesnuts, and the next gallnuts * ; which appearing so very extraordinary, I thought fit to mention it. Timur being arriv'd at the river of Jagatou, the empress Serai Mulc Canum, Canzade, and the other wives of the Mirzas, with their children, among whom was the Mirza Oulouc-Bec, came to meet his highness, and kiss'd his feet at Sineper, congratulating him on his conquests, and sprinkling upon him precious stones and pieces of mony. After having offer'd their presents,

---

* I believe the author is mistaken, supposing the oaks which produce gall nuts alternately with acorns, to be chesnut trees, which are very uncommon in Syria.

they

The history of Timur-Bec.

they decamp'd, and being arriv'd at Acziaret, encamp'd there. The Cherifs, doctors and principal lords of the empire of Iran, cloth'd with scarfs of Ihhrane which they wear in the mosques, came as far as this place to meet Timur, who gave 'em a handsom reception. They staid twenty days at this place; and the baggage and remainder of the army soon arriv'd. And as the most learned Imams, and doctors were assembled in this place, Timur, who was extremely desirous of being enlighten'd upon any questions of religion, invited 'em to dispute upon some point of doctrine, for the better clearing up of the truth: he employ'd himself in this exercise as long as he continu'd at Acziaret. Afterwards he gave leave to the Mirza Rouftem to return to Chiraz, with order, as soon as he shou'd arrive there, to send to court Haffan Yandar, and Jafan Jagadaoul.

CHAP. XXXIV.

Timur sends the Mirza Charoc to Arzendgian.

DURING Timur's stay in Syria, Bajazet, firnamed Ildurum or the Thunder, the Ottoman emperor, thro the instigation of Sultan Ahmed Gelair and Cara Youfef Turcoman, who had fled for refuge to his court brought an army into the field, and to revenge himself for the ruin of Sebafte, he march'd to besiege Arzendgian, which he made himself master of, having routed Taharten Mocbel, Taharten's lieutenant, was kill'd in the battel, and Bajazet sent the difconfolate wives and children of Taharten to Broufla; and then return'd

Book V turn'd himself. When Timur was departed from Acziaret, had pass'd by Oudgian [s], and was encamp'd at Hechtroud, that is to say, the eight rivers, he receiv'd advice that Bajazet was again marching towards the east: upon which he order'd the Mirza Charoc forthwith to fall upon the Ottoman, and make him repent of his boldness, he appointed the Emirs Solyman Chah, Chamelik, and other chiefs of Tomans, and colonels of Hezares, to accompany the Mirza. He then sent orders by the Emir Mezrab, to the Mirzas and Emirs who were gone out to make inroads in Georgia, and had stop'd in Mencoul, to depart directly to join the Mirza Charoc, which they accordingly did. The Mirza being set out from Avenic, and arriv'd at Nevine, met the Cheik Ali, nephew of Taharten, who brought advice that Bajazet, fearing the success of his bold undertaking, had besought Taharten to intercede for him with Timur, that he might obtain pardon for his hostilitys, on condition of his future obedience, that he wou'd send ambassadors with letters to make a treaty of peace, and a sincere alliance between the two empires, that so the Mussulmans might live quietly, and that he promis'd that if the peace shou'd be concluded by the intercession of Taharten, he wou'd send back his wives and children, whom he had carry'd to Brousa. The Mirza Charoc sent the Cheik Ali to the emperor, to give him an account of this affair; and staid himself some time where he was. Timur having decamp'd from the eight rivers, went to Oudgian, and staid some days in the Kiochk of Argoun.

---

[s] A town of Azerbijana near Tauris.

CHAP. XXXV.

Arrival of the second empress Touman Aga, and the young princes, from Samarcand.

WE have said before, that when the army decamp'd from Damascus, orders were sent to the empress Touman Aga to repair to court with her children. As soon as the princess receiv'd that letter, she hasten'd thither. When she arriv'd at Bocara, she went to visit the tombs of the saints, and among others that of the Cheik Seifeddin Bacrezi, whose intercession she besought. She cross'd the Gihon at Amouye, and passing the desart, came to Macan; and then going thro the desart of Bigen, she went to Machhad of Tous, where she visited the tomb of the great Ali, making vows, and distributing alms. When she was arriv'd near Oudgian, Timur went to meet her, and had the pleasure of seeing and embracing his dear children the Mirzas Ibrahim Sultan and Sad Vaccas. He return'd thanks to God for his favors; and aftrewards gave audience to the empress Touman Aga, and his daughter the princess Beghisi Sultan, as also his cousin Sadekin Aga, who paid their respects to him. After having staid several days at Oudgian, Timur took the road to Tauris, hunting in his way. When he was arriv'd there, he went into his imperial palace, where he inform'd himself of the affairs of all his people, and did justice to those who had been oppress'd by his officers. Then the Coja Ali Semnani arriv'd from Herat, and the Coja Sureddin from Sebzuar; they saluted the emperor,

peror, and made their presents. Timur gave 'em a place in the Divan, in consideration of their services.

CHAP. XXXVI.

Timur marches into Georgia, and to Carabagh Arran

TIMUR having staid some days at Tauris, resolv'd to march into Georgia: he went to encamp at Comtoupa, where he order'd the Coja Ismael Cavafi to be hang'd before the market-place of the camp, to punish him for the tyrannys he had exercis'd upon the people. He afterwards cross'd the river Araxes, and went to encamp with all the army at Nakchivan. And as the castle of Alengic was near Nakchivan, he was desirous to see that strong place, which had been taken by his soldiers in so short a time, and carrying with him the empresses, with the princes his sons, and his favorite Emirs, he carefully examin'd the place, and return'd to his camp.

About this time Taharten arriv'd at court, where on his knees he presented Bajazet's letter, gave an account of his repentance, and begg'd pardon for him; which he did with so much eloquence, that he appeas'd the emperor's wrath, and obtain'd his desire. Timur staid some days at this place, during which time he sent an ambassador into Georgia, to Malek Ghourghin, to demand the tribute of him. Then the Mirzas, Pir Mehemed son of Omar Cheik, Sultan Hussein and Aboubecre, with the Emirs who had been sent to Mencoul, to join

the

The history of Timur-Bec.

Mirza Charoc, arriv'd at court, and saluted the emperor. The army decamp'd from the meadow of Nakchivan, went to the defile of Chahboz, and enter'd into the mountains. Timur being arriv'd at Gheuktcheytonkez, had a desire to take the diversion of hunting, and when the circle began to close as usual, they took a very great number of stags After this place they encamp'd, and the Mirza Charoc return'd with his Emirs, and had the honor to salute the emperor at that place. Afterwards they departed, and when they were encamp'd at Chemkour [6], which is a delicious place, Idecou, son of Coja Seifeddin Berlas, arriv'd there from Kirman, he kiss'd the imperial carpet, and made his presents The commissary, whom Timur had sent into Georgia to receive the tribute impos'd on Malek Ghourghin, likewise return'd to the same place. That prince sent with him his own brother, loaded with curious presents, among which were horses and animals proper for the chace, he also sent the tribute impos'd on him. He had an audience of the emperor, by the intercession of the great Emirs; and having offer'd his presents, related the subject of his embassy He said that the king his brother had resolv'd to continue obedient to the laws of the emperor of the Mussulmans, that if he had committed any fault, he sincerely repented of it, and if his highness wou'd pardon him, he wou'd not let one opportunity slip of rendring him his services; that the wou'd faithfully pay his annual tribute, and always keep troops ready to march where his highness shou'd please to order 'em.

---

[6] A own in Georgia, long. 83. lat. 42.

Timur pardon'd Malek Ghourghin; he look'd upon his brother with a favorable eye, and giving him a veft, permitted him to return home. He order'd him to acquaint his brother that he forgave him, and wou'd quit his country, on condition that he kept within the bounds of his duty, that he treated the Muffulmans of Georgia civilly, and protected 'em from all infults and oppreffions; and that he rais'd an army, which he fhou'd fend directly to the imperial camp.

Then Timur fent to Samarcand Temour Coja fon of Acbouga, with other Emirs, to ferve under the Mirza Omar, in quality of lieutenant-general in the government of Tranfoxiana. The army departed from this place, and went to encamp at Caraoultopa, where they receiv'd advice that the Mirza Mehemet Sultan, who had orders to return from Samarcand to court, was arriv'd at Nichabour, and that the Emir Hadgi Seifeddin, his lieutenant-general, was dead. Timur was fenfibly touch'd with this news, and melted into tears, becaufe of the good fervices he had always receiv'd from that faithful fervant.

CHAP. XXXVII.

Timur paffes the winter at Carabagh. Arrival of the Mirza Mehemet Sultan from Samarcand.

AFTER a month's ftay at Caraoultopa, Timur departed, and having pafs'd by Ghendge and Berdaa, went to encamp at Carabagh Arran the 22d of Rabiulakher 804, which anfwers to the year of the Serpent, the fun being

Dec 12. 1401.

in the middle of Sagittarius. They built houses for Timur and the Mirzas his sons; and within the inclosures they erected tents and pavilions. And as Timur's intention was to make war in Capchac in the spring, the face of the pavilions was turn'd towards Derbend, and every one took up his winter-quarters, after Timur had distributed the mony in his treasury among the soldiers and Emirs. But at this time ambassadors arriv'd from Capchac: they obtain'd an audience by the intercession of the great Emirs, and on their knees assur'd the emperor of their Can's submission and perfect obedience. The respectful terms they us'd appeas'd his anger, who granted 'em pardon, and assur'd 'em of his friendship.

Then advice was brought that the Mirza Mehemed Sultan had pass'd by Ardebil, and was arriv'd at Actam, at the head of his army. The Mirzas Miran Chah, Charoc, and others, accompany'd by all the great Emirs, hasten'd to meet him: they cross'd the bridge of the Araxes, and join'd the Mirza on the bank of the river Agbuc. The Mirzas embrac'd their brother with tenderness and affection, testify'd their joy, and congratulated him on his happy arrival. The Mirza Mehemed Sultan went to cast himself at the emperor's feet, with the ordinary ceremonys. Timur embrac'd him, discours'd with him on the fatigues and length of his journy, and gave him a thousand benedictions. The Mirza offer'd his presents, as did also the Emirs of his court. For joy of this happy arrival the emperor made a great feast for several days, where the empresses and ladys appear'd with extraordinary splendor.

Timur particularly distinguish'd the Mirza Mehemed Sultan; he plac'd a crown of gold on his head, and gave him a belt of the same mettal,

tal, with nine sets of Arabian horses, with saddles of gold. When the feast was over, Timur again took upon him the care of the public affairs, and the first thing he did was to finish the process against the Mirza Eskender, whom the Mirza Mehemed Sultan had bound for a fault he had committed: he was interrogated in a full Divan, and being cast, receiv'd the bastinade appointed by the laws of Yasa, but at length his chains were taken off, and he set at liberty.

CHAP. XXXVIII.

Timur sends troops to make inroads in divers places.

WE have before remark'd, that the Sultan Ahmed Gelair, for fear of Timur's troops, had fled from his city of Bagdad for refuge into Natolia to Bajazet. Upon the rumor of Timur's march, the same Sultan departed from Bajazet in the neighborhood of Cæsarea in Cappadocia, and went towards Chaldea, which is call'd Irac-Arabi: he pass'd by Calat-Erroum, and along the banks of the Euphrates; he went to Hit, and thence to Bagdad, which city he endeavor'd to rebuild, tho entirely ruin'd, and he got together all those of his party who were dispers'd, and wander'd about as vagabonds in the deserts. Timur being inform'd of this, resolv'd to exterminate 'em before they shou'd be able to gather to a head: to which purpose he held a council with the Mirzas and Emirs, and order'd four bodys of the cavalry to march each a different route. The Mirza Pir Mehemed, son of Omar Cheik, had

The history of Timur-Bec.

had orders to go towards Lorestan, Couzestan and Vaset: the Mirza Aboubecre, with several Emirs of Tomans, was to depart for Bagdad: the Mirzas Sultan Hussein and Calil Sultan were order'd to go with several Emirs into certain places of Chaldea, and the Emir Berendac was nam'd to march with a good troop, to pillage Gezire, and endeavor to exterminate the rebels. And as the Courdes had dar'd to commit insults against our army, on its return from Bagdad, and had rob'd some of our soldiers who were scatter'd, the emperor order'd that the first of these robbers they met shou'd be destroy'd without mercy.

Tho it was winter, and the cold exceeding violent, because of the snow, so that it was impossible to pass without laying felts before one; yet the Emirs readily obey'd their instructions. This execution was begun upon the Courdes robbers, who, forc'd by the snow and violence of the cold, were come down from their mountains, and had encamp'd in the plains of Derbend Tachi Catoun: an infinite number were put to the sword, some wou'd have fled into the mountains, but were hinder'd by the snow and cold, and constrain'd to submit and beg quarter, which was not granted, because their own wickedness had brought upon 'em the wrath of Timur.

The Mirza Aboubecre, having the Emir Getanchi for his lieutenant-general, took the road to Bagdad, and blocking up the ways on all sides, arriv'd there in the evening, when the Sultan Ahmed least expected him. The Sultan was so surpriz'd and press'd, that he cast himself into a boat in his shirt, pass'd the Tigris, and accompany'd by his son the Sultan Taher, and

P 2   some

some officers of his houshold, took the road to Hille. Our troops repos'd themselves that night at Bagdad, and next morning, when they were assur'd of the Sultan's being gone to Hille, the Emir Gehan Chah was detach'd in pursuit of him, and went as far as Hille, but as the Sultan, who had caus'd the bridge to be broken, was gone towards the lower part of the Euphrates, into the isles of Khaled and Malek, Gehan Chah wou'd not march so far, but staid at Hille, and sent a horseman to give advice of it to the court.

The Mirzas Sultan Hussein and Calil Sultan pass'd by Cherchemal, and pillag'd Mendeli, from whence the Emir Ali Calander, who was governor of it for the Sultan Ahmed, fled, pass'd the river, and having got together some fugitive troops, posted himself on the bank of the Tigris. The Mirza Calil Sultan sent by the upper part of the river the son of Gehanghir Berlas, at the head of five hundred brave men, with orders to swim over the river, and attack 'em in the rear, while himself, with his army, lay in their view to amuse 'em. This detachment cross'd the Tigris, attack'd the enemy's rear, while the Mirza's troops swam over the river, charg'd the enemy on both sides, and having defeated 'em, pillag'd and brought 'em away prisoners of war, after having burnt alive their commander, who had had the boldness to defend himself.

The Mirza Pir Mehemed, with his lieutenant-general the Emir Solyman Chah, pillag'd at Doubendar the hords of Saki and Fili. He was join'd by the Mirza Roustem, who, according to his instructions, was come from Chiraz to pass the winter at Chuchter: and they went together

The history of Timur-Bec.

ther towards Abada [7] and Vafet. The Cheik Avis, a Courde, offer'd himfelf to be their guide, and advis'd 'em to ford the Tigris at Coupefer, they afterwards march'd all night, and came to Mabedia, where they vifited Sidi Ahmed Kebir. From thence they march'd two days journy, to plunder the Arabians of Abada, from whom they brought away great fpoils of horfes and camels. They went no farther; but repaffing the Tigris, return'd to Chuchter, the government of which the Emir Solyman Chah confirm'd to Doucom, and that of Dezfoul to Mehemed Adjab Chir, as likewife that of Haviza to Temour Coja, and that of Couzeftan with its finances to Chamfeddin Dehdar, but by way of retaliation he exacted of 'em great fums of mony Then the Mirza Rouftem departed, in order to return to Chiraz

All the Mirzas and Emirs, who were gone to make inroads into divers parts, ftaid the whole winter in Chaldea, where they feveral times beat the enemy, and brought away a great quantity of booty · and in the fpring they took the road to the imperial camp; and being all join'd at the bridge of Cales near the mountain Dgebelhamri, twelve leagues from Bagdad, and four from the dome of Ibrahim Lic, they march'd together to court, to give an account of what they had done

---

A town in Arabia, frontier of Chaldea, on the Perfian gulf, near Bafra or Baffora.

CHAP. XXXIX.

The causes which oblig'd Timur to return to make war on Bajazet the Ottoman emperor.

AS Cara Youſef, prince of the Turcomans, had begun afreſh to commit diſorders in the Muſſulman country, robbing all paſſengers of whatever quality, and even inſulting the great caravan which goes yearly to Hidgiaz and Mecca[1], and afterwards fearing the juſt indignation of our monarch, was fled for refuge to the country of the Ottomans, which was a ſure aſylum to all the robbers of Aſia Timur, who made it a point of conſcience to quell the diſorders which affected the Muſſulmans, reſolv'd to make war upon Bajazet. This prince receiv'd the news with indignation, and all the people of Natolia were ſo ſeiz'd with fear, that the principal men of the ſtate, as well lawyers as Cheriſs, waited upon him, and gave him the following advice.

The Counſel to Bajazet

" The prince who deſigns to march into our country, is ſo formidable and powerful, that he has deſtroy'd all who have refus'd to obey him. Whatever his armys undertake, they eaſily accompliſh, and they have never yet attack'd a province, city or fortreſs, which they have not ſoon reduc'd. It is impoſſible, mighty emperor, to execute ſo great deſigns without the favor of God, which makes us preſume that to wage war with ſuch an enemy,

---

[1] Every Mahometan kingdom ſends yearly a caravan for the pilgrims to Mecca.

"is against the rules of prudence. We believe it Chap. 39.
"best to act with him in the ways of peace and
"mildness, and that your highness shou'd use
"all your efforts to do what he desires of you,
"and to maintain a good correspondence with
"him."

The fear which had possess'd Bajazet made all this appear reasonable to him. He wrote a letter to Timur, full of submission and obedience, which he sent by a Cadi of the law, accompany'd by an eloquent Emir skilful in negotiations, who went in quality of ambassadors to our conqueror. They arriv'd in the imperial camp at Carabagh Arran, and by the intercession of the Mirzas and great Emirs were admitted to an audience: they fell on their knees, and having kiss'd the imperial carpet, presented their letter, and gave an account of the subject of their embassy. The letter imported, "That *Bajazet's* "since by the infinite favor of the great ruler *letter to* "of heaven and earth, your highness has been *Timur.* "rais'd to the throne of the empire of Asia, "we willingly resolve to be entirely obedient "to you: and if for the time past we have "acted contrary to our duty, we assure your "highness that we will repair the fault by our "zeal in embracing all opportunitys of paying "our homage and services."

Timur having heard the ambassadors harangue, and read Bajazet's letter, answer'd 'em in these terms. "Inasmuch as we have been inform'd, *Timur's* "that your master wages war with the infidels *answer to* "of Europe, we have always cast off all de- *Bajazet's* "signs of marching into his country with our *dors.* "army, not being willing to consent to the "destruction of a Mahometan country, which "will cause a great deal of joy to the infidels. "But there can be nothing more disagreeable to
P 4 "us,

"us, than to hear that he grants a protection
"to Cara Iousef Turcoman, the greatest rob-
"ber and villain in the whole earth, who pil-
"lages the merchants, murders passengers on the
"high-ways, and commits a thousand other in-
"sufferable disorders and what is most dange-
"rous is, that this wretch resides in the midst
"of the Mussulman country, where he is as a
"wolf among the sheep, and the evil he does
"is a thousand times worse than what a stran-
"ger cou'd do, tho he was the most powerful
"monarch in the world If your master has
"a real desire to remove the causes of our quar-
"rel, and keep a good correspondence with
"us, he must resolve upon one of these three
"things, either first, to put Cara Iousef to
"death as a criminal, after a legal process,
"or secondly, to send him to us bound in
"chains, that being convicted of his crimes,
"he may receive the punishment due to 'em,
"or thirdly, that he at least expel him out
"of his dominions On these conditions we
"will maintain a friendship with your master
"as far as possible, and give him proofs of it
"by the powerful succours we shall send him,
"to carry on the war against the infidels more
"vigorously.

The ambassadors receiv'd the emperor's answer with all possible marks of respect. Then
his highness took horse to follow the diversion
of the chace, he pass'd the river Araxes, and
the plain of Actam was chosen for the place
to hunt in. This vast country was surrounded
as usual, and the circle growing less, the emperor and the Mirzas enter'd, and with their
lances slew what game they pleas'd Timur
permitted Taharten and the Ottoman ambassadors to enter the circle with the Mirzas several

...ral officers of the houshold, as Mehemed Azad, Jeuchul Baourtchi, and others, had the same honor, and they flew a prodigious number of beasts. In the mean while the circle press'd closer, and there were five or six ranks of soldiers behind one another: and then the Mirzas and Emirs came out of the circle, and order'd the kettledrums to be sounded. The beasts, terrify'd at this noise, fell upon one another in such great numbers, that they form'd a kind of mountains. Then all the cavalry were permitted to kill and bind the beasts; and the chace was so great, that every one took five or six with his own hands.

After this hunting, Timur return'd to the camp, and in few days made a most magnificent feast, in which he did particular honors to the Ottoman ambassadors, gave 'em caps of gold, and belts, and told 'em that he wou'd take up his winter-quarters in this place, and at the spring set out for the frontiers of Natolia, where he wou'd wait the arrival of the ambassador whom he shou'd send to their master; that if he brought a reasonable answer, he shou'd be glad; if the contrary, the sword shou'd determine who was in the right. Then Timur sent with 'em, in quality of ambassador, Bayazid Tchembai Eltchikede, with a letter to Bajazet; he gave 'em a numerous attendance, and then dismiss'd 'em all. The tenor of the letter was as follows.

"After the usual compliments, we declare *Timur's* to you, that if what your ambassadors have letter to "said be sincere and true, it is requisite that Bajazet. "what we have propos'd concerning Cara You- "suf Turcoman shou'd be immediately put in "execution; and that you send to us forthwith "one of your Emirs you can most confide in,

" to

"to confirm with an oath the articles of a trea-
"ty of peace between us. After that, by am-
"basladors and letters a good correspondence
"shall be maintain'd between us, so that the
"Musulmans shall no longer fear any insult
"from either of us, otherwise you may expect
"to see our army enter your country, and ruin
"your monarchy. Safety be to him who fol-
"lows the right way."

CHAP. XL.

Timur digs the river of Berlas.

IT is a common observation, that the grandure of princes is known by the monuments which remain of 'em after their death. Never any potentate left so many of these marks of power as Timur. Some antient prince had dug a canal into which the Araxes was brought, but this canal was at length overflown, and its banks demolish'd. While Timur was hunting in these quarters, he by chance cast his eyes upon this beautiful relique of antiquity, and at the same time his ambition, and the desire he had to immortalize himself, excited him to repair this canal. To this purpose, he cross'd the Araxes and regulated the manner in which this project shou'd be executed the Tavatchis distributed the work among the Emirs, who were to take care that the soldiers wrought at it. This work was carry'd on with so much vigor, that in a month two entire leagues of the canal deep enough for a boat to swim in, were dug. The place where it discharges it self into the Araxes is call'd Kiochke Tchenghichi, and the spring

The history of Timur-Bec.

[read is it] a place nam'd Surcapil Timur gave [the] name of Nehri Berlas, that is, the river [of Ber]las: and on its banks have since been built [sev]eral towns, villages, mills, vineyards, gar[d]ens and pleasure-houses. Tho Timur employ'd [al]most all his time in war, with design to ren[de]r himself master of Asia, using all the means [of] policy, which seconded by fortune, hath fa[cil]itated to him the conquests of this great em[pi]re, by a chain of almost incredible victorys; yet [th]is prince, the better to transmit his memory to [pos]terity, has erected so many stately edifices [and] other famous monuments, that this canal, [wit]h all its beauty, ought to be accounted one [of] his least undertakings, since if compar'd with [the] others, 'tis but as a rivulet to the ocean.

CHAP. XLI.

Timur departs from Carabagh for the plains of Chemkour.

THE sun was now in Pisces, and the spring was advancing, when the emperor [was] as much resolv'd upon marching into the O[tto]man country, the prince whereof was his [ene]my, as he was set against it by the conside[rat]ion of the religious war which Bajazet at [th]at time so zealously maintain'd against the in[fi]dels. His heart being agitated by two dif[fe]rent motives, he remain'd in suspence. The [va]st extent of the Ottoman empire, the num[be]r and valor of its troops, who were perfectly [ski]ll'd in war, and prepar'd to defend themselves, [did] not a little contribute to keep up his irreso[lut]ion. Moreover, our troops, having been

employ'd

employ'd for three years in attacking place[s], fighting battels, and making inroads upon sev[e]ral enemys, were so fatigu'd, that the Em[irs] and generals fear'd they wou'd be dishearten['d] by this new enterprize, yet they dar'd not d[is]cover their sentiments, for fear of being though[t] guilty of cowardice or weakness. They judg['d] it most proper to reveal their mind to Chamse[d]din Almaleghi, who for his great wit, eloquenc[e] and clearness of thought, had obtain'd so mu[ch] access to Timur, that he cou'd declare his se[n]timents at any time, without being in the le[ast] thought ill of. The Emirs hereupon addres[s'd] themselves to him, and unanimously besoug[ht] him to lay hold on some favorable opportun[ity] to make known to his highness their thoughts o[n] his march into the Ottoman country, the[y] conjur'd him to let him know the consequence o[f] it, and advise him to think seriously on it, be[-] fore he began it, and they even engag'd him t[o] apprize Timur of the astrologers opinion, tha[t] in the campain against the Ottomans, there ap[-] pear'd in the heavens an inevitable misfortu[ne] attending the Zagataian army. Chamseddin wil[-]lingly undertook this commission, and represent[-] ed the Emirs sentiments to Timur, which were confirm'd by the prediction of the stars. Ti[-] mur having heard him, order'd Moulana Ab[-] dalla Lesan, one of the most famous astrologers of the court, to be call'd before him, and to take away all fear from the Emirs, he interro[-] gated him in public, and order'd him to declare freely the different aspects of the planets, and the judgment which might be form'd from thence. Abdalla hereupon deliver'd the following pre-

Admirable prediction of an astro-loge-

diction. "It appears by the Ephemerides of " the present year, that the ascendant of this " empire is in the highest degree of strength,
" and

The history of Timur-Bec.

and that of the enemy in the lowest degree of weakness. A comet will appear in Aries, and an army which comes from the east, will make an entire conquest of Natolia, the prince of which will be taken prisoner."

The 13th of Regeb 804, Timur departed from his winter-quarters, and went to encamp in a meadow dependent of Carabagh, Arran. *April 3. 1402.*

The 7th of Schaban 804, which answers to the year of the Horse, and is the first day of the Gelalian year, he departed from Carabagh Arran for Chemkour, and in the mean while the Mirza Mehemed Sultan cross'd the river of Cyrus, and advanc'd along its banks. Then Timur sent Moulana Obaid Allah Sedre to Ispahan to guard the imperial treasure there, he sent to Chiraz Moulana Cotobeddin Garmi, to regulate the expences of the Divan, and the revenues of the kingdom of Fars. and this monarch having pass'd by Berda and Ghendge, went down to the plains of Chemkour. They staid here some days, that the cattel might graze, and then they march'd towards Alatac. *April 27*

When the army was encamp'd at Tabadar, which is on the frontiers of Georgia, on the 4th of Ramadan 804, which answers to the 16th of the month Ourdibehicht 324 of the Gelalian epocha, a son was born to the Mirza Charoc under the horoscope of Cancer. The emperor return'd thanks to God, and nam'd the prince Mehemed Dgiouki. the empresses, Mirzas, and great Emirs congratulated his highness and the Mirza Charoc on this happy birth, and the princess Canzade was appointed his governess. The Mirza Mehemed Sultan, who had pass'd the river of Cyrus, pillag'd the inhabitants of the mountain Alburz Couh, and then return'd to the camp at Tabadar. *June 13. Birth of Mehemed Dgiouki.*

When

Book V.

When the army was on their march, Timur order'd the empresses, and the Mirza's wife to return home with the young princes, and they were conducted by Cohlugadgi. They staid at Tauris the rest of the summer, and towards autumn they went to Sultania. Timur at his arrival at Mencoul, not being willing to do any thing against the rules of policy, sent a second ambassador to Bajazet, with a letter in these terms.

Timur's letter to Bajazet.

" After the usual compliments, we give you
" advice, that tho we are on our march to meet
" you, yet our word is the same as we have be-
" fore declar'd · if you consent to what we de-
" sire, and put into the hands of our lieutenant
" the fortress of Kemac, which has been al-
" ways subject to the countrys under our obedi-
" ence, we will let you peaceably enjoy the king-
" dom of Natolia, that you may continue the
" war against the enemys of the Mussulmans,
" and we will not refuse the succour which you
" may expect on that account. Do what you
" think best for your good."

CHAP. XLII.

Taking of the castle of Tartoum.

TIMUR having been inform'd that there was a strong place in those quarters, nam'd Tartoum, in which were two hundred Georgians who refus'd to pay tribute, and insulted the Mussulmans and passengers, and that the prince who commanded 'em was absent, and had left in his place a lieutenant nam'd Ghurdgibec, his highness commanded the Emirs Chamelik, Cheik Noureddin, and others, to attack the place, and take it at any rate. They accordingly

The history of Timur-Bec.

..., came before it; and sent to acquaint the enemy, that if they wou'd willingly surrender, and pay the tribute, they shou'd have quarter: but they refus'd so to do, and trusting to the strength of the castle, prepar'd to defend themselves. Our soldiers made the great cry, Alla Ecber, and Salli Alla Mehammed[1]; and having invested the place, they gave several assaults, discharging infinite showers of arrows. The besieg'd vigorously defended themselves for five days, and the sixth the place was taken: our men put all the Georgians to the sword, and having overthrown the walls, they raz'd the place, even to the very foundations. The governor, who escap'd, came to the foot of the throne to beg pardon, and obtain'd quarter for his life.

Timur staid at Avenic till the return of the ambassadors he had sent to Bajazet. When two months beyond the time agreed on were past, and he had no news from the ambassadors, he grew impatient. " In truth, said he, extraction
" is a strange thing. Whatever mildness we use
" with regard to Bajazet, in order to preserve
" Natolia, as being the frontiers of the Mus-
" sulman country, and hinder as far as we are
" able its being destroy'd by our troops; yet
" the Turcoman blood of this ignoble person
" won't permit him to deal civilly with us,
" and preserve peace and friendship between us.
" He does not send back our ambassadors, but
" carrys his hatred and hostility so far, that we
" are constrain'd to enter his country with an
" army, tho we have no desire to seize by force
" on his dominions and effects. But this is the

---
[1] That is to say, God is the most great, and God bless Mahomet.

" result

"result of providence, whose depths we are not "able to fathom: and we know not whether "the effects are design'd for good or evil till "they happen."

Timur sent back to Sultania the second empress Touman Aga, with the Mirza Sadvaccas, son of the Mirza Mehemed Sultan; and he afterwards continu'd his march towards Natolia. When he was arriv'd at Erzerom, he was join'd by the Mirzas and Emirs who had pass'd the winter in Courdistan and Chaldea, where they had pillag'd and exterminated the enemys, as we said before, and had departed thence in the spring, with great quantity of booty, by the road of Coulaghi, and the mountain of Sounatai.

CHAP. XLIII.

Taking of the castle of Kemac. Arrival of ambassadors from Bajazet.

THE castle of Kemac is one of the most noted in Asia, it is situate upon a high steep rock, and is surrounded with a defile in form of a labyrinth. At the bottom of its walls are gardens and parterres of flowers on the bank of the Euphrates, and no prince has ever taken it by force. Several poets have compar'd it to the terrestrial paradise, because yearly for three days together, little birds, as big as sparrows, and unfledg'd, fall out of the air, the inhabitants gather 'em up, salt 'em, and preserve 'em in pots. If they don't take 'em in three days, their wings grow large enough to fly away.

The Mirza Mehemed Sultan besought the emperor to honor him with a commission to conquer this place, which having obtain'd, he departed with the Emirs of Tomans and Hezares, with all the arms and machines necessary for a siege. Timur being arriv'd at Arzendgian, sent the Mirzas Aboubecre, Calil Sultan, Sultan Hussein, and Eskender, with the Emirs Gehan Chah, Cheik Noureddin, and Berendac, to join the Mirza Mehemed Sultan; which they had no sooner done, than they besieg'd the place in turn. The siege continu'd ten whole days, during which our soldiers stop'd the water which flow'd into the place. The eleventh night they made rope-ladders, on which the Mecrit soldiers, who run upon the steepest mountains like roe-bucks, got to the top of the mountain; and when they were there, they fix'd cords, which they let down to the bottom. The Mirza Mehemed Sultan order'd a number of brave men, whose names he wrote down, to mount by these cords, which they did, arm'd with their cuirasses, during the darkness of the night. The besieg'd perceiving 'em defended themselves, and cast down great stones upon 'em. Alicher, nephew of the Emir Abbas, and others, miss'd the steps, and fell. The next morning our soldiers mounted to the assault, at the sound of drums and kettle-drums; and the wild-fire in pots were cast with machines from both sides: our men also attack'd 'em with arrows and stones; and every one gave marks of the greatest valor. The Mirza Mehemed Sultan us'd all his endeavors to encourage his soldiers. The Mirza Aboubecre did wonders; and his officers first scal'd the walls, and erected their horse-tail. At the same time the others mounted on all sides

sides, and enter'd the place, of which they made themselves masters

Timur having advice of the taking of this place, departed from the meadow of Arzendgian, and came before the castle of Kemac, the government of which he gave to prince Taharten, because it was no more than seven leagues from Arzendgian

From thence he began his march in earnest for the conquest of the Ottoman empire and as several peasants and laborers were retreated into caverns and steep places, he sent Emirs to attack 'em But these men having at a distance perceiv'd the number of his troops, were seiz'd with fear so they came up to 'em, and with submission beg'd quarter, which was granted 'em. The army being encamp'd at Sebaste, Bajazid Tchempai Eltchik arriv'd there from theOttoman Porte, accomany'd by fresh ambassadors from the emperor Bajazet, he gave an account to the emperor of his negotiation, and presented the answer to the letter he had writ to the Ottoman This answer, which was very haughty and arrogant, made appear that fate had resolv'd the ruin of this monarchy and Bajazet, to excuse his not surrendring up the castle of Kemac, alledg'd reasons very unsatisfactory to Timur's council

The Ottoman ambassadors being admitted to audience thro the intercession of the princes of the blood, they kiss'd the imperial carpet, offer'd their presents, which consisted of ten horses of great price, several animals proper for the chace, and divers other raritys, and on their knees declar'd the subject of their embassy The emperor having heard 'em, fell into a great passion, refus'd their presents, and thus address'd

him

"... If to the person who had been the speaker.
" If it were not an infamous action for princes
" to put to death an ambassador, I wou'd this
" hour separate your head from your body."
He having a little moderated his fury, he said:
" When fortune ceases to be propitious, counsel
" becomes useless, for tho we had no intention
" to hurt your country, yet we are constrain'd
" by that faithless prince's manner of acting, to
" make war upon him. Had he sent Cara Yousef
" to me, and deliver'd up the castle of Kemac
" to my lieutenants, he might have remain'd
" quiet in his kingdom. God be thank'd, this
" castle has been reduc'd to obedience by the
" valor of our soldiers. Tell him from me, that
" since he has refus'd to attend to my counsel,
" and has carry'd his obstinacy so far, he must
" prepare himself like a brave man to sustain the
" attacks of our ever-victorious army."

CHAP. XLIV.

Timur reviews his army.

TIMUR having resolv'd to attack Bajazet in his own dominions, order'd the troops to rendezvous in the plain of Sebaste to pass in view. He posted himself upon an eminence to examine their ranks, arms, and countenance. When any squadron pass'd before him, the captain advanc'd, fell on his knees, and holding his horse by the bridle, made his compliment to his highness generally in these terms. " Our " lives shall always be employ'd in the service of " our great emperor: we will not leave a plant " or shrub in the enemy's lands; but we'll sack
" Na-

Book V "Natolia, and deftroy the Ottoman" Timur anfwer'd thefe compliments, by encouraging 'em always to behave themfelves like brave men, rather to acquire honor, than in hopes of a reward.

Thus all the army march'd one after the other by Tomans, Hezares and Couchons, with great ceremony. But when the troops of the Mirza Mehemed Sultan, which came frefh from Samarcand, pafs'd by, Timur admir'd their beauty, order and magnificence: for as good order in an army is the fole and primary caufe of victory, this Mirza had divided his into feveral bodys, which had each a ftandard of a particular color, that they might rally when at a diftance from each other, and be known in the heat of a battel. A certain number of fquadrons had their ftandards and enfigns red, as likewife their cuiraffes, faddles, quivers, belts lances, bucklers, clubs, and other arms, of the fame color. Another body of the army was yellow, and another white: there were likewife violet and other colors in the fame order. One regiment had all coats of mail, and another cuiraffes. The Mirza having made his troops pafs in this pompous manner, paid his compliments to the emperor.

The review lafted from break of day till afternoon, when Timur went to prayers. He order'd the Ottoman ambaffadors to be conducted thro all the ranks: they admir'd the arms and beauty of the equipages, and were feiz'd with fear at the fight of this great multitude of foldiers, having never feen any thing like it. Next day Timur gave prefents to the ambaffadors and at the audience of leave made the following fpeech to 'em: "Tell Bajazet, that becaufe he employs the whole ftrength of his "empi

empire to make war on the infidels, we are
... we must be constrain'd to conduct our
army into his country, that notwithstanding
... our reasons to make war with him, we
are yet willing to adjust matters with him,
and pardon him He need only restore to us
the officers belonging to prince Taharten,
whom he hath seiz'd, and send to us one of
his sons, whom we will regard as our own
child, and treat with more courtesy than he
has ever receiv'd from his father. On these
conditions the empire of Natolia shall remain unmolested; the war shall cease, and
the inhabitants of his country shall continue
in peace and tranquillity, and have reason to
praise their prince's clemency, on whom the
merit of this action shall fall."

CHAP. XLV.

Taking of the castle of Harouc.

AFTER the Ottoman ambassadors return, the spys who had orders to give
notice of every thing which pass'd, inform'd the
emperor that in those quarters there was a
castle nam'd Harouc, into which a great number
of inhabitants were retreated, having fortify'd the
place, with design to make an obstinate defence.
The Emirs Cheik Noureddin and Berendac
were order'd to ruin this fortress: they departed
at the same time, and being arriv'd before Harouc, they cast into it so great a quantity of
wild fire, that they made the inhabitants retire from their walls, and no one dar'd shew
their heads. In the mean while the sappers
work'd

work'd with a great deal of brisknefs, and foon cast down the walls. A general affault was immediately given, and all the peafants put to the fword.

CHAP. XLVI.

Timur marches to Cæfarea in Cappadocia, and to Ancora.

WHEN the army was encamp'd in the neighborhood of Sebafte, the guides brought advice that the road of Tocat was full of forefts, the paffages of which are extremely narrow, that Bajazet was arriv'd at Tocat with a numerous army, and had feiz'd on the paffage of the river [1]. This oblig'd Timur to turn towards the fouthern fide of Natolia. He took the road to Cæfarea in Cappadocia, and fent before Ali Sultan Tavachi to hinder the troops going into the city. Timur was fix days in his march from Sebafte to Cæfarea, where he ftaid fome time, and granted quarter to the inhabitants, as well the criminal as the innocent. Some fled for refuge into caverns and caves, whom the foldiers perceiving, pillag'd their effects, becaufe of their being fo fufpicious. As it was the feafon for reaping the corn and pulfe in that country, the foldiers had orders to gather enough for the ammunition appointed to 'em. Timur nam'd the Mirza Aboubecre, and the Emir Cheik Noureddin for leaders of the

---

[1] The river of Cozel Irmac, which falls into the Euxine or black fea, and paffes by Amafia.

scouts and he departed for Ancora, arm'd with his cuirass and helmet. He march'd three days on the bank of the river nam'd Youlgoun Sou, and the fouth he encamp'd at Kircheter ², where he had advice that Bajazet's army had been seen.

Hereupon he gave orders for the army to march that way and encamp; and round the camp to dig a trench, which shou'd be fortify'd with bucklers and palisadoes: Timur sent the Emir Chamelic with a thousand horse to gain intelligence. This Emir being favor'd by the night, advanc'd about two leagues towards the enemy's cavalry, and at break of day he discover'd he was near Bajazet's camp: so he hid himself in an ambuscade to wait a good opp'nity. As soon as the enemy's scouts appear'd, he fell upon 'em, and a bloody skirmish ensu'd. Bajazet was very much surpriz'd, to hear that a handful of Tartars had dar'd attack his scouts so near his camp; and cou'd not refrain from expressing his sorrow at it to his Emirs: whereupon he decamp'd at sun-rise, and took the road to Kircheher. Chamelic sent a courier to Timur to give him an account of the skirmish, and of Bajazet's march. Then Timur sent Elias Coja, Sainte Maure, Mourad, and others, to the number of sixty, to gain intelligence of Bajazet: and the Emir Chamelic return'd in the evening to the imperial camp.

At break of day, Timur deliver'd his sentiments to the Mirzas and Emirs in the following manner. " There are, says he, two
' different opinions with relation to our con-
' duct in the present conjuncture. one is, that

---

² A city between Cæsarea and Ancora, long 66. 30. lat. 39.

Book V. "we wait the enemy here, to give time to our
"soldiers and horses to repose themselves from
"the fatigues of a long journy; the other,
"that we march into the midst of his country,
"and ravage it, which will oblige him to pur-
"sue us with expedition; and so we shall de-
"stroy his army, which for the most part con-
"sists of infantry." He resolv'd upon the last,
and order'd his army to march. He left in the
camp the Mirza Sultan Hussein with two thousand horse, and he sent before to Ancora ¹ the
Emirs Berendac, Belleri, and other captains of
companys, with orders to shut up the passage
against the enemys they shou'd meet; some infantry were order'd to march with 'em, to dig
wells in those places where they were to encamp
at night. These Emirs march'd according to
order, and were follow'd by Abderrahman Tavachi at the head of the infantry. Those who
had been sent out the preceding day to gain
intelligence, met a party of the enemy, whom
they put to flight, cut off the head of one,
and took another prisoner.

In the mean while the emperor Bajazet's son
advanc'd at the head of a thousand horse towards our camp, to observe our motions. He
pass'd the night near our army without being
perceiv'd, and laid in ambuscade in a defile. In
the morning, when our men return'd from making inroads, he attack'd 'em, and as they were
but sixty in number, he had certainly defeated
'em, tho they fought bravely, and always advanc'd towardss our camp, had he not perceiv'd
the squadrons of the Mirza Sultan Hussein, who

---

¹ A great city in Natolia, the same as Anghuria, long. 65.

The history of Timur-Bec.

were come to their assistance: so he was constrain'd to abandon 'em, and retreat.

The Emirs and infantry, who had taken the road to Ancora, acquitted themselves exactly of their orders. The cavalry march'd as far as the city, pillaging all the country: and the infantry who follow'd 'em, dug wells in the road, to get water for the rest. Timur finding the way so good, went in three days to Ancora, and encamp'd near it with all his army. An Emir, nam'd Yacoub, was governor of the fortress for the Ottoman emperor: and the garison consisted of several of the bravest men in that country, who were resolv'd to defend themselves to the last. Next day Timur took horse, and rode round the city to view it. Then he gave orders for the water of a rivulet which runs into the city to be cut off, and the walls to be sapp'd, while the sappers shou'd be back'd as usual. Some of our brave men even scal'd a bastion which looks upon the rivulet, and almost made themselves entire masters of the town: but advice was brought from our scouts, that Pajazet was advancing with design to fall upon our army in the rear, and was but at four leagues distance. On this Timur forthwith order'd the siege to be rais'd, and that those who were mounted on the bastion shou'd come down again, and they forthwith decamp'd.

The army march'd not far that day, but encamp'd, leaving the river behind 'em. Then a trench was dug round about the camp, and fortify'd with bucklers and palisadoes, fires being made all the night. There was a little fountain at the foot of a hill near the passage of the enemy's army: and as the Ottomans had no other water than this, Timur sent a great body of soldiers to destroy this fountain, and corrupt the water. When

When night came, Timur enter'd his closet as usual, to humble himself before God, and beseech him to give him the victory, when in the most devout manner he offer'd up the following prayer: "O Lord, who art the great creator "of the universe, and my particular benefactor; "it is of thy grace alone that I hold the victo- "rys I have obtain'd during the whole cour[se] "of my life; for what am I? Does not the "union betwixt my soul and body depend on "thy will? And thus, Lord, what thou hast "done for me, redounds to thy glory, and "thou art the conqueror and the triumpher. "On this occasion therefore I beg the continua- "tion of thy favor, which thou hast never ye[t] "refus'd me. Why then shou'd I despair?"

CHAP. XLVII.

Timur ranges his army in order of battel, to fight Bajazet.

TIMUR having spent the night in prayer, at break of day gave orders that the drums shou'd be beat, and that every one shou'[d] march out of the entrenchments with their ar[ms] to prepare for battel. Then he rang'd his army in order. The left wing was commanded by the Mirzas Charoc and Calil Sultan, who [had] for their lieutenant-general the Emir Solym-[] Chah; and the vanguard of this left wing was led by the Mirza Sultan Hussein, who had under him Ali Sultan. The right wing was under the command of the Mirza Miran Chah, who ha[d] for his lieutenant-general the Emir Cheik No[t-] reddin; the vanguard of this wing was given the Mirza Aboubecre, whose lieutenant was the Emir Gehan Chah.

The main-body consisted of a vast number of the greatest lords in Asia: forty colonels at the head of their regiments were on the right, and as many on the left. The Mirza Mehemed Sultan was general of the whole body; and before him was carry'd the great staff, on whose top was a red horse-tail, and upon that a half-moon. he had for his lieutenants-general the Mirzas Pir Mehemed, Omar Cheik, Eskender, and other princes his brothers, with the Emirs Chimseddin Abbas, Chamelic, Elias Coja, and others Timur commanded the body of reserve, compos'd of forty compleat companys well arm'd, with which he design'd to succour that part of the army which shou'd have most need of assistance. He order'd several ranks of elephants to be posted at the head of the whole army, as well to intimidate the enemy, as to serve for trophys of the spoils of India. They were cover'd with the most splendid trappings, and as usual arm'd with towers on their backs, in which were plac'd archers and casters of wildfire, to spread terror and disorder wherever they shou'd go.

Bajazet also took care to range his army in order of battel. The right wing was commanded by Pesir Laus an European, his wife's brother, with twenty thousand cavalry of Europe, all arm'd in steel from head to foot, so that nothing cou'd be seen but their eyes. Their armor is fasten'd below the foot by a padlock, which except they open, their cuirass and helmet can't be taken off.

The left was led by Mussulman Chelebi son of Bajazet, and compos'd of the troops of Natolia. The main-body was under the command

mand of Bajazet himself, having for his lieutenants-general his three sons Mouffa, Aifa, and Muftafa. The moft skilful of his five sons, nam'd Mehemed Chelebi, and firnam'd Kirichtchi, was at the head of the rear, and had for his lieutenants Balfouh Pacha, Ali Pacha, Hafan Pacha, Mourad Pacha, Aidbe, and Pachadgic, with a great number of brave captains

Thus the Ottoman advanc'd in good order, and well equip'd, full of ardor to come to blows with our Tartars, who were not lefs defirous of that than himfelf.

About ten in the morning, the infantry with their bucklers before 'em pofted themfelves on the neighboring hills. The drum was beat for the battel to begin, and the great cry Souroun made, at the found of the large trumpet Kerrenai.

CHAP. XLVIII.

Timur gives Bajazet battel, and gains the victory.

THE two armys rang'd in order of battel came in view of each other, being refolv'd either to conquer or die. The drums and kettle-drums were beat, and Timur got off his horfe to go to prayers, following the counfel of the Santon Abdalla Evfari. then he remounted, and gave orders for attacking the enemy

The Mirza Aboubecre, at the head of the vanguard of the right wing, began the battel by a difcharge of arrows on the enemy's left wing, commanded by Muffulman Chelebi, Bajazet's eldeft fon The Emirs Gehan Chah and

and Cara Ofman did wonders, breaking thro the left wing Kirichtchi, the moſt valiant of Bajazet's children, perform'd very noble actions, but when he had prov'd the ſtrength and intrepidity of our ſoldiers, he found it impoſſible to reſiſt 'em, and ſo took up a reſolution to fly with his troops. The Sultan Huſſein, who commanded the vanguard of our left wing, advanc'd vigorouſly upon the enemy's right, of whom he made a cruel ſlaughter The Mirza Mehemed Sultan on his knees beſought Timur to give him leave to enter the field of battel; and our monarch perceiving our left wing had advanc'd too far, ſent this Mirza to back it. He accordingly march'd thither at the head of all the Behaders ' whom he commanded, and ruſhing full ſpeed into the midſt of the Ottoman army, he broke their ranks, and put 'em into great diſorder The Europeans on the other hand, falling upon our men, gave marks of a prodigious valor and invincible courage. Each party ſometimes repuls'd its adverſary, and were as often repuls'd by him: but at length our ſoldiers had the advantage by the death of prince Peſir Laus, as alſo by the ſlaughter of the infantry of the enemy's right wing. The Mirzas Pir Mehemed, Omar Cheik and Eskender, with the Emirs Chamelic, Cheik Noureddin and Berendac, chas'd the enemy's infantry from the hills where it was poſted. Timur perceiving the enemy begin to give way, order'd the Mirzas and Emirs to fall upon the Ottomans with all the army. Theſe generals accordingly advanc'd ſword in hand: and quickly made ſo terrible a ſlaughter, that the great

---

' The Behaders are the braveſt men of the army, as the forlorn hope are among us.

battel

battel between thofe of Iran and thofe of Touran, commanded by Rouftem and Esfendiar, was nothing in comparifon to it. Part of the Ottoman army was put to the fword, and the reft fled.

While the Mirza Mehemed Sultan routed the enemy's right wing, fix companys belonging to this Mirza afcended a hill, which properly was their poft. Bajazet, obferving their fmall number, attack'd 'em at the head of his main-body, and having chas'd 'em from that poft, drew up his own men there. Our foldiers having join'd the Mirza, rally'd; and being ftrengthen'd with feveral regiments, return'd with defign to attack Bajazet's main body. The Ottoman emperor having carefully examin'd from the hill the difpofition of his army, and perceiving the diforder, or rather defeat, of his two wings, was feiz'd with fear. And as feveral of his foldiers came to him, who had fled out of both his right and left wing, Timur advanc'd thither himfelf with the Mirza Charoc, and enter'd into the midft of the enemy. The Mirza Miran Chah, with the Emirs of the right wing, and the Mirza Sultan Huffein, with the Emir Solyman Chah, and others of the left wing, haften'd thither likewife; and at the fame time all the troops, falling upon Bajazet, furrounded him with his army, like beafts in the circle of a chace. The Ottoman defended himfelf like a brave hero, and skilful warrior: he maintain'd his ground all the day, notwithftanding the miferable ftate he was reduc'd to, and when night was come, he defcended from the hill, and fled. Our foldiers difcharg'd a fhower of arrows upon him, and flew feveral of his men, while himfelf efcap'd from that danger. Several of our brave warriors purfu'd him fword in hand, killing

The history of Timur-Bec.

...very one they met, and as the sun was in ...xth degree of Leo, it was so hot, that most ...ose who fled dy'd of thirst, there being no ...er in the place where they went to rest them-...

After the battel Timur return'd to his camp, ...gave thanks to God for this glorious victory. ...e Mirzas and Emirs on their knees congratu-...ed him, and sprinkled upon him gold and pre-...us stones. This victory happen'd on friday ...e 19th of Zilcade 804, which answers to the ...r of the Horse.

Chap 49.

July 1. 1402.

C H A P. XLIX.

...he taking of the Ottoman emperor, who is brought in chains before the throne of the conqueror.

BAJAZET cou'd not fly so swiftly, but that he was overtaken by our brave men, ...o went in pursuit of him. The Sultan Mah-...oud * Can seiz'd him, bound him as a prisoner, ...d sent him under a good guard to Timur, to ...hom he was presented at the hour of sun-set, ...ith his hands bound, by the great Emirs. Ti-...r perceiving him in this condition, cou'd not ...le the tenderness of his heart; but was mov'd ...h compassion, and taking pity on the misfor-...ne of so great a prince, order'd his hands to ...e unbound, and he to be brought before him ...th respect. When Bajazet was admitted to ...e chamber of audience, Timur went to receive ...m at the door of his tent, with great cere-...ony, and causing him to sit down by him, he ...ver'd himself to him after this manner.

* Grand Can of Zagatai.

" Tho

Book V

Timur's speech to Bajazet.

"Tho accidents in this world happen thro'
"the will of God, and no one, how powerful
"soever, can conduct 'em as he pleases, yet it
"may be justly said, that you are the sole cause
"of the misfortunes which have befallen you.
"They are thorns which your-self have planted,
"and a net which you have wove. You have let
"your feet stray beyond their bounds, and have
"constrain'd me to march against you, to re-
"venge my self for your insults. I cou'd not
"resolve upon any thing, because I knew that
"your troops were always at war with the infi-
"dels. I have us'd all possible ways of mildness,
"and my intention was, if you had hearken'd
"to my counsels, and consented to a peace, to
"have given you powerful succours, both of
"mony and troops, to carry on the war for reli-
"gion with greater vigor, and to exterminate
"the enemys of Mahomet. To prove your
"friendship, I entreated you to deliver up the
"fortress of Kemac, and to send back the family
"and officers of Taharten, as also to drive
"out of your country Cara Yousef Turcoman,
"and send to my court an ambassador who
"might be confided in, to confirm the treatys
"of peace between us, but you haughtily re-
"fus'd to grant these small trifles, and conti-
"nu'd in your stubborness till affairs were drove
"to an extremity. Every one knows, if God
"had favor'd you with the victory, as he has
"me, in what manner you design'd to have
"treated me and my army. Notwithstanding
"all this, to return thanks to God for my good
"fortune in this battel, I will neither treat you
"nor your friends ill, and you may rest satisfy'd
"as to that point."

Bajazet's answer to Timur.

Bajazet, full of confusion, confess'd his fault
in these terms: "I have indeed done ill in not
"follow-

The history of Timur-Bec.

' following the counsels of so great an emperor,
' and have likewise receiv'd the punishment I
' merited. If your majesty is willing to pardon
" me, I swear that neither my self nor children
' shall turn aside from the paths of obedience to
" your orders".

Timur then gave him a splendid vest, and comforted him by kind promises, and by treating him as a great emperor. Bajazet perceiving Timur's generosity, remonstrated to him, that his children Mouffa and Muftafa were with him in the battel, that his heart being tenderly affected to 'em, he befought him to order that search might be made after 'em, and if living, that they might be brought to him adding, that this wou'd be an addition to the obligations he shou'd be under to him during the remainder of his life

Then the emperor order'd the Tavatchis to search every where for Bajazet's children they found only Mouffa, whom they brought to Timur, who gave him a vest, and sent him to his father, for whom he had order'd a royal pavilion to be erected near his own, commanding Hafan Berlas and Bayazid Tchempai to keep guard at the gate, and furnish Bajazet with every thing he shou'd want. Timur, in ufing Bajazet after this generous manner, imitated the great prophet Mahomet, who, after the conquest of Mecca, return'd thanks to God, and thus addrefs'd the inhabitants : " How do you think I shall use you
" at this time ?" They anfwer'd in the proverb :
' You are a generous brother, and the son of a
' generous brother. and the generous man par-
' dons when it lies in his power." Mahomet
' said to 'em, " I tell you the same that Joseph
' told his brethren, who had misus'd him, I

Chap 49.

Timur treats Bajazet with honour and respect.

Vol. II.   R   " have

" have nothing to reproach you with, may God
" pardon you, for he is infinitely merciful."

CHAP. L.

Timur orders troops to make inroads in divers parts of the Ottoman empire. He sends relations of his victory to the citys of Iran and Touran, with orders to make public rejoicings.

TIMUR then decamp'd, and went down to the meadow of Ancora, the governor of which place, nam'd Yacoub, came out to cast himself at his feet, and beg his pardon, after having deliver'd up the castle to the officers of the court, who resign'd it to Ali Sultan Tavachi. Then the commissarys of the Divan began to receive the tribute impos'd on the inhabitants of conquer'd places, as a ransom for their lives

Timur sent the Mirza Mehemed Sultan northwards to the city of Prusa [a] in Bithynia, the seat of the Ottoman empire, and he was accompany'd by the Mirza Aboubecre, and the Emir Gehan Chah, Cheik Noureddin, Sevindgic, and others, with their Tomans. The emperor order'd the Emir Cheik Noureddin to stay at Prusa, and seize on all the treasures of Bajazet, and the riches of that city He likewise commanded the Mirzas and Emirs to ravage all the country as far as to the banks of Isara Yaca [b], otherwise

---

[a] Call'd Broussa by the Turks; it is situate at the foot of mount Olympus and was the seat of the Ottoman empire, before the Turks took Adrianople.

[b] A shore towards Europe.

nam'd the defile of Alexander. He also sent the Mirza Eskender with several Emirs towards Iconium ³, Akcheher ³, Caraifer ³, Olaya ³, and Satalia ⁴.

Afterwards Timur order'd an account of his victory, and the conquest of the Ottoman empire, to be drawn up by Moulana Chamfeddin Munchi, and sent into all the kingdoms of his empire, that public rejoicings might be made. One letter was dispatch'd to the empreffes at Sultania, another to the Mirza Omar at Samarcand, another to the Mirza Pir Mehemed Gehanghir at Cabul and Zabul in India; another to the Mirza Rouftem at Chiraz, the feat of the kingdom of Perfia, and others into Turkeftan, Cachgar, Cotan, Bedakchan, Coraffana, Carezem, Mazendram, Tabareftan, Ghilan, Azerbijana, Irac-Arabi, Irac-Agemi, Kirman, Kidget-Mecran, and the maritim countrys. The couriers who carry'd thefe letters had each of 'em a guide. On the arrival of one of them at Yezd, the Coja Cayafeddin Selar Semnani, who had refided there to receive Timur's revenues, built a magnificent chappel in the middle of the great fquare, which he nam'd the chappel of victory.

The Mirza Calil Sultan had orders to go with his troops to Samarcand, and from thence to the frontiers of Turkeftan, and to take care of the limits of the kingdom; he was accompany'd by the Emirs Mobacher and Dolet Timur Tavachi. As the Emir Acbouga, governor of Herat, was dead, the Emir Mezrab had orders to repair to that place, and accompany the Mirza as far as Coraffana, where he fhou'd ftop.

---

³ Famous citys of Roum.   ⁴ A town of Caramania.

Timur departed from Ancora, and in six days arriv'd at the fortress of Sourihhissar, the walls of which place he ascended, and observ'd the neighborhood with circumspection. He sent the Mirza Charoc to Ghulhissar⁶, Estanous⁶, and Ketir⁷, with ten Tomans of the left wing. The emperor afterwards went in two days to Khiontahia⁸, a delightful town, as well for the pureness of the air, and the charming taste of the fruits, as for the beauty of its pleasure-houses, and the number of its fountains. As this place exceedingly pleas'd him, he staid here a month, and granted quarter to the inhabitants, on paying the accustom'd ransom to his commissarys, who at the same time seiz'd on the goods which Temour Tach had laid up for a long time in this place. As soon as Timur was arriv'd there, he sent the Emirs Chamelic, Abdelkerim, and Hadgi Seifeddin, with several captains of companys, to Kiarada⁹, Coja Eili¹, and Menecha².

Timur, being highly pleas'd with the conquest of Natolia, and the taking of the Ottoman emperor prisoner, resolv'd to make solemn feasts and rejoicings, to recreate himself after the fatigues of war. The most beautiful ladys of the court were at these diversions, where the best wines of Asia were drank, and the musicians perform'd extraordinarily. In the mean while the troops sent out to make inroads,

---

⁶ Towns of Roum towards the north.
⁷ A town of Roum northwards, long. 62. lat. 43.
⁸ Or Choutava, a noted city of Roum, long 61. lat. 41.
⁹ A town of Roum near Rhodes.
¹ A province of Roum near Rhodes.
² A province near Satalia, which has a town of the same name.

The history of Timur-Bec.

plunder'd and ravag'd all Natolia. The meanest soldier became in a manner a great lord by the booty he had gain'd; and he who before had not a single horse, was now master of several tables throng'd with 'em The whole army return'd thanks to their Creator, who had so enrich'd 'em. Timur distributed the treasures of Tocou Tach among the Emirs, which were in the custody of the commissarys, and he reserv'd nothing for his own use, to shew 'em that he fought rather for them, than for himself.

CHAP. LI.

The continuation of the history of the Mirza Mehemed Sultan, who had been sent to Prusa in Bithynia.

THE Mirza Mehemed Sultan being departed from Ancora for Prusa, according to the emperor's order, made so much haste in the five days he was marching, that of the thirty thousand horse he had, but four thousand arriv'd with him at Prusa Yet he cou'd not get there soon enough to execute the design he had in hand, for Mussulman Chelebi had got there before him, and fled with all the treasures belonging to his father, which he cou'd get along with him. The principal inhabitants of the city also fled with their effects and families, some to mount Olympus, otherwise nam'd Kechich Daghi, at the foot of which the city of Prusa is situate; and others to the sea-shore Our soldiers pursu'd 'em, pillag'd and brought em away bound. The grand Cheik Chamseddin Mehemed Jazari, with the chief men of Prusa, was

was met in the plains of Kurya, by the Cherifs Mehemed Bocari, and Chamfeddin Fanari, and others, who were gone out to make inroads: the pillag'd the Cheik, and brought him with his son to the Emir Cheik Noureddin Bajazet's wife and two daughters, who had hid themselves in a house in the town of Yenicheher[1], were taken; as was likewise the daughter of the Sultan Ahmed Gelair, king of Bagdad, whom Bajazet had demanded in marriage for his son Muſtafa, and who staid at Prufa with her attendants, while her father return'd to Bagdad from the country of the Ottomans, to which he had fled for refuge from our troops.

As for Cara Youſef, as ſoon as our army arriv'd in the neighborhood of Cæſarea in Cappadocia, he fled from Prufa to Hille, and from thence to the deſart of Arabia.

After Prufa was reduc'd under the emperor's obedience with very little reſiſtance, the Emir Cheik Noureddin enter'd the caſtle, and ſeiz'd on what was left of Bajazet's riches, among which were a great deal of ſilver-mony, veſſels and furniture of gold and ſilver, pearls and precious ſtones, rich ſtuffs, ſplendid habits, and other curioſitys which had been laying up together a long time. Ali Semnani and Seifeddin Tofni, Bitilchis or ſecretarys to the imperial council, wrote an inventory of theſe riches.

Burning of the city of Prufa. When they had carry'd away the wealth of the place, the city and caſtle were pillag'd by the ſoldiers, and afterwards the houſes were ſet on fire, which being built of wood, were ſoon conſum'd.

---

[1] Four leagues from Prufa and ſix days journy from Conſtantunople, the ſame as Yenicheher.

The history of Timur-Bec.   263

As soon as the troops which had been left be- Chap. 51.
hind were arriv'd, the Mirza Mehemed Sultan
march'd to the sea-shore, and sent to Nice [1] the
Mirza Aboubecre with ten thousand men;
which is one of the most famous citys of Natolia, the air and water being very wholesom.
Near it is a lake two days journy in circumference, whose water is exceeding sweet and
agreeable This city is situate near the Thra-
cian Bosphorus.

Timur sent the Emir Sevindgic with a great
body of the army to Kianende [2], and along the
sea shore, and this Emir pillag'd all that country The Mirza Aboubecre being come to
Nice, march'd as far as the sea, slaying and
plundering all he met Musiulman Chelebi was
there with several peasants · but having again
perceiv'd the fury of our soldiers, he found it
was impossible for the Ottomans, in ever so
great numbers, to resist 'em : so he embark'd,
and cross'd the sea *A seasonable retreat,* says
the proverb, *is sometimes as good as a victory.*
Having pass'd the Bosphorus, he went to Sara
laca, and his wife and effects fell into the hands
of our soldiers. After the pillage of Nice, our
soldiers ruin'd that town, and went as far as
Ienitche, ravaging every thing, and making
the people slaves The Mirza Aboubecre sent
advice of the taking of Nice to the Mirza Mehemed Sultan, assuring him that all the country
was reduc'd under the emperor's obedience, and
that Musiulman Chelebi was fled with great difficulty into Europe. The Mirza receiv'd this

---

[1] A city of Bithynia, famous for the first general council
held in it long. 58 35. lat. 43.
[2] A town on the gulf of Nice.

R 4   news

news at his camp in his meadow of Micalidge, of which he sent word to the emperor, as also of the state of other affairs, by a hundred men, who immediately departed. He also sent by the same persons a Choncar, which is a very large bird of prey, besides several other presents of great price. The Mirza Aboubecre also sent a Choncar by Ac Sultan.

Between Prusa and Kioutahia, which are two days journy from each other, is a mountain full of very close trees, above four leagues in length, into which several peasents had fled for refuge; they attack'd the Mirza's messengers in a defile with advantage. Our men, tho far inferior to 'em, stood their ground, and thro Timur's good fortune, Mehemed Couroumichi Yesouri, Ibrahim Ahmed, Facreddin, Mehemed Calander, and Kefer, defended themselves with so much bravery, that a great slaughter ensued, and the enemy were constrain'd to retreat, and let 'em pass by. They had the honor to salute the emperor at Kioutahia, and offer their presents, after having given him an account of all that had happen'd.

The Emir Cheik Noureddin having separated the gold and precious stones from the other riches of Bajazet's treasury, of which he had taken possession, deliver'd 'em to Chamseddin Almalighi, whom he sent to Timur under a convoy of several brave men. Chamseddin carry'd all to his highness at Kioutahia. The Mirza Mehemed Sultan being return'd from Micalidge, took up his quarters at Prusa, where he was join'd by the Mirza Aboubecre, who was come from making inroads. The Emir Sevindgic also came there, after having pillag'd the villages on the sea-shore, and ruin'd Kianende. Then the Mirza Mehemed Sultan decamp'd with all his troops,

troops, and went down to the meadow of Yenicheher, contiguous to that of Prusa, where
the Mirza Aboubecre, with the emperor's permission, marry'd Bajazet's eldest daughter.

CHAP. LII.

Account of the Mirza Sultan Hussein, and the Emir Solyman Chah, who were gone out to make inroads.

THE Mirza Sultan Hussein, and the Emir Solyman Chah, who were gone out to make inroads in the southern parts of Natolia, plunder'd Kepec a Turcoman prince, and took the towns of Akcheker and Caraiser, in which places the Emir Solyman Chah establish'd governors to defend the inhabitants from insults He plac'd Tcherkes Soutchi in Akcheker, impos'd a tax on the towns for the ransom of the inhabitants lives, and plunder'd every one who oppos'd him. He pillag'd the town of Tchaker Boulagh, and the hord of Caoumi Hamid; and seiz'd on so many horses, camels and sheep, that the soldiers were not able to bring 'em away. After having taken the town of Chehermata, he stop'd at Ic nium he took the tribute of Gane¹ from the soldiers he had made prisoners, which he sent to Timur The Seid Coja, son of Cheik Ali Behader, went to the country of Aidin, which he ravag'd, killing all the enemys he met as far as the sea-shore. Bajazet's treasure was carry'd upon mules and camels to Kioutahia, where it was presented to Timur by the

---

¹ The tribute due to a prince from captives.

Book V. Emir Cheik Noureddin, with Bajazet's family and his beautiful slaves, who were good dancers, cou'd sing well, and play finely upon music. The generous emperor sent to Bajazet his wife, nam'd Destina [a], daughter of Laus a European, with his daughter and all his domestics, but he was desirous that that princess who till then had been tolerated in the Christian religion, even in Bajazet's seraglio, shou'd embrace Mahometanism. The Cheik Chamseddin Mehemed Jazari, who had been carry'd away prisoner of war, was likewise presented to the emperor. They brought to court the Emir Mehemed, son of Caraman, who had for twelve years been kept in chains by Bajazet. Timur honor'd him with a vest and belt, and gave him the government of all the province of Caramania, with Iconium, Larenda, Ac... erai, Anzarya, Alaya [b], and their dependences, and thro the protection of our monarch all these provinces remain'd without opposition in the hands of this Emir, and after him in his children.

CHAP. LIII.

Timur departs from Kioutahia.

AFTER Timur had staid a month at Kioutahia in the delights of banquets and plays, he departed from thence, and was join'd

---

[a] The European romances call her Roxana, and say that Timur kept her for his own use; the truth of which this ...

[b] C...ys of Natol a.

in his way by the Mirza Mehemed Sultan, who had left the Emir Chamfeddin Abbas with the baggage at Cheherno *, and was fet out with the Mirza Aboubecre, the Emir Gehan Chah, and Sevindgic Behader, to return to court, where he kifs'd the ground before the emperor, and offer'd his prefents.

Chap. 93.

* Or Yenicheher.

Timur, who as emperor was oblig'd to take care both of church and ftate, iffu'd out a fevere order that the brave Sainte Maure and his brother Mourad fhou'd be put to death, for feveral crimes they had committed; and that even his fon and other brothers fhou'd be fought for, and treated in the fame manner: which order was immediately put in execution.

The Mirza Mehemed Sultan, with the Mirza Aboubecre, and the Emirs of his court, return'd to join the baggage, which had been left at Prufa and Cheherno. Timur march'd towards Tangouzliq, pafs'd the mountain of Alcountach, and encamp'd in an agreeable meadow near it He then gave orders that the Co-Firouz, prince of Ifra Yaca, fhou'd be put to death, and he afterwards made preparations for feafts and banquets, with mufic and dancing, and the wine was ferv'd about by the moft beautiful damfels of the country. Timur invited Bajazet to thefe entertainments; that as he had tafted the bitternefs of his wrath, he might alfo partake of the fweetnefs of his friendfhip. Bajazet was conducted into the affembly with great honors, and Timur did every thing he cou'd to pleafe him: he fpar'd neither careffes, nor expreffions of kindnefs and affection; and in fine, he even granted him the inveftiture of the kingdom of Natolia, which he had poffefs'd before his difgrace: then the crown was plac'd on his head, and the fcepter put into his hand, with
the

the patents usually given to princes for their governments. After this feast Timur departed and continu'd his road towards Tangouziiq.

CHAP. LIV.

Timur dispatches couriers into divers countrys. The arrival of several ambassadors.

TIMUR sent the doctor Bedreddin Ahmed son of the Cheik Chamseddin Mehemet Jazari, into Egypt, in quality of ambassador to the Sultan Farrudge son of Barcoc, the subject of whose embassy was compriz'd in this letter.

Timur's letter to the Sultan of Egypt.

" By the grace of the Almighty, the empire
" of Natolia is now reduc'd under our autho-
" rity, and join'd to our dominions. Our will
" at present is, that the mony which is coin'd
" at Grand-Cairo, and throughout all Egypt
" have our inscription, and likewise that the
" prayer of the Coutbe be made in our august
" name, and with our titles. We will also that
" without delay you send Atilmich to our court
" and if, inspir'd by your evil genius, you don'
" readily execute these orders, we let you know
" that at our return from the Ottoman country
" which will be shortly, we shall march to
" Grand-Cairo at the head of our ever-victo-
" rious army. And that you may not pretend
" ignorance, we send you this ambassador
" whose merit you are sufficiently acquainted
" with."

Octob. 25. 1402.

Bedreddin departed with full instructions the first of Rabiulevel 803, accompany'd by several couriers, who carry'd relations of the conquest of Natolia into Syria, with orders to make
publi-

...blic rejoicings. Moulana Omar conducted the ambassador as far as Satalia, where he embark'd for Alexandria, from whence he was to go to Cairo, and Omar return'd after they had ...sail

Timur likewise sent two ambassadors to Constantinople, vulgarly nam'd Eſtanbol, to the Tecour, or Greek emperor, to ſummon him to pay the tribute and cuſtoms. He afterwards ſent two meſſengers to find out Muſſulman Chelibi, Bajazet's ſon, who had fled to Iſra Yaca, and reſided at Ghuzelhiſſar[1], which his father had built over-againſt Conſtantinople. Theſe meſſengers had orders to tell him that he muſt repair to court forthwith, or at leaſt ſend ſome envoy to Timur, otherwiſe the army wou'd immediately croſs the ſea to ſeek him, which he wou'd have cauſe to repent. Some time after, the ambaſſadors who had been ſent to the Greek emperor return'd, accompany'd with two others, who came to make their maſter's ſubmiſſion to Timur. They had the honor of an audience; and having notify'd the Tecour their maſter's reſpects and obedience to his highneſs's orders, he declar'd his conſent to pay an annual tribute, and the cuſtoms, and to do every thing he cou'd deſire of him. At length the ambaſſadors offer'd their preſents, which conſiſted of gold florins, and ſeveral curioſitys. Timur impos'd on 'em the tribute he thought reaſonable; and they confirm'd it by a ſolemn treaty. Afterwards he gave 'em veſts, and permitted 'em to return home

Embaſſy to the emperor of Conſtantinople.

---

[1] A town in Europe, built by Bajazet. There is another of the ſame name in Natolia, near Tire, on the river Menſuas.

When

Book V. When Timur was arriv'd at Boulouk[a], was join'd by the messengers he had sent to M[u]sulman Chelebi; and with them came the Ch[e] Ramadan in quality of ambassador, with se[ve]ral presents of animals, horses and florins. T[he] ambassador, who was a very illustrious pers[on] having been prime minister to Bajazet, and gr[and] Cadi of the empire, brought a letter from [his] master to Timur in these terms. "I have [the] "honor to call my self your highness's serv[ant]. "If you have had the goodness to pardon [my] "father, and have done him the honor to gr[ant] "him a place in your imperial assembly, acco[rd]"ing to his rank, I have all the reason in t[he] "world to confide in your highness's bount[y] "and whenever you shall order it, I will co[me] "to the foot of your imperial throne, and p[er]"form the dutys of a faithful servant in wh[at] "ever you shall please to command me."

Timur receiv'd the letter and the ambassad[or's] speech very graciously, and return'd the follo[w]ing answer. "All that ought to have happe[n'd] "in this affair has happen'd: fate has execu[ted] "its project. We have pardon'd all that [is] "pass'd: and so your master need only co[me] "here without any fear, that there may rem[ain] "no more animosity between us, but tha[t I] "may give him some marks of my fav[or]." Then Timur presented a belt and a cap of g[old] to the ambassador, and dismiss'd him.

Advice was afterwards brought that the S[ul]tan Mahmoud Can, titular emperor of Zaga[tay] who by Timur's order was gone to make [in]roads in the Ottoman country, had been se[iz'd] with a violent distemper at Ketchic Bourlou[,]

---

[a] A town of Nat[o]lia, long. 61. lat. 40.

The history of Timur-Bec.

Chap. 55.

and had pass'd from this world into the other: at which news Timur was very much afflicted.

In the mean while the Emirs ravag'd the maritim countrys of Natolia. The Emir Chamelic pillag'd Ketchic Bourlough, Acyaca, and Satalia, situate on the sea-shore. The Cheiks Ali Seblai and Hadgi Selduz were slain. The provinces Mentecha and Teke Eili were afterwards ruin'd; and the Emirs return'd to court laden with booty. During autumn Timur lay encamp'd at Tangouzliq, to which place the Seid Coja return'd, after having pillag'd Aidin. As it was exceeding hot, and the air infected at Tangouzliq, several soldiers fell sick and died; and even Seid Coja was near the point of death, but the joy he conceiv'd at the good reception his highness gave him, restor'd him to his health.

In this place is a fountain, whose water petrifies when it stagnates; and some soldiers, who being ignorant of its effects, had drank of it, lost their lives.

A petrifying water.

CHAP. LV.

Timur regulates the winter-quarters.

TIMUR held a council with the Mirzas and great Emirs touching the distribution of the winter-quarters: he appointed a town to each colonel, and sent orders to the Mirza Mehemed Sultan to pass the winter at the town of Magni Siah ¹ in the province of Serhan Eili *. This Mirza departed from Prusa to Micalidge,

* Or Saroucan Eili.

¹ Long. 60. lat. 40.

where

Book V. where he staid several days; from whence he march'd to Balikisra, which he pillag'd, and encamp'd in a meadow. In the night he was attack'd by Elias Soubachi at the head of a number of peasants, of which Vesador had given advice, tho too late; for the enemy came to surprize our camp, while part of the soldiers were gone to make inroads, and the others were asleep in the camp without any precaution. The Mirza immediately took horse, and sally'd out of the camp; and the Emir Gehan Chah with the other Emirs having join'd him, they fell upon the enemy, and having slain several, and constrain'd the rest to fly, they encamp'd in that meadow, till the Mirza's equipage arriv'd there. The Emirs Gehan Chah and Sevindgic were sent from this place to the town of Birana to pillage it. The Mirza after that went to Magni Siah, where he pass'd the winter; this town is situate at the foot of a mountain, wash'd by many rivulets, the waters of which are wonderfully good, and the air is sweet, even in winter.

The Mirza Charoc, with the troops of the left wing, had the province of Ghermyan-Eili for his winter-quarters; and he encamp'd between Olouc-Bourlough and Ketchic-Bourlough.

Timur departed from Tangouzliq, and march'd to Dougourlic, a town full of goods and all sorts of delicious fruits, to the inhabitants of which he granted quarter on the payment of the tribute for their ransom. Then he cross'd the river of Mendouras [a] on a bridg which Temourtach had built, and encamp'd on the other side,

---

[a] Or Madre, a river which passes by Tire in Natolia, and Aidin, and falls into the Archipelago.

where he gave audience to the Emirs Mehemed and Esfendiar, sons of the Emir Mehemed prince of Mentecha, who made him a present of a thousand horses. Timur, after giving 'em an honorable reception, presented 'em with a vest, a belt and a crown. Esfendiar follow'd the court, and Mehemed consented to pay the tax, and return'd to the place of his residence, with the receivers Elias Coutchin, Firouz Chah, and Mirouz Chah Cherbetdar. Timur being arriv'd at Ghuzelhissar, staid there some days till the entire payment of the ransom was made. Near this place was a mountain, in which two hundred peasants had fortify'd themselves: these rash fellows slew and pillag'd our soldiers, who were gone out to fetch in wood and forage. Timur being inform'd of this, resolv'd to attack 'em in the night. Several of our soldiers who were enrag'd, invested the mountain, and at break of day fell upon these villains, whom they cut in pieces, and afterwards return'd to the camp. The doctor Abdelgebbar Carizmi fell sick, and died in this place.

Timur departed some days after from Ghuzelhissar, and went to encamp at Ayazlic, where he staid several days: he order'd 'em to pay the tribute for their ransom, and establish'd a governor, and a comptroller of the finances. From thence he went to encamp before Tire, one of the most noted citys of Natolia, the inhabitants of which he oblig'd to pay the ransom for their lives, and those who were gone with the Emir Mehemed prince of Mentecha, to receive the sums these people were tax'd at, return'd loaded with ready mony, jewels and divers curiositys, and bringing with 'em several horses and other beasts, from this Emir; all which they presented to Timur.

In the mean while the emperor was inform'd that there was an exceeding strong place on the sea-shore, built of free-stone, surrounded with the sea on three sides, and on the other with a deep ditch, entirely built with lime and mortar, from the foundation to the top, that it was inhabited by Europeans, and nam'd Ezmir or Smyrna, that the Greeks esteem it a holy place, and go in pilgrimage thither with great devotion; that near it is another fortress on the ridge of a mountain, also nam'd Ezmir, but inhabited by Mussulmans, who incessantly wage war with the others, because of the difference of their religion, and as the Smyrna of the Christians is surrounded by the sea on three sides, the Europeans supply 'em with ammunition and all necessarys, looking upon this place as of great importance, seeing it is at the extremity of Asia and of the Mussulman country that it had never been taken by any Mahometan prince, nor paid tribute to any; that Amura Bajazet's father, had several times appear'd before it at the head of a formidable army, but to no purpose, and that Bajazet had laid siege to it seven years in vain, that this place, strong as that of Caiber[5], very much molest the Mussulmans, whose blood was always flowing in o the sea like torrents.

---

[5] A place celebrated in the oriental romances.

CHA

CHAP. LVI.

Timur besieges Smyrna, and takes it.

WHEN Timur was inform'd of the state of Smyrna, his zeal for religion inspir'd him with the thoughts that it was his duty to deliver the Mussulmans from troubles, by exterminating their enemys. Whereupon he sent thither the Mirza Pir Mehemed, son of Omar Cheil, the Emir Cheik Noureddin, and others, to summon 'em forthwith to embrace the Musulman religion, according to Mahomet's order, which if they shou'd be so fortunate as to do, they shou'd be well treated, and partake of his favors, and if they wou'd leave their obstinacy, tho they still remain'd Christians, and pay the tribute, he wou'd fix the sum, and order the receit, but if they undertook to defend themselves, he wou'd order 'em all to be put to the sword.

The Mirzas and Emirs being arriv'd before Smyrna, sent an ambassador to invite the inhabitants to turn Mussulmans, as well by menaces as promises: but as they were predestin'd to perish, it all prov'd in vain. Mahmous, the governor, had sent to demand succours of all the European princes, so that there was assembled a great number of the bravest Christian captains, or rather a band of desperate wretches, who had laid up ammunitions in the place. Our generals sent advice of all this to Timur, who resolv'd to march thither in person. He left the baggage at the foot of the mountain of Tire; and tho it was winter, and great rains had fallen, yet he took horse that he might acquire the merit of this religious war. He arriv'd at Smyrna on saturday the sixth of Jumaziulevel 805, and sent orders to the Mirza Mehemed Sultan, who was in his winter-quarters at Magni-Siah, to repair to him. The same order was sent to the Mirzas Miran Chah and Aboubecre, as also to the Emir Gehan Chah and others.

At Timur's arrival before Smyrna, the drums and kettledrums were beat, and the great cry made by the whole army. The place was immediately attack'd on the land-side, and each general order'd the sappers to work, and the machines and battering rams to be got ready over-against his respective post, while arrows were shot, and pots of wild-fire thrown upon the gates of the castle. The Emir Chamelic built in the midst of the water, great scaffolds with three feet, near one another, on which they laid planks: and from the two sides of the castle, to the place where the feet of the scaffolds touch'd the ground, they made an even way, which they secur'd on each side, so that the soldiers might fight upon it with safety, as if they were on land. The Mussulmans, arm'd with their bucklers, mounted the scaffolds, from whence they gave assaults upon the castle: and as the way was shut up to the sea-side, it was impossible to bring any succour to the besieg'd.

In the mean while the Mirzas Mehemed Sultan and Miran Chah arriv'd, having left the baggage at Magni-Siah under the conduct of the Emir Chamseddin Abbas: which re-inforcement did not a little serve to forward the siege. Then Timur order'd a general assault. The Emirs of Tomans, and the colonels of Hezares, advanc'd with their troops, against their

...ir respective posts, and the assault lasted from
...ning till evening, and from evening till
...ning, wherein the bravest men of both
...s perform'd actions of the greatest valor.
...e attack was carry'd on with resolution,
...d ...nce was equally so. The battering-
...ms and other machines beat down the walls
...d towers, and the dauntless besieg'd never
...s'd throwing pots of naphtha and wild-fire,
...ows and stones In the mean while it rain'd
...such abundance, that a second deluge seem'd
...pproaching, notwithstanding which, the in-
...fatigable Timur was always giving orders to
...s generals, and exciting his soldiers. After the
...pers had done undermining, and prop'd up the
...tions and courtines with stakes, they put in
...great number of fascines done over with
...phtha, which having set on fire, the walls on
...ddden fell down, and with 'em several of the
...eg'd, who were thereby destroy'd. The
M...mans forc'd the enemy to quit the breaches,
...d then enter'd the place, returning thanks to
... and crying out, *Victory!* A few escap'd
...ter by casting themselves into the sea, and
...wimming to the vessels; while others were
...own'd After our soldiers had put the inha-
...nts of Smyrna to the sword, they raz'd the
...ses, as well of the city as of the castle, cast-
...eir arms and movable goods into the sea
...were come from certain parts of Europe
...t ships nam'd Caraca, with two masts, and
...e with more, which brought over soldiers
...rms to succour the inhabitants. When
...were come near the place, and beheld the
town and castle in ruins, they were struck with
...r, and anchor'd. Timur order'd that some
... the Christians heads shou'd be thrown into
... ships, which the flingers of wild-fire accordingly

cordingly did. The mariners seeing their companions heads, return'd in fear, and fruftrated of their hopes. From the beginning of the fiege to the ruin of the place there pass'd but two weeks, which very much aftonish'd the men of that country, who were acquainted with the ftrength of the place, and especially Bajazet. Every one acknowledg'd that Timur was the greateft and moft formidable monarch that ever appear'd in Afia. The author of this hiftory in his travels afterwards pass'd by the walls of Smyrna, which then belong'd to the Mufulmans, and one of his companions having related to him the hiftory of this place, the author expreft himfelf in thefe words. "Smyrna hath been ruin'd by "Timur in lefs than two weeks, tho the Ot-"toman emperor in vain befieg'd it feven years "judge from hence the power and conduct "each of 'em."

CHAP. LVII.

Second arrival of ambaffadors from Bajazet's fons

DURING thefe transactions the Che Ramadan, who came once before in quality of ambaffador to Timur from Mufulman Chelebi, arriv'd here again, and being admitted to an audience, offer'd large prefents of horfes and other animals, curious ftuffs, and florins of gold, and with abundance of submission made the following fpeech. "I take the liberty "reprefent to your highnefs, that fince you have "been pleas'd to pardon the emperor Bajazet "and load him with honors and favors, the

"one is freed from the fears he was in, and
"even hopes for advancement thro your high-
"ness's benevolence The prince Muſulman
"my maſter, who looks upon himself as one of
"the meaneſt ſervants of your court, and is re-
"ſolv'd to obey the orders with which you
"ſhall honor him, with all imaginable ſincerity,
"waits with impatience for an opportunity to
"give you the true marks of his reſpect, and
"his deſire to expoſe his life in your highneſs's
"ſervice, to whom may God continue ever-
"laſting glory and proſperity."

The ambaſſador having ended his ſpeech, Timur was touch'd with compaſſion for the deplorable condition to which Muſulman was reduc'd: he confirm'd him in the principality of all the country of Iſra Yaca[1], for which he iſſu'd out patents, which he ſeal'd as uſual with his red hand, he honor'd the ambaſſador with a magnificent veſt, and a horſe richly capariſon'd, with a ſaddle of gold, and having given him a veſt wove with gold, a crown, and a belt for Muſulman Chelebi, he diſmiſs'd him

About the ſame time arriv'd an ambaſſador, nam'd Cotobeddin, from Iſa Chelebi, another of Bajazet's ſons. being admitted to an audience, he kiſs'd the earth, and made his preſents; which Timur having accepted, the ambaſſador deliver'd his meſſage, declaring his maſter's reſpect, and obedience to whatever his highneſs ſhou'd order. Then he return'd, after having receiv'd the uſual honors, and the teſtimonys of friendſhip for his maſter

Timur afterwards gave orders to the Mirza Mehemed Sultan to beſiege the caſtle of Fodgia[2],

---

[1] Iſra Yaca is Turky in Europe.
[2] A town on the gulf of Smyrna.

situate on the sea-shore, a day's journey from Smyrna, because several European Christians had retreated thither. The Mirza immediately departed, and encamp'd before it, and was about to besiege it in form, when the governor of the place struck with terror at the name of Timur, came out to cast themselves at the Mirza's feet, and with submission and obedience gave consent to pay the tribute, provided quarter was granted the inhabitants. The Mirza agreed to their proposal, impos'd a tribute on 'em, and nam'd commissaries to receive it, after which he return'd with his Emirs and troops to Magni-Siah, where he had left his baggage.

CHAP. LVIII

Timur departs from Smyrna.

AFTER the destruction of Smyrna, and the extirpation of the enemys of the law, Timur took care to restore peace and quiet to the Mussulmans who inhabited the of their castle, giving 'em vests, bucklers, cuirasses, bows and arrows, sabres, lances, and all sorts of arms, to enable 'em to carry on the war of religion in these frontiers against the Europeans and hinder the Grecian Christians ever passing into Asia this way, and he order'd 'em to build a strong citadel near the place where Smyrna stood.

After Timur had deliver'd the Mussulmans from the continual insults they receiv'd from the Christians of Smyrna, leaved 'em with favors and succor'd 'em with arms and mony, he departed from this country, and went to encamp at Ayazlic, where he was join'd by the Emir Chap. 58. Solyman Chah, who had departed from Ancora to make inroads, return'd by Esouac, and join'd the Mirza Charoc at Caraigadge; but he came alone to court, and after his audience went back to join the said Mirza.

An European nam'd Soba, prince of the island of Chio [3], in which mastich grows, having heard by credible persons of the great valor and power of Timur, sent him several presents by an ambassador, whom he order'd to acquaint him that he was one of his meanest servants, willingly consented to pay the tribute, and was ready to obey his highness's orders, hoping Timur wou'd design to give him some marks of his clemency. The ambassador being arriv'd at the imperial camp, was admitted to an audience, where he made an harangue in the form his master had instructed him. Timur handsomly receiv'd the king of Chio's offer of service, promis'd protection to him and his subjects, and after having fix'd the sum for a tribute, made a peace with him: he gave a vest to the ambassador, whom he honor'd, and permitted to return home.

Embassy from the prince of Chio.

Timur then sent the Mirza Eskender, son of Omar Cheik, and Ali Sultan Tavachi, to plunder the country of Bezem, they enter'd the capital of it, and having taken the ransom for the inhabitants lives, return'd to the imperial camp.

After this Timur decamp'd from Ayazlic, and being arriv'd at Tangouzliq, he was join'd by the Mirza Mehemed Sultan, who had left his winter-quarters at Magni-Siah, and having taken the road of Alicheher before the rest, came

---

[3] An island in the Archipelago.

to court with a small number of his domestics Timur order'd him to march at the head of the troops of the right wing by the road of Ancora, and rejoin the imperial camp at Cæsarea. This Mirza staid at Tangouzliq till all his troops had join'd him. Timur departed from thence for Sdranhiflar, he order'd a great number of peasants, who were got together in the neighboring mountains, to be put to the sword, and he gave the towns of Chioutahia, Tangouzliq, and Caracheher, as well as the demesn of the province of Ghermyan-Eili, to Yacoub Chelebi, to whom the principality of these provinces fell by right of succession. This Yacoub had formerly fled from Bajizet into Syria, after the conquest of which kingdom he follow'd Timur's court. The emperor issu'd out his patents to this purpose, and honoring him with a vest and belt, left him in this place, the principality of which remains in the hands of his children to this day.

The court took the road of Oloue-Bourlouga where it was join'd by the Mirza Charoc, who was come from his winter-quarters. As this place had not yet surrender'd, Timur gave orders that it shou'd be attack'd. It was taken in a very short time and as the Emir Gelaleliflam had been slain by an arrow, all the men were put to the sword, and the women carry'd away captive, after the razing of the place.

CHAP.

CHAP. LIX.

Taking of the towns of Egridur and Nasibine.

IN the province of Hamid-Eili is a lake of sweet water, five leagues in length, and four in breadth, into which several rivers fall, and go out again by other passages; and round it are kitchen-gardens, orchards, and cultivated lands On the bank of the lake stands a town nam'd Egridur, built of free-stone, three of its sides are surrounded by the lake, and the fourth by the mountain. This lake is nam'd Falac Abad by some historians. Near the town, in the midst of the lake, are two isles; one nam'd Ghulistan, and the other Nasibine: in the latter, which is exceeding large, is built a fortress with houses and gardens. The people of the neighboring places had convey'd thither their mony and best effects, and abundance of soldiers were got into it, who had laid up stores of all sorts of ammunition, believing themselves safe, because of the lake which surrounds the place. Timur being inform'd of all this, conceiv'd it wou'd redound to his honor to conquer this place whereupon he order'd the baggage to be conducted by the road of Akcheher

About this time Bajazet falling sick, Timur order'd several skilful physicians of his court, as Moulana Azeddin, Masaoud Chirazi, and Moulana Gelaleddin Arab, to attend him with the same care as they wou'd use towards himself and Bajazet was conducted with the baggage

Book V
Feb. 28.
1403.

Timur departed from Olouc-Bourlough, and in two days and one night arriv'd at Egridur the 17th of Regeb 805 in the morning. Next day the Mirzas and Emirs march'd towards the walls of the town: some ascended the mountain while others attack'd the gate by the foot of the mountain, they gave assaults on all sides, and soon made themselves masters of the town, which they enter'd in a furious manner, and put most of the inhabitants to the sword, a few only escaping to Nasibine in boats.

Then Timur caus'd floats to be made of the skins of oxen and horses, on which the Mirzas and Emirs crost over to attack Nasibine, which they surrounded, ordering the drums to be beat, and the great cry made. The inhabitants were surpriz'd, not imagining they cou'd have been besieg'd by water. The governor Cheik Baba, perceiving he was unable to defend himself, went out, and besought the Mirzas to intercede for him. They brought him to Timur, before whom he kiss'd the ground, submissively begging pardon and quarter. Timur order'd that he and his family shou'd follow the army. Thus Nasibine was taken by our troops, who brought to the camp all the riches they cou'd find, which Timur distributed among 'em.

Then Mebacler's son arriv'd from the Mirza Mehemed Sultan, to give notice that this prince was fallen sick. Timur was exceedingly griev'd, and sent a skilful physician to him immediately, to discover the true state of his illness, and bring him back certain advice of it.

The court at length decamp'd, and march'd toward Akcheher, they met the troops of the left wing, and the Mirza Charoc's camp. This prince made a feast for Timur, and offer'd his presents, as did likewise the Sultan Hussein and

the Emir Solyman Chah, who strove to excel Chap 60.
each other in entertaining the emperor. At this
time the Emir Mehemed Caraman came to
court from Iconium; and under the name of a
custom, he presented such vast sums of silver
money, curious stuffs, and great numbers of horses and camels, that it was believ'd he did more
than he was able, considering the small extent
and power of his country: upon which Timur
distinguish'd him by several honors, and confirm'd him in his principality. As the emperor
had before deliver'd him from prison, where he
was detain'd by Bajazet, and had restor'd to him
his father's estates, so he again join'd other
countrys to his demesns, and dismiss'd him: after which the court departed, and continu'd its
march

CHAP. LX.

The death of the Ottoman emperor Bajazet, and of the Mirza Mehemed Sultan, Timur's grandson.

THE world is so inconstant, that we may rather look upon it as a continual destruction, than an agreeable habitation, since there is
nothing of a certain duration but God: a melancholy instance of which we find in Bajazet, who
died of an apoplexy at Akchcher on thursday
the 14th of Chaban 805; at whose death Timur March 23.
was so extremely affected, that he bewail'd the 1403.
misfortune of that great prince with tears. He
began to reflect how providence often baffles
human projects, for he had resolv'd, as soon as he
had finish'd the conquest of Natolia, to raise the
dejected

Book V dejected spirit of Bajazet, by re-establishing him on the throne with greater power and magnificence than he had before been possess'd of but fate had otherwise order'd it.

Timur being got to the frontier of Akcheher Dané Coja arriv'd from the Mirza Mehemed Sultan, with advice that doctor Farrudge had given some medicine to the prince, which had had an ill effect, and that the vapors having got into his brain, he was fallen into a delirium. This news very much afflicted the emperor, who dispatch'd away Dané Coja post, to acquaint the Mirza that he wou'd soon be with him.

Timur encamp'd at Akcheher, where he comforted Bajazet's officers by several largesses he bestow'd upon 'em. He made a present to his son Mousla Chelebi of a royal vest, a belt, a sword, and a quiver enrich'd with precious stones a load of gold, and thirty horses: he likewise gave him his letters-patent seal'd with the impression of his red hand, and then dismiss'd him, telling him that the coffin of the deceas'd emperor his father was laid by his orders in the tomb of the Cheik Mahmoud Hairan at Akcheher, and that it shou'd be convey'd to Prusa with all the pomp and magnificence us'd to the greatest king to be inter'd in the mausoleum, which he had built there himself.

Timur then left the baggage, and departed from Akcheher, for the place where the Mirza his grandson lay sick. On his way thither he learnt that the hord of Turcomans nam'd Durgot, whose chiefs were Kezerbei and Ibrahim had revolted, and were entrench'd in a mountain near the great road, hoping to defend themselves there. Some troops being order'd against 'em they block'd up all the avenues, and invested the mountain, and then attacking the Durgots with

their arrows, they fled. Our soldiers pursu'd Chap 6.
sword in hand, slew several on the spot,
seiz'd their horses, camels, oxen, and sheep,
and made their wives and children slaves, to
serve as an example to mutineers.

The sixteenth of Chaban, Timur met Dolet March 25.
Cuja son of Eltchi Bouga, who gave advice that
the Mirza's sickness increasing, his life was despair'd of This oblig'd Timur to hasten his
march, and being come to the place where he
was, he went up to his bed-side, where finding
him very ill, having lost his speech, he became
very disconsolate. Timur order'd the Mirza to
be put in a litter, and departed the same day.
When they had march'd three days journy, and
were come near Carahiſlar¹, they encamp'd;
and here the great and mighty prince, the Mirza
Mehemed Sultan, who was but nineteen years
old, pass'd from this life into the other, on the
18th of Chaban 805, which answers to the March 27.
year of the Sheep, the sun being in the last de- 1403.
gree of Pisces. Thus died this great prince,
who tho but a child in a manner, had already
obtain'd more victorys, and perform'd greater
actions of valor, than many famous heroes recorded in history.

¹ A city long. 70. lat. 38.

CHAP.

CHAP. LXI.

Mourning for the death of the Mirza Mehemed Sultan and the translation of his coffin.

THE natural love which fathers bear towards their children, was not the only motive that afflicted Timur for the death of the Mirza, but the great things which this young prince's virtue promis'd, were the principal cause of his excessive grief: he flung his crown aside, and quitted his throne, rent his clothes, and cast himself upon the ground in the most surprizing transports of grief. This caus'd a great change in his temper; and in this delightful season of the spring, instead of being chearful, the princes and lords of the court cloth'd themselves with hair-sacks, and black and blue habits, with felts about their necks. The ladys did the same; and they sprinkled earth upon their heads, and fill'd their bosoms with stones: they wou'd take no rest but upon chaff and ashes, instead of bedding; and nothing cou'd be heard in the court but groans and lamentations, especially from the princess Canike, wife of the deceas'd, who was so overcome with sorrow, that she often fell into swoons, and lost her senses.

Such is the stated course of affairs in this world; we shou'd not place our confidence in it, for those who do, will at last repent: but we belong to God, and must return to him. Timur order'd the Mirza's coffin to be convey'd in a litter to Avenic by two hundred horsemen, commanded by seven Emirs, and

that

that when they arriv'd there, Ouaifel and Ourdoucha fhou'd lay the corps in a new coffin, and carry it to the tomb of the prophet Caidar in the town of Sultania, from whence it was afterwards to be tranflated to Samarcand. and he likewife gave order that the other five Emirs fhou'd ftay at Avenic with a litter and an empty coffin, whofe covering fhou'd be nail'd up

Chap 62.

After their departure Timur return'd to the camp, and then fet out from the meadow of Akcheher to continue his journy. The grief was beyond comparifon; and not only the courtiers, but even the foldiers of the army, never ceas'd from weeping. When they had march'd fome days journy in this condition, the principal E-mirs and minifters of ftate came to the emperor, and falling on their faces, remonftrated to him, that all the foldiers of the army continu'd in fuch exceffive grief, that nothing was ever like it, that the continuation of this grief did not become the majefty of fo auguft a court; that it was better he fhou'd arm himfelf with patience, and endeavor to comfort his royal heart. They at laft perfuaded Timur, tho with great difficulty, to compofe his mind, and live after his ufual manner: fo he gave orders for every one to leave off their mourning-habits, as being of no advantage to the deceas'd.

CHAP. LXII.

Arrival of ambaffadors from Egypt.

WHEN Timur's ambaffadors, whom we before mention'd, were arriv'd at Grand-Cairo, they found a handfom reception. Far-rudge,

rudge, son of Barcoc, firnam'd Elmalekennaser, king of Egypt and Syria, having been inform'd of all that had pass'd between Timur and Bajazet, whom he had esteem'd the most powerful prince in the universe, was now convinc'd that it wou'd be wrong to think of dealing with Timur upon any other foot than that of an entire submission and perfect obedience, and he repented of the difficulty his father and himself had made of sending back Atilmich. He hereupon held a council with the principal persons of state; and with their approbation releas'd Atilmich out of prison, admitted him to an audience, treated him in an honorable manner, and made divers apologys for what he had done. He caus'd the mony to be coin'd, and the prayers read in the august name and titles of Timur, and sent back Atilmich, with two ambassadors, Ahmed and Acta, beseeching Atilmich to be his intercessor at the court. Farrudge order'd his ambassadors to make known to Timur his repentance for his former faults, his consent to pay the annual tribute, and what he had done in relation to the mony and the public prayers. He sent as a present, by the same persons, abundance of gold and silver mony, precious stones, belts, Alexandrian stuffs, swords of Cairo, horses of a fine breed, and other curiositys.

As soon as they enter'd the frontiers of the Ottoman country, Atilmich set out before 'em for the court, and having the honor to salute the emperor, he inform'd his highness of the affairs of Egypt, and of the Sultan and people's fears. The ambassadors soon arriv'd at court; and being admitted to an audience, declar'd to the emperor the intentions of the Sultan their master, and offer'd their presents.

Timur was again pleas'd to shew his clemency to the king of Egypt, and spake to 'em as follows. " I know that Farrudge lost his father " when very young, which will make it my " glory to take care of this young prince, and " be to him as a father If he continues firm in " his obedience, which is the only way of secu- " ring himself, we will give him testimonys of " our benevolence, and grant him succours, " with which he may preserve his kingdom, " provided he zealously continues in the service " of the two holy citys of Mecca [1] and Me- " dina." He afterwards presented vests, belts, and crowns to the ambassadors, and permitted 'em to return home; giving 'em a crown, a royal mantle, and a belt enrich'd with precious stones, for the Sultan Farrudge their master, to whom he promis'd his protection

CHAP. LXIII.

Timur marches against the Caratatars, or black Tartars.

CARATATAR is a nation of Turks, which Hulacou Can [2] lifted into his army when he was sent into Iran by Mangou Can, emperor of the Moguls. Hulacou being esta- blish'd on the throne at Tauris, and having ex- perienc'd the malice of this wicked people, ob- lig'd 'em to reside with their familys in the fron-

A. D. 1256.

---

[1] All Mahometan princes take upon 'em the title of the ser- vants of the two citys of Mecca and Medina.
[2] Brother of Mangou Caan, and grandson of Genghiz Can the great.

tiers of Natolia and Syria. When by the death of the grand Can Aboufaid [*], there remain'd no longer in Iran any abfolute emperor of the race of Genghiz Can, this people revolted, and divided themfelves into fifty-two hords, every hundred chufing a particular refidence, being all refolv'd to live independent. When Bajazet, after the reign of Cadi Burhaneddin at Sebafte, was become mafter of this kingdom, he enroll'd 'em in the Ottoman army, and gave 'em a refidence in his empire: and as there were no great taxes or tribute to pay in thefe parts, thefe Tartars enrich'd themfelves, and became exceeding powerful. But Timur, who defign'd to make 'em change the place of their refidence, and to fix 'em in the colonys of Gete, that they might repeople that country, treated their chiefs in an honorable manner when they came to falute him: he gave 'em robes wove with gold, belts and fwords of gold, with feveral largeffes. As no one infulted 'em in the leaft manner during the whole courfe of this war, but fuffer'd 'em to continue quiet in their hords, this fufficiently denoted that they were in obedience and fubjection, or at leaft ought to have been fo

When the ambaffadors of Egypt arriv'd at court, Timur ftaid three days among the Caratatars, and after having held a council, and maturely deliberated about the ways of bringing his enterprize to perfection, he refolv'd to remove 'em out of that country, and conduct 'em into Tranfoxiana But as there were between thirty and forty familys of 'em, he order'd the Mirzas and Emirs to furround 'em, each on their refpec-

---

[*] Son of Codabende king of Perfia, and of the race of Genghiz Can.

the sides, so that none of 'em might get away, but not to do 'em the least damage. Accordingly the Emir Gehan Chah, with the Emirs of the right wing, and the troops of the Mirza Mehemed Sultan, took the road to Tocat and Amasia. The Emir Solyman Chah, with those of the left wing, march'd by Cæsarea and Sebaste. Timur went by the plains of Amasia* and Cæsarea, the residence of the Caratatars; and he sent the Mirza Charoc, with the Sultan Hussein, to cut off their passage, and hinder any one's flight.

The emperor having pass'd the bridge of Kircheher, after several days march, arriv'd at the country of the Caratatars, whose chiefs he order'd to be call'd before him. There came two of 'em, Akhi Tebarec and Murvet they kiss'd the ground before the emperor, who gave 'em a handsom reception, presented 'em with vests and belts wrought with gold, and swore he wou'd never do 'em the least harm. " It is a long while, " says he, since your ancestors came out of the " country of Touran, which was their antient " residence, into these foreign lands, by the or- " ders of the emperors our predecessors. As " all that vast country is at present govern'd by " one master, God having brought it under my " obedience, you ought to look upon this op- " portunity as very fortunate to you ; and re- " turn from hence, with your wives, children, ' slaves, cattel, and other riches, under the " convoy of our soldiers, to the country of your " ancestors, where you may pass your life agree- " ably under the shadow of our protection "

---

* I believe it shou'd rather be Acsara.

The chiefs return'd thanks to Timur, and affur'd him that they were ready to obey his orders with pleasure; that they look'd upon it as a piece of good fortune to be under his protection, and that they were resolv'd to spend their lives in his service. Timur order'd they shou'd be divided into companys and regiments, and diftributed among the Emirs of the Tomans. Being thus made to decamp with their cattel, they began their march, they were prohibited buying any fheep or horfes, that they might be lefs embarafs'd in the roads, and that if they fhou'd endeavor to fly, they might the better be prevented.

CHAP. LXIV.

Timur returns from Natolia.

TIMUR was highly pleas'd with his conqueft of Natolia, of which he was become the abfolute and fole monarch, without any oppofition, and with the love of all the people, which great affair he had brought about by the ftrength of his arms and the valor of his foldiers, at the fame time that he won the hearts of the people by his good conduct. This vaft conqueft, by the divine affiftance, was finifh'd in lefs than a year; and thro-out all Afia Timur's name was ftamp'd on their coins, and the prayers were read with his auguft titles.

For thefe reafons his majefty refolv'd to return to the feat of his empire: he caus'd the great ftandard to be difplay'd, and began his march with all the army. He fent orders to the empreffes Serai Mulc Canum, Touman Aga, Tchelpan

pan Mulc Aga, and Canzade, mother of the deceas'd Mirza Mehemed Sultan, to come and meet him as far as the borders of Avenic. This new emperor of the lesser Asia, being arriv'd at Cæsarea in Cappadocia, the inhabitants fill'd with fear, conceal'd themselves in caverns: whereupon he sent Ali Sultan Tavachi, with a good troop of soldiers, in search of 'em, who having found 'em, they defended themselves against him, and shot him with an arrow in the Vena-cava, of which he dy'd upon the spot. Yet these rebels being vanquish'd and taken, Mehemed, brother of Ali Sultan, caus'd 'em all to be put to the sword, to revenge his death.

Afterwards Timur departed for Sebaste, where he confer'd several honors upon Cara Osman [6], and sent him back into his principality. From thence he went to Arzendgian, where Taharten, like a faithful servant, ofter'd his presents to the emperor, of horses, cattel, and other things, nine of each sort. Taharten follow'd the court two days journy: and then Timur, honoring him with a royal vest, permitted him to return home. He sent back the messenger who had brought advice of the empresses departure from Sultania, with orders that the princes shou'd hasten, that so they might arrive at Avenic before the ladys. Timur being come to Erzerom, was join'd by the Mirzas Oluc-Bec, Ibrahim Sultan, Mehemed Gehanghir, Aidgel, and Sadvaccas, his grand-children: he tenderly embrac'd 'em, and was over-joy'd to see 'em; but he cou'd not refrain from tears at the sight of the Mirzas Mehemed Gehanghir

---

[6] Made governor of Sebaste by Timur when at Malatia; he was son of the Cadi Burhaneddin, prince of Sebaste.

and Sadiaccas, because of the Mirza Mehemed Sultan their father's death.

CHAP. LXV.

The manner in which the death of the Mirza Mehemed Sultan, son of Gehanghir, was made known to Canzade his mother.

THE empresses who were set out from Sultania, made preparations at Tauris for mourning for the Mirza Mehemed Sultan; they cloth'd themselves in black, and then came to Avenic, according to the emperor's orders. When they were inform'd that Timur was near the place, they acquainted the princess Canzade with the death of her dear son: upon which she was so transported with grief, that she swoon'd away, and being a little recover'd, she rent her clothes, and twisting her hair about her fingers, began to pluck it off by degrees; she spit blood, and tore her lovely cheeks with her nails. She swoon'd away the second time, on seeing all the ladys, whose heads were cover'd with black mantles, and who cou'd utter nothing but crys and lamentations.

Timur being encamp'd, they began their crys afresh; and nothing was to be seen more dismal then this court; which at other times was the gayest and most magnificent of all Asia. He order'd that to moderate the princess's affliction, the empty coffin, nail'd down very strongly, and fasten'd with a lock, shou'd be presented to her. She twisted her self round it, crying and groaning "My eyes, said this disconsolate "princess, were continually looking towards the "public

The history of Timur-Bec.   297

"public road, in expectation of some news of
"my dear child, which wou'd have been the
"delight of my soul. I did not expect this cru-
"elty from fortune, this fatal dagger, which
"thus breaks my heart at the sight of this cof-
"fin. O deplorable condition! O wretched
"Canzade! O unfortunate prince! thou wast
"design'd for the throne of the empire of Iran;
"but merciless fate has snatch'd the scepter from
"thy hands. It is not without cause that a tor-
"rent of blood gushes from my eyes, and I make
"the earth red with my tears, since, my dear
"son, thou hast thus pierc'd my heart in thy
"tenderest age."

After this excess of mourning, Timur judg'd it proper to do something for the spiritual good of his soul, which lives as well in the other world as it did in this: he gave alms among the poor, and provided a funeral banquet. The Cherifs, doctors, grandees and nobles of all Asia assembled together for this ceremony: they sat down according to their rank at the emperor's table; and a Hafiz, with a Nazer, the lecturers, read over the Alcoran several times. The banquet was serv'd up by the emperor's stewards: and the Mirza's brass-drum was beat, at which the lords, the Emirs, and soldiers, as well masters as servants, on a sudden made a great cry, and wept bitterly; and then the drum was broke to pieces, according to the custom of the Moguls.

The doctors and Imams, who came from Tauris, Sultania, Cazuin, and other places, to salute the emperor at his return, and pay their
compliments of condolence, endeavor'd in several
conferences to comfort him and the princess:
they forgot not any of Mahomet's counsels on
this occasion, and strove to incite 'em to patience, assuring 'em that the deceas'd were tor-
mented

mented by the lamentations of their living relations, and that it was hurtful to their souls. By the force of their eloquence, they perfuaded the emperor to arm himfelf with patience againft the affaults of affliction caus'd by fo fad a misfortune. Timur then permitted an order to be iffued out for leaving off the mourning-habits, black fcarfs, hair-facks, and other marks of grief. He loaded the doctors with favors and honors; and after having given 'em vefts, fent 'em back to their refpective refidences.

The end of the fifth book.

BOOK VI.

A war in Georgia. Timur's return from a campain of seven years. The defeat and pursuit of Eskender Cheiki, prince of the race of the antient Persians. Timur's departure for the conquest of China. His death at Otrar near the river Jaxartes, and his interment at Samarcand. The strange revolutions which happen'd after his death. The Mirza Calil Sultan his grandson, son of Miran Chah, usurps the crown; and the ruin of that prince occasion'd by his prodigality, and passion for a woman.

CHAP. I.

Timur marches into Georgia.

TIMUR-BEC's greatest ambition being to merit the happiness promis'd to those who wage war with the infidels for the advancement of religion, and Giourghin king of Georgia, having fail'd in the prin-

Book VI. principal article of the treaty made the preceding year, which was to have come at a fix'd time to cast himself at the emperor's feet, and beg pardon, his highness took up a resolution to march again into his country. To this end, he departed towards Mencoul, where he receiv'd the submissions of Malek Issa prince of Merdin¹, who repenting of his fault in not coming before to pay his homage, and knowing he shou'd be ruin'd if he lost Timur's favor, confidently set out to come to court, where he presently address'd himself to the Mirza Charoc, whose protection he besought. This Mirza brought him to the throne, where with his head uncover'd, like a criminal, he beg'd pardon on his knees. Timur having reprimanded him, forgave his fault, and comforted him by his kind promises. This prince brought the tribute for several years past, which he paid exactly, and made abundance of handsom presents. The emperor gave him a crown, a royal vest, and a belt set with precious stones; and as an addition to the former favors confer'd on him, his daughter was betroth'd to the Mirza Aboubeere, and so he had the honor to be ally'd to Timur.

At the same time Youram grandson of Acbouga, a Georgian prince, came to pay his homage to the emperor, and made several presents of curious animals and fine horses, being introduc'd by the great Emirs, with Custendil brother of Malek Ghourghin, king of Georgia, who was at war with him. There came also the lords and princes of all the neighboring places, to pay their respects, and after their pre-

---

¹ A strong city and a principality, near the Tigris, in Mesopotamia.

ents. Timur receiv'd 'em with all manner of
civility according to their birth and quality, he
assur'd 'em of his favor, and presenting 'em with
vests, sent 'em back to their respective countrys.

CHAP II.

The government of Chiraz a second time given to the Mirza Pir Mehemed, son of Omar Cheik; and that of Ispahan to his brother the Mirza Roustem.

IN the neighborhood of Mencoul, Timur again invested the Mirza Pir Mehemed, son of Omar Cheik, in the government of the royal city of Chiraz, capital of Persia, for which he sign'd out his letters-patent, and made the Mirza set out for that country, after having given him a vest and a belt, and nam'd for his ministers Lutfallah, son of Beyan Temour, son of Acbouga, and Tchel Pauchat Berlas [1].

Then he dispatch'd orders to the Mirza Roustem at Chiraz to come to court. The messenger found him in the summer-quarters of the place of Cafrizer, and deliver'd his commission. The Mirza immediately set out, and being arriv'd at Canfar, a place dependent on Burbadecan, he receiv'd a pacquet from court, by which he learnt that the emperor had given him the government of Ispahan [2], ordering

---

[1] Two old men of great experience and trust.
[2] Capital of Hircania or Irac Agem, where the king of Persia at present resides.

him

him to send his baggage thither, and go to Ouroudgerd to rebuild the fortress of Ormyan. The Mirza Pir Mehemed, who was sent to Chiraz, also arriv'd at Cansar. These two brothers tenderly embrac'd each other, and entertain'd themselves with conversation on the present state of affairs; and afterwards they separated, and took their respective roads The Mirza Pir Mehemed departed for Chiraz, and Rouftem, having sent a lieutenant to govern Ispahan in his absence, went with expedition to Ouroudgerd, the fortress of which he rebuilt, and repeopled the city.

CHAP. III.

Timur sends the Mirza Aboubecre to rebuild the city of Bagdad, and gives him the government of Irac-Arabi and Diarbekir.

WHEN the court was arriv'd in the neighborhood of Cars[1], Timur order'd the princes his children, and the great lords of the state to come before him, and then made the following speech to 'em. " The war which
" the inhabitants of Bagdad have heretofore
" undertaken against us, having been obstinately
" continu'd by them, has been the cause of the
" desolation of their state, our vengeance having
" ing drawn upon 'em a total ruin. Nevertheless, if we consider that this is one of the
" principal citys in the Mahometan world, that
" the knowledg of the law deduces its origi-

---

[1] A city of Armenia near Georgia.

"from thence, and that the doctors of other
"countrys have drawn from this source the
"most sacred parts of religion, and the most
"useful learning; it wou'd be a crime utterly
"to destroy this famous city: wherefore we
"design to re-instate it in its former flourish-
"ing condition, that it may again become the
"seat of justice, and the tribunal both of reli-
"gion and laws."

The emperor's speech being universally applauded, he entrusted the execution of this commendable project with the Mirza Aboubecre, giving him the government of the provinces of Irac-Arabi, as far as Vaset, Basra, Curdistan, Mardin, Diarbekir, Oirat, with all their dependences, and appointing for the great officers of his court the Emirs Payende Sultan, Pir Hussein Berlas, Sevindgic, Sultan Sendger, Hadgi Seifeddin, Dolet Coja Einac, and others, with a great body of the army. Timur order'd the lords of Irac-Arabi to obey him, and mark'd out his road by the province of Diarbekir: he strictly enjoin'd him to exterminate all the disturbers of the public peace, who remain'd in that country, and to be in Irac-Arabi in the autumn, when the equinox renders the air more temperate. The emperor likewise instructed him to begin with ruining Cara Yousef Turcoman, who had made himself master of Irac-Arabi, and afterwards to encourage and comfort the inhabitants of the country, that they might rebuild their houses, and cultivate the lands, and in fine to employ all his care in restating Bagdad in its former splendor, that the following year there might depart people enough out of that city, to form a caravan for Mecca.

With

Book VI. With regard to Cara Youfef Turcoman, and his ufurpation, we muſt know that that prince for fear of our troops, fled into the country of Roum or Natolia; but when our army arriv'd at Cæfarea, he again fled from thence into Irac Arabi, where having affembled all the Turcoman hords, he ſtop'd at Payan-Hit. The Sultan Ahmed Gelair at that time went out of Bagdad, and retir'd to the Sultan Taher his fon, but the Aga Firouz, in whom the Sultan Taher repos'd the care of his affairs, excited a jealouſy in his maſter; whereupon he held a council with his father's Emirs, Mehemed Bei governor of Ormi, the Emir Ali Calander, Micayl, and Fatrac Chah, who likewife fear'd the Sultan Ahmed, and unanimoufly agreed to revolt; and having paſs'd the bridge during night, they encamp'd on this fide the river. When the Sultan Ahmed was inform'd of it, he broke down the bridge, and marching along the bank of the river, ſtop'd in prefence of his fon and the Emirs: he fent an expreſs to Cara Youfef to come and join him, which Youfef having done, they paſs'd the river together. The two armies being rang'd in order, a battel enfu'd, in which the Sultan Taher was vanquifh'd: he endeavor'd to fly, but coming to a brook, and ſtriving to make his horfe leap over it, he fell in with his horfe and armor, and perifh'd.

The Sultan Taher having been thus punifh'd for his revolt againſt his father, his Emirs and troops difpers'd, and the Sultan Ahmed, growing jealous of Cara Youfef, went to Bagdad. Cara Youfef came out of Hille with his army to the gates of Bagdad, and took the city. The Sultan Ahmed hid himfelf to fave his life, but was perceiv'd by one nam'd Cara Haffan, who affifted him in making his efcape during the

night

The history of Timur-Bec.

night, and taking him upon his shoulders brought him to a place near five leagues distance. On their way they met a man who had an ox, which the Sultan mounted, and went to Tecrit with Cara Hassan. Sarec Omár Ourit, governor of that place, made a present of forty horses to the Sultan Ahmed, with what money, arms, stuffs, and belts he was able. The Sultan was join'd in this city by several of his officers, as the Cheik Macsoud, Doler Yar, Adel, and others. From Tecrit he went to Damascus, while Cara Yousef became the peaceable possessor of Irac-Arabi. This digression was necessary for the better understanding of the history.

When Timur therefore made the Mirza Aboubecre depart for Bagdad, he sent orders to the Mirza Roustem at Ouroudgerd, to join Aboubecre before Bagdad, and march with him against Cara Yousef. The Emirs Toukel Arus Bouga of Hamadan, Tamun Soutchi of Nehavend, Chah Roustem of Sendgiar and of Dinaver, had likewise orders to march to Bagdad with the Mirza Roustem. The Mirza Aboubecre arriv'd at Arbele, and caus'd the governor Abdalla, and the other chiefs of the rebels, to be seiz'd and sent bound to court, with a present of Arabian horses, the care of which he gave to a Sultan. At this place died Payende Sultan Berlas; and the Mirza Aboubecre having left the baggage, march'd with expedition against Cara Yousef. The Mirza Roustem departed from Ouroudgerd, according to orders, and having taken the road to the dome of Ibrahim-Lic, he pass'd to Bagdad, and join'd the Mirza Aboubecre in the neighborhood of Hille.

CHAP. IV.

Timur's arrival at the frontiers of Georgia.

TIMUR having decamp'd from the neighborhood of Cars, enter'd Georgia After having pass'd thro Armenia, the Cheik Ibrahim prince of Chirvan, as a faithful servant, was gone before to make inroads into the enemy's country, and had already seiz'd on some passages and defiles Malek Ghourghin, king of Georgia, heard with a great deal of surprize of the march of the imperial standard. Fear exited him to send ambassadors to court with several presents, and the subject of the embassy was compriz'd in this speech.

"There is no comparison, great Sir, between
" you and me, who am your slave; and it is
" very astonishing that you shou'd have pro-
" pos'd to march against so mean a subject as
" I am, who am absolutely resolv'd to be-
" have my self as your faithful servant; and
" on the first order I shall receive from your of-
" ficers, whether to send in mony, or to march
" at the head of my troops in your service, I
" will not fail of acquitting my self faithfully
" and readily. I have not the confidence to
" come down directly to cast my self at the foot
" of your throne, for fear has too far seiz'd my
" heart: but if your highness shall please to grant
" me a short reprieve, till my fear is blown over,
" I will run to kiss your feet, as the prince of
" Merdin, and other governors have done, and
" I shall have the honor to prostrate my self be-
" fore you, and receive your orders as a slave, ac-
" knowledging this favor as an excess of your
" bounty."
Timur

Timur wou'd not hearken to what the ambassadors said, nor accept their presents: he told 'em, that their master's affair was no ways like that of the other princes, who were Mahometans, because the interest of religion pleaded for them, and render'd their faults more pardonable, but he being a Christian, ought not to expect the same favor; that if he was desirous of life, he must come directly to court; but if the grace of God shou'd not grant him sufficient assistance to enable him to embrace the Mahometan religion, he wou'd impose the tribute of the Carage * on him, leave him once more the principality of his country, send him back contented, and suffer his subjects to live in peace, without fear of being either murder'd, pillag'd, or made slaves; and thus his honor and reputation wou'd remain unblemish'd. He likewise told 'em, that the emperor of Constantinople, as a Christian, was on the same footing with him; that if Ghourghin had come to court, he wou'd have learnt how that prince had been treated, and what favors he had receiv'd, and that he ought to judge of his own case by the other: but if their master made the least difficulty of coming, none of his excuses shou'd be accepted of. At length the ambassadors were dismiss'd.

About this time Beyan Coutchin, governor of Tauris, came to court with the comptrollers and great officers of Azerbijana: they offer'd their presents consisting of a great number of horses, animals, and other things Ali Chacani, chief of the Divan of Corassana, for the Coja Ali Semnani, came also to offer his pre-

---

* A tribute which the Mahometan princes exact from the Christians or Jews who inhabit their dominions.

sents, which were distributed among the officers.

The season for the corn-harvest in Georgia approaching, it was requisite that the Georgians shou'd be hinder'd from reaping and carrying it in; whereupon Timur order'd the Emir Cheik Noureddin, and other Emirs, to enter the enemy's country forthwith: in effect, they chas'd out all the inhabitants, and destroy'd every thing with fire and sword, they reap'd all the corn and pulse, which they ground into meal, and so return'd laden with spoils to the imperial camp.

CHAP. V.

The taking of the famous castle of Cortent in Georgia.

THERE is a steep mountain in Georgia, a hundred and fifty cubits high, situate between two very deep defiles: on the south of it is a rock, which surpasses it in height, and which they ascend with ladders and cords. There is but one way to this mountain, and that very narrow and crooked; besides, the precipices which surround it hinder an army from encamping and besieging it. The Georgians had fortify'd this mountain on all sides, having built houses upon it, and a gate at the very extremity, with cisterns to preserve rain-water. It was commanded by a Georgian prince nam'd Tral, who had under him thirty great Osnaours, and a strong garison; they were not apprehensive of any scarcity, their cisterns being fill'd with water, their cellars furnish'd with delicious

cious wines, and the place ſtor'd with ſwine and ſheep.

Timur being appriz'd of the importance of this place, reſolv'd to take it, notwithſtanding the great difficultys which wou'd attend the ſiege, as it was in the midſt of the enemy's country, and wou'd require a great number of ſoldiers to carry it on, who wou'd not be able to find victuals and even water enough for 'em. Every one was ſurpriz'd at this undertaking, and believ'd it impoſſible to take the place; unleſs the ſole fear of Timur, who deſign'd to go there in perſon, ſhou'd ſeize the hearts of the beſieg'd, and make 'em ſurrender: but God had otherwiſe order'd it.

The imperial ſtandard arriv'd before the caſtle of Cortene on the 14th of Muharrem 806. The inhabitants immediately ſent to ſalute the emperor, offer him their preſents, and aſſure him of their ſubmiſſion, but ſeeing their flatterys cou'd not hinder the place being attack'd, they confided in the ſtrength of their walls, and declar'd war by a diſcharge of arrows and ſtones. Timur at the ſame time order'd the Emirs to take their poſts round about the place: the Emir Chamelic was fix'd on the ſide of the gate, having orders to build ſconces over-againſt it: two other Emirs had likewiſe orders to erect two ſconces in different places This was done, that if the ſiege ſhou'd laſt too long, a gariſon might be put in 'em, to incommode the place. Chamelic finiſh'd in three days one of theſe ſconces capable to contain three thouſand men; which excited the admiration of the whole army.

Timur encamp'd behind the fortreſs in a place proper to build battering-rams and other machines, and order'd a platform of ſtone and wood, which is call'd Meljour, to be built between his

Aug. 13. 1403.

camp and the castle, so high that it shou'd command the place, tho the Georgians had imagin'd that the height of their mountain wou'd have preserv'd 'em from all manner of insults. This work was not finish'd in less than a week;

Aug. 20. and on the 21st of Muharrem, a Mecrit, nam'd Bikidgek, who was skilful in marching over mountains, found means during night to get unperceiv'd upon a rock, south of the castle, there he caught a goat, and carry'd it to the very top of the rock, where having kill'd it, he plac'd it for a signal, and then descended without being seen by the Georgians. Next day Bikidgek related his adventure to the emperor, who applauded him, and gave orders for some very strong cords to be made of raw silk and thread, and ladders to be made of the cords: and then four Mecrits immediately ascended this rock, and drew up the ladders with long cords. On

Aug. 22. the 22d of Muharrem this design was executed they mounted by an arch, which a goat cou'd scarcely pass. A tree having grown out of the very ridge of this rock, they fasten'd the ladders to it, when they had drawn 'em up. The Emir Chamelic staid at the bottom of the ladders, and made fifty of the bravest Turks of Coraslana ascend, whose names he took down in writing: Argoudac was one of 'em. The Georgians were fast asleep while these things were passing. At break of day a Corassanian cried out with a loud voice, Allah Ecber, and bless'd Mahomet. Mahmoud, an officer of the Mirza Charoc, at the same time sounded his trumpet, and the Georgians surpriz'd at the alarm given 'em by the watch, ran to their arms to defend themselves. Timur took horse, pass'd the defile, and stop'd over-against the rock, which our brave men had mounted: he order'd order'd the brass drum to be beat, and the great cry Souroun made thro-out the whole army.

In the mean while, the way to the place by the rock being very narrow and dangerous, no more than three persons being able to march in front, one of our brave warriors march'd foremost, holding his buckler before him, he was sustain'd by two others, who advanc'd with him, but an arrow struck him in the mouth, which made him fall backwards, and the enemys seiz'd on his buckler. Abdalla Sebzuari advanc'd sword in hand, and slew some Georgians, till being mortally wounded in ten or twelve places, he fell down thro weakness. The Turk Mahmoud fell upon the enemys with a heavy club, with which he broke the leg of a very considerable Oznaour. In fine, of the fifty men who had mounted to the assault, several arriv'd at the gate of the castle, where a bloody skirmish ensu'd. Some also continu'd to attack the place from the Meljour before mention'd, so that the gate was broke, and the troops enter'd the castle.

This conquest happen'd the 23d of Muharrem, after a siege of nine days. The besieg'd begg'd for quarter on their knees: but most of the Oznaours or officers were precipitated from the walls· the governor, Tral, was bound and carry'd to the imperial camp with the whole garison, of whom not one escap'd. At the same time the Toughe [1] and standard of Mahomet was erected upon the walls, and the Muezins repeated the prayers of the Alcoran on the top of the church, and made the cry Yzan, which is

Aug. 22.

---

[1] A standard on whose top is a horsetail.

us'd to call the Mahometans to prayer. This conquest deserves to be recorded in history, and it is reported that the great Mahmoud Subectekin never gain'd so considerable victorys over the infidels of India, as our conqueror did over those of Georgia. Timur order'd Tral and all the garison to be beheaded, and their wives and children carry'd away captive, and he gave Tral's wife as a present to the Cheik Ibrahim, prince of Chirvan.

Timur afterwards order'd the machines, and Meljour, which had been erected against the place, to be burnt, and he return'd to his camp, where he heap'd honors and favors on Bikidgek and the other brave men who had first mounted the rock; he order'd money out of his treasury to be distributed among 'em, and gave 'em robes, sabres, belts, horses, mules, tents, umbrellas, young women, camels, furniture, and even gardens and villages in their respective countrys. He invested Mehemed Touran, sirnam'd the king of Bauran, who was one of the principal lords of Corassana, in the government of the place, assigning him a good garison of Corassanians: he gave him the revenues of the neighboring countrys, and enjoin'd him to preserve these frontiers for the Mussulmans, and not permit the Georgians to gain any more footing in the country; he order'd him to convert the church into a mosque, and build a niche in it instead of the altar, and in lieu of bells and crosses, to establish Muczins and readers of the Alcoran, according to the Mussulman law.

CHAP.

CHAP. VI.

Relation of what pass'd without during this siege.

DURING these transactions, the doctor Cotobeddin Carini came to court with all the great officers of Chiraz; he offer'd several presents of the finest stuffs, Arabian horses, mules for riding, and furniture, as pavilions, tents, umbrellas, and other curious things. Afterwards Hadgi Muzaffer arriv'd from the Mirza Roustem, and made his presents. The Cosa Muzaffer Neheuzi also came from Ispahan, and presented a great quantity of mony, pearls, precious stones, horses, saddled mules, stuffs, tents and pavilions, as likewise droves of horses and mules of carriage, with arms, and vessels and boxes of gold and silver. Timur distributed all these presents among the princes and lords of his court.

About the same time Idecou Berlas and Ahmed Daoud, who had been sent to Kirman, to receive and take care of the imperial treasures, as also Seifel Mulouk Hadgi Abdalla, receiver-general, return'd to the imperial camp: they had an audience of the emperor, who gave 'em a handsom reception, and to whom they offer'd their presents after the usual manner: they were accompany'd by the principal inhabitants of Kirman, and among others by Moulana Zyaddin Serradge, the Cheik Sedreddin, who were both Cadis, the Seid Hamza, and the Cheik Mahmoud Zendghi Adgem, author of the book call'd Dgiouch or Khourouch, which treats of the exploits of the glorious Timur, but this learned author had the misfortune to fall from off the bridge of Teflis, which is built over the river Cyrus, and be drown'd his son, who continu'd that work after his father's death, paid his respects to the emperor, who receiv'd him with a great deal of kindness, and comforted him by his favors for his father's death.

Yousef Gelil, Deroga of the city of Yezd, and Cayafeddin Salar Semnani, receiver-general of the revenues of the same city, as well as the commissarys of the Divan of Yezd, came also to court; as did all the great officers, and governors of the several provinces and citys of Coraffana and the two Iracs, who paid their homage at the foot of the imperial throne, and offer'd their presents, which consisted of the greatest curiositys of all Asia.

CHAP. VII.

Timur marches to Abkhaze.

AFTER the taking of Cortene, Timur summon'd the lords to a diet, where he made a magnificent banquet, and distributed his favors among the officers, according to their ranks He then took up a resolution to march to Abkhaze. he order'd the Emirs Cheik Nouredin, Chamelik, and others, to set out before with several squadrons, to ravage and lay waste Georgia, as far as Abkhaze, which is the northern frontier of that kingdom. They accordingly began their march, but as the ways were full of woods, the soldiers were oblig'd to cut down the trees to open a passage, and the ruin'

ruin'd every thing they met with in the countrys of the Armenians and Georgians. They were follow'd by the imperial standard; and Timur soon after enter'd into the middle of Georgia, where he plunder'd seven hundred towns and villages, laying waste the cultivated lands, ruining the monasterys of the Christians, and razing their churches to the very foundation, which were built of marble and free-stone.

But the Georgians having abandon'd their houses, were retir'd into caverns situate among rocks and high mountains, which they had ascended by ladders, which they drew up after 'em, and had fortify'd themselves in these caverns. Timur order'd a sort of boxes to be tied with chains, in each of which he plac'd several persons arm'd: these boxes were let down from the top of the mountain with great cords to the level of the caverns, where our dauntless soldiers attack'd the enemys with their arrows, and advanc'd to the mouths of the caverns with their swords and lances. They made their way into 'em notwithstanding the number of the enemys, and the advantage of their post; and tho in some of these caverns there were near a hundred Georgians, yet they leap'd out of their boxes into them, where they put all to the sword, making themselves masters of their spoils, and acquiring the merit of the Gazie. They punctually fulfill'd the Alcoran, which enjoins us to treat the enemys of the Mussulman religion with rigor; and they rooted up and burnt the trees, making havock every where.

The 14th of Rabiulevel 806, the Emirs and troops rejoin'd the imperial camp: next day they all pursu'd the chace, and took a great deal of game Timur hunted the day after, and continu'd to ruin the country, slaying all the Georgians he met.

Octob. 12. 1403.

CHAP.

CHAP. VIII.

Timur returns from Abkhaze. The cause of his return.

SEVERAL Georgian lords, who were slaves in Timur's army, having sent advice to king Ghourghin that this conqueror had render'd himself master of the country as far as Abkhaze, and that there remain'd no footsteps either of Armenia, or of the Armenians; that prince was seiz'd with fear, because this advice came from men of his own nation: whereupon he immediately sent ambassadors with presents to Timur. The remonstrance the Georgian slaves made to Ghourghin on this occasion, resembles the counsel the bishop of Nedgeran gave to his own people in the time of Mahomet. There goes a tradition that the inhabitants of Nedgeran being come to Medina, were so stubborn and proud as to dispute with Mahomet, and not receive the instructions he wou'd have taught 'em. Then the lord Ali, with Mahomet's daughter Fatima, and two grandsons Hasan and Hussein, came to the assembly to dispute with the Christian bishop: but this doctor, being surpriz'd at what he saw, far from disputing, said, "The men I now behold have "their faces irradiated. if they shou'd beseech "God to remove the mountains of the place, "he wou'd assuredly grant their request; and if "they shou'd be suffer'd to offer up their prayers "against the Christians, not one of 'em wou'd "remain alive." These words of the bishop struck terror into the Christians, who consented

ed to pay the annual tribute; after which they
return'd to Nedgeran, because their bishop had
on this occasion seen the lords of Mahomet's
family transform'd into angelical beautys. It
seems as if some such vision had engag'd the
Georgian slaves to write thus to Malek Ghourghin.

When the ambassadors of the king of Georgia
were arriv'd at court, they address'd themselves
to the generals of the army, and besought 'em
to intercede for them, humbly remonstrating
that their master was perfectly submissive and
obedient; beseeching 'em to employ their good
offices to appease Timur's wrath, and obtain
pardon for their master, who wou'd not fail of
sending immediately to court all his riches and
curiositys, and likewise the annual tribute; and
even promising that he shou'd send to the imperial camp, whenever he had orders so to do,
the troops which shou'd be requir'd of him.

This discourse touch'd the Emirs, who introduc'd the ambassadors into Timur's presence,
who gave an account of the subject of their embassy as usual: and the generals having found a
favorable opportunity, on their knees related to
Timur Malek Ghourghin's propositions, and
spake to him as follows.

" It is certain that your highness's intention
" in all your wars is only the increase and honor
" of the Mahometan religion: we see that
" God has bless'd your zeal in such a manner,
" that the Mussulman law has never before arriv'd at so high a pitch of glory in these countrys, for former emperors, and the most powerful Sultans of antiquity, accounted themselves happy when the Georgians gave only
" a few marks of their respect and obedience,
" either by sending a yearly present of horses,

" or

"or by furnishing a small number of troops when their occasions requir'd 'em in some war: and on these conditions the Georgians liv'd freely in Persia and the Mussulman kingdoms. But at present, thro your highness's great power, they esteem themselves happy, even in being shut up within the farthest parts of their kingdom, as long as they have quarter granted 'em for their lives. The Mussulmans have enter'd their capital citys, and enjoy themselves there, as if they were the masters of 'em. And thus, if your highness will grant 'em quarter on paying the tribute, and exactly obeying your orders, they will become faithful servants, and acquit themselves of their duty with entire submission and sincerity."

All the Emirs cou'd say, was not able to abate the emperor's zeal for the continuation of the Gazie, which oblig'd these lords to propose the affair to the doctors of the law and to the Muftis, who unanimously declar'd in the imperial council, that since the Georgians consented to pay the tribute, and not to injure the Mussulmans, they were oblig'd by their law to grant 'em quarter, without doing 'em any further harm either by slaughter or pillaging. According to the conclusion of the doctors, and in condescension to the prayers of the Emirs, Timur granted this favor to the Cheik Ibrahim, one of the intercessors, and nodded to him, in token that in respect to him he condescended to the request of king Ghourghin. He sent back the Georgian ambassadors between hope and fear: and afterwards he spent several days in these quarters in the diversion of the chace, till the return of the ambassadors, which happen'd soon. When they came back, they brought with
'em

'em a thousand gold medals struck in the name
and august titles of Timur, with a thousand horses, and great quantitys of curious stuffs, as also
vessels of gold, silver and chrystal, and a very
fine balass ruby, of a beautiful color, weighing
eighteen Medicales, there being few which
weigh so much. They presented the whole,
and oblig'd themselves by an oath to pay the
tribute.

Then Timur prepar'd to return home; he decamp'd, and after some days march arriv'd at
Teflis, having ruin'd all the churches and monasterys in the neighboring parts. When he had
gone two days journy beyond the river of Cyrus, he resolv'd to march to Carabagh to rebuild
the town of Bailacan: he set out before with
some of his favorite lords, and having pass'd by
Berda, encamp'd near Bailacan, where he was
join'd a fortnight after by the army and baggage, who also encamp'd there.

CHAP. IX.

Timur orders the town of Bailacan to be rebuilt.

THE Alcoran remarks, that the rebuilding
of places is one of the most glorious actions
which princes can perform in this world, and
which conduces most to the good of society.
When the army decamp'd in autumn, Timur was
incited to take up his winter-quarters at Carabagh where, not to lose time, and to keep the
troops in action, he resolv'd to rebuild the town
of Bailacan, which had been a long time ruin'd,
so that it was inhabited only by insects, scritch-
owls,

owls, serpents and scorpions. Tho the season was very cold, and the rains continually molested our soldiers, yet Timur soon after his arrival gave orders to the engineers and architects to draw the plan of the town, which shou'd consist of a wall, a ditch, four market-places, and a great number of houses, baths, caravanseras, squares, gardens, and other commodious places. They laid the foundations, and having mark'd 'em with lines, the emperor divided the work among the soldiers, under the inspection of the Chahzades' and Emirs. They wrought with so much diligence, that the buildings which were of brick, were finish'd in a month: the circumference of the walls was two thousand four hundred cubits of large measure, the thickness eleven cubits, and the height fifteen: the ditch was thirty cubits broad, and twenty wide: at each corner of the place was a great bastion, and in the middle of each courtine was a gallery with battlements, and a machine to cast stones. In fine, this prodigious undertaking, which the greatest emperors of antiquity were never able to finish in a year, was compleated in a month, notwithstanding the excessive cold and rains: the readiness with which Timur's orders were obey'd, was abundantly more surprizing than the execution of so vast a project. Never prince carry'd a more majestic and terrible air in his wrath; nor yet a more sweet and agreeable one, when he was pleas'd to bestow his favors.

Timur gave the government of Bailacan, Berdaa, Ghendgeh, the country of Arran, Armenia, Georgia, and Trebizond, to the Mirza Calil

---

' Chahzade, or Mirza, is the son or grandson of a king or emperor.

Sultan

Sultan. He honor'd Gelalelislam's brother, nam'd Behramscha, with the particular government of the town of Bailacan. And as water is what principally renders a country flourishing, inasmuch as it makes the land fertile, and nourishes the animals and vegetables, Timur form'd a design of cutting a canal, thro which to convey the water of the river Araxes into Bailacan. He issu'd out his orders to that effect, and the principal lords prepar'd themselves to put 'em in execution: the Tavatchis divided the ground the canal was to take up among the soldiers, which was six leagues in length, and fifteen cubits in breadth. The whole was finish'd in about a month; and it is one of the most magnificent monuments of Timur's grandure and power.

CHAP. X.

Timur sends intendants and doctors into all the provinces of his empire, to examine the affairs of particular persons, and to distribute his justice and favors among the people.

DURING Timur's stay at Bailacan, the principal lords of Iran and Touran came to court with all possible magnificence, where an assembly of the most learned men was held. The emperor, who was very curious in hearing the chief questions of the law explain'd, and the distinction between positive commands and those which contain only matter of advice, propos'd the most sublime and profitable controversys.

Book VI. One day the conversation fell very à-propos upon Mahomet's advice, wherein he tells us that God orders the princes of this world to practise justice and beneficence. the pious Timur attended to what was said, and seriously reflecting on it, wou'd not suffer this question to be ended by discourse only, but resolv'd to acquire the merits of it by practising good works, and then he spake to 'em as follows.

"Kings have always taken the counsel of doc-
"tors, when they excite 'em to do good, and
"strive to turn 'em from evil: how comes it
"then that you are silent, and neglect to tell
"me what I ought to do, and what I ought to
"omit the performance of?"

Then all the learned men modestly made answer, that his highness did not stand in need of the counsels of persons of their condition; but that on the contrary, others ought to learn how to conduct themselves by imitating his example

Timur told 'em, he did not approve this sort of compliments, by which they might expect to gain his favor; and that what he had said was neither thro' vain-glory or interest: "For thro the
"protection of God, says he, I am too great a
"lord in this world, to stand in need of such
"trifles, but my design in this results from the
"reflection I have made, that each of you
"coming from a different kingdom, must with-
"out doubt be inform'd of the affairs which
"pass there, and of the good or bad conduct
"of the Derogas, and commissarys of the Divan.
"Communicate therefore to me what you know,
"and tell me whether the governors and offi-
"cers observe justice and the commands of the
"law as they ought, that being inform'd of
"the evils they commit, I may remedy 'em,
"and deliver the weak from oppression."

Imme-

Immediately all the doctors freely declar'd their sentiments, applauding the emperor's intention, and they represented to his highness the condition the affairs of their respective provinces were in. Whereupon this just emperor made choice of the most learned among 'em, and those who were most vers'd in the laws of their country, and he nam'd an intendant to go with each of 'em, to whom he gave a full power to make laws, or to dispense with 'em, always approving whatever he shou'd do in relation to justice and the observation of the laws, so that right might be administer'd to those who were oppress'd thro-out all the kingdoms and provinces of his empire: likewise permitting these intendants to take out of the revenues of the imperial treasury of each country, what sums had been extorted from poor persons, by violence, against the ordinary rules, and to restore the same to 'em; and also to punish the tyrants in an exemplary manner: moreover they were order'd to register exactly every thing that shou'd pass during their commission, and at their return to give an account of it, that by this means the causes of vexation being entirely rooted out of the empire, the people may live in quiet and tranquillity. Then Timur made this memorable speech.

"My heart hath always been set upon the
" enlarging the limits of my vast empire: but
" now I take up a resolution to use all my care
" in procuring quiet and security to my subjects,
" and to render my kingdoms flourishing. I
" will that private persons address their re-
" quests and complaints immediately to my
" self, that they give me their advice for the
" good of the Mussulmans, the glory of the
" faith, and the extirpation of the wicked dis-
" turbers

"turbers of the public quiet I am unwilling
"that at the day of judgment my poor op-
"press'd subjects shou'd cry out for vengeance
"against me: I am not desirous that any of
"my brave soldiers, who have so often expos'd
"their lives in my service, shou'd complain a-
"gainst me or fortune; for their afflictions
"touch me more than they do them. Let
"none of my subjects fear to come before me
"with his complaints; for my design is that
"the world shou'd become a paradise under my
"reign, knowing that when a prince is just and
"merciful, his kingdom is crown'd with blessings
"and honors In fine, I desire to lay up a
"treasure of justice, that my soul may be happy
"after my death."

This speech of Timur, in which his piety is much to be admir'd, was taken down by a lord who was present at the assembly, and who wrote at the bottom of it these words of the Alcoran, *We give testimony only to what we have seen* After this the whole assembly lifted up their hands to heaven, and offer'd the following prayer: "O God, who art the lord both of
"this world and of the next, grant an ever-
"lasting reign to this just prince; hearken to
"his righteous petitions · and as thou hast sub-
"jected the universe to him, after a long and
"prosperous reign in this world, let him reign
"with thee in glory in the other."

CHAP.

CHAP. XI.

Continuation of the history of the princes who were gone into Irac-Arabi.

THE Mirza Rouſtem having join'd the Mirza Aboubecre near Hille, as already mention'd, theſe two princes, who were the Rouſtem and Esfendiar [1] of the age, paſs'd the river together, and met Cara Youſef Turcoman [2] over-againſt the town of Sib, on the banks of the river Nahrelganam, below Hille. They had then but three thouſand men, while Cara Youſef had entrench'd himſelf on the other ſide of the river with a numerous army, ready to give battel: and as the Mirza Rouſtem, being eldeſt, ought to have had the firſt rank, the Mirza Aboubecre prudently advis'd him to take his poſt in the main-body, but the Mirza Rouſtem anſwer'd him, that he was only come to bring ſuccours according to the orders given him; that it was better to ſeparate the army into two bodys, that they might each command one, and ſo attack the enemy on both ſides. In effect, the Mirza Rouſtem croſs'd the water, and attack'd Cara Youſef with all imaginable reſolution; and the Mirza Aboubecre did the ſame on his part: the attack was brave on our ſide, and as vigorouſly ſuſtain'd on the other. In the battel, Yar Ali, brother of Cara Youſef, was ſhot off his horſe with an arrow, and our men immediately

---

[1] Two famous heroes mention'd in the oriental romances.
[2] Prince of the Accoyunlus, or white ſheep.

cut off his head. The Emir Sevindgic distinguish'd himself bravely on this occasion, and contributed very much to the defeat of the enemy. Cara Yousef fled into Syria with some of his domesticks, but his subjects, who consisted of between ten and fifteen thousand familys, his oxen, sheep, and camels were pillag'd by our soldiers. Some of the Mirza Roustem's men brought Cara Yousef's wife, the queen of the Turcomans, to him in chains. She was the mother of Eskender and Espende, and was attended by the ladys of her court, and her relations.

Our princes also vanquish'd Noayr, who was absolute commander of all the Arabian tribes of the desart, and they likewise defeated several other princes of these quarters, who 'till that time had never submitted to any conqueror.

During the rebuilding of Bailacan, Sarel and Cotluc Coja, sons of the Dervich Buke, Aboubecre and Acbirdi Uzbec, officers of the Mirza Roustem, carry'd the happy news of these victorys to court, where they presented to Timur the head of Cara Yousef's brother.

After the causes of the disorders which Cara Yousef and other rebels had occasion'd, were remov'd, the Mirza Aboubecre employ'd himself particularly in rendring this country as flourishing as ever. He encourag'd the people, and oblig'd 'em to cultivate the lands; and he caus'd the city of Bagdad, which was almost ruin'd, to be rebuilt.

CHAP. XII.

Arrival of the Mirza Omar from Samarcand. Continuation of what happen'd during the building of Bailacan.

THE first of Jumaziulevel 806, the Mirza Omar, son of the Mirza Miran Chah, whom Timur had recal'd from Samarcand to take upon him the government of Azerbijana, arriv'd at the imperial camp before Bailacan, where he had the honor to pay his respects to his highness. At the same time came likewise to court a Circassian officer, the son of Toumen, with the head of Malek Azeddin king of Lor Coutchec, who had revolted: this officer brought advice that Malek had been flea'd, and his skin, stuff'd with straw, hung up in public view, to serve as an example to all future disturbers of the common tranquillity.

Nov 25. 1403

Timur about this time resolv'd to perform an act of justice on the person of the famous doctor Moulana Cotobeddin Carmi, who was come to court with the other officers of the Divan of Chiraz, because of his having tax'd the inhabitants of Fars at his departure from that place, at the sum of three hundred thousand Dinars Copeghi, under pretence of a present to the emperor. Moulana Saed, a doctor of the same country, who accompany'd him, accus'd him to Timur in a private audience, where the emperor had order'd him to give him what light he was able in relation to the affairs of Fars. This tyranny having highly offended his majesty, he immediately pass'd judgment

ment upon Cotobeddin, and iſſu'd out an order to the Cheik Dervich Aſlahi to bind his hands, and placing the fork'd branch about his neck, to ſend him in that manner to Chiraz, with the ſum he had extorted from the inhabitants, to be reſtor'd to thoſe who had paid it. Argoun, intendant to Cotobeddin, was condemn'd to be hang'd becauſe of the troubles he had brought on the people at his maſter's order. A declaration was alſo publiſh'd to inform the people of the deſtruction of theſe tyrants, in revenge of the wrong they had receiv'd: after which the intendancy of the finances of Chiraz was given to Coja Malek Semnani. The emperor order'd Moulana Saed to return to Chiraz, to declare to the inhabitants of Fars, that what Moulana Cotobeddin had done was not by his order, in proof of which Argoun was hang'd as ſoon as they arriv'd at Chiraz.

The following friday, the inhabitants of the city and neighboring villages being aſſembled in great multitudes in the old moſque, Moulana Cotobeddin was expos'd with his hands in fetters, and the fork'd branch about his neck, at the foot of the preaching-chair, which was of free-ſtone. Moulana Saed mounting the chair, told the people what the great Timur had order'd him, in alluſion to the words of Coja Amad Fakih. "If this kingdom, ſays he, has "been ruin'd, don't impute it to the emperor; "for Cotobeddin is only in fault." All the people applauded what he ſaid, and prais'd Timur, ſo that the moſque echo'd out their acclamations. The ſum of three hundred thouſand Dinars Copeghi, which Cotobeddin had extorted in the ſpace of two months, was entirely re-imburs'd, according to the regiſters of the Cadis,

Cadis, notarys, and Emirs of the kingdom, to those from whom it had been taken.

Thus justice was done in the person of one of the greatest lords of the kingdom, which ought to eternize the memory of Timur's equity. After this the Mirza Pir Mehemed, son of Omar Cheik, took off Cotobeddin's fetters, and fork'd branch, and sent him back to Samarcand.

CHAP. XIII.

Timur passes the winter at Carabagh-Arran. Relation of what happen'd there.

WHEN Bailacan was entirely rebuilt, Timur march'd towards Carabagh, where he had already given orders for Corias, or thatch'd houses, to be built, to pass the winter in. Being come to this place, he went down into the imperial Coria; and the Mirzas and Nevians quarter'd in those appointed for them, as did also the officers and domestics in theirs. Never was there seen before so magnificent a camp of such vast extent. The Mirza Rouftem came by the road of Coulaghi and Sunatai, according to the orders he had receiv'd to repair to the Couroultai or diet, which was to be held at Carabagh, to invest the Mirza Omar in the government of the kingdom of Hulacou Can.

In the mean while, on advice of the revolt of Eskender Cheiki, who with Timur's permission was return'd to his principality of Demavend and Firouz Couh, Solyman Chah had orders to go to Rei to observe Eskender's motions. The Mirza Rouftem was sent to assist Solyman in this affair: and they had orders, that if Eskender
shou'd

shou'd be so happy as to return forthwith to his obedience, to give him a handsom reception, but on the contrary, if he continu'd obstinate in his revolt, they shou'd draw together all the infantry of Com, Cachan and Deighuzin, and pursue and exterminate him wherever they cou'd find him. The Mirza Rouftem and the Emir Solyman Chah immediately departed to execute this order.

Then the Emir Cheik Ibrahim, king of Chirvan, prepar'd a great banquet to regale the whole court, he made a present to Timur of several pearls, beautiful women slaves, handsom boys, cuirasses, belts, arms, and a thousand led-horses, he also made fine presents to the empresses, princes, and chief persons of the state, and did what he cou'd to discover some marks of his affection to all the lords.

About this time Nour Elouerd, son of the Sultan Ahmed Gelair, about eighteen years of age, having been born during the war, was brought from Irac-Arabi. The venerable Cherif Seid Bereke then also arriv'd at court, the pious Timur went out of his tent to meet him. The Santon having perceiv'd him, flung off his turbant, and paid his compliments of condolence on the death of the Mirza Mehemed Sultan. Timur embrac'd him, and wept a long time with him.

The doctors, Imams, and lawyers of Transoxiana, Kech, Samarcand, Bocara, Termed, and other places, as the sons of the Can of Termed, Coja Abdelevel, Coja Afameddin, Coja Afdal Kechi, Abdelhamid and Abdelrahman, sons of the Cheik Eliflam of Kech, and other great lords of these kingdoms, came to court, where they were admitted to an audience, they paid their compliments of condolence on the death

death of the Mirza Mehemed Sultan, and endeavor'd to comfort the emperor by good counsels taken out of the Alcoran and the sayings of Mahomet. In effect, after they had somewhat moderated his affliction, he was pleas'd to have 'em dispute before him on some questions of learning and religion, which they did every evening, after Timur had done with the affairs of state.

One of the most considerable events which happen'd during Timur's stay at Carabagh, was that the secretarys of the Divan of Kirman had taken Idecou's account, in which they had set down in his name an excessive sum. Timur being inform'd of it during the building of Bailecan, apply'd himself to find out the truth of it in the Divan: but the princess Bouyan Aga, daughter of Timur's uncle *, presented her self big with child by Idecou, with her daughter Agatche, and compounded for it, by promising he shou'd pay a hundred Tomans Copeghi, and to which Idecou consented, obliging himself to pay that sum to the imperial treasury. Then he was confirm'd in the government of Kirman, and permitted to return home, with orders at his arrival at Kirman to send back from thence to court the Sultan Bayazid, his brother's son, who had been dispatch'd thither in his place, at Idecou's departure for court.

* Hadgi Berlas.

Timur sent Anoucherouan, son of Beyan Aga, of Tunis, to receive the revenues of Azerbijana: and he gave the government of Sari to Pir Mehemed Poulad, one of the Emirs of the Mirza Charoc. At the same time Bic Mulc Aga, wife of the Mirza Pir Mehemed Gehanghir, set out from Gaznin and Candahar for court, with her three sons Caled, Buzandger and Sultan Mehdi, who were then very young: she paid her respects to the emperor, and presented him with

several

several precious stuffs of India, and other curiositys.

CHAP. XIV.

The emperor sends the Mirza Charoc to Ghilan.

AS the princes of Ghilan were not come to court, but had only sent a few small presents, Timur resolv'd to march against 'em; he sent thither the Caraoul, or vanguard, commanded by Deryai Coutchin, Belal, Mehemed brother of Ali Sultan Tavachi, Bayazid, Borouldai, and Behloul Beilas, whom he order'd to pass the winter in the forest on the frontiers of Ghilan: and he likewise sent the Mirza Charoc to Kzelygadge at the head of his troops. This prince immediately set out, accompany'd by his son the Mirza Ibrahim Sultan, with his body of ten thousand men, the Emir Gehan Chah, the Cheik Ibrahim, Rouftem Tagi Bouga, the Seid Coja son of the Cheik Ali Behader, and other generals of Tomans with their troops: and they stop'd at Kzelygadge, expecting other orders.

As soon as the princes of Ghilan had receiv'd advice of the army's march towards their country, they were difquieted, abandon'd their former refolution, and confented to pay a great fum under the name of Carage. Charoc fent an exprefs to advertife the court of this; and made feveral perfons fet out to receive the tribute.

The Seid Razi Kya, one of the princes of Deylem, who was of Mahomet's race, and diftinguifh'd

The history of Timur-Bec. 333

Chap. 14.

tinguish'd by his knowledg of the belles-lettres, and the Emir Mehemed Kechti, also a prince of that country, departed together for court with magnificent presents: and each of the commanders of Ghilan sent presents and considerable sums of mony. Being arriv'd at court, they kiss'd the foot of the throne, and humbly offer'd their presents, saying that they were and had always been obedient to his highness; that they had us'd all their endeavors to collect the sums of the Carage, and that they had resolv'd to live and die in perfect submission to the emperor's orders.

Timur gave 'em vests, and highly honor'd 'em: and as the Seid Razi Kya was of Mahomet's race, he was pleas'd to treat him in a very handsom manner, and gratify'd him with ten thousand Mans of silk, that is, with fifteen thousand Mans of legal weight, with seven thousand horses and three thousand oxen, to be taken out of what the people had promis'd to pay for the Carage impos'd on their country: he gave the half of it to the Emir Mehemed, with a third of what remain'd due; and he issu'd out in order for the receivers to pay 'em these sums.

Timur likewise gave the Seid Razi the government of the castle of Kemac, on the frontiers of Natolia, which Chamis, a relation of the Emir Abbas, formerly possess'd; and he sent him thither with troops.

During the winter-quarters at Carabagh, the Cherif Seid Bereke fell sick: and tho his physicians employ'd all their skill, and administer'd the most excellent remedys, they cou'd do him no good; so that this great person pass'd from this world into the other with an entire resignation to the will of God. Timur was sensibly afflicted, and wept bitterly at the death of his

best

best friend; and afterwards he caus'd his coffin to be carry'd to Andecoud, to be there bury'd. Then he gave the governments of Hamadan, Nehavend, Ouroudgerd, Lircoutchek, and their dependences, to the Mirza Eskender.

CHAP. XV.

Arrival of some princes from Merdin and Vastan. A famous funeral banquet made for the late Mirza Mehemed Sultan.

WINTER being past, Malek Issa, prince of Merdin, came to court with several presents, bringing with him his daughter, who was betroth'd to the Mirza Aboubecre. Malek Azeddin Chir came also from Vastan with presents of abundance of horses to Timur, who gave him a handsom reception.

About this time the emperor issu'd out a general order to all the greater and lesser officers of the kingdom of Hulacou Can, residing in Azerbijana and Irac-Arabi, to send each a brother, or one of their relations, to reside at Samarcand: and that this project might be executed without delay, he order'd several officers to repair to the respective places, to bring 'em away forthwith.

In the month of Ramadan, Timur made a funeral banquet for the prince Mehemed Sultan, in which the poor were principally regal'd. The Cherifs, doctors, and Imams of all parts, were at the banquet, and took their places according to their ranks and dignitys. The entire Alcoran was read over, and the feast concluded with prayers for the repose of the Mirza's soul. Afterwards

rewards the princess Canzade went to Sulta- Chap. 13.
nia, and transported from thence to Samarcand
the Mirza's coffin, which had lain in the tomb
of the prophet Caidar.

Timur after this order'd a famous chace in the
plains of Actam, beyond the Araxes, in which
the utmost magnificence appear'd. The dogs
had coverings of lattin imbroider'd with gold,
and the hunting-leopards had chains of gold set
with precious stones about their necks: there was
an infinite number of Grecian grey-hounds, so
esteem'd for their swiftness, as also a very uncommon and excellent kind of beagles, but what
were most remarkable, were huge European mas-
tiffs, as strong as the lions of Africa, as terrible
as tigers rous'd up to the fight, and as swift as
arrows. After three days the circle began to
close, and the slaughter, which is call'd Camar-
michi, was made upon an infinite number of
wild beasts, as lions, antilopes, roe-bucks, as
well of the mountains as of the plains, and also
stags.

After the hunting was over, Timur return'd to
the camp, where he distributed among the Cherifs,
doctors and Imams of Samarcand, Kech, Bocara,
and other citys of Transoxiana, an innumerable
quantity of uncommon curiositys, which he had
taken from the kingdom of Natolia, among
which were several handsom stuffs, belts of gold,
beautiful horses, mules, women-slaves and boys;
after which he permitted 'em to return home,
which they did, loading his highness with their
praises and thanks.

CHAP

CHAP. XVI.

Timur's return from a campain of seven years

TIMUR having made himself master, during his campain of seven years, of the kingdoms of Natolia and Syria with their dependences; and having oblig'd the inhabitants of Grand-Cairo, the capital of Egypt, to coin the mony, and read the Coutbe, which is the friday-prayer for the reigning prince, in his name and titles; the Egyptians having also submitted to pay an annual tribute, and Timur having likewise fulfil'd the precept of the Alcoran in making war on the Christians of Georgia, whose pride and power he assuag'd: he found that to crown the triumphs of his happy life, he had no more to conquer in all Asia than the empire of China, the inhabitants of which were infidels. Whereupon he immediately resolv'd on that conquest, and departed from Ca-
April 8. rabagh the 14th of Ramadan 806, which an-
1704. swers to the year of the Monky, for Samarcand. He cross'd the Araxes on a bridge, and encamp'd on the other side in a meadow near Nimet-Abad, one of the towns on the canal of Berlas, which canal he had dug himself, as we said before; and he was join'd here by the Mirza Charoc, who according to order had taken the road to Kzelygadge

CHAP.

CHAP. XVII.

Timur invests the Mirza Omar in the empire of Hulacou Can.

ABOUT this time a great feast was made at court on occasion of the emperor's giving the Mirza Omar the government of the empire of Hulacou Can, for which he issu'd out his letters-patent sign'd with the imperial seal, which was the impression of his red hand. This empire contain'd the countrys of Azerbijana, the kingdom of Roum or Natolia as far as Constantinople; and Syria as far as Egypt. The princes who govern'd the kingdoms of Fars and the two Iracs, were commanded to obey his orders, and assist at his diets. Timur gave him the troops and officers of the Mirza Miran Chah, and permitted him to depart at the same time he nam'd for his principal officers, who were to have pensions, the Emirs Gehan Chah, Roustem son of the Emir Moussa, Tevekkul Berlas, Juneid Bourouldat, and others, and gave him ten thousand horse, recommending to him to do nothing contrary to the sentiments of the Emir Gehan Chah. Then Timur presented to this new king of the Medes a crown, a vest, a belt set with precious stones, and a horse with a saddle of gold, and to each of his Emirs a robe and a belt.

The prince then took leave, and paid his respects to the emperor, who tenderly embrac'd him as well as the Emirs, and then dismiss'd 'em. The Emir Gehan Chah cou'd not refrain from tears at parting from the emperor and court, because of his long affection to his highness. Timur

mur afterwards gave vests and belts to the Emir Cheik Ibrahim, Malek Issa the Sultan of Merdin, Malek Azeddin Chir, Kustendil a Georgian, Tizee, Dialeh, and Bestam, whom he order'd to attend on the Mirza Omar, who took his road thro the delightful country of Alatac.

Timur departed from this place, and hunted in his march. After a day's journy he encamp'd in a meadow on the bank of the river Abagloc, otherwise nam'd Tchaybelaroud, where he staid to the end of Ramadan.

Timur celebrated the feast of the grand Bairam with great devotion and pomp. Moulana Nezameddin Chanabi, one of the most eloquent doctors of the age, who had wrote part of the history of Timur, preach'd that day, read the Coutbe, and perform'd the ceremonys of prayer. Several alms and pious gifts were distributed, and the feast was finish'd by a magnificent banquet, in which were serv'd up abundance of the most excellent dishes and wines.

CHAP. XVIII.

Continuation of the history of the Mirza Roustem and the Emir Solyman Chah, who were sent towards Rei.

THE Mirza Roustem and the Emir Solyman Chah, who were gone to Rei to gain intelligence of what Eskender Cheiki was doing, being arriv'd at that country, found that Eskender had revolted, and having fortify'd the citadel of Firouz Couh, and plac'd in it his son and family, had fled to the mountains in the forests of Tchelaoun and Roustemdar. Our generals staid twenty days at Tahran in the province

...nce of Rei, and having got together the infantry of Rei, Com, Cachan, Savé and Derghezin, to the number of two thousand, they departed in pursuit of Eskender, enter'd the forest of Rouftemdar, and besieg'd the fortress of Nour, which they took and raz'd. Malek Kcoumerres came to find 'em in this place, and as he was at variance with Eskender, they seiz'd him, and sent him to Eskender. "Be-
"hold, say they, we send you your enemy,
"that you may see we are willing to accommo-
"date matters with you. therefore suspect no-
"thing, but come without delay to meet us
"If you return to your obedience, we'll make a
"treaty with you in the name of Timur you
"have spent part of your life in his service, don't
"root up the tree which you have planted

Eskender dar'd not come to 'em because of his revolt, but endeavour'd to strike up an accommodation with Kyoumerres, and as well by threats as promises, engag'd him to be of his party Then having sworn a reciprocal friendship, they join'd against us, and committed acts of hoftility Whilft the court was encamp'd on the bank of the river Agloc, a courier came from the Emir Solyman Chah, who gave advice to the emperor of what had happen'd. Whereupon Timur immediately resolv'd to march thither in person, and sent orders to the Emir Mezrab, lieutenant-general of Coraffana, to march with his troops by the road of Sari and Ancol, to revenge him on Eskender.

The 7th of Chawal 806, an officer of the Mirza Calil Sultan arriv'd from Tranfoxiana, who assur'd the emperor from that prince that the affairs of those parts were in a very good condition, and that the people enjoy'd perfect peace and tranquillity.

April 30. 1404.

CHAP.

CHAP. XIX.

Timur sends the Mirza Eskender and the Emir Chamelic before the rest towards Rei.

THE emperor being arriv'd at Ardebil, sent the Emir Chamelic and Pir Ali Selduz, with a thousand men, to Rei before the others, with orders to get together the soldiers of the Arabian tribes and the hords of Caladge, Turks who dwell about Savé, Com, Cachan, Tchara and Perahan, as far as Kerchroud, and to form 'em into a body to join the army: and he order'd the Mirza Eskender to join the Mirza Rousiem and the Emir Solyman Chah

Timur having pass'd by Ardebil and Myana, went down to Sertchem, where he found Douladi governor of Avenic, who was come thither to pay his respects to him Timur tenderly embrac'd him because of his former services, and having given him a vest and belt, said to him, "We are not certain we shall ever be able to "see each other again; but don't neglect in-"forming your self of what shall pass at my "court The Sultan Ahmed Gelair is at pre-"sent retir'd, and in a low condition, so there's "nothing to be fear'd from him but be upon "your guard against the Turcoman prince Ca-"ra Yousef." Then Timur dismiss'd his old friend

Timur departed from Sertchem, and arriv'd at Sultania the 20th of Chawal 806, to which place came the persons who had been sent into Ghila to receive the mony we mention'd before, they brought thence a great quantity of mony, horses

The history of Timur-Bec.

gifts, and curiositys. The emperor departed next day but one from Sultania, and after some days journy arriv'd at Casbin, to which place the Mirza Aboubecre came post in nine days from Ardebil by the road of Kelas, having for his attendance Pir Huffein Berlas and Serindgic. He paid his respects to his highness, and besought him to permit the Mirza Miran Chah, his father, to go to Bagdad, to reside there with him: which request was granted. Miran Chah receiv'd a gratification of four hundred thousand Dinars Copeghi¹, a hundred horses, and several toys, and then return'd to Sultania.

Timur being gone from Casbin to Saouc-Boulac, gave the Mirza Aboubecre two hundred horses, a hundred pair of cuirasses, and a huncred thousand Dinars Copeghi · he order'd him to meet the Emir Solyman Chah, and march with him against Eskender Cheiki. The emperor also made a present to Chahimulc, wife of Aboubecre, and daughter of the Emir Hadgi Seifeddin, of the lordship of Dudgyail, dependent on Bagdad, and this princess then return'd to Sultania.

Aboubecre having caus'd the snow to be remov'd, ascended the mountain of Acabay Talagoun, and join'd the Mirza Rouftem at Kudevour, the Mirza Eskender, and the Emir Solyman Chah, who were all encamp'd there with a good trench round 'em, fortify'd with branches of trees · and they staid here twenty days, till the arrival of the army. Having receiv'd fresh orders to fall upon Eskender, they departed to that end, and as the country was entirely cover'd with wood, they cut down the trees to

---

¹ A Dinar Copeghi is a ducat of gold, in value seven livres.

open a way cross, and mended the passages which had been ruin'd with planks, and thus they pursu'd Eskender, killing all the enemys they met.

Timur enter'd the meadow of Rei the first of Zilcade 806, and encamp'd in the plain of Sari Cam on he order'd the superfluous equipages to be conducted by the road of Rei and Khouvar Bic Mulc Aga, wife of the Mirza Pir Mehemed, had leave to return with her sons to Gaznin and Candahar The Emir Chamseddin Abas and others, who had the care of transporting the Caratatars and colonys, which had remov'd from Azerbijana, had orders to take the road of Kroutar and Semnan Then the Emir Chamelic, who had set out before, arriv'd at Rei.

Timur being come to the castle of Ghulkendan, which lay in ruins, situate at the foot of mount Demavend, examin'd it, and gave orders for its being rebuilt of stone and mortar, and render'd as flourishing as before. From thence having pass'd by Demavend at the head of his army rang'd in order of battel, he arriv'd at Firouzcouh

---

CHAP. XX.

The taking of the citadel of Firouzcouh.

AMONG the strongest places mention'd in history, none deserves more notice than the citadel of Firouzcouh, situate on the ridge of a mountain, with walls of the utmost strength On the 9th of Zilcade 806, the imperial standard arriv'd there, and the troops form'd the siege, encamping at all the avenues round about it. Every one having taken his post, the machines and

...d arms necessary were got ready the throwers of wild-fire began the assault, and were seconded by the bravest men of the army, who expos'd their lives with the greatest intrepidity. And as one of the towers of the place was built at the foot of the mountain, on the bank of the river, and the walls of that tower were rais'd as high as the level of the mountain, the besieg'd made use of it to draw up water out of the river; but our men turn'd the course of the river from the foot of the mountain, and spoil'd the water which was left. This oblig'd the besieg'd to sally out to hinder 'em, being resolv'd rather to die than suffer this.

During night an officer of the Mirza Ibrahim Sultan, accompany'd by Mehemed Azad, Cheik Behloul, Beyantencour, Acbouga, and other brave men, got up one after another to the foot of the walls. They were perceiv'd by the besieg'd, who ran thither in great numbers, fought with all their strength, and wounded several of our men; but day being come, all the soldiers ascended the mountain by different places, and gave a general assault. The son of Eskender Cheiki, governor of the castle, and all the others, perceiving the intrepidity with which they were attack'd, were seiz'd with fear, tho the garison consisted of three hundred men, or rather giants of Mazendran, or satyrs of the forest. Their inquietude oblig'd 'em to send several of their men to Timur, to beg quarter with submission. The emperor gave these messengers vests, and treated 'em with abundance of kindness; whereupon they were no sooner return'd to the place, than Eskender's son, and all the rest of the officers and soldiers, came to cast themselves at the emperor's feet, and deliver up the castle, which the troops enter'd, and made all the inhabitants go out, that they might be transported to another place. Thus this strong citadel, whose top seem'd to reach the heavens, was taken after two days siege. Timur left there, as governor, Zenghi Touni with a good garison.

June 2. Next day, the 11th of Zilcade 806, Timur took horse, and went to incamp in a meadow half a league from thence. He sent back to Samarcand the empresses Serai Mole Canum and Touman Aga, with the Mirzas Oluc-Bec, Ibrahim Sultan, Aidgel, and Sadvaccas, who departed by the road of Sultan Meidan: and afterwards the emperor march'd against Eskender Cheiki.

Then advice was brought that the Caratatars, being arriv'd near the town of Damgan, had wounded their Deroga, and were revolted; the Deroga of another band, which march'd after 'em, discover'd Tangribirmich, who lay upon the earth naked and wounded, and scarce alive, and carry'd him into the town to dress his wounds. The other bands hearing this, resolv'd to fly, upon which the Emir Chamseddin Abbas, Atilmich, Chalvch son of Sevindgic, and the other captains of companys who had the conduct of the bands, fell sword in hand upon these miserable wretches, of whom they destroy'd a great number, and either within the town of Damgan, or near it, slew about three thousand upon the spot, so that the dead bodies stop'd up the passage of the streets. Several fled into the forests of Estar-Abad, and the Emir Chamseddin brought away the rest.

Timur on advice of this immediately sent away Beyan Coutchin, Fazel, son of Seifelmulove, son of Hadgi Seifeddin, Dane Coja, Routem Pouled, and Comari Behader, with fifteen hundred horse, in pursuit of the fugitives. The Mirza

Mirza Ahmed Omar Cheik and the Emir Berendic were likewise sent after 'em on the same account, and went as far as Damgan: but they soon return'd to join the emperor, because they found that some of the Caratatars had been slain, others fled, and others brought away by the Emir Chamseddin and the Derogas Beyan Coutchin, and the others who went out first in pursuit of the fugitives, pass'd by Bestam, cross'd the mountain of Lengheroud, enter'd the forest of Mazendran, and join'd the Caratatars at Caratugan, on the shore of the Caspian sea; and tho the Tartars were far more numerous, yet they attack'd 'em immediately, and having happily defeated 'em, slew above a thousand, and took more than ten thousand familys prisoners. After this expedition Beyan Coutchin return'd to court.

When the empresses, who had taken the road to Samarcand with the baggage, were arriv'd at Bestam, the officers who conducted the Mirza Charoc's baggage, parted from the rest, and went to Herat by the way of Nichabour; and Serai Mulc Canum and Touman Aga went by the road of Jadgerom and Esferain with the greatest baggage.

CHAP. XXI.

Timur marches to Tchelao.

TIMUR being accustom'd to execute the greatest part of his enterprizes himself, he march'd in person against Eskender Cheiki: and as the Mirza Charoc was fallen sick, he return'd to Herat with the officers of his houshold,

while

Book VI while his Emirs and troops follow'd the imperial army to Tchelao, at which place they arriv'd in a few days, altho the ways were over high mountains, and thro deep vallys. The troops being arriv'd at the mountain of Tchelao, the ungrateful Eskender was oblig'd to fly, and retire into the defile call'd hell.

June 11. The 20th of Zilcade Timur arriv'd at Tchelao, from whence, not being able to find Eskender, he departed the same day. In this road is a very deep defile full of woods, always cover'd with mists and fogs, in the middle of which is a great and extremely rapid torrent, which can neither be forded nor swum over. The great difficulty there is in passing this defile is the reason of its being nam'd the defile of hell; and as Eskender had broke the bridge over the torrent, after having pass'd it, Timur was oblig'd to build another. The soldiers shortly built one of wood, on which forty brave officers pass'd first, and were follow'd by five hundred men, whom they commanded. Yousef Berlas afterwards cross'd it with Couthin Touchcal, as did the Seid Coja, son of the Cheik Ali Behader, and at length the Mirza Sultan Huffein, follow'd by the Emir Cheik Noureddin, who got up to the ridge of the mountain of the defile, cutting down the trees to open a passage in search of Eskender. Timur also pass'd the bridge, and encamp'd on the top of a mountain where there were no trees, but continual rains and fogs. At this place Timur gave audience to the Seid Ismael of Kersecan, one of the lords of Termed.

Timur sent soldiers into all the forests to find Eskender, assigning 'em for guides the Cherifs of Mazendran.

Among

Among those who went in search of Esken- Chap 21.
der, the captains Deryay Coutchin, Chadimulc
Berlas, the Cheik Mehemed Coutchin, Bic Temour Coutchin, Codadad Tchoura, and Vefadar, met him on the 26th of Zilcade 806, in June 17.
the middle of a wood near the Caspian sea. The
Cheik Dervich Allahi was seiz'd with fear, and
turn'd back on pretence of bringing Yousef Berlas
with more expedition to back 'em, he being
behind 'em with his troops.

In the mean while Eskender, at the head of
two hundred foot and thirty horse of his ac-
quaintance, sally'd out of his little camp, and
prepar'd to attack our men, who were but twenty
in number, and were not ignorant of Eskender's
valor, having seen him several times in action;
for intrepidity and courage were hereditary to
him, being descended in a right line from Bigen
son of Keyou, and Banou Kechaspe daughter of
the great Rouftem, as may be seen in the Chah
Namé or Fardaousi, which makes Bigen speak
these words, " My grandfather was a lion in
" battel, my father was the great Keyou: this
" day you shall behold my prodigious exploits "
Our twenty men, notwithstanding this, fearing
Timur's reproaches, resolv'd rather to die than
fly, reflecting that if the time destin'd for their
death was come, they might as well die here as
in another place: so they collected all their courage, and confiding in the ordinary good fortune
of Timur's arms, discharg'd their arrows Eskender, follow'd by his horsemen, attack'd 'em
several times with their pikes, but our men so
dexterously ply'd him, that he cou'd not only
gain no ground, but shamefully turn'd his
back before a handful of men, with all his soldiers Ingratitude is the source of all misfortunes. Eskender had preserv'd his honor, if he
had

Book VI. had not abandon'd Timur, from whom he had receiv'd so many favors.

After Eskender was fled into the forest, our scouts quarter'd in his camp, not knowing what road he had taken. Then Yousef Berlas arriv'd with Seifelmulouc and Hadgi Abdalla, who also enter'd Eskender's camp, which they entirely pillag'd, carrying away abundance of horses, mules, stuffs of gold, and other riches. They were join'd there by the Mirzas Roustem and Aboubecre, accompany'd by the Emirs Sevindgic and Solyman Chah, who came from the left. At break of day there appear'd in the mountain something glittering, which advanc'd towards 'em. The Emir Sevindgic march'd to the left towards the mountain and forests in search of Eskender: aking with him his nephew Leherasp and all his men, and met the Emir Ali, Eskender's son, with his daughter, wives and domestics, who were all made slaves.

CHAP. XXII.

Battel between the Mirza Sultan Hussein and Eskender Cheiki. The flight of the latter.

THE Mirza Sultan Hussein, and the Seid Coja son of the Cheil Ali Behader, join'd our scouts with seventy men, and enter'd with 'em into the woods in search of Eskender. They met him about noon in the midst of this forest, having with him two hundred foot and fifty horse, who prepar'd to defend themselves. The Mirza Sultan Hussein fell furiously upon Eskender, and immediately retreated as if he wou'd have fled. The enemy, who thought to im-
prove

...this seeming advantage, sally'd out of the ...d to fall upon our men, but they turn'd ...'em suddenly in good order, and made ...el slaughter of the foot. Vefadar perform'd ...er cou'd be expected from a great man; ... wounded with a lance in his face, which ...ck out his teeth: yet this did not hinder ...ghting Two horsemen of Tchelao were ...de prisoners by the officers of the Mirza Sul... ... Eskender perceiving himself ...quish'd, re-enter'd the woods, and went out ... the side towards Ghilan He was never heard of more, tho some say that he took the habit of a monk, while others assure us that he died thro grief in the woods.

The Mirza Sultan Hussein sent one of the men who were taken to Timur by Cazan Dervich. The emperor was then encamp'd in the moun...in we spoke of before, and order'd the man ...nform him what he knew of Eskender.

The Mirza Sultan Hussein at his return met on the shore of the Caspian sea the Mirzas Rouliem and Aboubecre, with the Emirs So-...im Chah and Cheik Noureddin, who had ...en in search of Eskender, they march'd toge-ther long the sea side near three leagues, ad-vancing towards Ghilan They encamp'd there, and were join'd by the Emir Mezrab Yacou, who had likewise been seeking Eskender with the troops of Corassana by the road of Amol and Sari. Then all the Emirs departed together for the imperial camp. Timur, notwithstanding all the fatigues they had undergone, reprov'd 'em ...not having continu'd to pursue Eskender, and sent 'em all back again on the same account with the Emir Chamelic They fatigu'd them-selves exceedingly in the woods, which were very miry, because of the continual rains, which

hinder'd

hinder'd their encampment. On advice of this Timur sent orders for 'em to return.

Then the emperor decamp'd from the mountain, and crossing the bridge over the torrent in the defile of hell, went to encamp before the castle of Nour in the province of Rouftemdar. The soldiers brought before him Eskender's nephew, and others of his relations, with several of his officers. he gave 'em a handsom reception, and granted 'em quarter.

During night an express came from the Mirzas Aboubecre and Sultan Huflein, and from the Emir Solyman Chah, with advice of their arrival at the torrent of the defile of hell, which they cou'd not pass by reason the bridge was broken. Timur immediately sent to 'em Mehemed Azad and Toukel Baourtchi, with thirty watermen of the Gihon, having for their chief Ourdouchah, who with their usual dexterity built a bridge, on which the Mirzas cross'd the torrent with their troops, and return'd to join his highness.

The army pass'd the night in the same place, and next day march'd to the castle of Harfi towards Ghilan: and Timur being arriv'd at Kelare Decht, encamp'd some days in that meadow, where the Emir Cayafeddin Ali, son of the Seid Kemaleddin, had a handsom reception from the emperor, who gave him the principality of Amol, because he had always carry'd on a war with Eskender Cheikhi.

CHAP.

CHAP. XXIII.

Timur returns to the seat of his empire.

AFTER the flight of Eskender, the taking of his wives, children and domestics, the conquest of his fortresses, and the pillage of his effects, horses and cattel, the emperor resolv'd to return to Samarcand. He order'd the Mirzas who had the government of the two Iracs to go thither, and likewise the Seid Azzedin Hezaregheri with his brothers, and the Seid Ali Mazendrani, to return to their respective governments and he gave vests to each of 'em. The Mirza Roustem, attended by the Emir * Said Berlas, departed for Ispahan, the Mirza Aboubecre for Bagdad, the Mirza Eskender for Hamadan, the Seid Azzeddin for Hezaregheri, and the Seid Ali for Amol.

At length Timur departed from Kelare Decht, and in few days arriv'd at the country of Lar, at the foot of the mountain Demavend, where the emperor Argoun Chah had built a pavilion in form of a dome, which is yet nam'd the Kiochk of Argoun.

The 20th of Zilhadge 807, he decamp'd, and march'd with so great expedition with the Emirs and his domestics, that on the 22d he encamp'd at the mountain of Firouzcouh. He gave the Emir Solyman Chah a vest wrought

July 10, 1404.

---

* Emir signifys commander: as also a prince of Mahomet's race, likewise call'd Cherif and Seid. But all Emirs are not Cherifs, for there are some Emirs who are not Mahometans, as among the Drufes, Maronites and others,

with

with gold, and a cap enrich'd with precious stones, leaving him in the government of the towns and provinces of Rei, Firouzcouh, and their dependences: and he permitted Beyan Coutchin, Deroga of Rei, to return to guard the castle of Ghule Khindan.

Ju'y 14. From thence Timur pass'd by Sultan Meidan, and the 24th of Zilhadge arriv'd at Bestam, where he visited Sultan Elaarefin, whose prayers he besought, distributing alms among the poor Pir Padichah, prince of Esterabad, who had follow'd Timur in this expedition, and had been permitted to go before the rest to his own town, return'd to this place to meet the court, and offer his presents, among which were nine sets of horses, nine in each. Timur gave him a vest, and sent him back.

Dané Coja, who had been sent in pursuit of the Tartars, arriv'd at the same place, and gave an account of what he had done. Timur order'd that the Tartar chiefs he had taken shou'd be laid in irons, and conducted to Samarcand by the Derogas of the countrys they shou'd pass thro. The emperor departed from Bestam the same day, and being arriv'd at the town of Jagaz, the lord Hasan Soufi Tercan came to him from the Mirza Charoc, to be inform'd where his highness wou'd appoint that prince to meet him. Hasan Soufi was sent back post, to let Charoc know he might meet the emperor on the bank of the river Joucoudgecan.

July 20 1404. Then Timur march'd with expedition, and the first of Muharrem 807, departed from Nichabour, and went down to Achcabad. The 3d he encamp'd at the tomb of Dgyam, where he paid his devotions, imploring the prayers of that Santon. Afterwards he set out from thence, and went to encamp on the bank of the river Joucoud-

The history of Timur-Bec.

Joucoudgeran, where the Mirza Charoc had the honor to kiss his hands, and offer his presents, which were generously distributed among the lords who attended the court. Hend bachan brought to this place Acbouga, and Carabougai Joun Garbani, whom he had made prisoners, because they had revolted during the emperor's absence, who order'd 'em to be hang'd in an hospital near that place.

About the same time Timur sent the Coja Ahmed Torsi, to be treasurer-general of the revenues of Corassana, and comptroller of the registers of the commissarys. this lord collected in forty days the sum of two hundred Tomans Copeghi from the monied-men and the commissarys.

Then Timur took leave of the Mirza Charoc, and departed. When he was arriv'd at Corlan, he encamp'd at the brink of a fountain near the hospital, to which place Temour Coja Acbouga came from Samarcand to meet the emperor, to whom he presented nine race-horses. From thence Timur went to encamp at the bank of the river Morgab, where he receiv'd the complaints of the inhabitants of Chichecrou, against the oppressions of Apactelpa, their Deroga, who was condemn'd on that account to have his feet bor'd thro, and himself hang'd with his head downwards, which was accordingly executed.

The emperor then departed, and on his road was met by the Derogas of the towns and the Kelanters of the tribes, who presented to him fresh horses, which the officers mounted, to make the more haste. Then he pass'd by Lengher Cheik Zade Bayazid, Andecoud, Ducca, the defile of Ghez, and Ali Abad; and encamp'd near the town of Adina Mesdgid, where he receiv'd the principal inhabitants of Balc who came to meet him. From thence Timur went to Syabghird, and crossing the Gihon in a bark, quarter'd at Termed in the palace of the lord Acalmulc, where this Can's son made a magnificent banquet, and considerable presents. Afterwards he pass'd by the iron-gate of Coluga, and by Chekedalic, and went to encamp at Doulburdgi. From this place he march'd to Kech, and lodg'd in Acserai: then he visited the tombs of the Santon Chamseddin Kelar, whose prayers he implor'd, and of the prince his father, the Mirza Gehanghir his son, and all his children and relations. At length he took horse, cross'd the mountain of Kech, and lay in the garden of Tact Caratche; from whence he went down to the garden of Caratopa, and quarter'd in the palace of Gehannuma, where he was complimented by the Mirza Caidou, son of the Mirza Pir Mehemed Gehanghir, being conducted by Coja Yousef, and Argoun Chah governor of Samarcand, who kiss'd the ground, offer'd their presents, and sprinkled precious stones upon the emperor. The empress Toukel Canum, with all the ladys and Emirs, also paid their respects, and offer'd their presents. As the emperor had made such haste, that no one cou'd know of his arrival, the Cherifs, Cadis, and principal persons of Samarcand, had not an opportunity of meeting and paying their respects to him at any other place than this

CHAP.

CHAP. XXIV.

Timur's entry into his imperial city of Samarcand.

TIMUR departed from Gehannuma in the month of Muharrem 807, and went down to the garden of planes in Samarcand, from whence having made his entry into the city, he visited the college of the Mirza Mehemed Sultan, which he had not seen since it was built; and afterwards he return'd to the garden of planes, where preparations were made for the banquets. The empresses and Mirzas, who had set out first with the baggage from Firouzcouh by the way of Baverd, Macan and Merou, not being yet arriv'd, Timur dispatch'd couriers to hasten their coming. The empress Touman Aga having cross'd the Gihon at Amouye, met the courier in the meadow of Bocara, who staid there three days to wait the great empress Serai Mulc Canum. Then leaving the baggage there, they went with expedition to Vabkyanab, thence to Rebatmulc, and the meadow of Tchacmounar, thence to Tatkent, and afterwards to Kutche Malek, where a feast was ready prepar'd for 'em, while a second courier arriv'd to advertize 'em to hasten. Hereupon they instantly took horse, and in a short time came to Samarcand. Serai Mulc Canum went down to Baghi Tchenar, and Touman Aga to Baghi Behicht, whither Timur immediately repair'd. But God was not pleas'd to suffer him to attain to this utmost pitch of glory and power, without some mixture of bitterness; for

July 1404.

this

Book VI — this good success in the conquests of Syria, Egypt and Natolia, was follow'd by a distemper which seiz'd him in Baghi Behicht, but did not last long. After his distemper was gone off, he went to Baghi Chemal to reside there for some days, where he gave a handsom banquet to all the Mirzas and lords of the court, on the birth of a son to Beghifi Sultan.

Timur afterwards enter'd Samarcand, and lodg'd in the palace of the late Mirza Meherned Sultan, for whom he caus'd a magnificent sepulchre to be built in form of a dome, close to the college built by that prince: the cincture of the dome was of marble set off with gold and azure; within it was dug a vault, to lay the prince's body in; and a charming garden was made round it on the ruins of some houses. Then the emperor apply'd himself to render justice to the oppress'd, and remedy the evils which had crept in among the inhabitants of Samarcand. When he pass'd by the great mosque, which himself had built, he thought the gallery, which had been erected during his absence, was too little: so he order'd another to be made, and reprimanded in the hall of audience the architect Coja Mahmoud Daoud for his not having done it as it ought to have been. Timur lodg'd in the college of Serai Mulc Canum situate over-against the mosque; and to render his justice the more conspicuous, he order'd the commissarys and comptrollers to be arrested and bound, who being interrogated, those who were found culpable receiv'd the punishment they merited, according to the wrong they had done the people, and Masaoud Daoud and Mehemed Dgilde, who had been the principal secretarys, and during Timur's absence perform'd the function of Visier

Visers, were both hang'd at Canigheul, during the banquet which we shall relate hereafter.

Afterwards Timur went to the garden of planes, where by the procurement of the Emirs he gave audience to an ambassador of Ideeou emperor of Capchac, who presented to him a Chuncar * and other things, and made his harangues, which contain'd his master's submission and testimonials of obedience.

* A bird of prey.

From hence the emperor went to the garden of Dileucha, where he staid several days, and receiv'd an ambassador from one of the greatest sovereigns of Europe ⁹, who made him several curious and magnificent presents, among which were pieces of tapistry, which the Europeans had work'd with so much niceness, that if they were to be compar'd with the great performances of the painter Mani on the cloth of Artene, Mani wou'd be cover'd with shame, and his works appear deform'd.

Then Timur order'd the architects, who had been brought from Damascus, to build a magnificent palace in the garden south of Baghi Chemal, which was square, each of its sides being a thousand five hundred cubits. This palace was the largest and most magnificent of any Timur had built. The chief ornaments of the buildings in Syria are of marble, and running streams are common in their houses: the Syrian architects are also very ingenious in mosaic work and sculpture, and in contriving curious fountains and perpetual jets-d'eau, and what is most remarkable is, that with stones of divers colors they do the same

---

⁹ From the king of Castile, of which we have an account written in Spanish, mention'd more particularly in the French author's preface to this book.

sort of work, which the artificers in inlaid work do with ebony and ivory, and that with equal niceness and delicacy. They likewise made several fountains in the palace, the beauty of which was augmented by an infinity of jets-d'eau of divers forms, with a surprizing and inimitable art. Afterwards the workmen of Persia and Irac enrich'd the out-parts of the walls with porcelane of Cachan, which gave the finishing stroke to the beauty of this palace. Then Timur order'd a noble banquet to be prepar'd, with all the delights which mortals can desire, or by which the senses can be gratify'd. He was there congratulated by the princes his children, the empresses and princesses, who sprinkled upon him gold and precious stones. The European * ambassadors were also invited to this great banquet, and partook of the diversions, for the Casses ⁕ have also their place in the sea ˢ.

* Spar.sh.

CHAP. XXV.

Timur holds a general diet. A great feast for the marriage of the princes at Canighul.

TIMUR having long since form'd a design of conquering all Asia, cou'd not refrain from finishing what he had intended. Neglectful therefore of the delights of repose, he

---

* A little animal, about the size of a barly-corn, which are seen upon the surface of the sea.
ˢ By this expression we perceive the great contempt the Zagataian court had of the Spanish ambassadors.

took

took up a resolution to subdue the empire of China, which was inhabited by infidels. But before he wou'd begin this great enterprize, he was willing to execute the command of the Alcoran by the marriage of his grandchildren. Hereupon he order'd a feast to be made; and sent out his circular letters to all the governors of provinces, generals of his armys, and Cherifs and nobles of his empire, to meet at a general diet, where they were to celebrate the nuptials The princes Taizi Aglen and Bachtemour Aglen, who were descended from Genghiz Can, intreated Timur to summon the Mirza Pir Mehemed who was at Gaznin, and the Mirza Charoc who was in Corassana, to this famous Couroultai: they obtain'd their request for Pir Mehemed, but as to Charoc, Timur answer'd, that it was not proper he shou'd come, he being the main support of the kingdoms of Irac and Azerbijana.

Canighul was the place appointed for the marriage-feast, and the first of Rabiulevel 807, which answers to the year of the Monky, Timur went to lodg there. This palace and the neighboring places were adorn'd with the greatest magnificence; so that this autumn-season render'd, in a manner, even the spring jealous. The tents were tied with silken cords, in which were abundance of carpets wrought with gold: the curtains were of velvet of Chuchter; and the cielings of ebony and ivory exquisitely engrav'd. The emperor's apartment consisted of four great inclosures, which are call'd Seraperd, built on very regular plans: his Kherghiah or imperial pavilion made two hundred tents, gilt and adorn'd with precious stones. Each tent had twelve columns of silver inlaid with gold; the out-side was scarlet and

Octob. 17. 1404.

seven

seven other colors, and the inside satin of all colors. The upholsterers, of whom there was a great number, had employ'd a whole week in erecting and furnishing this magnificent apartment. The Mirzas and Emirs had also each a Seraperd, a Barghiah, tents, and a great pavilion nam'd Kherghiah [6]. The columns of the tents were of masly silver, and the floor was cover'd with the richest carpets.

The governors of the provinces, the generals of the army, the lords and principal commanders of the empire, assembled in this place, and pitch'd their tents in good order. The people also came there from all nations, as China, Muscovy, India, Greece, Zabul, Mazendran, Corassana, Fars, Bagdad, Syria, and in short from all the kingdoms of Iran and Touran, that is to say, from all Asia.

During these entertainments Mengheli Bougai Hadgeb, one of the principal lords of the court of Melch Ezzaher Barcoc, king of Egypt, arriv'd in quality of ambassador from Malek Ennaser Farrouge, who had succeeded Barcoc his father. This Mengheli was endow'd with very rare qualities, cou'd repeat the whole Alcoran by heart, was master of a great deal of eloquence, and acquainted with several sciences, which render'd him the most agreeable person in conversation. He brought abundance of uncommon presents, ready mony, precious stones, rich stuffs, and nice toys. Among other rarities was a Ciraffa [7], one of the strangest animals

---

[6] Seraperd is an inclosure. Barghiah a great hall of audience, and Khergiah a great pavilion. The two last are [...] in the Seraper.

[7] A [...] creature about the bigness of a calf, bred in Africa, and, according to some, got by a camel upon a panther. It is call'd in latin Camelopardalus.

upon

upon the earth, and nine of the largest ofſtriches of Africa.

The Mirza Calil-Sultan came from Turkeſtan to this aſſembly, where he ſaluted the emperor, the great Emirs of ſtate, as Burdi Bei, Yadghiar Berlas, and others, who all made a very ſplendid appearance. The Mirza Pir Mehemed came from Gaznin, according to the orders he had receiv'd, he paid his reſpects to Timur, who embrac'd him, and by his tears teſtify'd his ſorrow at the death of his brother the Mirza Mahemed Sultan. The Mirza made his preſents, nine of a ſort: and next morning Timur gave him a veſt wove with gold, a crown and belt; and veſts to the officers of his houſhold, who left off their mourning-habits.

Then Coja Ahmed Touſi, receiver of the revenues of Coraſſana, arriv'd, and preſented the ſums belonging to the treaſury of Coraſſana, with abundance of curious toys, nine of a ſort. The emperor was not the only perſon who partook of the joys and diverſions; for both high and low had their ſhare. The moſt skilful artiſts prepar'd ſome maſter-pieces of their art, as trophys and cabinets of flowers to repreſent triumphs, which were adorn'd with garlands made up with perfect ſymmetry. There were in the jewelers ſhops necklaces of pearls and precious ſtones, eſpecially of grenadin and balaſs rubys, with an infinite number of pieces of rock-chryſtal, coral and agat, and ſeveral rings, bracelets and ear-rings; all which render'd Canighul a mine of gold and precious ſtones, inſtead of a mine of flowers, which its name implys.

An amphitheatre with four corners was built, call'd Tchartac, which was cover'd with pieces of brocade and Perſian carpets. There were ſeats for both the vocal and inſtrumental muſic, and

and also places for the buffoons and jesters, who with their facetious sayings excited mirth and laughter. There was likewise another Tcharta for all sorts of tradesmen, and a hundred of a different manner, fill'd with those who sold fruit, each of whom had made a kind of garden of pistachios, pomegranates, almonds, pears and apples, in great order; which perfum'd the air, and made an agreeable sight. The butchers were particularly taken notice of for the neatness of their representations: they dress'd up a sheep in a man's shape, and other skins in divers other ridiculous figures. There were speaking goats which had horns of gold, and run after one another: they appear'd outwardly like goats, but were handsom young women disguis'd in this manner: some were dress'd like fairys and angels, with wings, while others took the figure of elephants and sheep.

The skinners also appear'd in masquerades, some like leopards, others like lions, and others like other animals, with whose skins they were cover'd: there were those likewise who resembled foxes, and tigers. The design of the masquerade was to represent genii who had transform'd themselves into these several figures. The upholsterers likewise produc'd a masterpiece of their trade, for they made a camel of wood, reeds, cords, and painted linen, which walk'd about as if alive: and the man within it, drawing a curtain, discover'd the workman in his own piece. The manufacturers of cotton also made birds with cotton, which look'd as if they were alive. they also made a Minaret of the same material with the help of reeds, which every one imagin'd to be built with brick and mortar, and which was higher than the Minarets of the mosques; it was cover'd ver'd with brocades and imbroidery-work, carry'd itself about, and on its top was plac'd a stork. The saddlers were not behind the rest; for they gave proofs of their skill by two litters for women, which open'd at the top, and after the usual manner were laid upon a camel, in which sat two of the most beautiful women of the city, each holding a skin in her hand; and they made pleasant postures as well with their feet as hands, to divert the assembly. The matmakers likewise shew'd their dexterity, having very neatly work'd with reeds two lines of writing of Coufi [1], and other large letters.

On the other side were the rope-dancers, who by their agility attracted every one's admiration; their rope at the same time seeming to touch the heavens. Thus the whole company was employ'd either as actors or spectators, all endeavoring to contribute to the celebrating the marriage of the princes the emperor's children, that is, of the Mirzas Olouc-Bec and Ibrahim Sultan, sons of Charoc, Aidgel son of Miran Chah, Ahmed, Seidi Ahmed, and Biera, all three sons of the Mirza Omar Cheik.

The emperor order'd the astrologers to chuse a happy moment for an affair of such importance; which being done, the first officer of the houshold drew the curtain of the gate. The Cadis, Cherifs, Imams and doctors of the empire, met the emperor; and having agreed on the articles of marriage, the great doctor Cheik Chamfeddin Mehemed Jazari was chosen to read 'em to the assembly. The grand Cadi of Samarcand, Moulana Selahheddin, receiv'd the mutual consent of the partys, which he register'd; and then,

---

[1] The antient character of the Arabians.

Book VI. according to the maxims of the Hanafyan law he join'd the princes and princesses together in marriage, on whom every one sprinkled gold and precious stones

The emperor being seated on his throne order'd a banquet of the utmost magnificence to be serv'd up to the brides and the other ladys of the court, by the most beautiful young women of his seraglio, who wore crowns compos'd of flowers The princes of the blood, Emirs, Nevians, Cherifs, and foreign ambassadors, took their place according to their rank and dignity, as well as the Emirs of Tomans and Hezares. These lords were seated under a canopy of twelve columns, distant from the nuptial hall about a horse's course

The Yesaouls, or exempts, whom the Turks call Chaoux, were there backwards and forwards to perform the function of their posts, mounted in a magnificent manner upon horses of great price, with saddles of gold, adorn'd with precious stones, and habited in vests of gold brocade, with an air of authority * and command.

On another side there were elephants of a prodigious size, on whose backs were plac'd a kind of thrones, with abundance of ornaments Under the canopy with twelve columns, were plac'd earthern urns, with strings of precious stones tied about 'em, fill'd with gold and silver posts, and on the tops were cups of gold, agat, and rock-chrystal, adorn'd with pearls, and several sorts of jewels, all which were presented on salvers of gold and silver. The drink was

---

* The Yesaouls carry in their hands, as a sign of their office, a silver wand.

Cam-

Cammez [1], Oxymel, Hippocras, brandy, wines, Sirma, and other liquors. It is reported that the wood of several large forests was cut down to dress the victuals at this banquet. The head-steward with his under-officers constantly attended to give all necessary orders as to the serving up of the dishes, before which an officer always walk'd. There were tables furnish'd in different places thro-out the whole plain, and flaggons of wine set near the tables, with an infinite number of baskets full of fruit. Besides the flaggons for the emperor's use, and for the lords of the court, there were several jars rang'd in all the plain for the people's drinking: and that the joy might be universal, the emperor order'd a proclamation shou'd be publish'd that all the people might enjoy what pleasures they pleas'd, and no one take cognizance of 'em. The crier read the proclamation as follows; " This is the time of feast-" ing, pleasure and rejoicing. Let no one com-" plain of or reprimand another. Let not the " rich encroach upon the poor, or the power-" ful upon the weak. Let none ask another, ' Why have you done thus?" After this declaration every one gave himself up to those pleasures he was most fond of, during the feast: and whatever was done pass'd unobserv'd.

At length the feast was finish'd; after which, according to custom, a vast quantity of curious movable goods was laid upon mules and camels for the new-marry'd princes; among which were all sorts of rich habits, crowns, and belts

---

[1] Cammez is a drink us'd among the Tartars. The way of making it is mention'd in the history of Genghiz Can, book 5. chap. 10.

set with precious stones. The mules had coverings of satin embroider'd with gold; their little bells were gold, as well as those belonging to the camels: and both were handsomly adorn'd. This pompous equipage pass'd before the people, who were struck with admiration. The bridegrooms with their brides were cloth'd nine times in different habits, with crowns and belts set with precious stones; and each time they chang'd their clothes, they paid their respects as usual, while gold and precious stones, pearls, rubys, and balass rubys, were sprinkled upon 'em in great numbers, with which the ground was cover'd, and which became the domestics profit.

The following night there were every where illuminations with lanthorns, torches and lamps; and the new-marry'd princes enter'd the nuptial chamber. The next day Timur did 'em the honor to pay 'em a visit at their own apartments, being accompany'd by the empresses, and great Emirs and Cherifs of his court. The rejoicings were so great thro-out the whole empire, that from Canighul as far as Tous in Corastana, there was not one place, where the sound of drums and trumpets was not heard.

The ambassadors of Egypt, Spain, India, and Decht Capchac, Gete, and others, were witnesses of this magnificence, and particularly of the pleasures of the feast, which lasted two entire months. Timur distinguish'd 'em by particular favors, and gave vests to them, as well as to the Cherifs and other great lords, who were assembled from all parts of the empire; he did the same to the generals, the governors of the provinces, and all the officers.

After the marriage-feasts were over, Timur again betook himself to the administration of

public

public affairs, ordering every one to return to his proper employment. The licence which had been granted during the feast was recal'd, and for the future no one was allow'd to drink wine, or commit any thing unlawful. Afterwards Timur retir'd to his closet, to address himself to God by the following prayer.

"O Almighty-being, who art above whatever man can conceive, and whose essence is unknown to any but thy-self, being all in all; how can I recite thy praises, and how return thanks in proportion to the favors I have receiv'd, since they are infinite? Out of nothing hast thou created me; from poverty hast thou made me rich, and from a petty prince hast thou render'd me the most mighty emperor of the universe. To thy great bounty I owe the gaining of so many battels, and the conquest of so many kingdoms: for what am I, a poor and vile creature? I shou'd be incapable of every thing, were I not assisted by thy grace. In peace thou favor'st me with quiet and joy; and in war thou givest me victory, and maintainest me in sovereign authority, fear'd by my enemys, and lov'd by my subjects. Continue then, O thou great Creator thy goodness towards me: since thou hast chosen me in thy clemency, don't chase me away in thy wrath. I know that I am but dust; and that if thou dost not favor me with thy protection, all my glory and grandeur will be turn'd into vileness and dishonor. O Lord, put me not to shame because of my vices, who have been so long accustom'd to partake of thy favors: and then I shall rest contented."

CHAP.

CHAP. XXVI.

The causes which incited Timur to undertake the conquest of the kingdom of China.

IN the beginning of Timur's rise Asia was in the possession of usurpers, who had rais'd themselves to sovereignty, either by the extinction of the race of former kings and emperors, or by intrigues and revolts: but as the world cou'd not be peaceably govern'd by so many sovereigns, there were continual wars amongst 'em, and the poor people were drove into great extremitys. Virtue and tranquillity were banish'd the places which robbers only possess'd, security was no longer to be met with on the high-ways, which were full of thieves, and in fine, every thing was in confusion and disorder. The world might then be well compar'd to a human body, which being infected with some corrupt matter, necessarily falls sick, and can receive no benefit but from a strong medicine, which purges out the cause of the disease, and yet this purgation can't be undergone without some inconveniences which may arise from a deprav'd appetite. In the same manner, God, who was pleas'd to purge the world, made use of a medicine, which was both sweet and bitter, to wit, the clemency and the wrath of the incomparable Timur, and to that effect, inspir'd in him an ambition to conquer all Asia, and to expel the several tyrants thereof. He establish'd peace and security in this part of the world, so that a single man might carry a silver-bason fill'd with gold from the east of Asia

Asia to the west. But yet he cou'd not accomplish this great affair, without bringing in some measure upon the places he conquer'd, destruction, captivity, and plunder, which are the concomitants of victory.

After this hero was happily return'd from the conquests of Syria, Natolia and Georgia, and of consequence found himself absolute master of all the empires of Iran and Touran, he generously took up a resolution to make preparations for the conquest of China, which was inhabited by infidels, that by this good work he might rectify what had been amiss in other wars, wherein the blood of so many of the faithful had been spilt. Thus, after the marriage of the princes his grandchildren was consummated, he summon'd the Mirzas his children, and the great Emirs of his council to court, to whom he made the following speech.

"God hath favor'd us with such extraordi-
" nary good fortune, that we have conquer'd
" Asia, and overthrown the greatest kings of
" the earth; few sovereigns in past ages having
" acquir'd so great dominions, or attain'd so
" great authority, or had such numerous armys,
" or so absolute a command. And as these
" vast conquests have not been obtain'd with-
" out some violence, which has caus'd the de-
" struction of a great number of God's crea-
" tures, I have resolv'd to perform some good
" action, which may atone for the crimes of
" my past life, and to accomplish that which all
" the world besides is not capable of, that is,
" to make war on the infidels, and exterminate
" the idolaters of China, which can't be done
" without very great strength and power. It
" is therefore fitting, my dear companions, that
" those very troops which have been the instru-
" ments

"ments whereby those faults were committed
"shou'd also be the instruments of repentance
"and that they march into China, to acquire
"the merit of that holy war, in demolishing
"the temples of the idols of the fire, and erect
"ing in their places mosques and chappels
"By this means we shall obtain the pardon o
"our sins, as the Alcoran assures us, saying
"that good works efface the sins of this world."

Timur having finish'd this speech, the prince of the blood and Emirs besought God to bless his good intentions, unanimously applauding his sentiments, and loading him with praises "Let the emperor, say they, display his standard; and we his slaves will follow him, and sacrifice our lives in his service."

Then orders were given to the Tavachis to take an exact number of all the soldiers by thousands, and to augment and enroll the regiments Timur commanded all the Emirs of Oulous [1], and the governors of provinces, to assemble their soldiers: they took copys of the Toutcal [2] from the great Tavachis, that they might know in what order and with what arms they shou'd come; and they departed, to get together their troops in all the provinces

Timur then went from Canighul, and enter'd the city of Samarcand, where he lodg'd in the college of Serai Male Canem. He gave the Mirza Pir Mehemed a crown, belt and horse, and permitted him to return to Zabul; he also gave to each of his domestics a horse and a suit

---

[1] The Emirs of Oulous are the natural lords of the Tartar hords, who are inferior to the governors of provinces.
[2] The order for the war.

of clothes: he order'd the Mirza Sidi Ahmed [4], Chap. 26.
son of Omar Cheik, to accompany him. And
they took the road to Candahar.

The emperor did particular honors, and gave
vests and belts to the ambassador of Egypt,
who obtain'd leave to return home: he order'd
Moulana Abdalla Kechi to accompany him,
whom he sent with a convoy in embassy to the
Sultan of Egypt, for whom he gave him a letter
seventy cubits long, and three in breadth, wrote
in letters of gold by Moulana Cheik Mohemed,
son of the doctor Hadgi Bendeghir Tebrizi,
who won'd not yield to his father as to the beauty of his style and the art of writing finely.
The substance of this letter was an answer to
what the Sultan of Egypt had writ with regard
to the Sultan Ahmed and Cara Yousef. He sent
with his letter several curious presents worthy
of the greatest princes.

Timur likewise granted particular honors and
favors to the ambassadors of Europe [5], Decht
Cubchac, Gete and other parts, and permitted
'em to return home. He likewise dismiss'd the
princess Melket Aga, who had assisted at the
feast, and afterwards return'd to the Mirza Charoc at Herat. He sent to Hamadan the princess
Begum Sultan his daughter, to the Mirza Eskender her husband: and she pass'd by Bocara and
Macan

---

[4] I believe this Sidi Ahmed was the father of Baber Mirza, whose descendents reign in India at this present, under the title of the great Moguls.

[5] The Spanish ambassadors, whom we have mention'd in the preface, were dismiss'd at the same time as those of Egypt were without obtaining an audience of leave of Timur, who was reported to have been very sick, on which account, in the Spanish relation it is said thro mistake that he was dead.

Timur gave the Mirza Olouc Bec the government of the towns of Tachkunt, Seiram, Yenghi, Achira, and all the kingdom of Gete as far as China, and to the Mirza Ibrahim Sultan that of Andecan, Acfiket, Taraz and Cachgar, as far as Cotan, which he confirm'd by letters-patent seal'd with his red hand. Among the Emirs of the Mirza Pir Mehemed, Tagi Bouga and three others set out to assemble the troops of those provinces, and bring 'em to Tachkunt, which was the general rendezvous of the army. Temour Coja Acbouga was banish'd to Assigheul in Mogoliftan, for a fault he had committed.

Timur went from the college of Serai Mulc Canum to Arec [e], and lodg'd at Gheuc Serai, a palace he had built.

CHAP. XXVII.

Timur sets out for the war against the infidels of China.

THE Alcoran remarks, that if any one in his pilgrimage to Mecca shou'd be surpriz'd by death, the merit of this good work is written in heaven in his name, as surely as if he had had the good fortune to execute it: it is the same in relation to the Gazie, where with trouble and fatigues mix'd with dangers an eternal me

---

[e] Arec is the inclofure of the anuent royal palace of Samarcand.

rit is acquir'd; and he who dies during the expedition is deem'd to have executed his design. It was fitting that so great a hero as Timur shou'd die in the bed of honor, and that this inevitable accident shou'd happen during a journy he undertook for God's glory, and to acquire the rewards the Alcoran promises to the Gazie, that is, the war against the infidels. And as the death of this great man was nearly approaching, when he took up a resolution to march into China, God permitted that neither the season, nor the countrys he must pass thro, which were always cover'd with snow and frost, shou'd be able to divert him from his resolution, or oblige him to retard his departure till the spring.

He gave orders to the Emir Berendac to review the troops, and bring him an account how many men there were in the army he design'd to carry into China. This Emir reported, that the troops of Transoxiana, Turkestan, Balc, Bedakchan, Corassana, Sistan, Mazendian, the Caratatars brought from Natolia, the colonys from Persia, Azerbijana and Irac, amounted to two hundred thousand men compleat, capable of undertaking the greatest enterprizes. Timur, very much pleas'd at the good state of his troops, distributed his treasure among 'em, and commanded 'em to begin their march.

The Mirzas Calil Sultan and Ahmed Omar Cheik, accompany'd by the Emirs Codadad Hussein, Chamseddin Abbas, and other generals of Tomans and Hezares of the right wing, were order'd to pass the winter with their troops at Tachkunt, Chahroukhia, and Seiram, and the Mirza Sultan Hussein was to take up his winter-quarters with some troops of the left wing at Iassi and Sabran. Chahroukhia, which was formerly nam'd Fenakunt, was so ruin'd by Genghiz

ghiz Can's army, that there remain'd no footsteps of any edifices till the year of the Monky, which answers to the year of the Hegira 794, when Timur order'd his lieutenants to rebuild and repeople it; and as Timur then gave it to the Mirza Charoc, it was call'd from his name Chahroukhia.

The emperor having entrusted the government of Samarcand to Argoun Chah, and the care of his treasures to the Cheik Tchoura, order'd the great standard to be display'd, and he departed from Samarcand the 23d of Jumaziulevel 807, the sun being in the middle of Aquarius, in a sextile aspect with Jupiter, and the moon being in Libra, in a sextile aspect with the sun, and in a trine aspect with Jupiter. He laid hold on the happy moment which the astrologers had fix'd for his departure, and took the road to Acsoulat. He went directly to Caraboulac in Sogdiana.

Then the standard departed from Caraboulac, and took the road to Ilanoti, and after several days arriv'd at Tambic, where great rains and snows fell, the wind blew excessively, and the cold was extremely violent: yet this did not hinder Timur's departure and arrival at Acsoulat. And as this place was full of sands, and there was abundance of small wood for burning, orders had been given before to build cottages of reeds, and some houses fit to lodge in. The emperor being repos'd in his apartment, the Mirzas and soldiers encamp'd each in their respective posts. The sun was then enter'd into Pisces, the cold daily encreas'd, and the winter was more violent than usual.

CHAP.

CHAP. XXVIII.

An account of certain adventures, the knowledg of which is necessary to the understanding the latter part of this history. A relation of what pass'd at Acsoulat.

LOVE is often the cause of many disorders. The Mirza Calil Sultan, after having got with child the princess Dgehan Sultan, daughter of the Mirza Ali, Timur's sister's son, became desperately in love with one of the concubines of the Emir Hadgi Seifeddin, nam'd Chadi Mulc. This passion got so great an ascendent in his soul, that he cou'd not rest till he had marry'd her, which was during Timur's absence; of which the princess his wife being inform'd, so great a jealousy kindled in her heart, that she discover'd the case to the emperor at Samarcand. Orders were immediately given out for Chadi Mulc to make her appearance: but the Mirza conceal'd her, which so provok'd Timur, that he order'd diligent search to be made after her; and being found, she was condemn'd to die, and wou'd have suffer'd immediately, if the Mirza Pir Mehemed Gehanghir had not beg'd for a reprieve. Nevertheless advice was given the emperor at Acsoulat, that the Mirza Calil Sultan had again conceal'd her in his apartment: whereupon the Emir Berat had orders to go and seize her, and bring her away, which being done, Timur in a great passion commanded her to be put to death. The empress Serai Mulc Canum cou'd not bear to see the deep anxiety and despair the poor Mirza fell into: but considering moreover the great love Timur bore to the princes his children, she endeavour'd to accommodate this difference, by the help of the Emirs Cheik Noureddin and Chamelic, and persuaded 'em to inform the emperor, that this lady was with child by the Mirza. On this account the order was revers'd, and the princess entrusted to the care of the empress Bouyan Aga, that after her lying-in she might bring up the child, and commit the lady to some of her black slaves *.

The emperor being at Acsoulat, order'd the Mirzas his sons, the commanders of kingdoms, the governors of provinces, the Derogas of citys, and other grand officers and lords of his empire, to write to their lieutenants, to advise 'em to take great care during the expedition into China that the laws be duly executed, and justice dispens'd every where, so that the people might enjoy quiet and security, that they shou'd not give heed to the disturbers of the public tranquility, as knowing it was their duty to treat the people well, since they were entrusted to 'em by the Creator, that they behave themselves in such a manner, that when an account shall be demanded of their conduct, they may have no cause to repent, nor be the reason of Timur's blushing for shame before the throne of God, at the day of judgment. This order was carefully executed, and sent into all the provinces by men of probity.

---

* The black slaves are eunuchs, and the ordinary guardians of the Mahometan ladys. The reason of Timur's putting this lady into their hands, was to hinder the Mirza Calil Sultan's having any future commerce with her.

Then

Then the Mirza Calil Sultan went to Tachkunt, according to the orders he had receiv'd; and the Mirza Sultan Huſſein to Yaſſi and Sabran. There was nothing to be ſeen any where but carriages and waggons, which were brought from all the provinces, and fill'd with all ſorts of ammunition; and an infinite number of horſes brought from all parts to be ſold, which the emperor bought, and diſtributed among the Mirzas, Emirs and ſoldiers. Then the Seid Coja, ſon of the Cheik Ali Behader, came from Coraſſana from the Mirza Charoc, with advice of the good health of that prince.

The emperor ſent the Emir Berendac to Tachkunt, to bring away the proviſions · and he publiſh'd an order for all the generals and great officers to keep an exact account of the ſtate of their Tomans, Hezares and Sedes, that in this long expedition no one might be oblig'd to ſtay behind for want of either proviſion or arms. This order had ſo good an effect, that in this numerous army each horſeman had enough to ſuffice ten men, as well in victuals as in arms. Beſides this, ſeveral thouſand loads of corn were carry'd in the waggons which follow'd the army, to ſow the fields on their road, that at their return they might not have a ſcarcity. Several thouſands of ſhe-camels were alſo carry'd, that on a preſſing occaſion their milk might ſerve for nouriſhment to the ſoldiers. Theſe precautions were neceſſary to an army, ſo numerous as not to be match'd in antiquity. Thoſe who had ſeen the immenſe riches at the feaſt of Canighul, were ſtruck with admiration: and men of the beſt ſenſe reflected upon the Arabian ſaying, *That when a man has attain'd the higheſt degree of proſperity, he is upon the point of abaſement*. Moſt perſons ſaid, even in public,

after

after having seen the prodigious grandeur and magnificence which appear'd in the pleasures of Canighul, and the fine appearance which this innumerable army made, with the vast quantity of arms and baggage which were in the imperial camp, that they no longer doubted the prosperity of Timur being arriv'd at its utmost perfection, and consequently fear'd with reason the diminution of his good fortune. People began to mistrust some disgrace wou'd befall 'em; and their hearts fluctuating between hope and fear, they daily besought God to preserve the emperor from the misfortunes which attend the greatest prosperity, and to turn the evil and destructive eyes * from off this reign, which they hop'd wou'd endure a great while longer.

* See book IV. chap. 22.

CHAP. XXIX.

Timur departs from Acfoulat.

THE sun was yet in Capricorn, and the violence of the cold so great, that several men and horses perish'd in the road, some losing their hands and feet, others their ears and noses. the snows and rains were continually falling, the whole face of the heavens seeming to be cover'd but by one cloud, and the whole earth by one piece of snow. Astronomers remark, that at this time there was a conjunction of the three superior planets in Aquarius, which was a presage of some great misfortune. Yet the desire of acquiring the merit of the Gazie prevail'd in the mind of our conqueror above the greatest difficultys: he wou'd not wait till the cold abated, but inform'd himself of the nature and cir-

The history of Timur-Bec.

circumstances of the roads, of the water, pasturage, desarts and mountains, which he order'd to be taken down in writing, that all necessary precautions might be us'd.

Then Timur set out from Aesoulat; and sent fresh orders to the Mirzas Calil Sultan and Ahmed, accompany'd by the Emirs Codadad Husseini, Yadghiar, Chah Erlat, Chamseddin Abbas, Berendac, and eight others, who were in winter quarters with their troops about Tachkunt, Chahroukhia, and Seiram; as also to the Mirza Sultan Hussein, who was with his about Yassi and Sabran in Capchac, not to fail of leaving their winter-quarters at the beginning of spring, in order to join the court.

Timur having march'd two days and one night, went to Ouzoun-Ata to encamp, then to Yoscadgiai Cheik, from thence to Sourkent, and afterwards to Comarcha Ata, to Sultan Cheik, and at length to the town of Zernouc, from whence he departed, and crossing the Sihon upon the ice, encamp'd on the other bank. This river was froze so hard this year, that they were oblig'd to dig two or three cubits to get water; and from the sun's entring Sagittarius to his coming out of Pisces, waggons, men and beasts, cou'd pass either the Gihon or Sihon in any part of 'em.

Timur having decamp'd from the banks of the Sihon, arriv'd at Otrar on wednesday the 12th of Regeb 807, and lodg'd in the palace of Birdi Bei, where all the princes and lords had likewise each their respective apartments. The day of the emperor's arrival, one corner of the roof of the palace, where he was lodg'd, set fire, by the tunnel of a chimney running by it; but the fire was soon extinguish'd. This accident disquieted the lords of the court, inasmuch

Chap. 29.

Feb 27, 1405.

as

as most of 'em had had frightful dreams which prognosticated some misfortune, and it seem'd as if nature had given the people an insight into what shou'd happen to their prince. But fate is inevitable.

Timur sent Moussa Recmal to discover whether there was any passage over the bridge, who carefully examin'd the whole, and brought answer that it was impossible to cross it. Another, who had been sent towards Seiram and the mountain of Coulan, on his return declar'd that the snow of this mountain was two pikes high.

Then Cara Coja, an antient domestic of Tocatmich Can, heretofore emperor of Capchac, arriv'd at court in quality of ambassador from that prince, who had a long time wander'd about as a vagabond in the desart of Capchac Timur being pleas'd to grant him a magnificent audience, enter'd in state into the Divan Caré, and ascended his throne, the princes Taizi Aglen, of the race of Octai Caan[1], Bachtemour Aglen, and Cicr Aglen, of the race of Touchi Can, sitting on his right hand, and the Mirzas Olouc-Bec, Ibrahim Sultan, and Aidgel on the left. The ambassador was conducted to the audience by the Emirs Berdi Bei and Noureddin two brothers, Chamelic and Coja Yousef, and having prostrated himself, had the honor to kiss the imperial carpet · he made an harangue from his master in these words. " I have,
" says he, suffer'd the punishment my ingrati-
" tude merited. the slight acknowledgment I
" have made for so many favors receiv'd of your
" highness, hath drawn upon me the miserys
" I find my self reduc'd to. I have no other

---

[1] Caan signifys Can of Cans.

" refuge

"refuge than the hopes of pardon from your
"bounty. and if I can be assur'd you'll forget
"your servant's faults, I will discover a grateful
"sense of the favor by a constant submission to
"your imperial orders."

Timur, according to his wonted goodness, treated this ambassador with civility, and even assur'd him that at his return from the war of China, he wou'd again conquer the kingdom of Touchi Can, which he had a design to put into the hands of Tocatmich Can his master. After these civil treatments he dismiss'd the ambassador Cara Coja, sending by him a present to Tocatmich. And Timur's intention being to depart forthwith from Otrar to continue his expedition into China, he design'd to send back the empresses and the young princes his children, who out of ceremony were come thither to wait upon him. But fate had otherwise order'd it.

CHAP. XXX.

Timur's death at Otrar.

THE Alcoran remarks, that God created the world for the sake of man, but man for his own service. By this we see that the dignity of the human soul is too great to remain for ever in this material body; and that so pure and excellent a being can't find satisfaction but in the enjoyment of him who created it, and gave it immortality.

Timur, after the campain of seven years, in which he had conquer'd almost all Asia, turn'd the whole of his ambition towards the establishing of justice in the world, informing himself of

the

the state of his subjects, and redressing all evils if they were oppress'd by tyrants, he did 'em justice, and if in poverty, he enrich'd 'em by his favors; and by this means render'd the world flourishing, and rejoic'd the people's hearts. As soon as he was return'd to the seat of his empire, without reposing himself from his fatigues any longer than five months, he form'd a design to make war on the idolaters of China, hoping by that to obtain pardon of God for his former crimes and having set out for that expedition, he came to Otrar, seventy six leagues or parasangas distant from Samarcand.

March 25 1405

On Wednesday the 10th of Chaban 807, Timur was attack'd with a burning fever, and believ'd he heard the Houris* say to him, Repent, for you must appear before God. On this, he became sincerely penitent for his crimes, and resolv'd to make satisfaction for 'em by good works His sickness increasing, he found himself very much weaken'd, having no rest affliction seiz'd the heart of all the court, which appear'd the greater as the distemper augmented. Then neither empire, nor armys, nor riches, nor crowns stood him in any stead

And tho Moulana Fadlalla Tebrizi, one of the most skilful physicians of the age, employ'd all his care in prescribing the most excellent remedys, yet the sickness became more violent. Physic is useless when fate has ordain'd the death of any one. All hopes of the emperor's health were lost; his physicians having given him over But tho his body was weaken'd, yet his mind continu'd sound; and notwithstand-

---

* The Houris are continual virgins, who the Mahometans believe are appointed for their pleasures in their prophets paradise.

ing his violent griefs, he was always informing himself of the condition of his army. When he found his sickness so strong, that all remedys prov'd ineffectual, he resolv'd courageously to face death; and calling the empresses and principal Emirs into his presence, he made the following testament.

"I am satisfy'd that my soul is about to leave my body, and that my asylum is at the throne of God, who gives and takes away life at his pleasure. I beseech you to utter neither crys nor groans at my death; and instead of rending your garments, and running to and fro like madmen, pray to God to have mercy on me; say Allah Ecber [1], and the Fatiha [2], that my soul may find comfort. Since God has so highly favor'd me as to enable me to give laws to the earth, whereby at present thro' all the kingdoms of Iran and Touran no one dare encroach upon his neighbor, nor the great oppress the poor, I have hopes that he will pardon my sins, tho they are without number. I have this consolation, that during my reign I have not permitted the strong to injure the weak. Tho I am not ignorant of the instability of the world, yet I do not advise you to leave off caring for the affairs thereof; since that will cause disorders among men, banish safety from the highways, and be an obstacle to the people's quiet: and it is certain that at the day of judgment an account will be demanded of those, to whom the care of these things have been intrusted

---

[1] God is the most great.
[2] The first chapter of the Alcoran, which the Mahometans recite, as Christians do the Lord's-prayer.

Pir Mehemed Gehanghir declar'd Timur's successor.

"I declare my son Pir Mehemed Gehanghir my universal heir, and lawful successor to the empire. He must possess the throne of Samarcand with an absolute and independent sovereignty, that he may carefully manage both the religious and civil affairs, and take care of the necessitys of the army, and of the citys and countrys subject to my jurisdiction. I command you all to obey him, and unanimously to sacrifice your lives in maintaining his authority, that the world may not fall into disorder, and that my labor for so many years may not be lost. If you agree together, no one will dare to oppose you, or offer the least obstacle against the execution of my last will."

Timur then order'd all the Emirs and great lords of the court, and the generals of the army, to come before him, whom he strictly enjoin'd to see to the execution of his testament; and made 'em promise in his presence with solemn oaths not to consent that any one shou'd oppose it: and he sent orders to all the Emirs and generals who were absent to take the same oaths.

The lords having heard this discourse, were in the utmost consternation, melted into tears, and fell with their faces to the ground. The Emirs Cheik Noureddin and Chamelic, whose hearts were seiz'd with grief and despair, said to Timur, "We cou'd sacrifice our lives with a great deal of pleasure to purchase one single day more for our gracious master. If our death wou'd be of service to you, our lives shou'd cost us nothing: but it is impossible to alter the decrees of providence. We are your slaves; and tho being depriv'd of your presence we have no longer any joy or content-

"ment, yet we can assure your highness, that
"as long as we live, we will not fail of continu-
"ing obedient to your orders, tho at the hazard
"of our lives. May heaven never grant us suc-
"cess, if we have the least thoughts of doing
"any thing contrary to the will of our benefactor.
"We will always walk in the same paths of obe-
"dience after your death as during your life."

While they were thus speaking, tears gush'd out of their eyes, their minds no longer enjoy'd any quiet, and their bodys lost all their natural strength. They told the emperor that if he pleas'd, they wou'd write to the Mirza Calil Sultan, and the Emirs who were at Tachkunt, to come to court, that having the honor to see their master's face once more, they might learn from his own mouth his last will: "For, say "they, tho we shou'd declare to 'em the form "of your last will with all possible exactness, "yet it will not have the same force on 'em, as "if they had heard it themselves." But the emperor answer'd that his hour was approaching; that those who were absent cou'd not come time enough to see him, and that it was impossible for 'em to meet again till the day of judgment. "This, says he, is the last audience "you will have of me. I have no other desire "than to see the Mirza Charoc once more; but "that is impossible: God will not have it so." The ladys and princes, who were in the antichamber to observe the course of his distemper, on hearing this, lost all patience, and fell into the utmost consternation. Then Timur turning towards the princes his children, spoke to 'em as follows.

"Remember to do every thing I have recom-
"mended to you in relation to the public tran-
"quillity; and be constantly informing your-
"selves

"selves of the affairs of your subjects. Be valiant, and courageously keep possession of your swords, that like me you may enjoy a long reign and a vast empire. I have purg'd the countrys of Iran and Touran from the enemys and disturbers of the people's quiet, and have render'd 'em flourishing by my justice. If you do what my testament directs, and make equity and justice the rule of your actions, the kingdom will remain a long time in your hands: but if discord creeps in among you, ill fortune will attend your undertakings, your enemys will breed wars and sedition, which it will be difficult to put a stop to, and irreparable mischiefs will arise both in religion and government."

After this discourse the distemper increas'd: and tho there were several Imams and readers without the door of the chamber, who read the Alcoran from one end to the other, yet Timur was pleas'd to have the doctor Moulana Hebetulla, son of Moulana Obaid, to read the word of God at his bed's-head, and often repeat the belief of the unity of God. At night, between the evening-prayer and bed-time, (that is about eight a-clock) Timur several times made profession of his belief of Lailahillallah,*, remembring the promise of Mahomet, that he whose last words are, There is no other god than God, shall assuredly enter into paradise. Then he gave up his soul to the angel Esrafiel*, who call'd him in these words: "O soul, that hopest in God, return to thy Lord with resignation. We belong to God, and must return to him."

† Israel.

---

* There is no other god than God.

This fatal event happen'd on wednesday-night the 17th of Chaban 807, which answers to the 14th of Esfendarmez 326 of the Gelalian epocha, the sun being in the eighth degree of Pisces

Chap 31
April 1.
1405.

Several learned men have compos'd verses on his death, in which the date of the year is contain'd, and among others Moulana Behadedin Dgyami: they say he was seventy-one years of age, and that he had reign'd thirty-six, a number equal to that of his children and grandchildren, as we shall see in the last chapter.

CHAP. XXXI.

Relation of what happen'd after Timur's death.

TIMUR having pass'd from this mansion of pride to the paradise of eternal delights, fear and horror seiz'd both upon his friends and enemys, every one was jealous of disorders and wars, and did not in the least doubt but the security and tranquillity of the state wou'd entirely perish. The affliction wou'd have been insupportable, had not his horoscope predicted the continuation of the crown in his august family, and that the kingdoms he had conquer'd by the strength of his arm, and which he had render'd flourishing by his justice, wou'd remain in peace under the protection of his children who shou'd succeed him in the empire. Notwithstanding this, the princes of the blood cast their crowns upon the earth; the empresses and ladys tore their faces and their hair; the Emirs and principal persons rent their robes, and flinging themselves upon the ground, pass'd that dismal night in grief: and it seem'd as if the heavens had shar'd in this affliction, since rains and thun-

thunder, storms and tempeſt did not ceaſe all the night.

Next morning the grandees of the court ended their lamentations, to perform the emperor's funeral obſequys. The doctors Hendouchah Caznegi and Moulana Cotobeddin Sedre had the care of the ceremony. They order'd the prayers and verſes of the Alcoran, appointed on theſe occaſions, to be read. Then the body was waſh'd, and embalm'd with camphire, musk and roſe-water, and being wrap'd up in linen, was laid in a coffin of ebony, after having recommended his ſoul to God.

When they had finiſh'd this ceremony, the great Emirs who attended his perſon, as Birdi Bei, ſon of Sarbouga, and his brother the Emir Cheik Noureddin, Chamelic, Coja Youſef, and ſeveral others, ſolemnly ſwore they wou'd always aſſociate together, and uſe their utmoſt endeavors, even to the hazard of their lives, to ſee Timur's teſtament executed. And as the deſign of the war in China was not yet abandon'd, they kept Timur's death conceal'd, and forbad the ladys changing their habits, or ſhewing any exterior ſigns of grief, that the enemy might not have preſent advice of it.

Afterwards they went to meet the empreſſes, and held a council with 'em in relation to what muſt be done at this preſent conjuncture. They ſent advice of the misfortune to the Mirza Calil Sultan, and the Emirs who were at Tachkunt. They diſpatch'd expreſſes to Yaſſi and Sabran, to the Mirza Sultan Huſſein, to advertiſe him that the emperor's ſickneſs increaſ'd, and that he ſhou'd come to court with but ten of his men. They ſent Kezer Coutchin to Gaznin, with letters to the Mirza Pir Mehemed Gehanghir, to inform him of Timur's death, and of his will, in which he had declar'd him his universal heir and successor to the empire; and they besought him to repair immediately to Samarcand. They also wrote letters to all the Mirzas and governors of provinces, inviting 'em to observe all the vigilance necessary on the like occasions, to guard the countrys entrusted to 'em, and secure themselves from all reproach; praying 'em to inform themselves exactly of whatever shou'd pass on their frontiers, and give advice of it to court, in fine, to neglect nothing which might hinder any surprize, because the enemys and disturbers of the public tranquillity had kept themselves conceal'd for several years as it were in exile, and waited only such a favorable opportunity as this: that in the mean while they shou'd execute justice, and continue their favors to the people, that no one might have any thoughts of revolting. The Cheik Temour went express to the Mirza Charoc at Herat, Ali Derich to the Mirza Omar at Tauris, Aratmour to the Mirzas Miran Chah and Aboubecre at Bagdad, and another into Fars and Irac.

CHAP. XXXII.

Timur's coffin transported from Otrar.

THE Mirzas, empresses and Emirs, who were at Otrar, on thursday-night the 18th of Chaban 807, at the time of evening-prayers, cover'd the coffin with velvet and black damask, and with it took the road to Samarcand: they pass'd the river Jaxartes in the night upon the ice, and went into a wood on the bank of the river. from Otrar to the Jax-

April 2, 1405.

artes are but two leagues or parafangas. Next morning the grief became fo violent, that nothing was heard but the moſt piteous groans and lamentations, no one being able to abſtain from ſorrow. The Emirs, Haſekis and Coutchins caſt their turbants upon the ground, and cover'd their heads with duſt; while the ladys rent their hair, and tore their cheeks with their nails.

After theſe demonſtrations of affliction, the wiſe Emirs gave the following advice. "Since "fate, ſay they, begins to make us feel mif- "fortunes, we muſt give way to its force, no- "thing being able to hold out againſt its efforts. "The moſt refin'd politics can't retard its "courſe: death makes no difference between "kings and ſlaves. On this account, the beſt "method is to fortify our ſelves with patience, "ſince there is no other remedy, and endeavor "by alms, works of piety, prayers, and read- "ing of the Alcoran, to rejoice, if poſſible, the "ſoul of our deceas'd maſter. Death lies in "ambuſcade to ſurprize us; it gives the finiſh- "ing ſtroke to all affairs, as well to the con- "queſt of the world, as to the leaſt trifle: no "one is exempted from it, and he who never "dies can't be born again." Theſe counſels not being powerful enough to appeaſe the great deſpair in which every one was plung'd, the Emirs had recourſe to Mahomet's death, at the ſame time beſeeching him to intercede for the conſolation of the afflicted. They ſhew'd that tho this great prophet was the moſt excellent of God's creatures, and the ſeal of the prophets, yet the moment deſtin'd for his death being come, his pure ſoul broke the cords by which it was tied to his body, and with an entire reſignation took its flight towards paradiſe; that

ſince

since this illustrious man cou'd not be immortal, others must not expect to be so; and however afflicting this misfortune might appear, there was no other remedy to be us'd than to resign our selves to fate, and implore the assistance of God, whose orders we must obey.

CHAP. XXXIII.

The empresses and Emirs hold a council concerning the war of China.

THE reading of the history and death of Mahomet having a little moderated the universal grief, the Emirs took this opportunity to give the following counsel to the empresses and princes.

"There is no doubt, say they, that if so pow-
" erful and numerous an army, which was ne-
" ver exceeded by any in past ages, nor proba-
" bly ever will be in times to come, shou'd
" march into the enemy's country, we shall
" easily exterminate the infidels in a short time;
" and tho the news of our master's death shou'd
" be carry'd to the Calmacs and Chinese, yet
" all news being thought either true or false, if
" we lead our army as far as their frontiers, they
" will be jealous they have receiv'd false advice,
" and say that if Timur was dead, no one wou'd
" be powerful enough to head an army of that
" strength; and thus imagining he is yet alive,
" and that we spread the rumor of his death
" thro artifice and design, they will be seiz'd
" with fear, while we shall gain an easy vic-
" tory It is requisite that we put all Timur's
" intentions in execution, and confiding in God,

" carry

"carry our arms into China, where we may
"employ all our strength in prosecuting this re-
"ligious war with vigor, which the empe-
"ror had resolv'd to wage with the idolaters
"of China, in order to procure glory to the
"Muſſulmans And after we ſhall have ſatisfy'd
"our conſciences in this point, we will diſplay
"the victerious ſtandard, and return to Samar-
"cand, where we will employ all our joint en-
"deavors in the well-governing of the empire.
"Thro the grace of God, there are more than
"thirty kings or ſons of kings whom our maſter
"has left for his ſucceſſors to the crown, one
"of whom muſt neceſſarily inherit it. For
"wou'd it not be moſt unhappy that ſo mighty
"an army, equip'd with ſo much difficulty
"and care by Timur, after having began its
"march, and gone ſo many days journy with
"deſign to make war on the infidels, ſhou'd re-
"turn without having executed any thing of
"conſequence ?"

The princes, empreſſes, and great Emirs re-
volving theſe things in their minds, unanimouſly
reſolv'd, That the Emirs with their regiments
ſhou'd march under the command of the Mirza
Ibrahim Sultan, whom Timur had choſen to attend him in the expedition into China, and
that they ſhou'd join the Mirza Calil Sultan at
Tachkunt, to whom the Mirza Ibrahim Sultan
ſhou'd reſign the command of the army, as being the eldeſt of the Mirzas then preſent; and
that Calil Sultan ſhou'd bear the name of emperor thro-out the whole campain; but that the
great Emirs of the council ſhou'd adminiſter
the affairs of ſtate under him as uſual: and
laſtly, that they ſhou'd march into China in this
order, from whence, after having vanquiſh'd the
idolaters, ruin'd the towns, burnt the temples,
and

and seiz'd on the spoils, they shou'd return to Samarcand, where the empresses, Mirzas and Emirs shou'd hold a general diet, to execute Timur's last will and testament

CHAP. XXXIV.

Timur's coffin is transported to Samarcand.

THE foregoing resolution being taken, the Emirs Coja Yousef and Ali Coutchin, with several lords, took the road to Samarcand with Timur's coffin, where they arriv'd on monday-night the 22d of Chaban 807, and bury'd Timur with the usual solemnitys.

April 6. 1405.

After they were gone, the other great Emirs gave the following counsel to the empresses. " Tho our deceas'd master of happy
" memory has by his testament ordain'd the
" Mirza Pir Mehemed his successor in the em-
" pire; yet as this prince is at Candahar, and
" has perhaps pass'd into India, so that he is at
" a great distance from us; and if we wait his
" arrival to continue the Chinese expedition,
" we shall not get there in a proper season for
" making war, we will therefore immediately
" depart for that campain: and when that
" Mirza shall arrive at Samarcand, which will
" be in a little time, because he must soon re-
" ceive the news of the emperor's death, it is
" requisite that he enter the city with pomp
" and ceremony, and ascend the throne of the
" empire according to the will of his deceas'd
" grandfather, for to him the crown lawfully
" belongs. Timur has always cherish'd this
" Mirza's children more than those of any
" other,

Book VI. "other, because he was the son of Gehranghir,
"his eldest son, to whom and to his children the
"succession belongs according to the Mahome-
"tan law. We may also truly say, that good-
"fortune has always attended him, and that
"the majesty of kings may be seen even in his
"countenance, that he is of a pure faith, go-
"verns himself by good maxims, has a gene-
"rous and brave heart, a noble mind, and a
"princely behavior. His justice, equity and
"clemency towards the people are more conspi-
"cuous than the sun, and we ought to expect
"that this great prince's reign will add new
"splendor to the throne, great advantages to
"the subjects, peace and tranquillity in the king-
"doms dependent on this great empire, and a
"universal satisfaction among the people; so
"that the approaching installation of this
"prince may take away from ill-designing per-
"sons all means of sowing division, or procu-
"ring revolt."

This discourse being ended, the empresses Serai Mulc Canum, Tekil Canum, Touman Aga, and the other ladys, departed with the Mirzas Oluc-Bec and others for Samarcand, after the emperor's coffin. The Emirs recommended to 'em to use all imaginable precautions, especially where they encamp'd, and to send out constantly to gain intelligence for fear of being surpriz'd. This separation was not without a mutual affliction.

At ten in the morning of the same day, the Mirza Ibrahim Sultan, and the great Emirs took horse at the head of the army, with design to march into China, to execute the emperor's intentions in a Gazie against the infidels.

Timur's imperial standard, his drum and kettledrums, with the ensigns of his victorys,

were

were carry'd by a troop of horse of the Mirza Ibrahim Sultan's court. At the view of this great train an ingenious person made these reflections: "Behold the standards which are "the signs of command: to beat the drum, be-"longs only to kings: since the same has been "done by this young Mirza, he ought to hope "for the scepter. These are good omens: and "since he is the first who has taken the place "of empire, in all likelihood it will return to "him again in time." All this happen'd as predicted

When they had pass'd the Sihon, and march'd one league, they went to encamp on the bank of the river Ardge, near the bridge of Caldurma, east of Otrar An imperial tent and large pavilion were erected there for the Mirza; and the horse-tail of the deceas'd emperor was fix'd over-against the camp with the usual ceremony. From thence expresses were sent to the Mirza Calil Sultan and the great Emirs of the right wing, who were at Tachkunt and Charoukia, to inform 'em that they had sent Timur's coffin to Samarcand, and that the empresses were gone after 'em; that for their parts they had resolv'd to continue the war in China, and were set out with that intent. They also sent couriers with the same news to the Mirza Sultan Hussein, who commanded the left wing, desiring him to march immediately with his troops to join them at Jouclec, where they might see Timur's last will and testament, and prepare to march with 'em into China. Jouclec, which was the place of rendezvous, is a town five leagues east from Otrar.

CHAP

CHAP. XXXV.

The Mirza Sultan Hussein, Timur's grandson opposes the sentiment of the Emirs.

NOTHING is more certain, than that every enterprize which is not favor'd by providence will prove unsuccessful. Fate had not resolv'd on the design of making war in China, on which account all the efforts for that purpose were render'd useless, and fortune overturn'd this hopeful project · for the Mirza Sultan Hussein had no sooner heard of Timur's death than the desire of revolting, which had lain conceal'd in his breast so long, and the effects of which he had discover'd in the war at Damascus, where thro an unheard-of cowardice he abandon'd our party, when the Syrian army sally'd out of the city to attack us; the desire of revolting, I say, re-kindled in his breast on this occasion: and excited by a deprav'd imagination, he disbanded part of the troops of the left wing, and taking from 'em their horses, pass'd the Sihon at Cogende with a thousand men, each having two horses, with whom he took the road to Samarcand by the way of Cazac, designing to surprize the inhabitants of that place by a stratagem, that they might suffer him to enter the city. At noon of the same day the courier, who had carry'd him the express, return'd with this news. Every one was surpriz'd, and thought of taking the necessary measures for preventing his ambitious designs.

CHAP.

CHAP. XXXVI.

The Emirs write circular letters to give advice to all the provinces of the Mirza Sultan Huffein's undertaking.

WHEN the Emirs Cheik Noureddin and Chamelic were inform'd of the unjuft proceedings of the Sultan Huffein, they immediately wrote the following letter to the Emir Argoun Chah governor of Samarcand. "The " Sultan Huffein has begun to act his follys " afresh · he has disbanded the troops he com-" manded, and with a thoufand horfemen, each " having two horfes, has taken the road to " Samarcand : wherefore be upon your guard " for the defence of the city, and omit no " precautions. If this rash young prince ap-" proach the city, and you meet with an oppor-" tunity of taking him, fail not of fecuring " him; that no misfortunes happen thro his " means; for he ought not to be trufted." They wrote another letter with the fame advice to the empreffes, befeeching them to ftop wherever they then were, till they had join'd 'em. They alfo fent a courier to Coja Youfef to inform him of what had happen'd, advifing him to ufe all neceffary precautions in relation to the litter, and endeavor to convey it into the city as foon as poffible; left the Sultan Huffein, excited by his ambition, under pretence of feeing Timur's coffin enter Samarcand, fhould get in himfelf, and ftir up a revolt. They difpatch'd an exprefs to the Mirza Calil Sultan and his great Emirs who were at Tachkunt, which is diftant from Otrar

fix

six days journy in the caravan, to let 'em know of the ~~evil design~~ of the Sultan Huſſein, who had broke their meaſures in relation to the war with China; that it was proper for the Emirs at Tachkunt to return with their troops to Acar, which is a famous meadow full of good paſturage; to which place themſelves wou'd alſo repair, and make known to 'em Timur's teſtament, which he had order'd at the point of death; and which they had ſworn to execute, that afterwards they wou'd endeavor in concert to take care of the public concerns, as they ſhou'd agree together in the diets which were to be held.

When the couriers were ſet out, the Mirza Ibrahim Sultan, with the Emirs Cheik Noureddin and Chamelic, departed from Otrar, and took the road to Samarcand. The Emir Birdi Bei ſtaid in his government of Otrar; and as the revolt of the Sultan Huſſein had occaſion'd ſome conſternation, the whole army march'd in order of battel towards Samarcand. In the evening they paſs'd the Sihon, where the ice broke, and three camels laden with gold were drown'd. They march'd all night, and next morning the Emirs join'd the empreſſes.

On the other hand, there happen'd a very croſs affair, which was, that the Emirs of Calil Sultan's court, and even the ſoldiers of his body of the army, Turks and Tadgics, Iracians and Natolians, had had advice before the arrival of the expreſs who ſet out from Otrar, that the Sultan Huſſein had diſpers'd his troops, and taken the road to Samarcand with a thouſand horſe; that at the reception of this news the fear caus'd by Timur's death was much increas'd, and that imagining they ſhou'd in ſome meaſure remedy it, the Mirza Ahmed Omar Cheik,

Cheik, and the great Emirs Codadad Hussemi, Yadghiar Chah Erlat, Chamseddin Abbas, Berendac, and other principal officers, had assembled at Tachkunt; and without sending for the advice of the other Mirzas, the empresses, or great Emirs Cheik Noureddin and Chamelic, had advanc'd the Mirza Calil Sultan to the throne of the empire at Tachkunt; and sworn to obey him, not considering the ill success which must attend an undertaking of that importance.

CHAP. XXXVII.

A letter to the great Emirs who were at Tachkunt.

THE empresses, Mirzas, and Emirs Cheik Noureddin and Chamelic, having receiv'd advice of the oath taken by the great Emirs to the Mirza Calil Sultan, whom they had plac'd on the throne, wrote the following letter to 'em by way of reprimand.

"The great Timur our master, of blessed
" memory, has ordain'd by his last will the
" Mirza Pir Mehomed Gehangir his heir and
" lawful successor to the empire, whom we have
" sworn to obey, tho at the peril of our lives.
" At present you have acted contrary to the
" express will of our great master and bene-
" factor. By thus disobeying his last will, you
" have forgot the obligations you lie under to
" him. We did not doubt that if any one had
" but advis'd to do as you have done, you
" wou'd have oppos'd 'em with all your power
" We can't comprehend how lords of so great
" experience have dar'd to commit an action of
" such

"such ill consequence; which in the end must produce repentance and misery on your side. Your manner of acting will doubtless be charg'd as an excess of ambition: how come it then that you have wounded your reputation by ingratitude towards your benefactor? You have violated your oath of fidelity to Timur, which you ought never to have done, especially at a time when so many misfortunes have been caus'd by the death of our gracious master. Don't you consider the ill name you'll acquire by this action in history, which will remain to the end of time? How can you consent to this dishonorable deed, who have so often sacrific'd your lives in the pursuit of honor? How can you become traitors to an emperor, for whose sake you have so often and so generously expos'd yourselves to the greatest dangers? What is most surprizing is, that your consciences must reprove you at the same time that we do, since you are not ignorant of the crime you have committed. How can persons of your high quality, of so great understanding, and long experience, dare to commit so enormous a fault?"

This letter was seal'd, and sent by a messenger nam'd Abou Dgyoura; who having deliver'd it to the Emirs, they read it, and after a serious reflection, acknowledg'd their fault, and were sorry for it: but repentance was too late, they having resign'd their liberty to another.

CHAP. XXXVIII.

The Emir Berendac arrives at the empreſſes court, with an anſwer to the letter ſent the Emirs, who were at Tachkunt with the Mirza Calil Sultan.

THE Mirzas, empreſſes and Emirs being encamp'd at Acſoulat, the Emir Berendac, ſon of Gehan Chah, arriv'd from Tachkunt, and being admitted into their preſence, paid his compliments of condolence; and afterwards took his place in the council-hall with the Emirs Cheik Noureddin and Chamelic, where he preſented the following letter written by the Emirs Codadad Huſſeini and Chamſeddin Abbas.

" We have taken an oath to obey the Mirza
" Calil Sultan, for the good of both church and
" ſtate, and to maintain the ſucceſſion of the
" kingdom in our maſter's family for ever. The
" misfortune which has happen'd appear'd ſo
" terrible to us, that we fear'd ſome unexpected
" revolt, which it wou'd have been impoſſible
" to have remedy'd. All we have done was
" with a ſincere intention. A general was
" wanting to our troops, that no one might
" have any pretence for revolting, which wou'd
" have brought the ſtate into confuſion and diſ-
" order: we therefore imagin'd you wou'd have
" had the ſame ſentiments with us. But ſince
" our proceedings do not agree with the laſt
" will of our maſter, we receive his orders
" with reſpect and ſincerity, and God forbid
" we

"we shou'd in any wise contradict 'em We
"shall be always ready to join in whatever you
"judg proper to do as to the execution of the
"emperor's testament."

The Emirs Cheik Noureddin and Chamelic having read this letter, which was conformable to what the Emir Berendac had declar'd to 'em, told him they cou'd by no means consent to any thing done in contradiction to Timur's will, and that they wou'd never acknowledg the Mirza Calil Sultan. "If we disobey our emperor's "orders, say they, and acknowledg any other "for his successor than whom he has declar'd, "we shall deserve to be loaded with misfor- "tunes and shame, and to be for ever accurs'd. "We'll take great care as to what we do in this "affair, of which every sensible and impartial "man may judg."

Then the Emirs wrote a second letter to those at Tachkunt, whom they invited to submit entirely to the will, and annul the oath they had taken thro inadvertency; as likewise to remember the obligations they were under to the emperor, and not have cause to blush before him at the day of judgment. "This action, added "they, will look ill both in the sight of God "and man, and be an eternal blot upon you, "which you will never be able to wipe off."

This second letter was put into the hands of the Emir Berendac, to whom they spake as follows "You have committed a great fault "which you ought to repair by vacating the "oath you have so wrongfully taken, and by "following our master's orders, which we are "all oblig'd to obey. Submit your selves to the "Mirza Pir Mehemed, and persuade the Mirza "Calil Sultan to do the same. You must sign "an agreement to that purpose, and send it to

"us at Samarcand, that we may deliver it to
"the Mirza who is the true and lawful heir to
"the empire." Then the Emir Berendac set out
for Tachkunt.

Next day the Mirzas, empresses and Emirs departed to continue their road towards Samarcand. The Mirza Olouc-Bec, with the Emir Chamelic, at the head of one body of the army, march'd towards the right: and the Mirza Ibrahim Sultan with the Emir Cheik Noureddin, commanding another body, towards the left. These two Mirzas were then but eleven years old · and Olouc-Bec being eldest by four months and twenty days, the Emir Chamelic, when they were arriv'd at Caradgec, set out before, in pursuance of the resolution taken in the assembly; and being arriv'd at Samarcand, the governor Argoun Chah shut the gates against him, and even plac'd a guard upon the walls. The Mirza Calil Sultan had written a letter to him full of fine promises, by which he engag'd him to be of his side, telling him that if he was willing to gain his favor, he shou'd refuse entrance to the Emirs Cheik Noureddin and Chamelic.

Argoun Chah, puff'd up by this Mirza's fair promises, which flatter'd the ambition and ingratitude inherent in his Turcoman blood, abandon'd himself to folly, and was won over to the Mirza Calil Sultan. The Emir Chamelic went from the gate of Cheik Zade, which is upon that road, to the gate of Tchehar Raha, where the Emirs Argoun Chah, Coja Yousef, and other chiefs of the city commonly keep their stations Argoun Chah wou'd not suffer him to enter, pretending to stand by the orders he had receiv'd of Timur. He moreover told him that he was ready to believe the emperor had by his testa-

ment

ment ordain'd the Mirza Pir Mehemed his successor, but that he wou'd wait till all the Mirzas and Emirs being assembled together agreed on it, that he wou'd then open the gates to 'em, and they might proclaim the Mirza, and place him upon the throne; after which he wou'd deliver up the government of the city.

The Emir Chamelic believing that what Argoun Chah had told him was all grimace, and that he was resolv'd not to open the gate, return'd very much afflicted: he crofs'd the river Couhec, and being arriv'd at Ali Abad, a town of Sogdiana Kelana, he met the Mirzas and empresses, who had pass'd the mountain of Caradgec. He told 'em how affairs stood, and his thoughts of Argoun Chah's real designs. This renew'd their afflictions, and oblig'd 'em to encamp. Serai Mulc Canum and Touman Aga held a council with the Emirs on what was most fitting to be done, and agreed that it wou'd be best to go to Bocara, while they shou'd send the Emir Cheik Noureddin to Samarcand, to persuade the Emirs there to give 'em entrance.

April 14. 1405.

This Emir departed the the first of Ramadan 807, and being arriv'd at the gate of Tchehar Raha, counsell'd the Emirs within, who gave him the same answer as they had the Emir Chamelic Nevertheless Noureddin got off his horse, pass'd the bridge on foot, and spake to 'em before the gate "Emirs, said he, what we are
" now talking of is no trifling matter. Per-
" mit me then to enter alone into the city, that
" we may examine together the good and bad
" consequences of what you are doing, lest you
" have cause to repent at last." Whatever Noureddin cou'd say, signify'd nothing; for they were buoy'd up with the Mirza Calil Sultan's
pro-

promises. The Emir seeing his words had no effect, return'd to Ali Abad, where he gave an account to the Mirzas and empresses of all that had pass'd.

CHAP. XXXIX.

Relation of what happen'd on the Emir Berendac's return to Tachkunt.

WE said before that the Emir Berendac had made a treaty at Acsoulat with the Emirs Cheik Noureddin and Chamelic, which he had confirm'd with an oath, wherein he had promis'd to risk his life in the defence of Timur's last will; and that he went back to Tachkunt with letters to the Emirs there. These Emirs having read those letters, became very sorry for having proclaim'd and sworn to the Mirza Calil Sultan, and unanimously approv'd of what the Emir Berendac had told 'em from the other Emirs, saying that the throne belong'd to him whom Timur had declar'd his heir by will, and that they wou'd never consent to alter it. After which they drew up a manifesto, which every one sign'd and seal'd, and the Mirza Calil Sultan was likewise oblig'd to subscribe. The Mirza order'd Atilmich to carry this paper, with presents, to the Emirs Noureddin and Chamelic, from whence he was to convey it to the Mirza the lawful heir; and before his departure, he said to him, "When you have assur'd the Mirza "Pir Mehemed of my respects, tell him I am "his sincere friend, and according to the will "of the emperor our father and master, I ac-"knowledg him his successor in the empire."

In this the Mirza acted the part of a hypocrite, his sole desire being to command: and there were some Emirs who egg'd him on to the execution of his designs, tho they had had access to his person but for a short time. "The strongest, say they, ought to govern; and he who has any advantage shou'd make use of it You must, my lord, embrace this opportunity to depart immediately for Samarcand, and ascend the throne, after which you shou'd open the treasurys, and by your liberalitys make both high and low your servants, for man is a slave to favors. Arm your self with policy and courage for your advancement, and lose no time, for such an affair as this won't admit of delay or cowardice Such an opportunity may not be met with for several ages, do not therefore neglect it. The poet says, protract not the happy minute, for next moment an insuperable difficulty may be started."

These advices were so often repeated, that the Mirza's ambition surmounted his reason. he got together all the horses, mules and camels belonging to Timur, and to the Mirzas and Emirs of his attendance, which he had left to graze at Tachkunt and Seiram, and distributed 'em among the Emirs and other officers of Irac who were of his party, he gave 'em a great deal of mony, stuffs, belts, cuirasses, arms and utensils, which belong'd to the soldiers of the army who were in those quarters: and then he departed at their head for Samarcand. When he was come near the Sihon, he encamp'd, and afterwards resolv'd that the Emir Berendac, with the troops of the right wing, shou'd cross the Sihon forthwith on a bridg of boats above Charoukhia, and that himself wou'd pass over

after

after him, 'and then the Emirs Codadad, Chamfeddin Abbas, and the other Emirs.

The Emir Berendac had already made a secret proposal to these Emirs, that he shou'd join the Emirs Cheik Noureddin and Chamelic; to which they consented, saying, they wou'd do nothing repugnant to Timur's will, and that their intention also was to abandon the Mirza Calil Sultan, and march towards Atchic Ferkint 'Berendac advis'd 'em to stay some days near Tachkunt, that he might inform 'em of what shou'd happen; and that afterwards they shou'd unanimously prosecute what was just and reasonable, that so their designs might have the desir'd success

CHAP. XL.

The great Emirs oppose the Mirza Calil Sultan.

THE Emirs Berendac, Rouftem Tagi Bouga, and Abdelkerim son of Hadgi Seifeddin, being arriv'd at the Sihon, pass'd it on a bridg, after which Berendac broke it down, and then went to join the Mirzas and empresses who were on their road to Samarcand. The Emirs Codadad and Chamseddin likewise abandon'd the Mirza Calil Sultan, and march'd to Atchic Ferkint, on advice of which, that Mirza went to the Sihon, and having rebuilt the bridg, pass'd the river next day with his troops. The Emir Berendac being arriv'd in the neighborhood of Douabe, met Gelal Baourdgi, who on the Emir Chamelic's return to Samarcand had abandon'd the Mirzas and empresses, and was

Book VI. going over to the Mirza Calil Sultan: he gave Berendac an account of the Emir Chamelic's journy to Samarcand, and of Argoun Chah's refusing him entrance into the city.

The Emir Berendac surpriz'd at this news, and mov'd as well by his ambition as his cowardice, prefer'd policy to justice and reason, and regardless of his oath, or the observance of the rules of equity, immediately return'd to find the Mirza Calil Sultan. On the contrary, Roustem Tagi Bouga went to Ali Abad, where he inform'd the Mirzas of the Emir Berendac's return. This latter, asham'd and confounded, beg'd pardon of the Mirza Calil, and solemnly swore to him a second time. The Mirza with those of his party declar'd the paper void, wherein they had promis'd obedience to the Mirza Pir Mehemed, tho he had set his seal to it, and sent it by Atilmich; and at the same time he continu'd his road towards Samarcand, with design to usurp the empire. This news being come to the Emirs Cheik Noureddin and Chamelic, they thus address'd the empresses. "The
" evil counsel of seditious persons has at present
" obtain'd: the Emirs have again taken an
" oath to the Mirza Calil Sultan; they have
" violated the treaty which they subscrib'd
" and seal'd, and are all on their march to Sa-
" marcand. He who breaks his word and oath,
" ought to be abhor'd by every one, as an
" enemy to mankind. Every body's heart
" shou'd now be rent into a thousand pieces,
" for the most powerful emperor, who was in
" a manner the soul of the world, is dead: but
" scarce is he expir'd, when some raw youths,
" whom from the lowest state of life he has
" rais'd to the greatest honors, become trai-
" tors to him, and forgetting the obligations
" they

" they owe him, contravene his orders, and
" violate their oaths. How can we dissemble
" our grief at so terrible a misfortune? An
" emperor, whose equal is no where to be met
" with, who has oblig'd the kings of the earth
" to serve at his gate, and has justly acquir'd
" the name of conqueror, is no sooner pass'd
" out of this world, than his last will is tram-
" pled upon. Religion is barter'd for this
" world. What unheard-of ingratitude is it,
" that abject slaves, after so many benefits re-
" ceiv'd, shou'd become the enemys of their
" great benefactor? If rocks had but a heart,
" they wou'd mourn at the sight of so abo-
" minable an action. Why are not stones
" rain'd down from heaven to punish these un-
" grateful wretches? As for us, may God
" grant us his grace, that we may not forget
" our master's favors; but that after we have
" besought his intercession, we may employ all
" our care in the execution of his last will, and
" in being obedient to the young princes his
" children, and sacrifice even our lives as faith-
" ful servants, rather than disobey him in the
" least point."

CHAP. XLI.

The Emirs hold a council with the empresses, in relation to their marching to Bocara.

AFTER the Emirs Cheik Noureddin and Chameke had finish'd this speech, they represented to the empresses, that since affairs had took such a turn, it seem'd requisite that while their majestys shou'd go to Samarcand, the Emirs shou'd attend upon the Mirzas to Bocara, from whence they might go to meet the Mirza Pir Mehemed to shew him Timur's testament. The empresses approving their proposal, the Emirs took leave of 'em, and having assembled a great number of Emirs who were faithful to the deceas'd emperor, and resolv'd to execute his orders, they held a council with 'em, and spake as follows

"Every one knows that no body had freer
"access to the late emperor than we: if there-
"fore we forget the favors we receiv'd of him,
"we shall deserve to be made miserable for ever.
"And tho since his death every one has turn'd
"his back upon us, yet for our parts we'll ne'er
"quit our resolution to obey his last orders If
"others have no thoughts of blushing before
"him at the day of judgment, we have. Our
"intention is to seek the Mirza Pir Mehemed,
"who is declar'd by Timur's testament the
"lawful heir to the empire, and to offer our
"service to him and if to fulfil our benefac-
"tor's will, we must risk our lives, and for-
"sake our worldly goods, we'll do it a thousand
"times rather than fail in our promise, or vio-
"late our oath, for if we shou'd be guilty
"of so infamous an action, we cou'd never
"hope to enjoy one day in paradise You, E-
"mirs, who were the nearest officers of that
"happy emperor, let us know your sentiment
"with regard to this resolution"

The Emirs of this assembly, whose hearts were sensibly touch'd, unanimously answer'd, "Our sole intention is to obey our master's
"orders: since you are resolv'd to execute his
"last will, we'll follow you with the greatest
"alacrity, and in what relates to us, we'll em-
"ploy our utmost care, and sacrifice our very
                                    "lives"

"lives." The chief of thefe faithful fervants of the emperor, were Atilmich, Tevekul Carcara, Hafan Jagadaoul, Aflan Coja Tercan, Uftoui, Chamfeddin Almaleghi, Moufa Recmal, Berturi, Vefadar, and others.

CHAP. XLII.

The Mirzas and Emirs march to Bocara.

AFTER the refolution was taken of going to Bocara, the 3d of Ramadan 807, the Mirzas Olouc-Bec and Ibrahim Sultan took leave of the empreffes, who, after exceffive grief on both fides, embrac'd the Mirzas with the greateft tendernefs, and recommended 'em to the divine protection. Thefe princes took horfe, and departed from Ali Abad, trufting only in the affiftance of heaven. The Emirs Cheik Noureddin and Chamelic follow'd 'em, having with 'em Timur's treafury, which confifted of ready mony, jewels, habits, arms and other riches, which this emperor always kept by him · and they fent Rouftem Tagi Bouga to Bocara before the reft, to give all neceffary orders.

April 16. 1405.

CHAP. XLIII.

The empresses march to Samarcand. Their mourning, after the two Mirzas departure.

THE empresses, accompany'd by the young princes the Mirzas children, as Baiera, Aidgel, Sadvaccas, Siorgatmich and others, with several faithful domestics, departed from Ali Abad, and having the deceas'd emperor's horse-tail and drums carry'd before 'em, and his baggage following behind, they took the road to Samarcand, and arriv'd at the gate of Tchehar Raha, with their hair dishevel'd, and their eyes gushing out with tears. The Emirs of the city had the insolence to refuse opening the gate to 'em that day: on which the empresses went down into the garden of the Mirza Charoc near that gate, where they pass'd the night. Next day they enter'd the city with the Mirzas and officers of their houshold, and lodg'd in the Canicah of the Mirza Mehemed Sultan, where Timur's coffin lay. At their arrival there they uncover'd their heads, and tore their hair, they mangled their faces, and cast themselves on the ground, to testify their sorrow for the emperor. The princesses Canzade and Roukia Canica, the Mirza Mehemed Gehanghir, with several grandees of the empire, as the Coja Abdulevel and others, with the wives of the Cherifs and principal persons, having felts about their necks, and their faces torn, assembled together in different mourning-habits. The inhabitants shut up the shops and markets, and every one made lamentations over the

The history of Timur-Bec.

the emperor's corps. The affliction was not only among the inhabitants of Samarcand, but also spread thro-out all Asia.

CHAP. XLIV.

Account of what pass'd among the Mirzas and Emirs who were gone to Bocara.

THE Mirzas Olouc-Bec and Ibrahim Sultan, who had taken the road to Bocara from Ali Abad, arriv'd the fourth of Ramadan 807 at the walls of Debbous, a very high fortress, at the foot of which runs the river of Samarcand. They were met there by Beyan Temour Cazen, brother of Mengheli Coja, from Samarcand, who brought a letter from Coja Yousef and Argoun Chah, the tenor of which was as follows. " After the usual salutations, " we let you know that tho we have refus'd to " open the gates of the city to you, it was not " thro any motive of treason, or, with intent to " revolt: our design is only to observe Timur's " last will, to the alteration of which we'd never consent. If the Mirza Calil Sultan shou'd " come hither, we wou'd use him in the same " manner. We are resolv'd to preserve this " city, it being the seat of the empire, and not " deliver it up to any one till the coming of " the Mirza Pir Mehemed, the lawful successor " to the crown, into whose hands we will re- " sign it according to the emperor's testament. " We thus let you know the state of affairs, that " you may not be incens'd against us." At the end of the letter they swore to perform what they promis'd.

April 15.

The

Book VI. The Mirzas, notwithstanding the oath, suspected the promises of these flatterers. but not to irritate 'em in this bad conjuncture, they dissembled their suspicion, and order'd the messenger to salute the Emirs, and tell 'em that if their intention was to do what they had promis'd, it wou'd be better for 'em, since it was the way which every honest and sensible man wou'd take Besides this they wrote a letter, in which they mildly advis'd 'em to continue firm in the resolution they had taken, and to govern the city according to their duty, without hearkning to any instigations to the contrary, for if they kept their word, and acknowledg'd the obligations they had receiv'd from the emperor, in maintaining the city for the Mirza Pir Mehemed, they wou'd fulfil their master's will, it being an indispensable obligation on every one to do that which is well-pleasing both to God and man, that so their integrity might be mention'd with honor by posterity. They likewise order'd him to tell 'em they need not doubt but that, when the Mirza shou'd be fix'd upon the throne, he wou'd distinguish them above all others, as they had preserv'd it for him; but if they shou'd transgress the orders of their benefactor, they wou'd commit a very heinous and treasonable action, and besides the dishonor and infamy of it, wou'd incur a severe punishment, and must in the end repent in vain They seal'd up this letter, which they deliver'd to Beyan Temour Cazen, who immediately return'd with it to Samarcand

CHAP.

CHAP XLV.

The Mirzas and Emirs at Bocara receive advice of the Mirza Calil Sultan's arrival at Samarcand, and of the obedience paid him by the Emirs of that city.

BEYAN Temour Cazen being return'd to Samarcand, the Emirs continu'd their journy towards Bocara, and two or three days after receiv'd advice that the Mirza Calil Sultan, who had taken the road of Samarcand from Tachkunt, with the Emirs of his party and his troops, being excited by a desire of usurpation and dominion, had made great haste, that being arriv'd near the city, the Emir Coja Yousef went out to meet him with presents, and had receiv'd him as emperor, having cast gold and precious stones before him, and kifs'd his hand at Chiraz, a village four miles from Samarcand; that the Cherifs and principal persons of the city had done the same; that when the Mirza was arriv'd at the bank of the river of Couhec, Argoun Chah went out to make his submission to him, and had deliver'd the keys of the city and castle, with those of the treasury of that capital, into his hands, and that all the traitors of the city and of the Mirza's court had unanimously resolv'd to acknowledg him for their sovereign, regardless their oaths, or the obedience due to Timur's last testament

The Emirs Cheik Noureddin and Chamelic having heard this news, loaded the ingrateful perjurors with curses, and wrote a letter to em 'em full of reproaches, which they sent by an express. Then continuing their road, they met Rouftem Berlas, brother of Hamza, governor of Bocara, whom they had sent thither before, and was return'd to meet the Mirzas, who being arriv'd before the city went to visit the sepulcher of the prophet Job, whose affistance they implor'd. They made a new treaty in this holy place, which they confirm'd by solemn oaths.

Afterwards they took horse, and enter'd Bocara; they lodg'd in the castle, which they rebuilt, and augmented the fortifications. As to the guard of the city, they agreed that the gate which opens upon it, with one half of the castle, shou'd be under the care of the Mirza Olouc-Bec, affifted by the Emir Chamelic, and that the gate which looks upon the out-parts, with the other half of the castle and walls, shou'd be commanded by the Mirza Ibrahim Sultan, attended by the Emir Cheik Noureddin; that the city shou'd be guarded by the Emirs Rouftem Berlas, his brother Hamza, Atilmich, Teveckul Carcara, and others, each of whom shou'd have the care of a gate, as well as of the baftions and walls. Having all come to this refolution, they began immediately to put it in execution, and to rebuild the walls of the city.

CHAP

CHAP. XLVI.

Coronation of the Mirza Calil Sultan at Samarcand.

THE aftrologer Moulana Bedreddin having made choice of wednefday the 16th of Ramadan 807, which anfwers to the year of the Hen, the fun being in the fixth degree of Aries, for the coronation of the Mirza Calil Sultan, that prince made his entry the fame day into Samarcand, and took poffeffion of the great imperial palace, where the treafures of all Afia were amafs'd. Being feated on the throne in his imperial habits, he receiv'd the fubmiffion of the Mirzas, Emirs, and principal men of the ftate, who on their knees congratulated his acceffion to the throne. April 27. 1405.

As foon as he was inftal'd, to fhew he had an outward regard to Timur's teftament, he gave the title of Can to the Mirza Mehemed Gehanghir, fon of the Mirza Mehemed Sultan, and nephew of the Mirza Pir Mehemed, tho this young prince was but nine years of age: and his name was plac'd at the top of all the patents and imperial orders according to cuftom, tho the Mirza Calil Sultan had the fole difpofal of every thing, as if he had been the lawful fovereign of all Tranfoxiana

Two days after, this new emperor went to the Canicah of the deceas'd Mirza Mehemed Sultan, where Timur's tomb was, to pay his devotions, and perform the public ceremonys of mourning. The empreffes, Mirzas, Emirs, and all the people came there in black habits, and wept and made

made bitter lamentations. By the Mirza Calil Sultan's order the whole Alcoran was read thro, alms were distributed among the poor and sick, and a great funeral-banquet prepar'd.

Then the emperor's drum was beat in a very mournful manner, after which it was broke to pieces according to custom. The learned men and poets compos'd panegyrics and epitaphs upon the emperor, and among others the son of the Coja Mafaoud Bocari, and the Coja Afmet Ulla.

As the pious Timur, by reason of the love he always bore to the Cherifs, had several times desir'd that his tomb shou'd be plac'd under that of the great Cherif Seid Bereke, that Cherif's coffin was transported from Andcoud, and inter'd under the mausoleum Timur had erected near the alcove of the Canicah, and Timur's body was plac'd underneath that of the Cherif, according to the orders he had given, the corps of the Mirza Mehemed Sultan was also transported to the same mausoleum, and bury'd at the emperor his grandfather's side. May God enlighten their souls with the lamps of his mercy.

When the Mirza Calil Sultan was fix'd on the throne, he open'd his treasures, and distributed them very liberally among the Emirs, principal lords, and soldiers; but why shou'd it be call'd liberality? it was rather imprudence and prodigality, for he distributed his gold like measures of wheat, and it was carry'd away by loads, as corn out of barns, to the great amazement of the people.

CHAP.

CHAP. XLVII.

Abridgment of the history of the reign of the Mirza Calil Sultan: and the cause of his ruin.

LEARNED men have accounted kings the shadow of God, and acknowledg'd that the power of sovereigns is as a ray of the Divinity. But nothing is likewise more certain, than that he who believes himself capable of worthily acquitting that great charge without the divine assistance, gives credit to what is both absurd and impossible: for God always favors with his mercy the good man, and prefers above all other potentates those who regularly pay their devotions to him, and distribute alms to the poor. We may also be assur'd that a state is not well govern'd by its vast treasures and magazines, nor by the multitude of its troops or the great number of its captains, but by the protection of the Almighty. In fine, there is somewhat besides valor requisite for the governing of a great empire.

The truth of this plainly appears in the case of the Mirza Calil Sultan, who thro injustice and favorable conjunctures became master of so vast an extent of ground, as scarcely ever any one emperor possess'd so much. His birth, as grandson of the great Timur-Bec, drew on him the attention of the whole universe: and at his grandfather's death, most part of the Nevians and great Emirs were with him at Tachkunt. When they receiv'd the news of that misfortune, their hearts were fill'd with fear: and as of Timur's children, there were none at that place older than the Mirza Calil Sultan, every one took an oath to him, thinking by this means to preserve the crown for ever in Timur's family.

The Mirza at the same took the road to Samarcand, and at his arrival there perceiv'd a general consternation among the people, the chief of whom, judging it best so to do, went to meet him, and congratulate him on his coming to the crown. The Emirs who had the keys of the city and treasurys, likewise resign'd 'em to him, and so he easily became master of the throne of Samarcand. This city was then in a very flourishing condition, being inhabited by princes and great lords, learned doctors, and the most skilful artists in the world; for most of the tradesmen of the towns conquer'd by Timur, had left their own country to dwell in this great city, it being the seat of the empire of Asia. We will not mention the immense treasures of ready mony, precious stones, stuffs, belts, curious vessels and toys, which were innumerable; nor the arms, bucklers, tents, pavilions, canopys, thrones, and other marks of grandeur, riches and magnificence, which had been amassing for several ages by the princes of all the kingdoms of Asia, and had been pillag'd by Timur from the emperors and princes of the countrys of Iran and Touran, from the country of the Calmacs to the frontiers of Greece and Natolia; and from the farther part of India to the frontiers of Syria, and from Carezem and the great Capchac to the limits of Russia, Circassia, Bulgaria and Europe: besides which was the tribute of thirty-six years receiv'd from all Asia.

This city, tho so vastly rich, and fill'd with great quantitys of goods, and abundance of soldiers, fell into the hands of the Mirza Calil Sultan without his striking a blow for it: but this prodigal prince squander'd away all those treasures, brought all this grandeur to nothing, and entirely ruin'd th s vast power in less than four years; which was one means made use of by fate to ruin his good fortune.

The second cause was the Mirza's violent passion for Chadi Mulc, one of the concubines of the Emir Hadgi Serfeddin, whom he had privately marry'd in the emperor's absence, and cou'd never visit except in secret: but when he found himself an absolute sovereign, he resign'd every thing up to the will of this beauty, and took no pleasure but in her company, her charms being the subject of all his thoughts; while she shew'd no regard either to princes or nobles, but accounted every thing below her; and even the emperor, laying aside his sovereignty, became her slave, and breath'd only by her permission. This brought disorder upon the state, and upon the Mirza's affairs, so that nothing succeeded in which the sovereign authority had any concern. He squander'd away all his riches, and chiefly among those who were afterwards the instruments of his ruin: and tho he was so rich that all the wealth of Hatem and the tribe of Tai did not amount to a tenth part of one of his treasurys, yet he soon spent all. He had neglected the counsel not to be over-liberal, for fear of being at last left naked: and he seem'd ignorant, that one shou'd give only to those who deserve it, and that in moderation.

On this account, the first thing to be mention'd as done by this prince was his excessive pro-

prodigality. He sprinkled handfuls of precious stones on the heads of those, upon whom it wou'd have been a crime, in a manner, to fling a little earth; while persons of extraordinary merit cou'd obtain nothing, or at least but a trifle. It was then a perfect game of hazard, for he who put in a penny, carry'd away a million, and those who deserv'd vast treasures, died without having a tenth part. Moreover, the Mirza advanc'd several strangers of mean extraction, made 'em Emirs, and gave 'em the first places in the state, which discover'd a great want of policy and conduct, for it alienated the hearts of the great Emirs of his court, and the generals of his army from him; and even those upstarts whom he had enrich'd, fell into an excess of self-love and pride, which was the root of many disorders. "Bestow " not honors, says the poet, upon him thou " lov'st, unless by degrees, for if you advance " him on a sudden, he will become insensible " of the favors you have heap'd on him, and " of the obligations he owes to you."

Besides all this, as the Sultan Calil's mistress was inferior in rank to the deceas'd emperor's wives, and these empresses became jealous of her growing greatness, she conceiv'd a great indignation against 'em, and persuaded Calil to give each of 'em, as well as Timur's concubines, to some brave Emir in marriage, who might by that means, as she pretended, become more attach'd to his interest, and so bring the state into better order. Accordingly he behav'd himself towards those venerable empresses, whom he ought to have reverenc'd as his own mother, in a manner condemn'd by all men of sense, forcing them to marry those who were unworthy to be their porters. He cast angels into the
mouths

mouths of satyrs, gave eagles to crows, strung pearls with pieces of glass, and rubys with flints, which he did without the least remorse. But he did not consider, that a king who had cast off all thoughts of honor and justice, will shortly lose his kingdom. In effect, his actions drew on him the aversion of his soldiers, and even of all his subjects: and as he no longer acted with sincerity, the public affairs fell into the utmost disorder and confusion. "He run, "says a certain poet, the ship of empire a-"ground, both himself and his lady were cast "away; for the kingdom slip'd out of his "hands, and he fell from the utmost height."

The source of all these disorders was the great familiarity the Mirza had with strangers, and persons of no figure or merit. The good ought to avoid the wicked; for the wicked are the cause of their ruin. These events shew the great soul and admirable conduct of Timur-Bec in his governing the empire: they let us see that his ordering the death of this woman was not without the providence of God, tho at that time every one was ignorant of the ill consequence of her being suffer'd to live.

CHAP. XLVIII.

Conclusion of the history of Timur-Bec, wherein the qualitys by which that conqueror surpass'd all the kings who preceded him, are set down.
The names of his children who surviv'd him.

THE glorious perfections by which the incomparable Timur-Bec adorn'd the regal dignity, were his sincere piety, the great veneration he bore to religion, his strict justice, and unbounded liberality, the effects of which were daily seen and felt by his people.

As his great qualitys have been mention'd in the series of this history, our design at present is to take notice of certain which were peculiar to him. And among others, with regard to his birth, it is proper to be inform'd, that tho his ninth grandfather was Toumene Can, of the race of Buzendger Can, chief of a branch or the tribe of Cayat, who was descended from Turk, the son of Japhet, the son of Noah, on whom may salvation rest, (from whence we discover that his ancestors were Cans and emperors) yet the Emir Tragai his father, as well as his grandfather the Emir Berkuth, having abdicated the kingdom, and left the government of the principality of Kech, which they had preserv'd with the Toman of ten thousand men annex'd thereto, to the children of their uncles of the family of Berlas, we may say that Timur-Bec brought the crown into this august family, he being the first emperor in it

At the age of twenty-five he attain'd to the highest dignitys, with admirable courage, and an ambition admir'd by all the world, endeavoring to bring the great talents he had receiv'd from nature to perfection. He pass'd nine years in different countrys, where his good sense and great genius appear'd in councils and assemblys, while at the same time his intrepidity and valor drew upon him every one's admiration, whether in personal combats, or in pitch'd battels, wherein no conqueror before him cou'd boast performing even the tenth part of his actions.

The truth of what we advance may easily be conceiv'd, when we reflect on the actions related in this book; and we are not at all apprehensive that our history will be tax'd with exaggeration. He mounted the throne of the empire when thirty-four years old, and reign'd successfully for thirty-six years, during which time he gain'd a considerable number of conquests, for he made himself master of the three empires of Zagatai Can, Touchi Can, and Hulacou Can, he subdu'd the greatest citys, and kingdoms of Asia; and extended the limits of his dominions as far as the borders of that part of the world; so that his power, riches and magnificence were greater than we can possibly imagine. This is so certain, that we need only read the historys of other kings and princes, in whose familys the crown has continu'd a long time, to be assur'd of it. But the chief proof of his great power was, that to whatever place he march'd to wage war, he soon conquer'd it, and gave the government thereof to some of his children or officers, not acting like antient conquerors, who were contented with those tokens of submission which vanquish'd princes might make by a tribute.

Book VI. One thing further remarkable in this monarch was, that tho he always observ'd the wholesom maxim of holding diets, yet he never solely confided in 'em; but constantly did what his own good genius inspir'd in him, and had such good success in all his undertakings, that it seem'd as if he had been always the care of divine providence. He cou'd not be shaken in his resolutions: he had the policy to be present at the execution of his most important enterprizes, either as to the state or religion. Both in peace and war he wou'd put forward every thing himself.

Besides his great and continual employments in war and the government, there remain many monuments of his ambition and grandeur, in citys, towns, castles, and walls which he built, in rivers and canals which he dug, and in works of piety, as mosques, chappels, hospitals, bridges, palaces, monasterys, gardens, vineyards, and pleasure-houses, which he erected in divers parts of Asia, in so great a number, that it wou'd take up a large volume only to enumerate 'em, without describing each in particular. And it wou'd be no exaggeration to say, that a king wou'd be accounted very powerful and magnificent, who shou'd have employ'd thirty-six years only in building the great edifices which Timur did, and that he wou'd be thought to surpass all the kings of the earth on that account, without carrying on those long wars, and obtaining the surprizing conquests which he did. Are not all the caravanseras in the great roads of Asia for the accommodation of travellers, the magnificent monasterys and hospitals, from which the poor, the rich and travellers reap so great advantages by the alms distributed there, are not these,

ASIA
Divided into its principal parts after Tamerlan's expedition according to the Memoirs of M de la Croix & reshaped by ye Observations of the Academy by IB Nolin

I say, the good works of this pious emperor, who now reaps the fruits of 'em in eternity?

We may also consider the blessings this emperor receiv'd from heaven in the great number of children he left behind him, which were thirty-six sons, and seventeen daughters living, according to the following detail.

The deceas'd Mirza GEHANGHIR his eldest left eleven princes, for the deceas'd Mehemed Sultan had had three sons, Mehemed Gehanghir, then nine years of age, Sadvacoas six, and Yahia five. The Mirza *Pir Mehemed Gehanghir* twenty nine years old, had seven sons, Caidou nine years of age, Caled seven, Buzendger, Sadvaccas, Tendger, Cnser, and Dgehanghir.

The deceas'd Mirza OMAR CHEIK left nine sons, *Pir Mehemed*, twenty-six years old, who had one son, of seven years of age, nam'd Omar Cheik; *Roustem*, ag'd twenty-four, who had two sons, Osman six years old, and Sultan Ali one year; *Eskender* twenty-one years of age; *Ahmed* eighteen years; *Sidi Ahmed* fifteen, and *Bajera Hasan* twelve.

The sons of the Mirza MIRAN CHAH, thirty-eight years of age, were in all seven: Abo bere, twenty-three years old, who had two sons, Alengher nine years of age, and Osman Chelebi four, *Omar* twenty-two years old; *Calil Sultan* twenty-one; *Aidgel* ten, and *Siorgatmich* six.

The Mirza CHAROC, twenty-eight years of age, had seven sons. *Olon.-B* and *Brahim Sultan*, both eleven years old, *Rusaucar* eight years, *Siorgatmich* six; *Mehemed Joaki* three years, *Janaglen* two years, and *Yarou* one year.

<small>Timur's children.</small>

These

These thirty-six princes were all living at Timur-Bec's death: besides whom he had one daughter nam'd Sultan Bact Begum, and sixteen granddaughters: the Mirza Omar Cheik had three daughters, the Mirza Mehemed Sultan three, the Mirza Miran Chah four, and the Mirza Charoc one; the Mirza Pir Mehemed Gehanghir three, the Mirza Aboubecre one, and the Mirza Calil Sultan one.

The Mirza Sultan Hussein, twenty-five years of age, was the son of Timur's daughter nam'd Akia Beghi or Tagi Can; and his father was the Emir Mehemed Bei, son of the Emir Moussa.

And as it was written in the book of fate, that the crown shou'd continue in this illustrious family by the branch of the Mirza Charoc and his children· after having now finish'd the history of the glorious actions of Timur-Bec, we intend to compile a history of the Mirza Charoc, and give a true relation of his great actions, which prov'd him the worthy successor of the most illustrious conqueror who ever appear'd in the world.

The end of the second volume.

I HAVE read by order of my lord chancellor *the history of Timur-Bec, grand Can of Tartary*; and believe the public will receive as much pleasure as advantage from a work, in which the reader will discover the geography of the vast regions of Tartary, so little known in this part of the world.

Paris Decemb 24.
1720.

L. De VERTOT.

THE CONTENTS OF THE First VOLUME.

BOOK I.

CHAP. I. *Of Sultan Cazan, grand Can of Zagatai, his defeat and death. Mir Cazagan, a Turkish prince, takes upon him the government of the empire, and establishes a grand Can. The war of Mir Cazagan against Malek Hussein, prince of Herat.* Page 1

Chap. 2. *Of the government of the Mirza Abdalla, the son of Cazagan, and of the difference which happen'd between the princes of Zagatai.* 14

Chap. 3. *Toglu Timur Can, king of the Getes, marches into Transoxiana. The flight of Hadgi Berlas.* 18

Chap. 4. *The rise of Mir Hussein, grandson of Mir Cazagan; he is assisted by Timur-Bec.* 19

Chap. 5. *Several intrigues between Timur and Hadgi Berlas, as also between the other princes.* 22

Chap. 6. *The king of the Getes returns to Transoxiana with a great army. The death of Hadgi Berlas. The Can confirms Timur in the possession of his country of Kesh, and of a Toman of ten thousand men.* 28

Chap

The CONTENTS.

Chap 7. *Timur-Bec marches in search of Emir Hussein.* 31

Chap 8. *Several warlike exploits of Timur and Hussein.* 37

Chap 9. *The encounter of the army of Gete, and its defeat, caus'd by the policy of Timur-Bec, with the reduction of the city of Kech.* 44

Chap 10. *The death of Togluc Timur Can, King of the Getes; and the defeat of his army by the princes Timur-Bec and Hussein.* 47

Chap 11. *The assembly of the princes convea'd by Timur and the Emir Hussein, in which they elevated Cabulchah Aglen to the dignity of grand Can.* 52

Chap. 12. *The battel of Lai, or of the sloughs.* 55

Chap 13. *The Retreat of Timur-Bec and Hussein. Samarcand besieg'd by the Getes.* 61

Chap 14. *Departure of the princes for Samarcand, and the dissension which happen'd between 'em.* 66

Chap. 15. *Timur-Bec brings an army into the field against Emir Hussein.* 72

Chap. 16. *Several exploits of Timur, and intrigues of the princes. The march of Timur to Carschi.* 77

Chap. 17. *Mir Hussein brings an army into the field to oppose Timur.* 86

Chap 18. *The siege and taking of Bocara by the army of Hussein. Timur defeats the army of the Coronas.* 89

Chap 19. *Timur sends an ambassador to Malek Hussein at Herat.* 92

Chap. 20. *Timur defeats the army of the Emir Hussein in Transoxiana.* 94

Chap 21. *The Emir Hussein sends an army against Timur, which is defeated.* 101

Chap 22. *The Emir Hussein again seeks to make peace with Timur.* 105

Chap. 23. *The Emir Hussein brings an army into the field from Bedakchan.* 108

The CONTENTS.

Chap. 24 *Timur marches at the head of an army to repulse the Getes.* 111
Chap. 25 *Timur returns from Bedakchan* 115
Chap. 26. *A second rupture between Timur and Hussein* 117

BOOK II.

Chap. 1 *The establishment of Timur on the throne of the empire of Zagatai.* 130
Chap. 2. *Timur returns from the city of Balc to Samarcand, the building of the castle and fortress of that metropolis* 132
Chap 3 *The Couroultai, that is, the diet or assembly of the states, conven'd by Timur's orders.* 136
Chap 4. *Timur marches to Cheburgan at the head of an army.* 138
Chap. 5. *Timur sends an army to Balc and Termed.* 140
Chap 6. *Timur sends the Emir Yakou to besiege Cheburgan.* 141
Chap. 7 *Timur marches an army into the country of the Getes.* 142
Chap. 8. *A second expedition of Timur against the Getes.* 144
Chap. 9 *The embassy from Timur to Hussein Sofi, king of Carezem.* 147
Chap. 10 *Timur departs from Samarcand, to make war on the king of Carezem.* 149
Chap. 11. *Timur makes peace with Ysouph Sofi, who succeeded Hussein, and demands in marriage the princess Canzade for the prince Gehanghir his eldest son.* 155
Chap. 12. *Timur marches a second time into the kingdom of Carezem.* 157
Chap 13. *The famous embassy from Timur to the king of Carezem, to demand the princess Canzade* 158

Chap.

The CONTENTS.

Chap. 14. *Timur marches a third time into the country of the Getes.* 163

Chap. 15. *Timur's marriage with the princess Dilchadaga, daughter of Camareddin king of the Getes. Timur is in danger of losing his life by a conspiracy which he narrowly escap'd* 166

Chap. 16. *Timur marches a third time to Carezem, and returns on the revolt of Sar Bouga and Adelchah* 168

Chap. 17. *Timur's fourth expedition to the kingdom of the Getes.* 171

Chap. 18. *The death of Mirza Gehanghir, Timur's eldest son.* 174

Chap. 19. *Timur's fifth expedition against the Getes.* 176

Chap. 20 *Timur's fifth expedition to the country of the Getes against Camareddin. Tocatmich Aglen, descended from Touschi, son of Genghiz Can, arrives at court, and puts himself under the protection of Timur.* 178

Chap. 21. *Timur gives Tocatmich Aglen the principalitys of Otrar and Sabran, and assists him in making himself master of the empire of Capchac which he claim'd as his right; tho Ourous Can, descended from Genghiz Can, was in possession of it.* 180

Chap. 22 *Preparations for war. Timur brings an army into the field against Ourous Can, emperor of Capchac and grand Russia.* 183

Chap 23. *Timur's irruption into the country of Ourous Can Tocatmich Aglen plac'd on the throne of Capchac, otherwise call'd the empire of Touchi Can.* 185

Chap 24. *The birth of prince Charoc, son and heir to the emperor Timur.* 187

Chap. 25 *Timur sends Tocatmich Can to attack Timur Melic Can, emperor of Cpachac.* 189

The CONTENTS.

Chap. 26 *Embassy from the emperor Timur to Joseph Sofi king of Carezem.* 191

Chap 27. *Timur's fourth war in Carezem death of Joseph Sofi conquest of that kingdom* 194

Chap. 28. *Foundation of the walls of Kech, the country of Timur the building of the palace of Acserai.* 199

Chap. 29. *The Emir Hadgi Seifeddin sent ambassador to Herat, to Malek Cayaseddin Pir Ali, king of Corassana.* 200

Chap 30 *Mirza Miran Chah, son of Timur, marches into Corassana, to make war on Malek Cayaseddin Pir Ali, prince of Herat.* 202

Chap 31. *Timur's army marches to make war in Persia, and the rest of the empire of Iran* 204

Chap. 32 *Reduction of Fouchendge, a town of Corassana.* 207

Chap 33. *Reduction of Herat, capital of Corassana* 209

Chap. 34 *The army marches to Tous and Kelat.* 213

Chap 35. *Timur returns to Samarcand.* 215

Chap. 36 *Death of Akia Beghi, daughter of Timur, and wife of the Emir Bei, son of the Emir Moussa.* 216

Chap 37. *Timur's second expedition into the kingdom of Iran or Persia* 219

Chap. 38. *Reduction of the town of Terchiz in Corassana.* p. 225

Chap 39 *The arrival of an ambassador from Fars, or the true Persia, at the court of Timur.* 227

Chap 40 *Timur marches into the province of Mazendran* 229

Chap 41 *Timur marches to Samarcand. Death of the empress Dilshadaga, and of the princess Cotlu Turcan Aga, Timur's sister* 231

Chap.

The CONTENTS.

Chap. 42. *Timur sends a sixth army into the country of the Getes.* 235

Chap. 43. *Timur marches to Mazendran, and thence to Sistan.* 236

Chap. 44. *Town of Sistan besieg'd and taken.* 239

Chap. 45. *Timur marches to Bost.* 245

Chap. 46. *War against the Ouganians, inhabitants of the mountains, south of Candahar.* 247

Chap. 47. *Timur returns to Samarcand.* 250

Chap. 48 *Timur marches into the province of Mazendran* 251

Chap. 49 *Timur marches into the province of Irac Agemi.* 256

Chap. 50. *The emperor Timur marches to Sultania.* 257

Chap. 51. *Timur returns to Samarcand, the capital of his empire.* 259

Chap. 52. *Timur enters the kingdom of Iran, where he stays three years successively.* 261

Chap. 53. *Timur marches to Azerbijana, or the country of the antient Medes.* 263

Chap. 54. *Timur enters Georgia at the head of his army. The description of the Persian way of hunting; as also of the Gerke and Nerke.* 267

Chap. 55. *Timur returns to Carabagh.* 269

Chap. 56. *The march of Timur to Berda The motion of the army of Capchac. Defeat of the troops of Tocatmich Can.* 273

Chap. 57. *The arrival of the empress Serai Mulc Canum, and the princes her sons.* 277

Chap. 58. *Timur's army marches against Cara Mehemed, prince of the Turcomans.* 278

Chap. 59. *Timur marches to Van and Vastan. The letter which Cha Chuja king of Persia wrote to Timur at his death.* 282

Chap. 60. *Timur marches again into the countrys of Fars and Irac Agemi* 289

Ee 2　　　　　　　　　　Chap

The CONTENTS.

Chap. 61. *Timur marches to Chiraz, the capital of Fars or the true Persia*   294

Chap. 62 *Reasons which induc'd Timur to return to the capital of his empire.*   297

Chap. 63 *Timur returns to Samarcand; and gives the government of Fars and Irac to the family of Muzaffer.*   301

Chap. 64 *The emperor orders a process against some Emirs, whom he had left in Transoxiana.*   303

BOOK III.

CHAP. 1 *Timur-Bec departs for his fifth expedition into the kingdom of Carezem*   305

Chap. 2 *Some accidents during Timur's expedition into Carezem*   308

Chap. 3 *Timur departs to make war in Capchac, and is victorious over Tocatmich Can.*   317

Chap. 4 *Timur sends the Mirza Miran Chah into Corassana*   323

Chap. 5 *Timur's expedition into Mogolistan against Kezer Coja Aglen, and the prince Ancatoura, which made the fifth campain in that country.*   325

Chap. 6 *Timur holds a diet, and sends his armys into all the quarters of the Moguls, to fight the Getes*   331

Chap. 7 *Timur returns to the seat of his empire.*   338

Chap. 8 *The Couroultai, or diet, held by Timur's order.*   342

Chap. 9 *Timur sends his troops into the country of the Getes*   344

Chap. 10 *Timur marches into the desart of Capchac*   347

Chap. 11 *Timur reviews his troops.*   356

Chap. 12. *Timur sends the Mirza Mehemet Sultan at the head of the scouts.*   359

The CONTENTS.

Chap 13 *Battel between the scouts of the two armys. Death of the Emir Ascoutmur, and other famous men.* 367

Chap. 14. *The army rang'd in order of battel in an extraordinary manner. A terrible fight which ensu'd thereupon.* 371

Chap. 15. *Timur returns from the desart of Capchac to the seat of his empire.* 382

Chap. 16. *The government of Zabulestan given to Mirza Pir Mehemed, son of Gehanghir.* 384

Chap. 17. *Timur departs for a war of five years continuance.* 386

Chap. 18 *Timur departs from Jourdez after his recovery.* 388

Chap. 19. *The taking of Amol, Sari, and Mahanasar* 390

Chap 20. *Timur sends a letter to Samarcand.* 396

Chap. 21. *Timur makes war a second time on the kingdoms of Fars and Irac.* 399

Chap. 22. *Timur marches to the kingdoms of Lorestan and Courestan.* 402

Chap. 23. *An account of the motions of the princes of Fars, or of Persia and Irac, on which the present affairs depend.* 406

Chap. 24. *Timur marches to Chiraz against Chah Mansour.* 411

Chap. 25. *Battel between Timur and Chah Mansour. The death of the latter.* 416

Chap 26. *Timur seizes the princes of the house of Muzaffer, and disposes of their effects among his lieutenants.* 421

Chap 27. *Timur marches to the kingdom of Irac Agemi, or Hircania.* 424

Chap 28. *Timur invests the Mirza Miran Chah in the kingdom of Hulacou Can* 426

Chap. 29 *Timur vanquishes the Turcoman Hachan Sarec* 427

Chap 30. *Timur marches to Bagdad* 431

The CONTENTS.

Chap 31 *Return of Mirza Mehemet Sultan after the defeat of the Courdes robbers.* 438
Chap. 32 *Timur sends an ambassador to the Sultan Barcoc in Egypt* 439
Chap 33 *The taking of the town of Tecrit.* 441
Chap. 34. *Timur continues his journy, and sends his princes and Emirs to make inroads in several kingdoms* 448
Chap. 35. *Timur marches to Diarbekir.* 450
Chap 36. *Timur marches to Edessa* 452
Chap. 37. *Death of Mirza Omar Cheik, Timur's son.* 455
Chap. 38. *Timur marches to Gezire.* 460
Chap. 39. *Timur's second enterprize upon Merdin.* 461
Chap. 40 *Birth of the Mirza Oluc Bei* 463
Chap 41 *Timur marches to Amed or Hamed, capital of the country of Diarbekir.* 464
Chap 42. *Timur returns to Alatac.* 467
Chap. 43 *Timur sends bodys of soldiers into several countrys to enlarge his conquests.* 468
Chap 44. *The taking of the town and fortress of Avenic.* 471
Chap 45 *Timur's return after the taking of Avenic.* 477
Chap. 46 *Timur sends an army into Georgia.* 479
Chap. 47 *The birth of Ibrahim Sultan, son of Charoc.* 480
Chap 48. *Solemn rejoicings for the birth of Ibrahim Sultan, son of Charoc* 482
Chap 49 *Timur constitutes the Mirza Charoc governor of Samarcand* 484
Chap. 50 *Timur goes in person to the Georgian war.* 485
Chap 51. *Timur marches a second time into Capchac against Tocatmich Can* 487
Chap. 52. *Timur reviews his army.* 490
Chap 53. *Battel between Timur and Tocatmich Can* 493

Chap.

The CONTENTS.

Chap 54. *Timur goes in pursuit of Tocatmich Can, and instals a new Can of Capchac* 498

Chap. 55. *Timur marches into Europe; and pillages the western Capchac, as also Muscovy and Russia* 501

Chap. 56. *Timur makes war in Circassia* 505

Chap. 57. *Timur marches to Alburz Couh, or mount Caucasus.* 506

Chap. 58. *Timur attacks the fortresses of Coula, Taous, and others.* 507

Chap. 59 *Timur marches to Sensem.* 511

Chap. 60. *Timur marches into Capchac, and pillages the town of Hadgi Tercan, or Astracan.* 513

Chap. 61. *Timur returns to Capchac.* 515

Chap. 62. *Timur gives the government of Azerbijana to the Mirza Mirancha, who besieges Alengic.* 519

Chap 63. *Taking of the town of Seirjan; and the retreat of Behloul to Nehavend* 520

Chap. 64. *Timur sends the Mirza Mehemet Sultan to conquer the kingdom of Ormus. The reduction of Yezd.* 524

Chap 65. *Timur returns to the seat of his empire* 525

Chap. 66. *The building of the palace of Baghi Chemal.* 530

Chap. 67. *Timur gives the principality of Corassang to the Mirza Charoc.* 531

Chap. 68 *Timur stays some time at Kech. Return of the Mirza Mehemet Sultan from the campain of Fars.* 534

Chap. 69. *Timur demands in marriage for himself the daughter of Keser Coja Aglen. He celebrates the nuptials of the Mirza Eskender with the princess Beghisi Sultan.* 537

Chap 70. *Timur gives orders for making the garden of Dilencha, and building a stately palace in it.* 538

Ee 4 THE

THE CONTENTS OF THE Second VOLUME.

BOOK IV.

Chap 1. *The cause of Timur's war in India* Page 4

Chap 2. *Timur brings his army into the field, to make war against the Guebres in India.* 7

Chap. 3. *Timur marches against the inhabitants of Ketuer He defeats the Siapouches, who were cloth'd in black.* 8

Chap. 4. *Timur sends Mehemed Azad to gain intelligence of Mirza Roustem and Burhan Aglen. His return to Ketuer.* 13

Chap 5. *Timur sends Mirza Charoc to Herat.* 17

Chap 6 *The arrival of ambassadors from several places Taizi Aglen returns from the country of the Calmacs, and Cheik Noureddin from that of Fars* 18

Chap. 7 *The repairing the fortress of Irjab, and the destroying of the Ouganis robbers.* 23

Chap

The CONTENTS.

Chap. 8. *Timur marches to Chenouzan and Nagaz; and destroys the robbers of the nation of the Pervians.* 25

Chap. 9. *Timur passes the river Indus* 28

Chap 10. *Chehabeddin Mobarec Chah Temini commits hostilitys against the emperor after his submission.* 29

Chap. 11 *Timur's arrival at Toulonba.* 32

Chap. 12. *Timur marches in search of Nusret Coukeri* 34

Chap. 13. *Arrival of prince Pir Mehemed Gehanghir from Moultan.* 35

Chap 14. *The taking the town of Bend, and the fortress of Batnir; the inhabitants of which places are put to the sword.* 39

Chap. 15. *Timur departs from Batnir, for Seresti, Fatabad and Ahrouni.* 45

Chap. 16. *Timur marches against a nation of rebellious Getes* 46

Chap. 17. *A review of the whole army marching in order of battel.* 48

Chap 18 *Timur marches to the east side of the town of Louni. Massacre of a hundred thousand Indian slaves who were in his camp.* 52

Chap. 19 *Timur gives battel to Sultan Mahmoud, emperor of India.* 55

Chap. 20. *Flight of Sultan Mahmoud, and his general Mellou Can, prince of Moultan. Reduction of Deli capital of India.* 61

Chap 21 *Timur departs from Deli; and pursues his conquests in the remoter parts of India, near the Ganges.* 68

Chap. 22. *Conquest of Myrthe. The Guebres are flea'd alive* 69

Chap. 23. *Several battels upon the great river Ganges, against the militia of the Guebres.* 72

Chap 24 *Timur's three Gazies, or expeditions against the Guebres.* 74

Chap

The CONTENTS.

Chap. 25 *Timur exterminates the Guebres assembled in the famous defile of Coupele. Description of a marble statue of a cow ador'd by the Indians* 78

Chap. 26. *Timur's resolution to return to the seat of his empire.* 81

Chap. 27. *Timur's irruption on the mountain Soualec.* 82

Chap. 28. *Several combats in the woods near Soualec* 83

Chap. 29 *Timur's Gazies and expeditions in the province of Tchamou.* 87

Chap 30 *Relation of what pass'd at Lahor, with regard to Chicai Couker, prince of that city.* 91

Chap. 31. *Description of the little kingdom of Cachmir, or Kichmir.* 95

Chap 32 *Timur returns to the seat of his empire.* 97

Chap. 33. *Timur crosses the Oxus, and is met by the princes and princesses of the blood.* 102

Chap. 34 *Building of the great mosque of Samarcand.* 105

BOOK V.

CHAP 1. *The causes which oblig'd Timur to make war in the country of Lau, that is, in the western parts of Asia, from the river Gihon to the Mediterranean sea.* 108

Chap. 2 *Timur's departure for a campain of seven years* 113

Chap 3 *The transactions of the Emir Solyman Chah.* 117

Chap 4 *The arrival of good news from several parts.* 120

Chap 5 *Timur marches into Georgia, and to the defile of Conchi.* 126

Chap

The CONTENTS.

Chap. 6. *Timur's return from the defile of Comcha.* 128

Chap. 7. *Continuation of the history of the Mirza Roustem, who was gone from Dgiam to Chiraz. A great crime committed by his eldest brother, the Mirza Pir Mehemed.* 130

Chap. 8. *A diet in relation to the affair of Georgia.* 136

Chap. 9. *Timur marches against prince Jani Bec, a Georgian.* 139

Chap 10. *The taking of the fort of Zerit, and the town of Suanit.* 141

Chap. 11 *Timur marches against the Georgian prince Aivani.* 143

Chap 12. *Timur returns from Georgia.* 144

Chap. 13 *Reasons which oblig'd Timur to march against the city of Sebaste, capital of Anatolia.* 145

Chap 14. *Timur's letter to the Caiser Roum, that is, the Ottoman emperor* 147

Chap. 15. *Timur marches to Sebaste, and takes that city.* 151

Chap 16. *Timur marches to Abulestan.* 155

Chap 17. *The reasons of Timur's carrying his arms into Syria and Mesopotamia.* 157

Chap 18. *Timur marches into the kingdoms of Syria and Egypt.* 160

Chap. 19. *The taking of the castles of Behesna and Antapa* 162

Chap. 20. *The siege and taking the city of Aleppo* 165

Chap. 21 *The castle of Aleppo attack'd and taken.* 173

Chap 22. *The taking of the towns and castles of Emessa and Hama.* 177

Chap 23 *Conquest of the town of Balbec* 180

Chap. 24. *Timur marches to Damascus, capital of Syria,* 181

Chap

The CONTENTS.

Chap. 25. *Timur gives battel to the Sultan of Egypt, and gains the victory* 187
Chap. 26. *Taking of the city of Damascus.* 189
Chap. 27. *Taking of the castle of Damascus.* 194
Chap. 28. *Timur returns out of Syria.* 202
Chap. 29. *Timur crosses the Euphrates, and hunts in Mesopotamia.* 205
Chap. 30. *Timur marches to the town of Merdin.* 206
Chap. 31. *Timur sends troops into Georgia, and to Bagdad* 208
Chap. 32. *Timur besieges and takes Bagdad.* 211
Chap. 33. *Timur's return from Bagdad, and march towards Tauris.* 217
Chap. 34. *Timur sends the Mirza Charoc to Azendgian* 219
Chap. 35. *Arrival of the second empress Touman Aga, and the young princes, from Samarcand.* 221
Chap. 36. *Timur marches into Georgia, and to Carabagh Arran* 222
Chap. 37. *Timur passes the winter at Carabagh. Arrival of the Mirza Mehemet Sultan from Samarcand* 224
Chap. 38. *Timur sends troops to make inroads in divers places.* 226
Chap. 39. *The causes which oblig'd Timur to return to make war on Bajazet the Ottoman emperor* 230
Chap. 40. *Timur digs the river of Berlas.* 234
Chap. 41. *Timur departs from Carabagh for the plains of Chemkour.* 235
Chap. 42. *Taking of the castle of Tartoum* 238
Chap. 43. *Taking of the castle of Kemau. Arrival of ambassadors from Bajazet* 240
Chap. 44. *Timur reviews his army* 243
Chap. 45. *Taking of the castle of Harouc.* 245
Chap. 46. *Timur marches to Casarea in Cappadocia, and to Ancora* 246
Chap. 47. *Timur ranges his army in order of battel, to fight Bajazet* 250

Chap

The CONTENTS.

Chap. 48. *Timur gives Bajazet battel, and gains the victory.* 252

Chap. 49. *The taking of the Ottoman emperor, who is brought in chains before the throne of the conqueror.* 255

Chap. 50. *Timur orders troops to make inroads in divers parts of the Ottoman empire. He sends relations of his victory to the citys of Iran and Touran, with orders to make public rejoicings.* 258

Chap. 51. *The continuation of the history of the Mirza Mehemed Sultan, who had been sent to Prusa in Bithynia.* 261

Chap. 52. *Account of the Mirza Sultan Hussein, and the Emir Solyman Chah, who were gone out to make inroads.* 265

Chap. 53. *Timur departs from Kioutahia* 266

Chap. 54. *Timur dispatches couriers into divers countrys. The arrival of several ambassadors.* 268

Chap. 55. *Timur regulates the winter-quarters.* 271

Chap. 56. *Timur besieges Smyrna, and takes it* 275

Chap. 57. *Second arrival of ambassadors from Bajazet's sons* 278

Chap. 58. *Timur departs from Smyrna* 280

Chap. 59. *Taking of the towns of Egridur and Nasibine.* 283

Chap. 60. *The death of the Ottoman emperor Bajazet, and of the Mirza Mehemed Sultan, Timur's grandson* 285

Chap. 61. *Mourning for the death of the Mirza Mehemed Sultan and the translation of his coffin.* 288

Chap. 62. *Arrival of ambassadors from Egypt.* 289

Chap. 63. *Timur marches against the Caratatars, or black Tartars.* 291

Chap. 64. *Timur returns from Natolia.* 294

Chap. 65. *The manner in which the death of the Mirza Mehemed Sultan, son of Gehanghir, was made known to Canzade his mother.* 296

BOOK

The CONTENTS.

BOOK VI.

CHAP. 1. *Timur marches into Georgia* 299
Chap 2 *The government of Chiraz a second time given to the Mirza Pir Mehemed, son of Omar Cheik, and that of Ispahan to his brother the Mirza Rouftem.* 301
Chap. 3. *Timur sends the Mirza Aboubecre to rebuild the city of Bagdad, and gives him the government of Irac-Arabi and Diarbekir.* 302
Chap 4 *Timur's arrival at the frontiers of Georgia* 306
Chap 5. *The taking of the famous castle of Cortene in Georgia.* 308
Chap. 6. *Relation of what pass'd without during this siege.* 313
Chap 7 *Timur marches to Abkhaze.* 314
Chap 8 *Timur returns from Abkhaze. The cause of his return* 316
Chap. 9. *Timur orders the town of Bailacan to be rebuilt* 319
Chap. 10. *Timur sends intendants and doctors into all the provinces of his empire, to examine the affairs of particular persons, and to distribute his justice and favors among the people.* 321
Chap 11. *Continuation of the history of the princes who were gone into Irac-Arabi* 325
Chap. 12. *Arrival of the Mirza Omar from Samarcand. Continuation of what happen'd during the building of Bailacan* 327
Chap. 13. *Timur passes the winter at Carabagh-Arran. Relation of what happen'd there* 329
Chap. 14 *The emperor sends the Mirza Charoc to Ghilan.* 332
Chap 15 *Arrival of some princes from Merdin and Vastan. A famous funeral banquet made for the late Mirza Mehemed Sultan.* 334

Chap

The CONTENTS.

Chap. 16 *Timur's return from a campain of seven years.* 336

Chap. 17. *Timur invests the Mirza Omar in the empire of Hulacou Can.* 337

Chap. 18. *Continuation of the history of the Mirza Roustem and the Emir Solyman Chah, who were sent towards Rei.* 338

Chap. 19 *Timur sends the Mirza Eskender and the Emir Chamelic before the rest towards Rei.* 340

Chap. 20 *The taking of the citadel of Firouzcouh.* 342

Chap 21. *Timur marches to Tchelao.* 345

Chap 22 *Battel between the Mirza Sultan Hussein and Eskender Cheiki. The flight of the latter.* 348

Chap. 23. *Timur returns to the seat of his empire.* 351

Chap. 24. *Timur's entry into his imperial city of Samarcand* 355

Chap. 25. *Timur holds a general diet. A great feast for the marriage of the princes at Canighul.* 358

Chap 26. *The causes which incited Timur to undertake the conquest of the kingdom of China* 368

Chap 27. *Timur sets out for the war against the infidels of China* 372

Chap 28. *An account of certain adventures, the knowledg of which is necessary to the understanding the latter part of this history. A relation of what pass'd at Acsoulat.* 375

Chap. 29. *Timur departs from Acsoulat.* 378

Chap. 30. *Timur's death at Otrar.* 381

Chap 31. *Relation of what happen'd after Timur's death.* 387

Chap. 32. *Timur's coffin transported from Otrar.* 389

Chap 33 *The empresses and Emirs hold a council concerning the war of China* 391

Chap. 34. *Timur's coffin is transported to Samarcand* 393

Chap.

The CONTENTS.

Chap. 35. *The Mirza Sultan Hussein, Timur's grandson, opposes the sentiment of the Emirs.* 396

Chap. 36. *The Emirs write circular letters to give advice to all the provinces of the Mirza Sultan Hussein's undertaking* 397

Chap. 37. *A letter to the great Emirs who were at Tachkunt* 399

Chap. 38. *The Emir Berendac arrives at the empresses court, with an answer to the letter sent the Emirs, who were at Tachkunt with the Mirza Calil Sultan* 401

Chap. 39. *Relation of what happen'd on the Emir Berendac's return to Tachkunt.* 405

Chap. 40. *The great Emirs oppose the Mirza Calil Sultan* 407

Chap. 41. *The Emirs hold a council with the empresses, in relation to their marching to Bocara.* 409

Chap. 42. *The Mirzas and Emirs march to Bocara.* 411

Chap. 43. *The empresses march to Samarcand. Their mourning, after the two Mirzas departure* 412

Chap. 44. *Account of what pass'd among the Mirzas and Emirs who were gone to Bocara* 413

Chap. 45. *The Mirzas and Emirs at Bocara receive advice of the Mirza Calil Sultan's arrival at Samarcand, and of the obedience paid him by the Emirs of that city.* 415

Chap. 46. *Coronation of the Mirza Calil Sultan at Samarcand* 417

Chap. 47. *Abridgment of the history of the reign of the Mirza Calil Sultan and the cause of his ruin.* 419

Chap. 48. *Conclusion of the history of Timur-Bec, wherein the qualities by which that conqueror surpass'd all the kings who preceded him, are set down. The names of his children who surviv'd him.*

The end of the contents.

Printed in the USA
CPSIA information can be obtained
at www.ICGtesting.com
LVHW021943201024
794329LV00001B/59